Secret and Sacred

Secret and Sacred

The Diaries of
James Henry Hammond,
a Southern Slaveholder

Edited by

Carol Bleser

Oxford University Press
New York   Oxford

Oxford University Press

Oxford   New York   Toronto
Delhi   Bombay   Calcutta   Madras   Karachi
Petaling Jaya   Singapore   Hong Kong   Tokyo
Nairobi   Dar es Salaam   Cape Town
Melbourne   Auckland

and associated companies in
Berlin   Ibadan

First published in 1988 by Oxford University Press, Inc.,
200 Madison Avenue, New York, New York 10016

First issued as an Oxford University Press paperback, 1989

Oxford is a registered trademark of Oxford University Press

Library of Congress Cataloging-in-Publication Data
Hammond, James Henry, 1807–1864.
Secret and sacred: the diaries of James Henry Hammond, a southern
slaveholder / edited by Carol Bleser.
p. cm.   Includes index.
1. Hammond, James Henry, 1807–1864—Diaries. 2. Slaveholders—South Carolina—Diaries.
3. Plantation life—South Carolina—History—19th century.
4. Slavery—South Carolina—History—19th century.
5. South Carolina—Race relations. I. Bleser. Carol K. Rothrock. II. Title.
F273.H24   1988
975.7'03'0924—dc19
[B] 88-4204   CIP
ISBN 0-19-505308-7
ISBN 0-19-506163-2 (PBK.)

2 4 6 8 10 9 7 5 3 1
Printed in the United States of America

For Elizabeth and Gerald
and those who come after

Foreword

James Henry Hammond's recent emergence as a fascinating and important historical figure of the Old South is a remarkable phenomenon. Until a decade or so ago most students of nineteenth-century Southern history knew of him only as the ante-bellum South Carolina politician who had made the famous "Mud-sills" speech in the United States Senate. "No, you dare not make war on cotton," he had informed his fellow senators in 1858 during the Kansas difficulties. "No power on earth dares to make war upon it. Cotton *is* king." All great civilizations, Hammond declared, require menials to perform the drudgery of life; such an inferior class "constitutes the very mud-sill of society and of political government." The South had secured its menials, "A race inferior to her own, but eminently qualified in temper, in vigor, in docility, in capacity to stand the climate, to answer all her purposes. We use them for our purpose, and call them slaves." Both the sentiments expressed and the arrogant confidence with which they were delivered infuriated the North and the Midwest; "Mud-sills for Lincoln," banners at the Republican convention in Chicago in 1860 are said to have read.

Scholars of antebellum Southern literature had some knowledge of Hammond as a friend of William Gilmore Simms. William Peterfield Trent, in his biography of the novelist (published in 1892 and at this writing still the only biography), was eloquent in his comdemnation of slavery as the bane of the Old South's society and literature, yet he referred to Hammond as "a capital fellow if one may judge from his letters." Although the publication of Simms's voluminous correspondence, including numerous letters to Hammond, gave an indication of the complexity of Hammond's mind, still, the sole biographical work on Hammond was Elizabeth Merritt's 1921 Johns Hopkins doctoral dissertation.

How different it is today! Drew Gilpin Faust discussed Hammond to good effect in her stimulating study of a group of Old South savants, *A Sacred Circle: The Dilemma of the Intellectual in the Old South, 1840–1860* (1977). In 1981 Carol Bleser published an enthralling selection of four generations of Hammond family letters, *The Hammonds of Redcliffe* (1981), in which it is no exaggeration to say that almost every cliché and generalization about the nineteenth-century South received implicit contradiction. The picture of Hammond emerging from the correspondence was both fascinating and more than a little appalling. Here was no "capital fellow," no high-minded Southern planter, but an ambitious parvenu of New England parentage who set out to become a gentleman and slaveholder. He was a driving fury of self-aggrandisement, a political ideologue, a highly indulgent sensualist, a tyrannizing father and domineering husband, and also a self-pitying man who flaunted his sensibility and throughout his days personified the deluded Romantic opportunist—in sum, "a tough-minded son of a bitch," as Dr. Bleser put it both accurately and succinctly. The year following *The Hammonds of Redcliffe* came Drew Faust's *James Henry Hammond and the Old South: A Design for Mastery*, an excellent biographical study that convincingly filled in much of the portraiture that was sketched in the correspondence.

Now appears a book that I can only describe as unique among all the historical works ever published about the Old South. It is nothing less than the private diaries, astoundingly revealing, of this extraordinary man. *Secret and Sacred: The Diaries of James Henry Hammond, a Southern Slaveholder*, again ably edited by Carol Bleser, consists of a set of two previously unpublished diaries containing Hammond's private commentary on what was happening in his life and that of his state and nation. Incredibly, despite the inclusion of much revealing and mightily damning discussion of his sometimes scandalous sexual life, they appear to have been allowed to survive almost intact, except for one passage in which Hammond's acerbic comments on a son's recalcitrant ways appear to have angered that son so much that he removed some, but by no means all, of the offending pages. Otherwise, and despite their remaining in the hands of the Hammond family for one hundred years, they seem not to have been censored, bowdlerized, or even emended beyond some light annotation.

As Dr. Bleser notes in her illuminating introductory essay to the book, diarists do not write and keep such documents for themselves only; the diarist expects someday to be read. From time to time in his entries Hammond would address himself directly to his children, as if he intended his diaries to reveal to them what manner of suffering man their father really was. At the same time, it seems likely that he did not plan for such reading to take place until after his death, for he would almost certainly have not wanted much of what he had to say known to them while he was still around. However, neither will it do to characterize these diaries as a coldly calculated rhetorical performance for posterity. Obviously their author used them for purposes of emotional release, venting of spleen, the rehearsal of his own grievances, expression of private hopes and ambitions—as a way of giving a shape to his pent-up feelings such as was not otherwise available to him. Yet he must have presupposed an audience, even if in the future, because the satisfaction that such self-expression provided of itself could not be sufficient; he needed to know that his emotional outpourings would be *read*.

The dominant tone throughout is resentment, anger, lamentation. From time to time there is also an element of self-flagellation involved, but truth to tell, at such moments one has the feeling that the motif of *mea culpa* is being staged mostly for effect. Hammond will often blame himself for his real or imagined misfortunes, but in general terms only; when he gets down to the specifics the fault is seen as resting elsewhere.

There is no need here to comment on the specific relevance of the diary material to Hammond's life and career; Carol Bleser's introduction performs that task thoroughly and admirably. A few observations, however, on Hammond's personality as revealed in his diaries might be in order.

It may be presumed that anyone who performs the sustained labor of keeping a diary such as these must almost by definition be said to take himself and what he is thinking and feeling very seriously indeed, and also that such a person is not satisfied with the everyday reality of the world he inhabits. He must give it additional meaning through recorded language. Hammond's diaries do not importantly function as a record of events, so much as the occasion for discoursing upon them. As a planter he also maintained an extensive journal, in which, especially at times when he was not also keeping his diaries, his personal thoughts and feelings are sometimes interjected. For the most part the documentation entered in the "secret and sacred" diaries, as he called them, seems intended as a starting point to allow him to extemporize upon their personal significance for his own career and hopes. While anxiously awaiting word that the legislature has chosen him to be governor, for example, he anticipates almost every conceivable kind of betrayal, and is at pains to denounce the motives and impugn the character of everyone who might possibly do him in. His supporters are portrayed as weak and ineffective, his rivals as crass, vindictive, self-serving.

Like many another ambitious politico before and since, Hammond tended to identify his personal advancement with the public weal, and to ascribe motives of narrow private gain to all who opposed him. But in Hammond's instance it goes beyond that. His view of his public career takes on transcendent overtones, involving not merely the assumption of civic virtue in search of recognition and reward but something approaching a conviction that he possessed a fated destiny beyond and superior to what might lie in store for most other mortals. Believing himself unfairly relegated to the political boneyard because of conniving office-seekers and a hypocritical, scandal-mongering electorate, and observing what he considered to be the timidity and ineffectiveness of the South's leadership in failing to oppose Northern threats to the expansion of slaveholding, he deposes as follows:

> I have done with the Public forever, in every form and shape so far as it is in my power to keep clear of it, unless indeed by some marvellous turn of event I could be placed in the position which I feel myself entitled to occupy—and placed in it *in all respects* and without condition. [12 May 1852]

What could he have had in mind? The Presidency? The military and civil leadership of a seceded Southern Confederacy? A virtual dictatorship such as he noted on another occasion had been given by South Carolina to John Rutledge in 1778? Or more grandiose even than these, an historical role comparable to Cromwell's or Bonaparte's? It would be difficult to pronounce any limits upon Hammond's secret ambitions, or upon his estimate of his own capacity for greatness.

Yet Hammond also recognized, and frequently bemoaned, his inability to capitalize on opportunity when it arose. Repeatedly during his public career he had a way of caving in under pressure, which took the form of coming down with bodily maladies that were surely psychosomatic in origin. Aspiring to the mantle of John C. Calhoun both before and after that powerful political figure was removed from the South Carolina scene, he failed to rise to certain occasions. Not gifted at introspection, and like almost all others in his time largely unaware of the vital relationship between psychic and physical health, he lamented what he believed to be his wretched bodily constitution for its inability to respond to the demands his career placed upon it. Yet it is obvious, too, that he suspected that there was more to the matter than that.

Mainly, however, he blamed external factors for his failure to achieve public greatness—the electorate, crass times, conniving politicos, public pusillanimity, democracy, pettiness, jealous Charlestonian bluebloods, Jews, the unwillingness of the people of South Carolina to defer to true intellectual and moral distinction when encountered, their inability to recognize its incarnation in himself. Not a religious man in any meaningful way, he did not, however, shrink from ascribing his economic, social, and political setbacks to the Divinity itself, as in this remarkable but by no means isolated outburst of 30 August 1842, upon the occasion of a series of fatalities among his slaves:

> For I am pursued by "Envy, hatred and all uncharitableness." I feel like one hunted down by the jealousy of the world and that every man's hand is against me. I see no *real, sensible, appreciating* sympathy any where. For a mere exclamation of sorrow, which those round me only give and then dismiss the matter, is a mockery, and I avoid it—I reprove it. If God would only allow my negroes to live and thrive and give me reasonable health, I could stand the rest and fight it out with the world. But this he will not do.

Several years later comes another such outburst, triggered by agricultural woes, which produces this stirring tirade whereby, following an expression of seeming humility, the diarist vents his true feelings on the accountability of the Almighty to James Henry Hammond:

> I cannot fathom his [God's] purpose I do not know what to do. Sometimes I think my destiny is not here. He proposes me for other schemes. But I see no clue, no light to lead me elsewhere. All is darkness and I am bewildered. That I am not pleasing to him and that my ways and views do not meet his approbation is further shown in that after selecting every experiment for this year that I could believe likely to succeed here, after going to immense labour and expense to put large quantities of peat on the whole snow f[ield] and testing it also elsewhere, after trying plaster, manure, in various quantities, rice, tobacco, potatoes on a new and laborious plan, planting in various ways with different seeds, in short, after doing all that man could do, it seemed to me, when it became necessary for God to aid me, He *failed*. [15 May 1845]

As might be suspected, Hammond was nobody's gentle and kind slaveholder. He worked his slaves hard, so much so that, particularly at the outset of his career as a planter, they experienced an appalling mortality rate. Hammond's views in the "Mud-sills" Speech were genuinely held. Africans were in every way an inferior race, designed for his *use*. Proslavery rhetoric to the contrary, there was nothing remotely paternalistic about it, if we are to believe the evidence of his diaries. Indeed, as Dr. Bleser makes clear, not only did such usage include concubinism, but— and nothing could offer greater proof of Hammond's attitude toward the human inferiority of blacks—Hammond took for his mistress an eighteen-year-old slave with a one-year-old female child, and then when the child reached the age of twelve he made her his mistress as well!

What sent Hammond into political eclipse for 13 years following the end of his term as governor of South Carolina in 1844 was a sexual indiscretion of an altogether different sort. The four young daughters of his wealthy brother-in-law, Wade Hampton II, were accustomed to spend much time with the Hammonds, and eventually Hampton learned that all four of them were in the habit of engaging, apparently *en masse*, in the most intimate cuddling with their uncle. In Hammond's words,

> Here were four lovely creatures from the tender but precocious girl of 13 to the mature but fresh and blooming woman nearly 19, each contending for my love, claiming the greater share of it as due to her superior devotion to me, all of them rushing on every occasion to my arms and covering me with kisses, lolling on my lap, pressing their bodies almost into mine, wreathing their limbs with mine, encountering warmly every portion of my frame, and permitting my hands to stray unchecked over every part of them and to rest without the slightest shrinking of it, in the most secret and sacred regions, and all this for a period of more than two years continuously. Is it in flesh and blood to withstand this? . . . Nay are there many who would have the self-control to stop where I did? Am I not after all entitled to some, the smallest portion of, credit for not going further? [9 December 1846]

Hammond's outraged brother-in-law, who thought Hammond had gone much too far as it was, thereafter took it upon himself to see that influential friends knew of Hammond's misbehavior, and when a seat in the United States Senate became vacant the knowledge of Hammond's conduct was sufficient to keep him from being elected by the legislature. Typically, although continually asserting his own guilt and remorse, Hammond thereafter filled his diaries with censure of the Hamptons, charging them with every kind of hypocrisy, justifying his own conduct as no more than a regrettable but unavoidable weakness of the flesh, and complaining bitterly that the people of South Carolina had no right whatever to deny him political office merely because of such private goings-on! (Apparently the powers that be, or enough of them, eventually agreed, because when Senator A. P. Butler died in 1857, Hammond was named to fill the unexpired term, and afterward could have been reelected in his own right.)

In almost every respect James Henry Hammond seems to have resembled nothing less than a monster. Yet there must have been more to him than that, for otherwise how could he have gained and held the close friendship of a man like Gilmore Simms, whose moral and ethical standards were of the highest, and who, though likewise a parvenu in the South Carolina establishment, was generous, loyal, compassionate, indulgent to his slaves, and a devoted family man?

Perhaps the diaries that Dr. Bleser has so ably edited may offer clues to the matter that I have failed to perceive. I would, however, in closing note one thing more. When *The Hammonds of Redcliffe* appeared in 1981, more than one reviewer made the point that if one could imagine the counterpart of Thomas Sutpen in William Faulkner's *Absalom, Absalom!* who unlike Sutpen was also highly articulate and gifted at rationalizing away his misdeeds, he would come close to resembling James Henry Hammond. Like the protagonist of Faulkner's novel, Hammond too possessed a "design," and in its service he subordinated all human considerations, including those of family and fatherhood. Hammond used people as if they were commodities, just as Sutpen did. Hammond too was of humble origins, though not so lowly as those of Sutpen. He aspired to the plantation aristocracy, married not for love but in order to advance his social status, fathered children on a slave mistress and would not recognize them, dreamed grandly and failed massively. Like Sutpen, too, however more articulate in voicing his dismay at what was happening to his design, Hammond could not understand where or why he had gone wrong, and sought to explain away his moral transgressions as no more than unfortunate mistakes in tactics. To a degree, like Sutpen he was "innocent"—not in the sense of being blameless but of failing, for all his great intelligence, to recognize that the world did not exist solely for his benefit.

Life, as has been observed, has a way sometimes of imitating art. Isn't it odd that, a half-century following publication of Faulkner's great novel of the Old South, a James Henry Hammond should emerge from unremembered obscurity with a personality, and with recorded deeds, that seem so strikingly to resemble the protagonist of *Absalom, Absalom!* And what is more, readers familiar with Faulkner's fiction will have recognized at once that Hammond's deed of taking first a slave woman and then later her daughter for his mistress constitutes a sickening parallel with the behavior of a character in yet another of Faulkner's works of fiction, old Carothers McCaslin of "The Bear."

Readers of these diaries of James Henry Hammond—and henceforth his diaries must be required reading for anyone who would understand the history and nature of the Old South—will discover that at one point in his career Hammond himself wanted to write a novel. He was quick to plead his lack of capacity for doing so. "The great points of human character have been forced on my consideration," he wrote in his diary on 28 August 1841, "and I have reflected much upon the workings of the human heart. But even if I could convey my ideas of these things fully, I could not make up for the want of minute practical knowledge in the innumerable variety of positions in which men and women must be exhibited in these works." And he concludes, "I wish I could get [rid] of the idea finally, but I doubt if I ever shall until I write and fail, that I think will cure me."

So perhaps these "secret and sacred" diaries that Hammond left for posterity might be said, in a way, to represent *his* novel, his work of fiction. Not an invented tale or tales, perhaps, but "real life" as subject matter to be shaped and formed to his heart's desire. If so, there is no happy ending to the tale, and the protagonist largely fails to gain our sympathy or to achieve a suspension of disbelief. A "typical" Southern planter Hammond was not, but in his naked acquisitiveness, his intense ambition, and his willingness to use whoever or whatever comes to hand to advance his fortunes and achieve his goals, he represents all too aptly the terrible capacity for evil existing within a system that based its achievements and aspirations upon the ownership of human beings as slaves. The question that Harriet Beecher Stowe asked in her Afterword to *Uncle Tom's Cabin*, "Is *man* ever a creature to be trusted with wholly irresponsible power?" is appropriate here. But it is not Mrs. Stowe's novel that is likely to come to mind as one reads the Hammond diaries. Rather, it is Faulkner's great tragedy of the Old South, and in particular what young Quentin Compson finds himself thinking as he listens to Miss Rosa Coldfield telling about Thomas Sutpen:

> *It's because she wants it told*, he thought, *so that people whom she will never see and whose names she will never hear and who have never heard her name nor seen her face will read it and know at last why God let us lose the War: that only through the blood of our men and the tears of our women could He stay this demon and efface his name and lineage from the earth.*

Louis D. Rubin, Jr.

Preface

James Henry Hammond (1807–1864), a prominent South Carolina planter and politician, aspired to be recognized by his peers as the preeminent statesman and leader of the antebellum South. His goal through nearly all of his life was the dissolution of the Union, leading to a South independent and free of Northern constraints, rich and powerful in the community of nations, able to carry on into the future under the leadership of the planter aristocracy, an aristocracy based on the firm foundation provided by that essential institution—black slavery. Dreadful, impracticable, and immoral as we may now view his dream, it was apparently shared by millions, and hundreds of thousands of people died trying to realize it. We still marvel at their misguided valor, and we still ask why.

The work at hand does not deal directly with such a cosmic question, but rather, a personal diary, it deals with the motives and beliefs of only one man. However, Hammond was an important figure and more significantly for us he was an articulate intellectual, given to thoughtful and penetrating analysis of his times as he saw them. His diary offers many insights into the mind and ideology of that near mythic creature, the Southern planter and slaveholder. Hammond was a prolific writer, leaving behind many public papers, a great profusion of private letters, and many plantation records. He also left his "secret and sacred" diaries, which remarkably survived largely unexpurgated in the hands of his family for over half a century after his death. A portion of these diaries subsequently has been closely held by the South Caroliniana Library for over another half-century, and only now has permission been given for their publication. Through his voluminous writings Hammond has long been a subject of interest for historians, and his unpublished diaries should be fascinating for both the historian and the general reader. In tracing the legacy of the past, the problem for the historian always is to discern not just the facts of what happened but the facts of why it happened, what were the views of the protagonists, what did they believe in, what were they trying to do. The danger for the historian always, professional as well as amateur, is to assume that his historical personages have a set of beliefs, values, and world views which are similar to his. Thus since slavery is abhorrent in the modern world, it is easy to dismiss all slaveholders as abhorrent and immoral. It is easy but ahistorical, for such a view does not help to understand them. Most slaveholders perceived themselves as Christian, moral, God-fearing, decent people, Hammond typically claiming in his diary, "But I do not remember that I ever intentionally did wrong, and I do not think that I ever deliberately or otherwise, wronged any human being. If any accuse me of it, I am ready to meet the accusation openly, before any Tribunal. Human or Divine."[1]

Which brings us to James Henry Hammond and his diaries. By his own testimony we can judge him flawed. He owned hundreds of slaves, who died off at a great rate. Almost alone among the planter aristocracy, he clearly documents his proclivity for sexually exploiting his female slaves. In addition he debauched the young, the very young daughters of a fellow planter, his brother-in-law, a despicable practice then as now and certainly very dangerous then, when the *code duello* was still in fashion.

And yet his wife devoted herself to preserving his memory, his children revered him, his slave mistresses stayed on his plantation lands decades after emancipation, and his state turned to him for leadership and guidance as the final crisis approached. An extraordinary and fascinating man, in his "secret and sacred" diaries we have a rare opportunity to draw our own conclusions based upon one of the most remarkable documents in American history, written by a prominent and prosperous slaveholder, the owner of over 300 slaves and twenty-two square miles of plantations, living in a pivotal Southern state, during the heyday of the Cotton Kingdom. He poured into them his thoughts and views and rages and dreams. These ring with his true authentic voice, visionary, caustic, ironic, whining, anguished, outraged, petty, bombastic, vain, but never dull.

They cover many topics: the crises and strains of operating a large plantation; the deals and details of state politics; his comments, always penetrating and usually acrid, on the political figures of his day; the grand play of the national political scene; his personal cares; his concerns for his

1. James Henry Hammond Diary, October 3, 1854, James Henry Hammond Papers, The South Caroliniana Library at the University of South Carolina in Columbia, hereafter cited as SCL.

family and friends; the state of his stomach and bowels; and the complications of his sex life.

What is equally interesting for us is what he does not say. In his most private diary, in which he is given to discoursing on whatever may be troubling him, we might expect to find his private views on slavery, as opposed to his oft-stated public political views—in reality his private views seem to have been his public views, for he never questions the peculiar institution, never agonizes over it.

Finally, almost as in any good novel, the diaries can be read for insights unknown or unrecognized by the protagonist. Could he have done more and been more than he was? Did he have the natural talent? Probably. Did he have the strength and will and perserverance? Probably not. For twenty-five years we see that when he was faced with great opportunities and great responsibilities, he would self-destruct, either through illness or flagrantly foolish sexual misadventures. Thus late in his life, as secession was becoming a reality, to our not great surprise he resigns with unaccustomed quietness from the Senate, and returns home to his plantation in the country and his diary. He may have been too old, too sick, and too tired to play a leading role in the secession crisis, or he may have been following his lifelong pattern. An alternative speculation arises from noting that Hammond had recently, with great foresight, moved away from secession as a goal, feeling it was too late, would be ultimately unsuccessful, and would only result in a vast and terrible bloodletting. Probably no one man could have stayed the rush of events, but Hammond with his great skills of analysis and exposition might have made an interesting attempt. It is clear to the reader, however, that it was not in his character to do so.

The significance of these Hammond diaries lies in the range and versatility of their contents, the years they cover, and the remarkable talents of the diarist. As Thomas Mallon has noted in A Book of One's Own, we cannot read a diary and remain unacquainted with its author. "No form of expression more emphatically embodies the expresser," than a diary which is like "flesh made word." Although these diaries are not a daily compendium, Hammond frequently let a week or a month go by, he tended to keep his book on a more regular basis during times of personal trouble. As his diary unfolds, Hammond is revealed to be a keen participant of the nineteenth-century Southern slaveholding world, but he appears also to be an astute observer and critic of the Old South, an "outsider," in part, because he was labeled by his political foes as "the son of a Massachusetts adventurer," in part, because he was stigmatized by his sexual misconduct. In 1853 he was led to write that he was "nobody in politics, in society and in domestic life—wholly without *real place.*"[2]

These diaries of course must be used carefully as all primary material must be. For although Hammond had the capacity for self-analysis, he also had the talent for monumental self-deception. Unwilling to assume personal responsibility for his troubles, and thinking that as a very successful slaveholder he never had to say he was sorry, he at times is arrogant and insensitive, and at other times, he appears to be suffering from bouts of depression and neuroticism, but, whatever his mood, he is vividly self-expressive, and the reader gains access to Hammond and the rich texture of his life and times without the filter of an intervening author.

While we wait for the definitive study on the Southern planter class, the contents of Hammond's diaries can reveal much about the mind and life of one preeminent Southern slaveholder as well as impart some of the prevailing views of the Old South's master class. The pages of the "secret and sacred" diaries better document the thoughts and actions of one successful member of the slaveholding elite than those of any other known diary left by any other significant nineteenth-century American slaveholder.[3] In them, we can focus on a whole range of subjects including politics and politicians, patriarchy and plantation life, slavery and secession. Of John C. Calhoun, Hammond wrote bluntly that his "whole strength in this State—and he has none elsewhere—arises from the confidence our people have in his devotion to our peculiar interests. Let them once think he has sacraficed [sic] us, as I think he has, to his own ambitious views and he is prostrated."[4] On the secession of the South he wrote as early as 1844 that separation of the states is inevitable. "It might now be effected peaceably and properly," but he predicted that in "a few years hence it must take place in blood or the South remain in it as a subjugated region."[5] Hammond did modify his views on secession, and had come to believe by the late 1850s that it better served Southern interests to remain within the Union and take a firm stand against what he considered to be the North's violation of Southern rights. Yet when it appeared inevitable that South Carolina intended to secede he wrote, "We must go out at

2. James Henry Hammond to Marcellus C.M. Hammond, [1853], James Henry Hammond Papers, SCL; Thomas Mallon, *A Book of One's Own: People and Their Diaries* (New York: Ticknor and Fields, 1984), xvii.

3. *The Journal of Thomas B. Chaplin*, edited by Theodore Rosengarten and Susan W. Walker, and published by William Morrow & Company in 1986 (along with Rosengarten's *Tombee*), is a remarkably rich, and skillfully edited, record of an unsuccessful slaveholder of St. Helena Island in Beaufort District, South Carolina.

4. James Henry Hammond Diary, December 26, 1844, James Henry Hammond Papers, Library of Congress, hereafter cited as LC.

5. *Ibid.*, November 24, 1844.

once, and for good. Nothing half-way."[6] On owning slaves there is not a trace of defensiveness in Hammond's papers, and frequently in his accounts he lumps his human chattel with his livestock. For instance, he wrote in his diary on November 2, 1841, "for ten years I have been working hard, overwhelmed with anxiety and care and all I have made has been regularly swept off by death. . . . Negroes, cattle, mules, hogs, every thing that has life around me seems to labour under some fated malediction."

Hammond's narcissism always placed him at center stage. A restive Hammond, from the depths of self-pity, wrote in his diary on June 7, 1852, "I am left alone. My Mother never comes to see me. My wife never even sends a message unless it is something to annoy. Friends I have none. Neighbors none." Hammond cried out, "My God! What have I done or omitted to do to deserve this fate?" Raging and rationalizing, Hammond emerges from the pages of his diaries to answer his own question. The secret and sacred diaries of James Henry Hammond are a one-character melodrama.

Hammond, as we shall see, openly flaunted the mores of society. He was made to pay for that behavior, which outraged him, since he claimed he was far from unique. However that may be, what does seem to be unique was the preservation by his family of the detailed records of his behavior. His voluminous and uncensored papers deposited for the most part in the Library of Congress as the James Henry Hammond Papers and in the South Caroliniana Library at the University of South Carolina as the James Henry Hammond Papers and the Hammond-Bryan-Cumming Papers have attracted many scholars in Southern history to write on Hammond. This writer acknowledges a vast debt to those who have built up an extensive body of work on James Henry Hammond including the editors of his speeches and addresses; three biographers, Elizabeth Merritt, Robert Tucker, and Drew Faust, the last having done the most comprehensive and widely acclaimed study of him; and Clement Eaton and Charles Wiltse, who have each written profiles of Hammond (Wiltse, the biographer of Calhoun, described Hammond as a person "of great ability with a mind probably second only to Calhoun's").[7] For their studies on the South, John Barnwell, Bertram Wyatt-Brown, Orville Vernon Burton, and John B. Edmunds, Jr., made extensive use of Hammond's papers as did the editors of the William Gilmore Simms Papers. Also there is Drew Faust's

6. James Henry Hammond to Colonel Beaufort T. Watts, November 28, 1860, James Henry Hammond Papers, SCL.

7. John C. Calhoun, *Sectionalist, 1840–1850* (Indianapolis: Bobbs-Merrill, 1951), 54.

work on the leading intellectuals of the Old South, in which Hammond figured prominently, and my study of four generations of the Hammond family beginning with the founder of the dynasty, James Henry Hammond. My greatest debt is to Hammond's great-grandson, John Shaw Billings II, a gifted journalist, who became the second in command in Henry Luce's Time-Life empire. Billings amassed, arranged, and donated to the South Caroliniana Library at his death in 1975 the massive Hammond-Bryan-Cumming Papers upon which many historians now draw extensively for their studies of Hammond, slavery, politics, plantation life, and Southern family history.

Seemingly no aspect of Hammond's life has gone unnoticed. In addition to studies exploring Hammond as an agriculturist, slaveowner, politician, patriarch, and intellectual, his possible homosexual behavior has been described by Martin Duberman, and in a recent article Lawrence McDonnell depicted Hammond as a possible suicide and his death as a metaphor for that of the Old South.[8] In spite of all that has been said about James Henry Hammond, it is not all that could be said. His own story in his own words has not yet been told.

There are four unpublished diaries that Hammond labeled "secret and sacred," and they cover the years 1836–1862. Two volumes, one and three, are held by the Library of Congress, are open to the public and available on microfilm. Two volumes, two and four, have been held by the South Caroliniana Library and were not available to the public. Volume one was written in intermittently from the spring of 1836 until September 1839,

---

8. *Selections from the Letters and Speeches of the Hon. James H. Hammond of South Carolina* (New York: John F. Trow, 1866); Clyde N. Wilson, ed., recently reprinted the 1866 edition; Elizabeth Merritt, *James Henry Hammond 1807–1864* (Baltimore: Johns Hopkins University Press, 1923); Robert C. Tucker, "James Henry Hammond, South Carolinian," Ph.D. dissertation, University of North Carolina, 1958; Drew Gilpin Faust, *James Henry Hammond and the Old South: A Design for Mastery* (Baton Rouge: Louisiana State University Press, 1982); Clement Eaton, "The Hamlet of the Old South," in *The Mind of the Old South* (Baton Rouge: Louisiana State University Press, 1964), 44–68; Charles Wiltse examined Hammond's political role in South Carolina in *John C. Calhoun, Nullifier, 1829–1839* (Indianapolis: Bobbs-Merrill, 1949), and *John C. Calhoun, Sectionalist, 1840–1850;* John Barnwell, *Love of Order: South Carolina's First Secession Crisis* (Chapel Hill: University of North Carolina Press, 1982); Orville Vernon Burton, *In My Father's House Are Many Mansions: Family and Community in Edgefield, South Carolina* (Chapel Hill: University of North Carolina Press, 1985); Bertram Wyatt-Brown, *Southern Honor: Ethics and Behavior in the Old South* (New York: Oxford University Press, 1982); John B. Edmunds, Jr., *Francis W. Pickens and the Politics of Destruction* (Chapel Hill: University of North Carolina Press, 1986); Mary C. Oliphant, Alfred Taylor, and T. C. Eaves, eds., *The Letters of William Gilmore Simms,* 5 vols. (Columbia: University of South Carolina Press, 1952–56); Drew Faust, *A Sacred Circle: The Dilemma of the Intellectual in the Old South, 1840–1860* (Baltimore: Johns Hopkins University Press, 1977); Carol Bleser, *The Hammonds of Redcliffe* (New York: Oxford University Press, 1981); Martin Duberman, " 'Writhing Bedfellows': 1826 Two Young Men from Antebellum South Carolina's Ruling Elite Share 'Extravagant Delight,' " *Journal of Homosexuality,* Fall/Winter 1980/81, pp. 85–101; and Lawrence T. McDonnell, "Struggle Against Suicide: James Henry Hammond and the Secession of South Carolina," *Southern Studies,* Summer 1983, pp. 109–37.

and volume two covers the period from September 26, 1839, to December 26, 1840, when Hammond ran an unsuccessful and bruising campaign for governor. Volume three was written in continuously from February 1841 to March 1846, and volume four, an intensely personal document, illuminating events ordinary and extraordinary, covers the period from April 1, 1846, to September 20, 1862, and includes Hammond's several versions of his involvement with his young nieces, almost the only extant records. Following the fall of Fort Sumter in April 1861, Hammond's health, which had always been precarious, began to fail him completely, and in his diary on September 20, 1862, he recorded in an unsteady hand, "I shall not probably go further in my story." The diary abruptly ends. Hammond, fortunately for the editor, was unable to give up the habit of a lifetime, and had, in fact in the autumn of 1861, resumed writing in his plantation journal, a task he had earlier relinquished to his son Paul. Hammond had kept an almost uninterrupted plantation journal since his marriage in 1831 (which is on deposit and open to the public at the South Caroliniana Library) in which he recorded in brief entries the day-to-day planting operations on his estates including the weather, planting schedules, crop conditions, comments on slaves, *etc.*, as well as notations on the comings and goings of family and friends. Among these wartime journal entries, however, with no other diary to keep, he frequently broke out from the narrow confines of his task and made lengthy and sometimes censorious comments on wartime disasters both on the battlefield and at home. On October 22, 1864, this journal ends. Hammond died twenty-one days later on November 13, just two days before his fifty-seventh birthday and just three days before General William Sherman began his March to the Sea, a calamity for the South foreseen by Hammond. Volume one, which is more a collection of random jottings than a diary, is not published here, nor is volume two, which is not a chronicle of the times, but is almost exclusively a personal record of Hammond's unsuccessful pursuit of the governorship in 1840. Volume three held by the Library of Congress and volume four on deposit in the safe at the South Caroliniana Library are brought together here in the publication of this book.

On February 6, 1841, Hammond seated at his desk in the library of his Columbia town house began volume three of his diary and wrote on its first page, "I want a friend to whose sympathetic bosom I could confide anything to whom I could speak of myself as I am. . . . Such a friend," he concluded, "I can now only find in this book." The private side of the life of James Henry Hammond recorded here begins on that gloomy February day in 1841 and spans over two decades.

Acknowledgments

I wish to thank the former director of the South Caroliniana Library of the University of South Carolina, Les Inabinet, for granting me permission to publish those parts of the "secret and sacred" diaries of James Henry Hammond that were in his possession. These intimate and sensitive documents had been locked away in a safe at the library for more than fifty years, and were shown only to selected scholars, who could read them but not take notes or make direct quotations. Before they came to the library, the family had carefully preserved them, largely unexpurgated, since Hammond's death in 1864. In light of the resurgent interest by American historians in the life of James Henry Hammond in particular and in American slaveholders in general, Mr. Inabinet decided that these unpublished diaries, although containing some very controversial material of both a public and private nature, should at last be made available to general readers and scholars interested in the lives of nineteenth-century Southern planters, of whom Hammond was a well-known and flamboyant example. Without Les's full cooperation this study could not have been undertaken.

I am as always deeply indebted to Allen Stokes, the current Director of the South Caroliniana Library, for his wide-ranging knowledge of all the manuscript collections in his care and for his sustained interest and his valuable assistance which enabled me to see this project through to completion. He is also a wise friend whom I hold in very high esteem. I am most appreciative, too, for the aid of Herbert Hartsook, Henry Fulmer, Eleanor Richardson, Tom Johnson, Charles Gay, Laura Costello, and the rest of the staff of the South Caroliniana Library. I wish to thank the staff of the South Carolina Department of Archives and History, especially the former director, Charles Lee, who has unstintingly supported my work,

---

assistant director, Charles Lesser, reference archivist, Wylma Wates, the director of the Search Room, Alexia Helsley, and her very able staff including the exceptionally helpful Ruth Trice. In addition I want to thank the staff of the South Carolina Historical Society, especially its director, David Moltke-Hansen, and his second-in-command, Harlan Greene. I also wish to express my appreciation to the staffs of the Manuscript Divisions of the Library of Congress, the National Archives, the Southern Historical Collection at the University of North Carolina, and the William R. Perkins Library at Duke University. My thanks go also to the librarians at the New York Public Library, Colgate University, Clemson University, the University of South Carolina, and on Long Island to the Bellport Memorial Library and the Patchogue-Medford Library (under the directorship of Sara Courant).

I am deeply grateful for the help and encouragement of Walter Edgar, director of the Institute for Southern Studies at the University of South Carolina who has given me shelter and scholarly assistance at the Institute on numerous occasions, even after I went to a rival institution, Clemson University. In addition graduate assistant Megan Lembach was unstinting in her efforts to track down information, and I am as well deeply grateful to Nancy Ashmore, the administrative assistant, and to Tibby Dozier of the staff. I know I owe a particular debt to Tibby, much greater than that of secretarial support.

I owe a very special acknowledgment to Louis D. Rubin, Jr., Professor of Southern Literature at the University of North Carolina at Chapel Hill, a journalist, critic, and the director of his own press, Algonquin Books, who read the entire manuscript, and to whom I am deeply grateful for placing these diaries in a literary perspective in his most kind and graceful Foreword to this book. The only restrictions placed on me by Mr. Inabinet were that I not have the manuscript typed locally or sent out to colleagues in the field before publication, only Professor Rubin was exempted because of his special literary perspective, which I felt was needed.

Many other persons, however, shared with me their mutual interest in Southern history or the life and times of James Henry Hammond. Of especial importance has been the wisdom of my good friend Drew Faust of the University of Pennsylvania. My debt to her is vast. The late James Henry Billings, a well-known painter and the great-grandson of James Henry Hammond, Susan Cerasano of the Colgate University English Department, Catherine Clinton of Harvard University, Michael Foley of the South Carolina Department of Parks, Recreation and Tourism, Elizabeth Fox-Genovese of Emory University, Frederick Heath of Winthrop College, George Rogers and John G. Sproat of the University of South Carolina,

ACKNOWLEDGMENTS

Kenneth Stampp of the University of California at Berkeley, and Wylma Wates of the South Carolina Department of Archives and History were early sources of encouragement and raised questions that I am sure in the answering made this a better study. Mary Giunta, Assistant Director of the Publications Program of the National Historical Publications and Records Commission, shared with me her vast knowledge of historical editing and helped clarify my thoughts on solving the particular puzzles of editing Hammond's diaries. I am deeply grateful.

Photographs have been provided through the courtesy of the South Caroliniana Library, the University Archives of the University of South Carolina, and Clemson University.

I had one typist, Rosalie Hiam, of Colgate University, formerly of Great Britain; she not only typed the manuscript, but rendered important assistance by recognizing immediately all of Hammond's Britishisms. Roger Bell of Seneca, South Carolina, put the unedited first draft of the manuscript on that modern convenience, the word-processor. I thank him for the hundreds of hours he saved me and for his very expert work.

I consider myself very privileged to have Sheldon Meyer as my editor, and my gratitude goes to Leona Capeless for her editorial wisdom and patience.

I am especially thankful for the financial support provided by the National Endowment for the Humanities, the American Philosophical Society, the Colgate Research Council, and the Clemson University Provost Award. I owe a special debt of gratitude to Colgate president, George Langdon, and to the provost, Charles Trout (both historians), who generously supported my work at Colgate, and to my former departmental chairman, Briton C. Busch, who understood my need to work in Southern manuscript collections and arranged my schedules accordingly. In my new surroundings at Clemson, I am most appreciative of all the members of the History Department, especially my chairman, John Wunder, and my colleague, Alan Schaffer. My thanks also go to Kathryn and Calhoun Lemon, and Dean Robert Waller.

Finally, I should like to acknowledge the loving support of both my husband, who has served unsparingly as my computer expert, and his parents, who celebrate their eightieth birthdays this year.

Bellport, New York
February 1988   C.B.

Editorial Procedures and Policies

The first objective of the editor was to maintain the integrity of Hammond's diaries for the scholar. The second objective was to make them readily accessible to the general reader. Fortunately Hammond wrote his diaries in narrative form, so these objectives are not mutually exclusive and the diaries are easily comprehensible.

Of James Henry Hammond's four personal diaries, covering the period 1836–1862, this book brings together and publishes for the first time the last two volumes, spanning the years 1841–1862, and, to fill in the last several years of Hammond's life, supplementary entries from his plantation journal, 1861–1864, two letters exchanged between Hammond and his eldest son, Harry, in November 1861, and an eyewitness account of his death by his son Spann. Less than 10 percent of the 1841–1862 diary text of 365 pages, written in a small hand, of which only a few words were finally indecipherable, was deemed extraneous and repetitious and not transcribed, and these occurrences, which include some rambling theological disquisitions, are indicated in the text by ellipsis points; in addition the omission of a whole entry is indicated by ellipsis points preceding the heading of the next entry. Those entries dropped in their entirety are: August 26, 1841; August 31, 1841; April 10, 1845; and September 10, 1854 (8 pages on "My Religion"). In Chapter 9, drawn from the Plantation Journal in which Hammond made almost daily entries, I have used only a fraction of the entries and the ellipsis points indicate only omissions within the entry.

I have let stand Hammond's British and archaic spellings, as well as the following words that for twenty-five years he consistently misspelled: cemetery, negotiate, sacrifice, and separate. For aesthetic reasons I have corrected his consistent misspellings of believe and relieve. His other infrequent misspellings I have let stand, but noted by *[sic]*. To prevent misunderstanding, I have, without notice to the reader, introduced a pronoun, a conjunction, or an article. I have in addition added to the punctuation as an aid to the reader, again without notification, principally through the introduction of a limited number of necessary commas. In the text of the diaries, editorial interventions are enclosed in square brackets (i.e., [   ]). The paragraphing remains as Hammond arranged it, but the chapter divisions and chapter titles are my own selections.

Manuscript volumes one and three, as previously noted, may be consulted in their entirety at the Library of Congress and are also available on microfilm. Volumes two and four are to be made available to researchers at the South Caroliniana Library following the publication of this book, but they are not included in the Library's selections for the microfilm series, *Records of Ante-Bellum Southern Plantations from the Revolution through the Civil War.*[9]

In the interest of the general reader, I have used editorial interventions in the text of the diaries instead of footnotes, and I have provided a biographical directory of some of the principal characters who parade back and forth across the pages of this narrative, emphasizing their personal or political relationship to Hammond. The Introduction is my account[10] of the first 33 years of Hammond's life until he starts volume 3 of his diary on February 6, 1841. On that date, with Chapter I, the diary proper begins, Hammond providing his own brief summary of his life and then going on to record the occurrences of the year, not fully finding his voice, I feel, until Chapter II. Chapter V marks the start of volume 4 of his diaries. An Epilogue and a Biographical Directory of family, friends, and foes conclude *Secret and Sacred: The Diaries of James Henry Hammond, a Southern Slaveholder.*

9. Hammond's plantation journals, however, are included in the microfilm series on antebellum plantation records being published by University Publications of America, under the general editorship of Kenneth M. Stampp.

10. I have drawn freely upon volumes one and two of Hammond's diaries, 1836–1840, as well as upon *The Hammonds of Redcliffe* for the introductory chapter to this work.

Contents

Secret and Sacred

Introduction

Young James Henry Hammond,
1807–1840

James Henry Hammond compared his life to that of the mythical Sisyphus, compelled to roll a stone to the top of a slope, the stone always escaping him near the top and rolling down again except, Hammond added melodramatically, that "the stone rolling back has always broken some limb of mine and utterly crushed some body connected with me."[1] He might have added that his father spent his life rolling a stone up a hill but never got it high enough to cause damage when it escaped.

Elisha Hammond, the father of James Henry Hammond, was born in New England just before the American Revolution at New Bedford, Massachusetts. As a youth, Elisha Hammond was a manual laborer, but in 1795, at the age of twenty-one, he began attending the local academies, working half of each year so that he could study the other half. In that way he gained enough education to enter Dartmouth College. Elisha's life at Dartmouth was a hard one for he was a good ten years older than most of his classmates and he had constantly to break off his education to go out and earn money for tuition and living expenses. Nevertheless, he was graduated in the class of 1802 when he was twenty-eight years old. Setting off to seek his fortune, he went, for reasons unknown, to Charleston, South Carolina, arriving there in the late fall of 1802 without money or contacts. His first job was as a teacher at the Mount Bethel Academy in Newberry, almost 150 miles from Charleston. There Elisha remained until 1805, when he unexpectedly received an appointment as professor of languages at the newly opened South Carolina College (now the University of South Carolina), forty miles away at the state capital, Columbia.

In the quicker paced world of Columbia, the thirty-one-year-old New Englander met twenty-year-old Catherine Fox Spann of Edgefield, South

---

1. James Henry Hammond Diary, August 26, 1856, SCL.

3

Carolina, who was living in town with her recently widowed mother. Although Catherine like Elisha had no fortune of her own, she hoped some day to inherit a portion of the estate of her rich bachelor uncle John Fox. Catherine and Elisha were married in 1806, and soon thereafter they returned to Newberry, where Elisha became the principal of Mount Bethel Academy. Catherine, besides keeping house for her husband and overseeing the residential life of the boarding students at the Academy, gave birth between 1807 and 1814 to three daughters and two sons. In 1815, a disgruntled Elisha, already forty-one years old and still struggling to make ends meet, decided to try his luck again in the fast growing capital, taking with him to Columbia his wife and their four surviving children, one daughter having died in 1814. Although the Hammonds had several more children only four lived to maturity: James Henry born in 1807, Caroline Augusta in 1810, Marcus Claudius Marcellus in 1814, and John Fox in 1820.[2]

Prosperity continued to elude Elisha. However, his eldest child, James Henry, entered the junior class at South Carolina College in 1823, at the age of sixteen, having been tutored by his father at home in Latin, Greek, and other classical studies. At college James Henry, considered by his father the brightest of his offspring, rubbed shoulders with the sons of the South Carolina gentry, for by the 1820s the school had come to be regarded as the training ground for the leaders of the Palmetto State. Hammond, like many of his peers, tells us that while he was at college he gave himself up "to idle associates and neither read nor studied until the close of my time,"[3] but unlike his classmates Hammond did not succumb to the touchy fractious behavior of the sons of South Carolina's antebellum aristocracy who rushed to the field of honor upon the slightest pretext. Hammond sought prominence through oratory, becoming active in and eventually president of the prestigious Euphradian Society, a college debating club. At the college commencement in December 1825, Hammond managed to graduate fourth in a class of thirty-one.

Some flavor of college life, and after, in South Carolina in the 1820s can be gained from a set of twenty-four letters to Hammond from Thomas Jefferson Withers,[4] his close friend, and eventually a leading South Carolina jurist. Withers tells us that Hammond's motto at college had been

2. As noted in the preface, footnote #10, information in the Introduction is also drawn from Bleser, *The Hammonds of Redcliffe*.

3. "Thoughts and Recollections," February 24, 1852, Janes Henry Hammond Papers, SCL.

4. Thomas Jefferson Withers to James Henry Hammond, 21 letters, 1826–28, in James Henry Hammond Papers, SCL; Thomas Jefferson Withers to James Henry Hammond, 3 letters, 1826–27, James Henry Hammond Papers, LC.

"Women, wine and cigars," in that order. However, after college they were without any real wealth or social status and had to stand on the fringe of Southern society. "We cannot be independent without money," Withers lamented to Hammond, and though "we may despise the aristocracy of wealth and try to scorn its frowns . . . they press too hard and gall too much to be treated with levity."[5] Most of his correspondence to Hammond concerns his preoccupation with the opposite sex and is bawdy and scatological. In one letter he confessed to feeling so "horny" but feared getting the "Clap," especially since "pale faces among the raking youth of town evince its existence and having passed thro' the fiery furnaces of fear during last June I feel as wild as a brick."[6] It has been suggested that Withers and Hammond may have had a homosexual relationship when they were roommates at college.[7] However this suggestion results from a rather tortured reading of passages from just two of the twenty-four letters. These passages can more easily be viewed as deriving from the fact that Hammond and Withers shared a bed, the norm for those times, and from the fact that young men, Hammond was sixteen to eighteen years of age in college, are frequently tumescent without any specific sexual stimulation.

Although educated with the best of South Carolina society, Hammond, upon graduation at the age of eighteen, felt pressed to take a teaching job away from the capital, a move he resented. Since his birth, his restless and unsuccessful father had been a teacher and then the principal at Mount Bethel Academy, a professor at South Carolina College, a farmer, a merchant, and a food steward at the college. Not only had Elisha failed to provide his son with the means to live comfortably, but much to James's shame, his parents by the late 1820s were heavily in debt, and with several children still at home, forced to take in boarders after Elisha's latest failure as a barge operator on the Savannah River. Moreover, after twenty years of marriage, the senior Hammonds had given up all hope of receiving any substantial gifts from Catherine's uncle, although in 1820, in a gesture meant to flatter John Fox, they had named a son for him. Elisha wrote his son James in 1827 that they could expect nothing from the old man in his lifetime, and he "is tending more crabid [sic] than ever, crosses and injures me in everything he can, but I will bear it in patience and mean

5. Thomas Jefferson Withers to James Henry Hammond, April 14 and November 10, 1826, James Henry Hammond Papers, SCL.
6. Ibid., October 31, 1826.
7. Martin Duberman, " 'Writhing Bedfellows' ": 1826 Two Young Men from Antebellum South Carolina's Ruling Elite Share " 'Extravagant Delight,' " Journal of Homosexuality, Fall/Winter 1980/81, pp. 85–101.

to bear it."[8] Two months after the death in 1828 of his daughter Adele, Elisha confided to his son that John Fox had attempted "to destroy the chastity of your sisters," a thing, Elisha wrote, "I never intended to have related to you, yet he did it more than one time." If ever, he swore to James, "I come in contact with him again I will break his head."[9] The image of his compromised father who had been willing to overlook the attempts of a rich old man to molest his daughters in order to secure an inheritance for his family was not lost on James. He himself, he vowed, would not live in the shadow of wealth nor would he allow any of his family to do so. Years later he wrote to his younger brother named for John Fox that he was glad that John's engagement to a local belle had been broken, because the young woman's father "will never surrender one cent before he dies," and John no doubt would have had "to struggle on through life with a family and fretful wife, hanging on the skirts of a miserly father who will live for 40 years."[10]

Although Elisha Hammond apparently never applied his superior intellect to ask what he really wanted to do with his own life, he freely lectured his son James on health, diet, exercise, regulating his bowels (a concern that almost bordered on being an obsession among the Victorians), improving his mind, and reading the Scriptures. From his lips came no praise. As for his son's career, Elisha urged his eldest child to become a lawyer, and he thought that his own life would have been vastly different and by implication very much better if he himself had studied law. Since James considered the time he had taught school as "time most unprofitably spent," he took his father's advice, gave up teaching, and began reading law in the offices of several leading attorneys. Of this apprenticeship he later recalled, "at least I was in all these offices, but I do not remember that any of these gentlemen asked me a question about law. I read their books and in return did some little filling of blanks for them, that was all." Nevertheless, in 1828 at the age of twenty-one, Hammond was admitted to the bar and opened an office in Columbia.[11]

The times were inauspicious for beginning a law practice, the field seemed overcrowded, and the economic depression that had struck the United States following the Panic of 1819 continued its hold in the South throughout the 1820s. The seaboard states were especially hard hit. Land values, exports, and slave prices all fell, and South Carolina planters found it difficult to compete in cotton production with planters opening up newer

8. Elisha Hammond to James Henry Hammond, April 12, 1827, James Henry Hammond Papers, SCL.
9. *Ibid.*, November 5, 1828.
10. James Henry Hammond to John Fox Hammond, May 2 1841, *ibid.*
11. "Thoughts and Recollections," February 24, 1852, *ibid.*

and richer lands in Alabama and Mississippi. In the summer of 1829 Elisha Hammond died suddenly, apparently of yellow fever, leaving a widow and several dependent children. James Henry soon felt the pressure to look after them and to become as well his mother's emotional anchor; at twenty-two years of age Hammond had the responsibilities of a fifty-year-old. Nevertheless, Hammond, a popular young attorney, attracted clients and began to prosper. A career in politics beckoned. In early 1830, Hammond was hired to edit a new publication, *The Southern Times*. In it he advocated states' rights and nullification of the tariff of 1828, positions popular with South Carolina voters. He began to communicate regularly with John C. Calhoun, Robert Y. Hayne, George McDuffie, James Hamilton, and the other "leading spirits" of the day in South Carolina. Vice President Calhoun even sought Hammond's advice on the strategy he should pursue to obtain the presidential nomination in 1832.[12] This attention and social contact must have been immensely flattering to the twenty-three-year-old son of a schoolmaster. But Hammond unerringly knew that being a popular lawyer and editor though making him personally well-known would not bring him the power he craved. He needed to look elsewhere, to the acquisition of land and slaves, for that was the prerequisite for success in antebellum South Carolina society. To become a member of the master class he needed a rich wife.

Many women, intrigued by James Henry's good looks, his slightly licentious smile, and his slightly tarnished sexual reputation, were attracted to the dark-haired, dark-eyed, and quite handsome young man. His friend Withers thought him capable even of catching a daughter of Wade Hampton I. Hampton at the time was considered to be one of the richest planters in all of the South and was the father of five daughters. Instead, in 1829, Hammond met Catherine Fitzsimons, the young sister-in-law of Wade Hampton II, at the Columbia home of Catherine's sister, Ann Fitzsimons Hampton.[13] Their father, Christopher Fitzsimons, after inheriting some Charleston property from an uncle, had emigrated to South Carolina from Ireland following the American Revolution. An ambitious young man, he became a very successful cotton factor, handling the sale of his clients' cotton in both the European and Northern markets. In 1788, he married Catherine Pritchard, the daughter of Paul Pritchard, a Charleston ship builder who had emigrated to Charleston from Scotland. The newlyweds prospered and soon became a part of the Charleston planter aristocracy

12. *Ibid.*; James Henry Hammond Common Place Book, March 18, 1831, James Henry Hammond Papers, LC.

13. Virginia G. Meynard, *The Venturers: The Hampton, Harrison, and Earle Families of Virginia, South Carolina, and Texas* (Easley, S. C.: Southern Historical Press, 1981), 1955.

investing less and less of their capital in mercantile interests and sinking more and more of their funds into plantations and slaves in South Carolina and Georgia.[14]

A painting of Catherine Pritchard Fitzsimons holding her daughter Catherine was done by Charles Willson Peale, the Philadelphia society portraitist, when young Catherine was about twenty months old. In it, Catherine, with a round sweet face and large dark eyes, appears to be an alert looking child. The youngest of ten children, little is known of Catherine's childhood, except that her family lived in a grand style, vacationing nearly every year in Philadelphia, New York, or Newport. In 1807, Christopher Fitzsimons purchased the William Rhett mansion in Charleston, where Catherine was born in 1814 and where her sister Ann was married three years later to Wade Hampton II in what has been described as "one of the most elaborate weddings Charlestonians had ever witnessed." Ann's wedding dress of white lace was embroidered with pearls, and her attendants wore gowns of rich white silk. After the wedding service an elegant supper "was served by six waiters wearing white gloves, and the many tiered wedding cake, decorated with small swans and rabbits of spun sugar, was displayed on a stand of plate glass." Christopher Fitzsimons at his death in 1825 left an estate estimated at $700,000 to be divided between his widow and their four surviving children. Catherine, only eleven years old when her father died, inherited several plantations in and around Beech Island, South Carolina, just across the Savannah River from Augusta, Georgia.[15]

Plain-looking, fatherless, shy, and awkward, Catherine met James when she was only fifteen years old. The dashing young lawyer swept her off her feet, but the courtship between the vulnerable young heiress and the ambitious Hammond was troubled from the outset, the match being vigorously opposed by Catherine's mother, her brothers, and the Hamptons.[16] To them, Hammond, although personally attractive and well-educated, was without social rank or money, an obvious fortune hunter. Hammond continued to press his suit, and, when Catherine refused to give up her suitor, her family asked him to renounce her dower. Outraged, and most certainly remembering his father's humiliating experience at the hands of

14. *Ibid.*, 149; John Shaw Billings, Ms. vol. bd. Jan. 1956, Christopher Fitzsimons, 1762–1825, John Shaw Billings Collection, SCL.

15. Meynard, *The Venturers*, 149–50; John Shaw Billings, Christopher Fitzsimons, 1762–1825, John Shaw Billings Collections, SCL.

16. Thomas W. Brevard to James Henry Hammond, June 18, 1830, April 12, 1831, James Spann to James Henry Hammond, July 19, 1830, July 26, 1830, James Henry Hammond Papers, SCL; Faust, *Hammond: A Design for Mastery*, 58–61.

John Fox, Hammond refused. At an impasse, and with the strain on Catherine, a lovesick teenager, immense, Mrs. Fitzsimons relented. The wedding took place in June 1831.

Catherine's relatives were of course right. Hammond's future conduct and his views on marriage and on women make it doubtful that he ever loved her. In 1852, he wrote in an often quoted letter to his eldest son, that he expected large dowers for all his sons, "not only in virtues but in palpabilities: Somehow—God forgive me—I never could bear poor girls [even] when pretty and pure spirited . . . [I] avoided them. Even the sweetest pill of that kind should be gilded." In Hammond's view "women were made to breed—men to do the work of this world. As a toy for recreation, and one soon tires of any given one for this, or as bringing wealth and position, men are *tempted* to marry them and the world is kept peopled."[17] In pursuit of his worldly ambition, Hammond, twenty-three years old and at the height of his vigor, took possession of a seventeen-year-old bride and her handsome dowry. Marriage to Catherine, he later wrote, was his greatest achievement. Ironically, the vision of success to which Hammond was wedded—a plantation economy based upon slavery—had become by then increasingly repugnant to much of the Western world.

After an extended honeymoon, Hammond returned to Columbia and closed his law office. Accompanied by his wife, he went to Beech Island to take control of Catherine's dowry, which, as he described it in his plantation journal, consisted of Silver Bluff plantation of approximately 7,500 acres, other properties totaling in all about 10,800 acres, 147 slaves, a residence, household furniture, 26 farm animals, 90 to 100 head of cattle, 180 to 190 hogs, bushels of corn, potatoes, and wheat, bags of ginned cotton, and hams and poultry of various kinds.[18] The Beech Island region, where Catherine's plantations were located, was one of the most naturally productive regions of South Carolina. In addition, the lands lay within a dozen miles of Augusta, the second largest city in Georgia, an industrial and cotton-shipping center with access via the Savannah River to Georgia's largest city, Savannah, one of the principal ports in the United States.

Even with Catherine's fortune, Hammond could not settle down at Silver Bluff to live a life of ease as a cultured country gentleman, fulfilling the stereotypical image of the antebellum planter in the Old South. His wife's father had done little or nothing to improve Catherine's properties,

17. James Henry Hammond to Harry Hammond, December 20, 1852, Hammond-Bryan-Cumming Family Papers, SCL.
18. James Henry Hammond Plantation Journal, December 8, 1831, SCL.

much of which were swamp land. Hammond alleged that when he married Catherine her property brought in a net income of only $600 a year.[19] Although Hammond knew little about large-scale planting, he threw himself energetically into learning to become an agriculturist and eventually achieved great success at it. Inexperienced also as a slaveholder, in the beginning, he tended to be an extremely harsh master and sought to compel his slaves to clear and drain large bodies of swamp land "never before penetrated by the foot of man." Many slaves died in those early years and in the pages of Hammond's diary their sufferings are documented. By 1841 his net income increased to $7,000 and by 1859 to $21,000 annually.[20] Despite his success as a planter, Hammond soon felt restless and isolated at his Beech Island plantation. He yearned for public office. With his newly acquired wealth, social position, and close connection by marriage to influential South Carolina families he tried first to become a delegate to the South Carolina Nullification Convention set to be held in November 1832. He lost by a narrow margin. When the Convention met, the delegates defiantly nullified within South Carolina's borders the tariffs of 1828 and 1832. President Andrew Jackson responded to South Carolina that he intended to enforce the federal laws within the state despite the nullification ordinance. The state immediately prepared for a military showdown with the national government. Governor Robert Y. Hayne, of Webster-Hayne-debate fame, signed Hammond's commission to be one of his aides-de-camp, and put Hammond in charge of military preparations in his district of Barnwell. Hammond raised a regiment of Barnwell volunteers and they in turn elected him their colonel. There were musters and parades, but when the danger of war ended in the spring with the passage of the Compromise of 1833, his regiment disbanded.

The crisis receded, but the split between the Nullifiers and Unionists begun over the nullification issue in the 1820s continued. For the most part, the members of the much smaller Unionist party had a hard time getting elected to office in the 1830s. The coast was clear for Nullifiers as visible as Hammond. He ran for Congress and won. At the age of twenty-eight, Hammond, late in the fall of 1835, set off to Washington with his wife and four children, Catherine having produced four sons in a little more than four years. The new representative of Barnwell District expressed some misgivings about bringing his family to the capital and referred to his young sons as a "gang" and commented that he "had no idea

19. James Henry Hammond to Harry Hammond, July 16, 1859, Hammond-Bryan-Cumming Family Papers, SCL.

20. Ibid.; Harry Hammond, "Sketch of James Henry Hammond," ibid.

at first that children would be such a nuisance."[21] Catherine who was very shy and self-effacing found life in Washington extremely intimidating. She rarely made social calls except when accompanied by James and spent most of her time at their lodgings looking after their children, mingling with the other families of South Carolina politicians, all of whom lived together in the same boardinghouse, and serving as her husband's scribe. From the letters she wrote home, the twenty-one year-old Catherine apparently performed all these duties without complaint.[22]

Hammond, although only a freshman Congressman, was hardly timid. Almost immediately upon taking his place, he took a stand in defense of slavery by leading a fight in the House to reject unequivocally all petitions in favor of the abolition of slavery and the slave trade in the District of Columbia. He argued that Congress had no jurisdiction over slavery in the District, that the abolition petitions were therefore unconstitutional, and that Congress must refuse to receive such petitions. In the past such anti-slavery petitions had been either tabled or referred by the House to its Committee on the District of Columbia and ignored. Hammond's demand that Congress should refuse to receive such petitions was an escalation of Southern demands. Hammond said on the floor of Congress on February 1, 1836, that "slavery is said to be an evil, that it impoverishes the people and destroys their morals. If it be an evil, it is one to us alone, and we are contented with it—why should others interfere? But," he asserted, "it is no evil." On the contrary, Hammond considered slavery to be a positive good, "the greatest of all the great blessings which a kind Providence has bestowed upon our favored region," and the cornerstone of the Republic. Furthermore, he threatened that if Congress were to be given jurisdiction over slavery in the District, he would abandon his seat and go home "to preach and if I can, to practice disunion, and civil war if need be. A Revolution must ensue, and this Republic sink in blood."[23]

Hammond's speech in the House in 1836 called into question not only the issue of federal authority over slavery but also the right of petition. His Northern colleagues in Congress were unmoved by his address, but back home he was greatly praised. However, Henry Pinckney, his colleague from Charleston, took the whole South Carolina delegation by surprise, when on February 4, he introduced a compromise proposing that petitions for the abolition of slavery in the district in the future would be received

21. James Henry Hammond to William C. Preston, November 4, 1835, James Henry Hammond Papers, Perkins Library, Duke University.
22. Catherine Fitzsimons Hammond to Marcellus C. M. Hammond, January 25, and April 18, 1836, James Henry Hammond Papers, SCL.
23. Wilson, ed., *Selections from the Speeches of Hammond*, 34–35.

by a select committee of the House, reported on to the House, and then automatically tabled. As one historian recently noted, the crucial difference between the resolutions of Hammond and those of Pinckney was that Hammond asserted Congress had no constitutional right to interfere with slavery anywhere whereas Pinckney's resolutions, although considering Congressional interference with slavery in the district as inexpedient, implied it was constitutional.[24] Pinckney's resolutions eventually passed in May, but at home he lost his seat in the next Congressional election. Out of Pinckney's resolutions emerged the famous "gag rule," which according to House rules required renewal at every session of Congress, and which stirred up angry debate at each session until it was rescinded in 1844 on the motion of John Quincy Adams, who since 1836 had led the opposition to its passage.

In the midst of all this notoriety, Hammond took suddenly ill. Late in February 1836, while walking in the Capitol with his colleague Samuel Hoar of Massachusetts, Hammond fainted. A doctor was sent for who bled the Congressman and sent him home to rest. Hammond, who suffered with an ulcerous stomach throughout his adult life, may have had a flare up of that ailment; he, however, blamed it on the "mephitic air" of the Capitol. After six weeks of convalescing in their Washington boarding-house, Hammond grew impatient with the slowness of his recovery and set off to consult physicians in Philadelphia. In the pages of his diary he recorded dramatically, "broken down at twenty-eight . . . . dying of decay in the very blossom . . . . But twenty-eight is very young to leave the stage." Both doctors whom he consulted diagnosed his complaint as a nervous disorder, both recommended a strict diet, and both suggested an extended trip abroad. That settled the matter.[25] Hammond returned to Washington and resigned his seat in the House without a backward glance. At important moments in Hammond's life, when he seemed on the brink of experiencing some great success, he would suddenly retreat into bouts of depression, into self-destructive behavior, or succumb to real or imagined illnesses. The abrupt abandonment or undermining of his success was to be a recurring pattern in Hammond's life.

Hammond wasted no time in making his escape to Europe. In addition to the pursuit of a cure, he may also have viewed the taking of the Grand Tour of Europe as the means of achieving a life-style that money could buy. For James, the son of a struggling schoolmaster, here was the oppo-

24. Barnwell, *Love of Order*, 36–37; Edmunds, *Francis W. Pickens*, 42–43.
25. James Henry Hammond Diary, April 12, 15, and 18, 1836, James Henry Hammond Papers, LC; P. S. Physick to James Henry Hammond, April 19, 1836, James Henry Hammond Papers, LC; Granville Pattison to James Henry Hammond, April 19, 1836, James Henry Hammond Papers, SCL.

runity to acquire a cultural polish so far denied him. Back in South Carolina, he arranged for the management of his plantations and provided for the care of his mother and his two younger brothers, Marcellus and John, both of whom were fully dependent on him since his marriage in 1831. Much more difficult, Hammond said, was leaving behind his four young children "Hal [Harry] my bright boy, and my honest Christopher, and my dear little Edward, and William my baby . . . . which shall I leave— which shall I take." A family story told is that he called to his two older sons Harry, aged four, and Christopher, aged three: "First one to me goes to Europe."[26] Harry won. The other children were to be looked after at home by a white nurse under the supervision of their grandmothers, who would take turns managing the lively household. Before they left for Europe, Catherine knew she was pregnant.

The sea voyage, begun in mid-July 1836, turned sour even before they lost sight of New York habor. Both Catherine and James were seasick until they reached Liverpool, twenty days later. After this bad beginning they remained in England only seventeen days. To his old friend Francis W. Pickens, with whom he had been in Congress, he wrote that either he had not recovered from the effects of sea sickness or it was the cold damp climate of England, "or the petty vexations to which every one is subjected in that land of sharpers, or all together produced a very bad effect"; he began to wonder if he had not made a very grave error in coming to Europe. During the time he was in England, however, he did visit the most "splendid castles" including Warwick and Blenheim, made a pilgrimage to Stratford-on-Avon, and in London visited the Houses of Parliament. The House of Lords made a deep impression on him, although he thought it "does not equal our Senate (U.S.) in point of hard sense, but as an assemblage of gentlemen of high tone, whose ideas are elevated, language chaste, sentences polished and pointed, and whose whole remarks are full of fine illustrations and apt quotations from the ancient and modern classics," none, he thought, equaled it in America, except that the South Carolina Senate came closest to it "and in dignity surpasses it. In England there is no dignity, from the king down. I did not see a man who possessed any." The House of Commons, Hammond dismissed as "a rabble."

"Like sunshine after darkness," Hammond described France. The difference he attributed to the French people who "looked pleased and smiling," or, perhaps, "there is more *nature* in France, which after all possess a charm beyond all that any can invent to enliven the heart." One loved

26. James Henry Hammond Diary, April 19, 1836, LC; John Shaw Billings, "The Hammond Family," SCL.

13

Paris, he guessed, "because every body seems to have leisure to be in good humor." Hammond, nevertheless, did not like the buildings which "are all plastered on the outside and look like dirt houses though very high, nor the streets which are generally very filthy, the people here too will take advantages as they do everywhere, though they are not such Burkites as every man woman and child in England is."[27] For fifteen months, the length of the time they were abroad, Hammond kept an elaborate set of books in which he recorded his impressions of the people and places they visited in Italy, Great Britain, France, and various other parts of the Continent from Amsterdam to Naples, and noted also along the way the cost of the paintings and sculptures he was buying to bring back home, including works attributed to Mouton, de la Tour, Gilbert Stuart, and Sir Thomas Lawrence.[28]

While Hammond was occupied in Rome collecting art works with which to impress his friends at home, his wife prepared for her confinement. Caught up in an unending cycle of childbearing since her marriage less than six years before, Catherine gave birth in Rome to her fifth child in late January 1837. Except for James and their young son Harry, Catherine was among strangers and had as her primary support only a maid who spoke no English. A month after safely delivering the baby, whom they named Charles Julius, she wrote to her mother-in-law at Silver Bluff that they probably pitied her being alone without "the comforts of home," missing dreadfully "her little ones" back in South Carolina, and looking after an infant whom she sometimes deemed cross, "because I have so much of him myself, at home there would be so many to nurse him." Moreover, after three months in Rome, James, having grown bored with the place, proposed to take the family to Naples, "earlier," Catherine wrote, "than I wished to travel," and in spite of a reported cholera outbreak. A few months later in Belgium the baby died.[29]

The year 1837, memorable to the Hammonds as the year of their Grand Tour and of the birth and death of their infant Charles Julius, was also memorable to them for being the year that Hammond's Uncle John Fox died. The old man, it turned out, left his relatives entirely out of his will preferring to give the bulk of his estate to the city of Augusta and to nu-

27. James Henry Hammond to Francis W. Pickens, September 6, 1836, James Henry Hammond Papers, Duke University.
28. James Henry Hammond Account Book, August 6, 1836–April 7, 1837, with specimens of bills paid while traveling in Europe, passim; James Henry Hammond Diary of European Trip, 1836–37, 2 vols., passim, James Henry Hammond Papers, SCL. For a summary of the Grand Tour see: Faust, *Hammond: A Design for Mastery*, 186–203.
29. Catherine Fitzsimons Hammond to Catherine Fox Hammond, February 26, 1837, James Henry Hammond European Diary, II, May 30, 1837, Catherine Fitzsimons Hammond to Marcellus C. M. Hammond, September 11, 1837, James Henry Hammond Papers, SCL.

merous charities, including two churches. Hammond, later, as his diary reveals, successfully broke Fox's will and gained legacies for his mother and all the other relatives. The senior Mrs. Hammond's share came to twenty thousand dollars,[30] a sum which made her, until her death in 1864, financially independent. Eighteen hundred and thirty-seven was also the year of a serious financial depression in the United States, which struck not only the cotton market but also the whole of the American economy. Many of the letters Hammond received in Europe spoke of the Panic and especially of the numerous planting disasters. In one disquieting letter, a friend wrote that he had asked Hammond's manager how things were going at Silver Bluff and that the man had simply shaken his head and uttered some discouraging words.[31] Letters of this sort were bound to cause Hammond much anxiety, and after more than a year-long absence, James and Catherine, longing for children and homeland, set sail for New York on October 1, 1837.

Upon their return to Silver Bluff, Hammond threw himself vigorously back into the workaday world of the plantation. Temporarily satisfied with his life, he boasted that planting was the "only independent and really honorable occupation," and compared planters in the South to the nobility of Europe: "both stand at the head of society and politics." As for his health, he wrote, *"No better! Worse? I fear So!"* In fact, he had, since coming home, restricted his diet to "a bird and three slices of stale bread and two gills of hot tea."[32] On March 27, 1838, Catherine, with scant mention from Hammond, gave birth to their sixth son. They named him Paul Fitzsimons after the brother who had most opposed Catherine's marriage, thereby signifying that the breach between Hammond and the Fitzsimonses had been bridged. Two weeks after Paul's birth, Hammond, impatient with his Barnwell land, set off on a month's journey on horseback in search of cheap and fertile land in Georgia and Florida. Hammond soon realized, the further south he went, that "good land was high and cheap land poor." He rode back home to Silver Bluff and began to drain and ditch his land in an effort to improve what he already had. In February 1840, with the region still in the grip of the depression, he estimated that his land was worth $70,000 in the best of times and "in the worst of times (and none can be worse than these with cotton at 6 to 8 cents) $44,650." Most likely, $50,000 "may be realized for them."[33]

30. James Henry Hammond Diary, June 13, 1842, LC; John Shaw Billings, "The Hammond Family," SCL.
31. William Longstreet to James Henry Hammond, July 23, 1837, James Henry Hammond Papers, LC.
32. James Henry Hammond Diary, December 8, 1837, LC.
33. James Henry Hammond Diary, April 13–May 14, 1838, LC; John Shaw Billings, comp.,

Hammond, quickly tiring again of his isolation at Silver Bluff, bought some property in Columbia and, in December 1838, began construction of a fine town house. Ostensibly, it was to be the residence for his growing family while his young sons attended schools in the capital, but the building of the house, described as "outstanding for its elegance and beauty," signified Hammond's emergence from political retirement. Confiding in his diary that he had declined to run again for Congress and had refused to be considered for a seat in the South Carolina Senate, Hammond acknowledged, however, that he hankered after a brigadier-generalship in the state militia. When that appointment went to another, he wrote that the idea of becoming governor appealed to him, especially since "there is now no prospect for me" in the United States Senate.[34] An arrogant Hammond let his friends in the state legislature know of his gubernatorial availability—until after the Civil War the legislators in South Carolina chose the state governor—his new home presumably could serve as the governor's mansion.

Even while pursuing the governorship, Hammond, who had an eye for the women and who was probably bored by sweet, modest, and compliant Catherine after seven years of marriage and six children, began looking elsewhere for personal gratification. In the spring of 1838 he had noted in glowing prose how attractive he had found an innkeeper's wife he had seen during an overnight stay on his Southern tour. He described her in his diary as being beautiful and young and "clad in striped homemade homespun without a corset to correct the squareness of her figure . . . she has one of the sweetest of faces and softest of voices . . . . her complexion is clear but not ruddy, soft and transparent indicating health but not robustness." She was, thought Hammond, "a flower of the wilderness" with her blue eyes and Grecian nose and who "with sufficient culture would have been a bright one in any hot house in the world."[35] In December 1838 he committed to his diary his impressions of sixteen-year-old Mary DeSaussure who was on a two-week visit to Silver Bluff. Catherine described her too in a letter to her brother-in-law, Marcellus, stationed at Fort Gibson, Arkansas. "As she is something of a belle," Catherine presumed Marcellus would want to hear all about her. "She is," she wrote,

"Compilation of Silver Bluff, Cowden and Redcliffe Land Papers," Album C, James Henry Hammond Papers, SCL; Merritt, *James Henry Hammond*, 44.

34. James Henry Hammond Diary, May 26, June 1, 1839, LC; F. W. Pickens to James Henry Hammond, March 9, 1838, James Henry Hammond Papers, LC; James Henry Hammond to Marcellus C. M. Hammond, November 26, 1838, James Henry Hammond Plantation Journal, December 25, 1837, John Shaw Billings, "The Hammond Family," and a copy of Recorded and Registered Mesnes Conveyance Office, Richland District, February 12, 1839, all in SCL.

35. James Henry Hammond Diary, April 17, 1838, LC.

"pretty but not beautiful tho' your Brother thinks she is at times—her figure is good, her neck could not be formed more beautiful, but her face is childish tho' her manners are very confident almost to bolsterness [sic]." Hammond wrote Mary the day after her departure how he longed "for a glance from those bright eyes and a burst from that gay heart of yours to send life and gladness thro' us. I can scarcely realize that you were here in our midst but yesterday—it seems an age ago!"[36] Several weeks later he wrote a poem entitled the "Enchantress," most likely about her.

> When first we met I did not dream,
> It eer would be so hard to part:
> Tho' beautiful, thou didst not seem
> The being formed to win my heart,
> But gazing on that lovely face
> I ceased to think that fault could be
> Where heaven had lavished every grace
> And Love lent all his winning witchery.
> How little power—too late I learn,
> Hath Reason to combat with Love,
> For how can earth's dull armour turn
> Bright weapons brought from heaven above.
> Long years of toil and sternest thought
> Was blighted in one fatal hour,
> And glory's votary cheaply caught,
> Fell at a glance beneath thy peerless power. . . .[37]

Apparently neither marriage nor fatherhood could deter Hammond from fancying the young belle, but a powerful deterrent to trying at that time to make a conquest of "Miss Mary" might have been his equally powerful desire to re-enter politics. Perhaps more readily tolerated and certainly less difficult and dangerous than the seduction of teenage "hot house" flowers were the very discreet sexual liaisons between planters and their female slaves. In January 1839, the master of Silver Bluff purchased for $900 a seamstress named Sally and her one-year-old daughter Louisa.[38] Soon after their purchase, Hammond made eighteen-year-old Sally his mistress and by her he acknowledged he had children. When Louisa reached the age

36. Catherine Fitzsimons Hammond to Marcellus C. M. Hammond, January 10, 1839, James Henry Hammond Plantation Journal, December 7 and 20, 1839, James Henry Hammond Papers, SCL; John Fox Hammond to James Henry Hammond, January 11, 1839, James Henry Hammond to Miss Mary, December 20, 1838, a copy in James Henry Hammond, "Occasional Thoughts," LC.
37. James Henry Hammond, "Occasional Thoughts," January 9, 1839, LC.
38. James Henry Hammond Plantation Journal, January 8, 1839, James Henry Hammond Papers, SCL; a Bill of Sale, January 12, 1839, Hammond-Bryan-Cumming Family Papers, SCL.

of twelve, Hammond took her as his mistress and by her he had several more children.

The relationship of the slaveholder and his female slaves has always been a vexed question, and much attention has recently focused on Thomas Jefferson and his slave Sally Hemings. The possibility of a sexual relationship between the two is hardly shocking to the modern reader, but the possibility that Jefferson not only fathered children by a slave but also kept them in bondage and passed them on as slaves to his heirs is shocking. Thus for the modern sensibility, the real question is, Can an enlightened and sensitive human being keep his own children enslaved? For Jefferson the evidence is circumstantial at best and in the eyes of many, non-existent. What is unexpected is that, despite the plethora of dramatic fictional accounts of miscegenation, there is almost no documentary evidence involving the planter aristocracy. What little there is, is found usually in wills in which a slaveholder singles out a female slave and her children for special consideration, perhaps even setting them free and sending them north. In most cases the modern historian has only been able to speculate on the motives for such acts. This absence of proof is understandable, Hammond, himself, having on one occasion written that in his society "he who takes a colored mistress—with rare and extraordinary exceptions—loses caste at once—." The intermixture of the races was severely frowned upon and was not generally acknowledged. In addition the human capability for self-delusion is immense as was noted by Mary Boykin Chesnut, who observed that, "the Mulattoes one sees in every family exactly resemble the white children—and every lady tells you who is the father of all the Mulatto children in everybody's household, but those in her own she seems to think drop from the clouds or pretends so to think."[39]

In such an atmosphere it is most surprising that Hammond's personal papers contain proof of Hammond's illicit and long-term relationships with two slave women and that this documentation survived the natural instinct of heirs and executors to prettify their family history. Hammond records that he took eighteen-year-old Sally Johnson as his mistress and that he eventually became enamoured of her twelve-year-old daughter Louisa. The seriousness of this affair with Louisa is indicated by the fact that Catherine Hammond, who had stood by her husband during an earlier scandal with

39. James Henry Hammond to Thomas Clarkson, January 28, 1845, in Clyde N. Wilson, ed., *Selections from the Letters and speeches of the Hon. James H. Hammond of South Carolina* (Spartanburg: The Reprint Company, Publishers, 1978), p. 137; C. Vann Woodward and Elisabeth Muhlenfeld, *The Private Mary Chesnut: The Unpublished Civil War Diaries* (New York: Oxford University Press, 1984), 42. For other documented examples of planter miscegenation see especially, Helen Tunnicliff Caterall, ed., *Judicial Cases concerning American Slavery and the Negro*, 3 vols. (New York: Negro Universities Press, 1968).

her nieces and, in fact, later bore Hammond another child, left him when he refused to give up Louisa. Hammond's diary contains numerous rather elliptical references to his family being away, but other materials make clear the reason. After two years, Hammond reluctantly sent Louisa away, but when Mrs. Hammond refused to return home, Hammond recalled Louisa. Several years later, after the Hammonds had reconciled, Hammond wrote to his eldest son Harry, then twenty-two years old, an astonishingly frank letter.

Redcliffe, 19 Feb. 1856

My Dear Harry:

In the last will I made I left to you, over and above my other children Sally Johnson the mother of Louisa and all the children of both. Sally says Henderson is my child. It is possible, but I do not believe it. Yet act on her's rather than my opinion. Louisa's first child *may* be mine. I think not. Her second I believe is mine. Take care of her and her children who are both of *your* blood if not of mine and of Henderson. The services of the rest will I think compensate for an indulgence to these. I cannot free these people and send them North. It would be cruelty to them. Nor would I like that any but my own blood should own as Slaves my own blood or Louisa. I leave them to your charge, believing that you will best appreciate and most independently carry out my wishes in regard to them. Do not let Louisa or any of my children or possible children be slaves of Strangers. Slavery *in the family* will be their happiest earthly condition.

Ever affectionately,

J.H.H.[40]

There are certain ambiguities inherent in this letter which need not be dwelt upon other than to note that Harry is probably not involved in fathering any of these children, but apparently members of his mother's family may be. Moreover both Sally and Louisa are in other documents described as mulattoes, suggesting that their children by Hammond would be of mostly white parentage. The two main points to derive from this letter are first that it presents clear cut evidence for planter-slave sexual relationships and secondly it shows the attitude of at least one planter toward his resulting offspring. Despite the mostly white parentage, as we assume, of his children, Hammond felt it would be a cruelty to free them and send

40. James Henry Hammond to Harry Hammond, February 19, 1856, James Henry Hammond Papers, SCL.

them north. How could he justify this but by a complete and untrammelled racism. He believed without any doubt that blacks were inferior to whites and the least component of black blood made one a black, an inferior, and fitted for slavery. Hammond accepted the logic of his position, enslaved his own mixed blood children, and firmly concluded that "Slavery *in the family* will be their happiest earthly condition."[41] Since he felt this way about his own mixed-blood children, we can better understand his unquestioning acceptance of slavery.

As aggressive politically as sexually, Hammond was a political arriviste, and although he said he knew that the governorship "cannot be sought," he asked in 1840 for backing from John C. Calhoun (then in the United States Senate), both to give his candidacy legitimacy and to unite behind his nomination the former Nullifiers and the moderates in the legislature. Several letters passed between them but Calhoun disappointed him, having already encouraged John Richardson, a Unionist from Clarendon. Calhoun earlier had decided on a course to bring forth a Union man for governor to signal the end of animosities between the Nullifiers and the Unionists. In the end, the most Calhoun promised Hammond was his neutrality. Hammond disparagingly described Richardson, a member of Congress, as "a fourth rate man of no talent, little information and an arrant coward but a most artful knave and greate hypocrite."[42] Encouraged, however, by some of his friends, Hammond continued to push his candidacy because as he put it, "I prefer striking at higher game," than to take a seat in the state legislature for now, and wait until 1842 for a crack at the governorship. "I had enough of political drudgery for a lifetime," he wrote, "when I was Editor." Even though it was a mostly honorific post, his political arrogance in seeking out the governorship in 1840 must have astonished political friends and foes alike, for in antebellum South Carolina the ruling oligarchy usually controlled the nomination. Eventually almost all the newspapers in the state endorsed Richardson; and Hammond began to wish he "had never entertained the question of being made governor."

Hammond confessed, "I am rather sick of everything,"[43] but, in the

41. *Ibid.* By the time of Hammond's death in 1864, Louisa and Sally each had four or five children, and since he kept the women and their children living apart from the other slaves, he may well have been the father of these children. After the war Louisa and Sally remained on the Hammond plantation, their presence accepted now by Hammond's widow, and as late as the 1880 census they were still in residence with their families.

42. James Henry Hammond Diary, October 6, 1839, January 20, March 6, 1840, SCL; John C. Calhoun to James Henry Hammond, January 25, February 23, April 2, and May 16, 1840, James Henry Hammond Papers, LC. See also the account of the 1840 gubernatorial campaign in Edmunds, *Francis W. Pickens,* 52–56.

43. James Henry Hammond Diary, January 6, 29, and February 12, 1840, SCL.

pages of his diary—and Hammond is no exception to the charge that no one ever kept a diary just for himself—he keeps tugging at our sleeve to allow him to tell us his side of what happened during this unusually heated campaign. Convinced as he was that he could not confide in his wife, whom he dismissed as a "good soul" who would not hear half of what he said, and that "it would distress her if she did, more than it would comfort me," Hammond confided all to his diary. In mid-February 1840, a very agitated Hammond rushed off to Charleston to look up the "dear sweet girl," probably Miss Mary. Back at home again after a ten-day visit he recorded in his diary that he had spent a delightful time in Charleston and was relieved finally of much stress by free and frequent visits "with the beloved and by the hearty support of my friends."[44]

By July 1840, Hammond, again unhappy and unwell, wrote that the strain of the gubernatorial campaign and the betrayal of many of whom he considered his allies, including his friend Francis Pickens (who had encouraged Hammond to run), had reduced his health to wretched, that he had seldom felt worse, and that he needed "to go somewhere." On August 11, he fled from his plantation and from his family and went to New York City, to buy furnishings for the newly completed residence in Columbia. Catherine could not travel; she was almost eight months pregnant, her seventh pregnancy in nine years. While Hammond went about the city buying silver, linen, and furniture, she remained at Silver Bluff during the hot and muggy summer, looking after the crops with the aid of her brother, caring for the sick, and presiding over a house full of family and guests. Hammond wrote her breezily that he did not doubt that she got through it all well. "I expect too that you have found yourself excellent at plantation matters."[45] Hammond stayed away for six weeks and arrived back home only three days before Catherine gave birth on September 26, 1840, to their seventh child and first daughter. They named her Katherine for the many Catherines in the family. In all, Catherine Hammond would give birth to eight children, five of whom—Harry, Edward Spann, Paul, Katherine, and a second daughter, Elizabeth—lived to maturity. In fact, Elizabeth, born to the Hammonds after a nine-year interval in 1849, lived to be ninety-two years old, not dying until 1941.

Six weeks after the birth of the infant, Katherine, Hammond left his wife and seven children at Silver Bluff in the care of Catherine's mother and hurried off to Columbia to be on hand when the state legislature assembled in late November. While awaiting the balloting for the gover-

44. *Ibid.*, February 16, 24, and March 16, 1840.
45. *Ibid.*, July 23, 1840; James Henry Hammond to Catherine Fitzsimons Hammond, August 25 and September 4, 1840, James Henry Hammond Papers, Southern Historical Collection, Chapel Hill.

norship, Hammond kept himself occupied by visiting and receiving callers at his new house, by catching up with his correspondence and writing in his diary, and by hanging the pictures and engravings acquired in Europe. As the election drew near, Hammond wrote Catherine that he had "already sacrificed more in this canvass than any office in America is worth."[46] When it was over on December 9, 1840, Hammond had been badly defeated by a vote of 104 to 47. More than two weeks passed before Hammond could bring himself to record his failure in the pages of his diary.

Inveighing against John Richardson and his supporters especially, Hammond rationalized his defeat and accused his opponents of being "selfish and unprincipled intriguers who do not care one straw for the honor or the interest of the State, in whom no faith is to be placed whatever." In short, they were politicians "with whom no *honest man* could act and whose overthrow it is the duty of every patriot to desire and if in his power effect." Hammond emerged from this final diary entry for 1840 convinced that only he could tame the politicians and effect the needed change to claim by 1842 the rewards, both public and private, he now considered due him. Nothing else mattered.[47] Having been obsessed for over a year with running a campaign to become governor and recording it all in his diary, Hammond, the day after Christmas, abruptly quit writing in the leather-bound volume. Early the next year he took up his pen again and started a fresh new book in which he wrote that the year 1841 probably would fix his destiny for life. In fact, in 1841, he embarked on sexual indiscretions with his four teenage nieces, transgressions that would be neither forgiven nor forgotten.

The picture of Hammond is that of a handsome, intelligent, ambitious, and restless individual who was frequently afflicted by illness, real or imagined. After successfully making his way through South Carolina College and the reading of law, Hammond proved himself to be perfectly capable of ruthlessly marrying for her fortune a shy, insecure, and homely seventeen-year-old Charleston heiress. After marrying for money, he proceeded to develop his wife's property to the fullest—hauling enormous amounts of muck up from the Savannah River to enrich the land he was cultivating, and clearing and draining swamps to bring into production new land as rich as any in the South. Although this grueling, dangerous, and unhealthy work was carried out by slaves, Hammond always took immense credit in his letters and diaries for supervising much of this work himself rather than relying solely on overseers. Not only did the master of

46. James Henry Hammond to Catherine Fitzsimons Hammond, November 27, December 4 and 6, 1840, Southern Historical Collection.

47. James Henry Hammond Diary, December 26, 1840, SCL.

Silver Bluff seek domination over the land and his slaves, he also felt compelled to rule oppressively over his family—his wife, their children, his mother, and his two brothers, Marcellus and John. Each of his children, except for his youngest, sought to struggle free from his control, and their "rebelliousness" is discussed by Hammond in his letters and diaries. In one place an angered son years later ripped from the diary the record of his confrontation with his father (one of the few examples of censorship in this vast collection of family papers). His brother, Marcellus, for whom James Henry felt a deep bond, rocked the family with the news of his devotion to Rachel Huey a Cherokee Indian by whom he had at least one child. Marcellus bent to the will of James, nevertheless, and married a young woman from nearby Augusta, Georgia, recommended by Hammond to Marcellus as "rich enough for you." His betrayals of his wife, Catherine, were legion, and his failure to consider the emotional cost to her of his deceptions is astounding. Nevertheless, after his death she sought to memorialize him, despite having suffered through his alliances with other women, his overbearing behavior, and perhaps even his physical abuse of her, mentioned only elliptically by Hammond in his diary. Only his mother in the end escaped his grip. Hammond, believing himself to be his parent's major source of emotional support throughout her long widowhood of thirty-five years, as well as her financial adviser and the executor of her will, felt thoroughly betrayed to discover at her death in June 1864, just five months before his own, that his mother had drawn a secret codicil leaving most of her estate to a niece despised by Hammond.

Hammond's secret and sacred diaries record the insecurities, the anxieties, and even the courage of a man who brought himself back again and again from public and private disgrace by sheer determination. Hammond noted that in his diaries "I have painted myself as I am." A tormented and self-destructive man, he bemoans his misfortunes in love, on the plantation, in politics and society, and among his family, and believes he has been singled out for numerous misfortunes by some personally vindictive and ironic fate. Yet Hammond created much of his own torment and disasters, as if, in some unconscious way, he sought to render valueless what he had won at such cost. But much of this dark chronicle lies ahead.

I

Defeat is not pleasant and would not do a second time

---

6 FEBRUARY 1841 – 12 MAY 1841

Columbia S.C. 6 Feb. 1841

I begin this diary from almost purely selfish motives—Alas how few things do any of us do from better ones. "I want a friend." Circumstances—my own frequent change of residence and of occupations—the migration to the West of nearly every one of the young men with whom I was brought up and with whom I was or might have been very intimate—the ups and downs of political parties—have combined to prevent me from having a friend to whose sympathetic bosom I could confide *anything*–To whom I could speak of myself as I *am*, as I was; as I expect or desire to be—in short of *myself* without reserve at all times and in all humours. To whom I could also speak with equal freedom of others and of passing events. Such a friend I can now only find in this book, on whose responsive page I can at will engrave my own heart, and if I cannot secure for them appreciation and sympathy at least [I can] perpetuate for my own times all its emotions. With this book I can converse as with the sincerest of friends of all that interests me in life, and though it returns me no answer, I am sure that it will at all events listen patiently to all that I may have to say whether of myself, of others, or of the affairs of the world, and I doubt if the best of friends would after all serve me a more useful purpose—that is, afford me a higher gratification. Nor will it be wholly mute. Should I be spared to collect here the reminiscences of past years and to add for a few more the records of passing incidents and reflections, it will not be long ere many, very many, of the questions that it would be interesting to solve, may be illumined if not rendered fully transparent by a reference to its earlier pages. Life moves in a cycle. To-day reviews the difficulties of yes-

25

terday, and tomorrow explains what yesterday had revealed also to our treacherous memory, or too hasty observation.

I have just returned to reside in Columbia, [South Carolina] after having for near ten years made my dwelling place in other and various parts of the world. There seems to be a fatality which has in this respect attended my family before. At least there is a coincidence that did not occur to me until now. My Father lived in Columbia—married here—removed, and, after about the same length of time, returned again. He married in 1806—returned in 1815. In 1823 he removed again alas never to return. He died in Macon in 1829. I was born at Stoney Battery in Newberry in 1807—the 15th Nov. On my Father's removal in 1823 I was left here. I entered College that fall and graduated in December 1825. In the [year] of 1826 I left Columbia to wander about—teaching school in Orangeburg at Poplar Spring and near Cheraw in the family of C.B. Pegues Esq. afterwards studying law in Augusta and at Cambridge. I was admitted to the Bar in November or December 1828 and opened an office here the January following and was married 23 June 1831. Soon after which event I abandoned the Bar and Columbia to settle at Silver Bluff [Plantation] and became a planter. I now return to Columbia [over nine years later] with six children. Four of them are school boys and the fifth looking forward to become a member of some infant establishment. I come to educate them—to get from the woods into the world. I have besides many motives which will be revealed in this diary from time to time—many of them vague and immature, yet all combining to bring me here. Not one of them however looks to pecuniary advancement, which in the present times and under the prospects for the future, should be a primary object with all prudent men. They may all be doomed to disappointment. I am not without misgivings. But my temper is sanguine. I do not despond or give up easily. I will try it. Time will show.

[Columbia] 7 February [1841]

Supped last night with Professor [Francis] Lieber. Went at 8. Supper at 9. Turkey, ducks, tongue, *poisson aux truffles*, potatoes etc., afterwards salad— a treat for this season which I forgot to inquire how he came by. Sherry, Hock, and a french *vin ordinaire* that was quite pleasant. I think it was an Italian wine, but he did not. Then afterwards, a sort of mixture that looked like pea soup, for which he had no name. It was a mulled claret with rum in it, sweet and sickening stuff. Nothing remarkable occurred—our company was Prof. Eliot, McCord, De Saussure, Dr. Gibbes, A. S. Johnston,

Clark, young Cheves, and Deveaux, the painter. [William F.] De Saussure told me how his father [Henry William] was one of the Directors of the Mint in '93 or 4 and had the first gold coin of the U.S. struck off at the request of Gen. Washington, and after several previous failures of his predecessors. Little was said of political matters and we broke up between 10 and 11. These suppers are pleasant and with a little pain a very interesting literary or political cast may be given to them. They are cheaper than dinners—not so stiff—not requiring display, and will be more generally given. I have no position in the literary world. I have never written a book, nor even an essay or critique. I am therefore at the beginning in that line. Politically it is very different.

[Here and in the next entry, February 8, Hammond recapitulates his career in politics and the state militia in detail, material perhaps of interest only to the specialist.]

In the year 1830 I began my political career by starting a new paper in Columbia under the name of the Southern Times. Spencer I. McMorris was the owner, I was the Editor. I was getting a good practice at the Bar for a beginner and I hardly know what induced me to embark in it, especially as I had not up to that time been a very warm politician. The questions of the time however were very exciting. Nullification had just been broached and I threw myself into the conflict—in favour of it, of course. It was a dark hour for the South and a dangerous question, and I may hereafter recur to many incidents of the contest. When I married I gave up the paper. My friend Isaac W. Hayne, a grandson of Col. Isaac Hayne of the Revolution, now living in Montgomery Alabama, a gallant fellow and highly talented, but very lazy, succeeded me. I retired to Barnwell where I bore a part in the elections of 1832 by taking to the stump occasionally. When R[obert] Y. Hayne was elected Gov. after the act of Nullification [passed the state legislature], he appointed an aid for each district to organize the volunteers who came forward to defend the State from Federal Invasion. I was his aid for Barnwell. I had been Hamilton's [Hayne's predecessor] aid before. I raised a Volunteer Regiment of near 1000 men and was elected to command it. I came very near to being sent to the [Nullification] Convention previously. The nominating committee did so by ballot and I came within 1 vote of being nominated from my Battalion instead of old Mr. Stephen Smith, although I had just come into the district. In the fall of 1833, or, in December, rather, I was brought out as a Candidate for Congress to succeed Maj. J. M. Felder who declined reelection. Col. F[ranklin] H. Elmore opposed me, but in April declined on a plea of ill health. I was of course elected and in Dec. 1835 took my seat there and in a few days after demanded the question of reception to be taken on the Abolition Petitions. It was a bold move made more from impulse than reflection, but was well sustained and we made a hard fight on it until Henry I. Pinckney one of [our] colleagues, betrayed us and moved a compromise. Anon I may recur to these things. In February 1836 I was taken ill. In April Dr. Physic recommended me to go to Europe for my health and I resigned my seat and sailed for Liverpool in July. I did not return home until Nov. 1837. I took my wife [Catherine] and eldest son [Harry] with me. On my return home Elmore, who [had] succeeded me, offered to decline if I would resume my seat, but I declined. I was repeatedly solicited from various quarters—and among others by Mr. [John C.] Calhoun to return to Washington. The people of Barnwell would have sent me to the State Legislature but I declined that also. In the mean[time] I saw that things were going wrong in So. Ca., as I thought, for Nullification and Abolition having both lost their predominant importance, the pecuniary crisis in the country and Bank suspension in the Spring of 1837 made the Banks the all absorbing subject of political interest. Mr. [President Martin] Van Buren proposed at the extra Session in Sept. '37 to establish for the Gov. places for the special deposit of their revenue, as it was collected, under the eye of the Collector or Receiver, and thus dispense with and as far as possible discontinuance [of the] banks. He also proposed to collect the revenues in specie. Calhoun embraced his views. [Senator William Campbell] Preston [of South Carolina] opposed [and began a campaign to organize the state against the independent treasury.] The State of So. Ca. went almost unanimously with Mr. C., only about a dozen members of the Legislature voting against the resolutions in Dec. '37 approving the Sub-treasuries. Elmore, [John] Richardson, and other members of Congress (all of whom, however, except [Francis W.] Pickens and R[obert] B[arnwell] Rhett, agreed with Preston) now united with Mr. C. and instantly formed the idea of controlling the State through him and by means of intrigue and management. I saw it early. In this district [Richland] a war grew up and parties were nearly divided as Preston lived here. His friends were however beaten by a few votes. They were my brother-in-law [Wade] Hampton, Gen. Adams, B. F. Taylor and C. Bookter. Elmore, being the member of Congress, was the champion of the Sub-treasury parties and his brother B[enjamin] T. Elmore, who was also a candidate for Gov., was [re]elected [to the South Carolina House.] [Patrick] Noble however beat him [Benjamin Elmore] for Gov.[in 1838]. Noble was an intimate friend of Calhoun and a relative of Pickens—who it was said brought him out. This I expected would produce a split in this new party. It did so as far as Pickens was concerned, but the E's would not, could not, give up Calhoun. Richardson, who was a leader of the old Union

party, and the Rhetts—Albert Rhett being a brother-in-law of F.H.E.—
went with the Elmores. This *clique* concealed their hostility from P[ickens]
until he became a candidate for the [U.S. House] Speakership in Dec.
1839, when they defeated him by running [Alabama Representative Dixon
Hall] Lewis, another brother-in-law of the E's. [Robert M.T. Hunter of
Virginia was elected Speaker on December 16, 1839.] B.T.E. not being
considered [in 1840] an available candidate for the Gubernatorial Chair,
Col. J.P. Richardson was brought forward under pretence of harmonizing
the old parties by giving the Union men a Governor. At the solicitation of
Pickens. . .and many others I consented to oppose him. We had a warm
contest and there were many apparent oscillations of the victory, but at
length R. was elected by an overwhelming majority. The vote Richardson
104, Hammond 47, B. K. Hannegan 2, Johnson (Judge David) 5. . . .

[Columbia] 8 Feb. [1841]
Tom Whitmore writes me that he will very soon assume the command of
the 3rd Brigade and that I will have no opposition as his successor. My
connection with the office is somewhat singular. In 1833 I happened to
be on the military Board which matured for the Legislature a militia system. There was a general vacation of all the offices of the State and the
Major Generals and Brigadiers were elected by the Legislature. I was requested then to offer for the Command of the 3rd Brigade, but declined
as I was about to offer for Congress and did not wish to appear too grasping
for honors. Gen. Henry Arthur was elected. He resigned in a year. I was
again solicited and might have been easily elected, but having just been
elected to Congress, the same reason again induced me to decline. Gen.
Trotti was elected. Col. [Robert] Goodwyn, now Cashier of the Branch
Bank here, was his opponent, and Col. Caughman of Lexington, a vulgar
and dissolute Dutchman, also ran. In 1837 Gen. Hayne resigned the
Command of the Division. I was in Europe. Gens. Trotti and Brisbane,
and Col. Ford offered for the succession, and Ford was elected, the election contested and broken. They were again candidates and Ford elected.
Before the last election it was arranged that I should succeed Trotti. The
qualifying Commission which I held before I went abroad was vacated by
my long absence, but I was re-appointed by Trotti (the incumbent having
died just as I returned home), and he was, if defeated, to hold on until I
had been a Commissioner a year and then give way. But he died before
the election for Maj. Gen., and a new Brigadier was necessarily elected
before I was qualified by time. This was Gen. J. H. Hogg. Within a year

Hogg resigned suddenly, and before I was aware of it candidates were popped out. My most intimate friends at Barnwell had supposed that I would not take the office as I was leaving the District, they supposed, altogether [having built a house in Columbia], and I had been but little with them for a year before. I went to the village soon after, and many were anxious for me to offer. At one time I agreed to do so, but Col. Walker had been announced and was anxious for it, with a good prospect of success. I went so far as to tell him that I would oppose him, but it seemed to mortify him so much, and he had always been so warm a friend of mine, that I forthwith declared I would yield the field to him. I did so and did what I could for him, but Whitmore beat him and Caughman both, Caughman, bye the bye, had also opposed Hogg. Last year Gen. Ford died. Whitmore and Edwards were the candidates to command the division. It was arranged now that if Whitmore was elected I should succeed him. Edwards however beat him a long ways. Whitmore spoke of resigning but did not. Shortly after the Gov. election, Col. Lartigue of the Beaufort Reg^t (a gallant fellow and warm friend) came to me and said that Whitmore was about to resign, and that, if I would consent to offer, he would not, and he had no doubt I would be elected by acclamation. After consulting with Cols. Jamison and Quattlebaum I consented to do so. Whitmore however has hung on this long and altho he has written to me that he will resign *immediately*, I am not sure he will do so. The fact [is], after having had an opportunity of being elected, and each time solicited for, four times within the last seven years, and each time prevented from doing so from some circumstances rather accidental than otherwise, I do not feel any great assurance of ever obtaining the command. I desire it for many small reasons. I am fond of the military, it would carry me in an agreeable manner on my reviews through a part of the State where I should very much like to go, it would give me some additional influence, it would change my title of which I am very sick and altho' militia titles are of no consequence, since they will stick to us, we had as well have the highest. My residence here [in Columbia] might be made a difficulty, but I take the ground that as I shall divide my time between Columbia and Silver Bluff, I have a right to say of which I consider myself a citizen, and I prefer for many reasons to remain a citizen of Barnwell, and, in fact, this command is desirable as demonstrating that fact. Besides the Brigade includes Lexington and on the other side of the river—a mile from this I am in it.

[Columbia] 9 Feb. [1841]

Rec'd a letter to day from M[illedge] L. Bonham—he is one of my fast friends and very much opposed to this Regency. He is not however of an equable temperament, being either full of hope or plunged in despair. He writes me that he expects soon to have a difficulty with a young duellist named [Louis] Wigfall, who resides at Edgefield also and who lately distinguished himself by killing a fine young fellow named Bird on Saturday, exchanging shots with J. R. Carroll the Wednesday following without effect, and on the next Wednesday having two fires with young Preston Brooks, at the second of which both fell severely but not mortally wounded. I hardly think any difficulty will occur between him and Bonham, who is a gallant, highspirited fellow and not one whom a duellist would select to experiment upon.

The question, perhaps of most interest to me at this moment, is whether I am to be the candidate for the Gov. the next time. Before the [1840] election the succession was offered me by the Clique [In Hammond's view, the Clique or Regency consisted in large part of the members of the Rhett and Elmore families and their associates.], nay a *carte blanche*, if I would decline [in 1840 to run for governor], but I scorned it, sent back a defiance (though certain of being defeated), and declared I would have nothing from them. Had I however withdrawn without any such understanding, I think there is no doubt I should have been the next Gov. But having made so bad a run, I rather think it has disheartened most of my friends and made them suppose me an "unavailable." This [is] not true and if I sink under it, I shall probably rise no more, yet I have not yet made up my mind to make any—even the most indirect efforts to produce a contrary impression—I do not appreciate office, I fear. I certainly consider the evil greater than the good in 9 out of 10 cases, and I would accept of few stations in public life : The Gubernatorial chair—the U.S. Senate for a year or two, or a good mission abroad if every thing suited, [these] are the only appointments not military that I would accept. I have by many of my friends been solicited to run again for Gov., but I have uniformly said we had better wait a year and then start our strongest man. I will not run again, if I think I am to be defeated. I did so this time, knowing pretty well my fate, but it was necessary to make an issue with these men and to persevere in it to the last. To have allowed them to walk over the course without opposition would have been to surrender the State for 10 years to come. But defeat is not pleasant and would not do a second time. Duty will hardly require it. [Francis W.] Pickens (who wishes to be Gov. himself) writes me that I will have no opposition and offers me his support, but he is at Washington and was not here after my defeat. He is not therefore a judge of public sentiment here. I do not propose to trouble myself about the matter much.

[Columbia] 12 Feb. [1841]

The most important news of the day is the third suspension and supposed failure of the U. S. Bank of Penna. It resumed specie on the 15 Jan. and suspended on the 4 Feb., having during the interval paid out nearly 6 millions of dollars. This Institution for a long time sustained the highest reputation abroad and raised that of the U. S. to a high eminence. Even the withdrawal of the Gov. deposits in 1834 and the subsequent expiration of its charter from the U. S. and renewal of it by the State of Penn. did not affect it seriously in point of credit. When the crisis of 1837 occurred, it came forward to relieve the country by throwing into circulation an immense amount of post notes, payable in London at 12 months. To meet them it had to purchase cotton largely, and was an immense loser on it. It also speculated, largely in State stock, which, in the embarrassed state of the finances of the world, proved to be a dead weight on their hands. These things have destroyed it—if, as is pretty generally believed, it is bankrupt. It is computed that 2 millions will be lost by it in S. C. The shock I fear will be severely felt in Europe by those who have an interest in American securities and will bring down American credit there below its present low ebb. In a country town like this it produces little or no effect. Money is already as scarce here as it can well be. The Banks discount scarcely anything but drafts for 60 days and those sparingly. At the last discount day at the Br. Bank, $100,000 were offered and only $7,000 discounted. Yet prices are fair. Prime cotton will bring 11¢, corn 56¢, fodder 1.25, fowls 5 to the dollar, and surloin of beef 12¢. It has been excessively cold to day. I am yet in great hurry and confusion, and find myself getting "fixed" but slowly. Dined with [David] McCord to day. Small party to Dr. Carter of Virginia—a common sort of man. He told me that in Virginia now planters realized nothing except from raising slaves and the increase in the value of their lands in consequence of improvements from marling [fertilizing with deposits rich in calcium carbonate, typically from oyster shells] and increase of population. I suspect the rise in lands is rather imaginary and that on the whole the wealth of Virginia does not increase more than that of the oldest countries. Such, I fear, will soon be the case with So.Ca. when the culture of cotton will be abandoned in consequence of its fall in price. The current expenses of raising cotton here on our fair lands is 5¢ per lb., and values of our negroes at $300 round, and on land at $10 per acre, we must get 10¢ nett to realize 7 per ct per annum, leaving out the increase of negroes. Dr. C[arter] said that the small farmers on the wheatlands made $100 nett per hand he thought. This is very light wages and can only be done, I imagine, by small farmers who own no more slaves than they overlook with their own eyes. Slaves can be worked in large gangs only on rice, cotton, and sugar estates, where the operations are regular and systematic for whole seasons, and the owner is not required to be present daily and hourly.

The weather is very cold. It has for a month been very inclement. I have seldom known in this country so long a spell of wet weather, except occasionally in July or August, last year for instance. An eclipse of the moon took place a few days ago and eclipses always bring extraordinary seasons.

[Columbia] 14 Feb. [1841] Sunday

This has been the most fitful day as regards the weather I ever knew. We found an inch [of] snow on the ground this morning when we awoke, and it has been an alternation of bright sunshine and the most fierce snow storms all day long. There have been four or five such changes. The snow melts at every whim of sunshine and by morning there will be only a speck remaining here and there. The skies are murky and there is no telling when it will break off mildly. This is race week in Charleston, and they are no doubt anxious for a clearing up. The winter with us has been severe on the whole. After the extraordinary rains of last August and September and, in fact, of June and July, we had a dry fall and winter until about new year, since when it has been raining, but not very cold. In Europe the cold has been intense. The remains of Bonaparte were brought from St. Helena and deposited in the Hotel des Invalides on the 15 Dec. Many of the spectators died from the effects of the coldness of the day. 3000 persons are said to have died from cold in Sweden. In Bohemia and Moravia, the ponds were frozen to the bottom and the fish destroyed, 80,000 head of horned cattle have frozen in Hungary and even Birds and game in the forest have shared the same fate.

The[re] is no political news of importance. Gen. [William Henry] Harrison, the Pres. elect, entered Washington on the 9th inst. when the great parade intended for the occasion was defeated by a tremendous storm of sleet. The Globe thinks it ominous—it adds that the journals announced an earthquake on his setting out, and at Baltimore he was met by an explosion of the Banks which followed that of the Philadelphia Banks. It is also mentioned by the Globe, as an indication of approaching disaster, that on New Year's day the scroll bearing the motto of the Union, "E pluribus unum," fell from the talons of the Eagle in the Senate Chamber, and the hand of the Goddess of Liberty in front of the Capitol, bearing the constitution, fell off also. In ancient times such events would have filled a whole people with consternation. Altars would have smoked with offerings to the gods and solemn embassies would have been sent to the oracles. Nowadays they scarcely occasion a passing remark. Such is the effect of Christian civilization.

The Philadelphia banks have nearly all suspended and the alarm and confusion of the money market at the North is represented as unprecedented. Even in New York where specie has been paid ever since the resumption in 1838–9, there is an universal panic.

[Columbia] 15 Feb. [1841]

I started my boys to school to-day. The three eldest to Mr. W. A. Irving and Willie to Miss Jane Bryce. Harry went with delight, Spann seemed willing, but Kit and Willie were opposed. Poor fellows, my heart ached for all of them. Their troubles have now fairly begun. It is a long and thorny road they have to travel. When a boy, I hated school. I look back to it now with abhorrence, nor would I again pass my school and college days to be restored to youth and live life over. I must be peculiar in my constitution, or the delights of childhood, which poets paint with so much rapture and which most people pretend to look back to with regret, are only imaginary. I must be peculiar, I think, for so many would not concur in a falsehood, and it is not only childhood that brings no happy reminiscences to me, but really I know of no part of my past existence that I would recall. In every epoch that I do remember, pain predominated. The sunshine made no lasting impression favorably on my morbid mind, and only the gloomy days are chalked down in my collect. The demon of Dyspepsia—the cognomen under which are classed all the horrors of indigestion, nervous excitement or lassitude, weakness, giddiness, and sinking of the soul and body—has been my companion from my earliest recollection, and whenever I look back I see nothing but his wan visage and despairing frown. They blighted every joy in its bud. I never was allowed to realize any thing. I was always looking to the future, not so much because I was sanguine in temperament as because I could not dwell on either the present or the past, and the soul demanded some outlet. On!

on! has been the cry with me from the first. The thorn in the flesh has whether for good or evil pressed me on to what I am, and, in spite of all I can [do], dictates so much of my conduct now. My poor dear boys, may a better fate await you. I shall be careful not to make you too ambitious or too anxious, but to enjoy the present moment as far as reason and prudence will allow. You have good tempers and pure hearts, and I trust a father's precepts and a mother's example will preserve both to you. May God be with you through your education and your life and grant you a safe deliverance through both.

[Columbia] 20 Feb. [1841]

I have been very busily engaged for this week. The mornings have been devoted to the fatiguing business of hanging pictures, every thing about which I have to do with my own hands. Dining and evening parties, of which there have been a round to Dr. Carter, have taken up the remainder of time that was not required for gardening and little matters about the house. The weather has been pleasant and favourable, but every thing is yet in confusion. We are only gradually emerging from chaos. The people too have been kindly calling on us in shoals. They are truly kind for almost every hour in the day brings us some present of vegetables or something in the way of provisions very acceptable to new beginners, as we are here. Time has not of course begun to hang heavy on my hands, but I am growing anxious to visit my plantation.

The only political news is that the Intelligencer has officially announced the new Cabinet. I should perhaps say semi-officially, as Harrison has not yet been inaugurated and of course has not nominated them. The Cabinet is thought to be a strong one. It is wholly Federal, of course all Whigs. The conservatives—that is the Republicans who left Van Buren on the Sub-treasury question—have no representation in it. A most remarkable feature, as they had some strong men who were pressing for office, it is said. [Senator William Campbell] Preston and Rives are the leaders of that squad. The Cabinet, I have very little doubt, like the great Whig party will *explode* in less than two years. They have no principle in common but their opposition to V[an] Buren, and when he is out of the way the cement will dissolve and the edifice fall. It is now pretty certain that an extra session will be called to repeal the Sub-treasury [Bill], establish a [third] U.S. Bank, distribute [to the states] the revenue from the [sale of] Public Lands, and adjust the Tariff [upward]. [Henry] Clay rules the roost in every thing, is driving like Jehu and will upset the whole concern.

He is a bold, open, fine fellow, with more spirit than talents, more energy than judgment, and wholly wrong-headed in politics. A man for a monarchy where there are but two sides and every thing conducted on the highest national principles, regardless of constitutional scruples, of state rights, and money. But for a rigid republican government he is not the man.

[Columbia] 25 Feb. [1841]

I do not have time just now to keep up my Journal altho I have much to say that I really wish to say. The round of gaiety still continues here, and between that and my continued household, yard, garden, and street occupations I am even in arrear in my correspondence. Events of much interest are transpiring at home and abroad. Washington is now the scene of important changes as a new administration is just coming in and every mail brings us something new and of pressing interest, while I see daily here new movements on the social, financial, and political board. The financial pressure is tremendous and God knows who will stand it. I owe nothing myself worth speaking of, but I am embarrassed for current expenses. Nobody that owes pays me and my Factor in Charleston is about breaking. He has about a thousand dollars of mine in his hands which it will embarrass me greatly to lose just now. [Pierce Mason] Butler has spent the evening with me. He starts to-night for Washington—*office-hunting*. He has three strings to his bow: The Charleston Collectorship, The Governorship of Florida, and the General Indian Agency in Arkansas. I advised him warmly to take the last and told him plainly that he would get into a hornet's nest by going to Charleston. The truth is he has a blemish and they know it there. He is a shrewd man, overshrewd. He thinks "too precisely on the event" and joined to a desponding temper this makes me [sic] too gloomy in his views. It makes me unhappy to be with him long.

[Columbia] 28th Feb. [1841]

I christened my new House yesterday by giving a dinner party. There were present Prof. Henry, Prof. Lieber, Maj. T. Taylor, B. F. Taylor, J. M. Taylor, Mr. Coles of Virginia, Dr. Carter of Va., J. C. Singleton, W. F. De Saussure, A. S. Johnston, Col. R. H. Goodwyn, Dr. Gibbes, Col. McCord, J. L. Clark, Dr. J. Fisher, J. S. Preston and W. Hampton Jr. Col. [Wade] Hampton [II, Hammond's brother-in-law,] came in afterwards. It went off very well, but was rather too large for social enjoyment of the highest character. Another such will pay off all my friends and conclude the last of all to whom I propose to extend such invitations. After that I can invite whom I please. I gave them half an hour to examine my pictures in the Parlour. As usual I was wholly disappointed in any little expectation I might have had that there would be any enjoyment. They gazed at them with the apathy of Indians. A few looked over the catalogue, but none seemed to feel them at all. It is throwing pearls before swine. Doubtless they think they are mighty fine and an eclat of a thing is as great as if they were really appreciated, but the pleasure of sharing communion in my own enjoyment is entirely lost. So of my House. Few understand the points of it. But as every man lives in a house and many have built one, all feel authorized to express an opinion and find faults without feeling obliged to propose corrections. Many odd remarks are made and all have tried their wit. On the whole I believe the admirers far exceed those who condemn, tho' all perhaps see faults. The fact is, however, that there are faults. I see and know them myself and could easily correct them in another house and would have done so, had I been here. The chief one is that the stories are one foot too low each, and the roof is rather too pointed. I am fearful the pillars would not bear stretching and to make them larger would have covered the house with them, and I saw that a flat roof would give the house a very squat appearance. Trees and shrubbery will relieve it very much, and when a pillar is seen peeping out here and there from a bower of limbs it will be much handsomer. Time I hope will effect this. The truth however is that my house and position have (to my surprise so much have I lived out of the world) created no small degree of jealousy, and I fear my dinner yesterday did not lessen it. I endeavour to bring my manners to the simplest standard and to show that not pride, but taste has launched me into these expenses—extravagancies it may be. I hope time will correct these feelings of jealousy, and I shall do all I can towards it. But I have no favours to ask and am determined to be independent in all things.

[Columbia] 1 March [1841]

Had Clark and C[hristopher] F. Hampton [son of Wade Hampton] to potluck and J[ohn] S[mith] Preston [Preston was a brother-in-law of Wade Hampton and the brother of Senator William Campbell Preston] after. P. and myself consulting about schools which is an interesting subject to us as we have large families of boys coming on. There is the worst assortment of them in Columbia of any place of similar size in this country and under the worst management. Most of them, even the infant schools, open at 9 and close at 3, and during the intermediate time the boys run wild, go a-hunting, riding, or traverse the streets forgetting all they have learned and rendering themselves incapable of bringing their minds to bear on their books that night or even the next day. I find no parents in favour of it, and yet there is not a sufficient spirit of resistance among them to prevent the teachers from practising this fraud upon the community. I intend to exert every influence to break it up.

To-morrow I contemplate, and with much pleasure, returning on a visit to Silver Bluff. I am not only anxious to see my family and my people and plantation there, but I want to shake myself clear of town once more. I fear I shall make a bad citizen. Many of the little forms of Society are irksome to me, although I appreciate their importance, and desire to see others observe them towards myself. Unless habit shall make them more agreeable, I shall, I fear, withdraw myself too much from intercourse and incur a strong suspicion of pride. This would soon render me odious and make [me] in consequence still more exclusive, until I shall cut myself off from the world entirely and become a recluse in the midst of it. The truth is my disposition is rather of a contemplative, solitary cast, and I am as it were acting a part among the social world. As I have only occasionally made my appearance in it for some years past, I have without any effort sustained my part when there, but now that I am to play it every day and every hour, I find it very irksome and I fear I shall not be able to keep it up very well. The struggle at all events is severe. A few months will decide what position I am to occupy on the new stage, and may settle my prospects for life. Nous verons.

[Columbia] 2nd March [1841]

The weather has been so bad that I did not go [to Silver Bluff] to day. Passed the morning reading English papers and other trash and the evening from 3 o'clock to 7 most stupidly at Clark's playing Backgammon with bad luck, smoking segars which always make me sick, and in dull twaddling conversation with John Preston who happened to step in and Sid Johnston who came afterwards. I learnt nothing important, nothing, and overstaid my time from mere apathy. I had as well been in bed, and before I again twaddle away my time so I will go to bed, I believe. It is surprising what mere trifles these grown men will talk about, and how little wit is developed by them. But how can it be [otherwise] when men have no information themselves and no taste for acquiring it from others. Not only never asking for any, but looking coldly, if not sneeringly on any one who gives them any. I soon feel blocked up when I get among them and become as stupid as they are. [John] Preston is a good-hearted, good meaning fellow, without any knowledge of any kind whatever, and who really appears never to think. He has just appreciation of knowledge sufficient to make him a little ashamed of his deficiency and induce a retreat behind a certain pomp and formality, which constitute his idea of gentility, when any matter of consequence is on the tapis. [James L.] Clark [a teller at the branch bank of the Columbia Commercial Bank and Hammond's next door neighbor who sold him some lots in Columbia on which he built his house] is a plain, blunt, shrewd, practical man, as ignorant as a bear and not pretending to be otherwise. When the scandal of the day is exhausted he is at his wits end and receives all ones flights of imagination, or philosophic croakings, or sentimental sallies with a sceptical smile or abrupt pshaw. Johns[t]on is a man of considerable information and some wit, but labours to give to every thing some odd and trivial point, which effectually dampens all attempt at intellectual conversation. I will seek them no more except when purely to lounge, and will never overstay my time again. I wish I were settled down so that I could commence some regular course of reading and fill up my time without having to resort to such Society. There is better here, but they are all occupied as I should be. I wish I could rely upon my health, but an hour's reading makes my head swim and my blood coagulate. I must be abstemious and study, quit segars and wine, and ride into the country. This singing in my ears is a terrible music.—Perhaps were I to undertake some great work I might by having a strong motive regulate my diet and exercise so as to enjoy more health, but taking things as they come, one can put no restraint on themselves or avoid falling into careless and bad habits. But what work can I undertake of an abstract character when I have so many exciting, tho' not occupying realities, to break into upon one. The little arrangements here, my plantation at Silver Bluff, a contemplated trip to the west, or a large purchase there, delayed by the expectation of having to take command of my Brigade and go on the Spring reviews, which depends on the movements of the present Brigadier whose promised resignation I have been expecting every day for more than two months.

[Columbia] 3 March [1841]

Again detained by constant rain to-day. We have late foreign news by the mails. The Eastern Question has been settled by giving to Old Mahomet Ali Egypt as an hereditary Pachalic. He claimed that and Syria also. But the bombardment of Beyrout and Acre by the English soon brought him to the feet of the Allies. I do not know that this result will be likely to affect us in America at all, except as demonstrating the prospect of a war in Europe. They seem however to be preparing for it, all of them. There is a war spirit abroad, I fear. The cankers of a long peace are beginning to itch. The English seem also to have settled their affairs in China by exacting peace, renewed trade, and indemnity. That affair has not, however, been brought to a close, and there will probably be much delay yet. If peace is restored there, the Chinese will afford a market for some 40,000 bales of East Indian cotton and for a considerable quantity of English Cotton manufactures. This will benefit us. I fear however that when the news reaches England of the failure of the U.S. Bank, it will produce a very bad effect on our cotton. We were beginning to think that matters were taking a change for the better, and on the strength of the late resumption in Phil^a. and Baltimore, large orders were sent abroad, and the prospect for a spring trade seemed very flattering. But these orders must be countermanded. A stagnation in the Manchester trade will follow, and cotton fall in the face of a short crop.

The political news is void of interest. [Edward] Stanly from N. C. in a late debate in the House spoke very insolently of S.C., prefacing it however with a disclaimer of any personal disrespect for our representatives, or insult to the State. Our Reps nevertheless took it up. Holmes, Campbell and Pickens. The latter warmly, a contest ensued, the result of which has been I fear unfortunate for Pickens. He has shown no anxiety for fight and half the world will call it a *hack*. The general impression at Washington and elsewhere seems to be against him. The fact is Stanly insulted the State and bullied the whole of them. South Carolina chivalry is at a low ebb indeed. It seems to be generally understood that [Senator William Campbell] Preston was a candidate for some of the Departments of the New Administration and defeated. He writes to his friends here that he was offered any post after that of Sec. of State. If this be true, he manages badly to maintain before the nation the attitude of a defeated aspirant. I hardly know what to believe myself. He is such a Jesuit that I have but little confidence in what he insinuates, tho' I hardly think he would tell a downright lie.

Silver Bluff 7 March [1841]

Hea me miserabile! I never felt more unhappy in my life. I can hardly find a cause for it. I came over here a day or two ago to see how all was going on, and I found every thing so altered at the Hill that I became melancholy. Mother and Caroline [Hammond's sister] were there, but the rooms were empty and cold and those I was accustomed to meet there were all, all gone. It was no longer home, yet every thing reminded me that it once was. The weather too, that prolific source of melancholy, has been dreadful and although the sun shines to-day, there is a brisk chilling blast that goes to the marrow. I found a birth to greet. Puck had a child, but I met old Johnny at the point of death. He thanked God he had lived to see me, when I called yesterday morning, in a cheerful tone, and I gave him last night something warming and stimulating to sweat off some of the water in his swollen legs. Alas it has timed the inevitable catastrophe. This is enough to make one sad. But there are other things. I am not well myself and feel weak and feeble, and I am so. I can undergo nothing, fatigue, excitement, study, all knock me up, and it makes me dread to undertake any thing for fear I shall drop in the middle of the adventure. This is the old complaint one would say, hypochondria, hypochondria. Agreed, but is it not horrible? Yet I am feeble I feel it on all occasions, I can stand nothing. And it adds to my melancholy to reflect how much I should do and do now. Here I am wearing out my negroes on poor land where they do not increase, tho' I take every care, and they make me comparatively nothing. With 70 hands I hardly average 300 light bags, in fact I never but once have made 100,000 lbs nett., while in the cotton country I might as easily make an average 200,000 lbs. I should remove there, at least summon my forces. Here I can make only a low living, with all my forces I cannot do more than support myself in Columbia and educate my children. They are growing up and in a few years will need advancements and then what am I to do. This makes me sad. I am looking a long way ahead for causes of uneasiness to-be-sure, but this is nature with me. I never was one of those who could feel that "sufficient for the day is the evil thereof." It is a miserable thought that one should fill the world with paupers. It does not always make me wretched, but it often does, and this is one of the times. I feel that I should be up and doing, I know what to do, and how to do, but this cursed mill stone is around my neck. Oh that I could feel like other men. What a glorious thing is health! rich, bounding health, a stomach that never faints, blood that never flags, muscles that do not tire, and nerves that never snap. These are happiness, wealth, honor, *real* life! For this at least it seems we were all made, and freely would I give up all for it. If genius is a disease, let me be cured, and farewell genius.

[Silver Bluff] 10 March [1841]

To-day I intended to have gone up to Augusta on my way home, having got every thing snug here, and things going on to my satisfaction. But how little are we able to foresee. The rain fell in torrents last night, and instead of waking to a comfortable fire in my new cabin this morning my slumbers were broken by a succession of dull lumbering sounds like the distant heaving of the lead at sea. It proved to be masses of clay falling from my undried mud chimney, which by daylight filled my fireplace within and left the stanchions bare without. The rain was still falling heavily and not a hand could stir out to work. While I was swallowing a lonesome breakfast and musing on the uncertainties of life, the news arrived that 2 mills were blown up on the creek above. All hands were piped away to mine, and after an hour had elapsed, the rain still pouring, I went down myself. I found the water falling slowly and little or none vented thro' the saw mill. The gates were not sufficient. I had the breast knocked off as far below the water as it could be done, yet it ran but little faster. I then discovered that the gates of the fore-bay were closed. Another hour was passed in fruitless efforts to prize them open, and we then knocked them to pieces as well as we could. It did not occur to me, in my unpardonable ignorance of such matters (for I have always been about saw mills tho' never in such a crisis before) that we should have let down the gates and put down planks on the breast when the fore-bay gates would have swung round on their hinges with perfect ease. Nor did it occur to my millers or my overseer who has had much experience. When understanding this we got the water down 4 feet by 2 o'clock, when I called off all hands leaving only a watch. Muddy water and floating bonnets were coming down, and I thought we had received the contents of the broken dam above. About six o'clock the watch gave the alarm that the water was rising. We hurried down. I saw at a glance that the danger was imminent for the pond had filled 2 feet and, I soon ascertained, was rising an inch every 5 minutes. The rain which had scarcely slacked all day, now came down in a deluge. All the gates were taken out with no effect, and I commenced laying slabs along the whole length of the dam by which means I raised it some 6 or 8 inches. It soon however became dark, and such darkness as I never saw before. The lightning's flash alone revealed the dam, the water, or the mills. Torches were brought but could with difficulty be kept alive. After 2 hours of incessant labour and repeated failing of our light, we were once more left in Cimmerian night. I thought we had done all we could, and tho' the water was then in many places only kept in by our breastwork of slabs and still rising rapidly, I called in all hands, and we groped our way back in a perfect flood, overshoes in water everywhere, and without a hope of saving the dam. A huge tub of pepper tea, well sweetened, was ordered for the people, the overseer and myself changed our clothes and took a cup of coffee and at 9 o'clock I sent down to ascertain the fate of our mills. The report was that the water was running round the dam beyond the saw mill and over it under the slabs between the 2 mills. Both these things I predicted as certain, and had very little hope that the disaster was not even by that time more extensive. I sent back and the overseer went also to stop the insidious attempt of the water beneath the slabs and if it must run over to make it find its way above. Should this succeed and the pond be as is reported (tho' I do not credit it fully) to be on a stand there is a chance. The overflow beyond the saw mill will be some relief and cannot do much harm. But the rain still falls as steadily as ever and the lightning flashes vividly, the streams and rills from every little hollow are pouring in a heavy tribute, and six miles above are emptying their floods upon us. My hope is but a faint one therefore. An hour, or perhaps a fourth of one, will settle the matter. But if it must go, let it choose its own channel. I will not make one for it. I will trust to Providence to make the breach when it sees fit and to give me Philosophy to bear it cheerfully. Never have I known so much water to fall in the same length of time. Not even last May when we had the memorable flood which surpassed the Yazoo in many places. There has been a fresh and a smart one in the river for a week, every where the ponds and streams are overflowing, and if this rain has been general there will be a deluge that will cast all we have heretofore had into the shade. For others sake I trust it may not be. Beyond the loss of my dam, my recently planted corn (about 1/3 of my corn crop), my loss of time, and a few head of cattle yet in the swamp, I cannot sustain much injury. I shall be water bound, but that is nothing if the soaking I have had does not make me sick, and my people and overseer escape it likewise. Never was such a season known. It began to rain on 1st day of January and there have been but few, very few, fair days since. The ground has never been ordinarily dry in all that time. And the wind is in the East with the prospect of several days at least of rain ahead.

After all the loss, [what] I feel most is that of my poor mud chimney. It has driven me from my snug cabin, where I last night rejoiced in a glorious lightwood and black jack fire, crackling, roaring and with its flood of cheerful light dissipating every shade of murky melancholy.

It is now 1/2 past 10 o'clock. All hands have returned and I have given them a dram. The first I believe I have ever given them. The water is running over freely beyond the saw mill which vents a great quantity and *may* save the dam if the barricades stand firm.

[Silver Bluff] 11 March [1841]

It is morning and the dam yet stands, sadly wasted but standing yet. The breastwork alone saved it. The water barely receded from it and now stands almost level with the brink and still runs out beyond the saw mill thro' a channel it has cut some 6 inches deep and 10 feet wide. The rain fell in heavy showers all night. It is pouring down this morning, with the wind still East and as gloomy a sky as ever frowned on sinful man. Have not yet heard from the river. It is not time for it to become *interesting* yet, altho' I have some 80 cords of wood in jeopardy there.

4 o'clock

At 10 o'clock the pond began to rise again and soon swelled up a foot. It is still raining tho' slowly, about 3/4 of an inch an hour. We were once more driven to our breastworks which we raised and strengthened. We can now bear 12 inches more of water, and if this rise has been occasioned merely by the rain, we shall have it, for it is still falling heavily. I fear however that some other dam has broken up ahead. If so and we can once more get it to a stand, we will be safe. It seems incredible but the rain had fallen to the depth of 12 inches this morning. There is a pot standing in the open yard remote from house, tree, or any conduit for water, which all declare was empty before the rain. It holds at least 10 gallons, probably 12 and was brim full this morning. The river has not yet risen to an extraordinary height down here, but will do so. The disaster must be immense. My fields are sheeted with water.

[Silver Bluff] 12 March 1/2 p[ast] 10 [1841]

It is morning again and the dam is still standing, but the water made another breach about daylight this morning which was stopped with great difficulty. Were it not for our barricades it would be running over half the dam. Yet it has risen only about 6 inches since 4 o'clock yesterday and is standing still now. The river comes up to our assistance in the shape of back water slowly. It is now about as high as the great April fresh of 1833. Four feet are required to meet the May fresh of 1840, and, if the rains have been general, these it will have, for it must rise as rapidly at least as it is now rising (2 inches an hour) for 36 hours more. The rain has not yet *relaxed* but the sky is not so gloomy. The pot which was half emptied yesterday afternoon is nearly full, and the cook affirms that it was emptied

44

entirely, after the first night's rain. If this be true it has been as good as twice filled in the last 60 hours.

[Silver Bluff] 13 March [1841]

The rain fell for 66 hours without a cessation of an hour at any time and only [stopped] as long as 15 minutes. It ceased yesterday at noon, and last night both the pond and river fell. It is evident the rains have not been near so heavy up the country. The fresh however has been higher by some six inches than the great one of April 1833, but not so high as that of last May by nearly 5 feet.

Leesville 17 March [1841]

I ought to mention as a part of the history of my times that I found yesterday in Augusta that Geo[rgia] R[ail] Road B[an]k bills, which constituted their entire currency, now were 14 to 15 pr ct. below par. I drew on Charleston and received a premium in them of 12 pr ct. The Bankers would have asked 14 to 15 for the same bill. Yet these bills pay debts every where, even in the banks, and the branch at Augusta will take them on dep[osit] and pay 8 pr. ct. pr ann. interest. What a state of things. Yet it will be worse and probably stay low, and relief bills will be next resorted to. All the other Banks in Aug[usta], and nearly all in Geo[rgia], are paying specie, having been compelled by law to resume on the 1 Feb. last. This B[an]k resumed also, but soon suspended and so will all do, that have any circulation. I have however seen no Augusta or Savannah Bill, save these, for a year or more.

I read Harrison's Inaugural to-day for the first time. It is the most perfect specimen of "non-committal" that has yet been issued from any American Statesman in a responsible station. Its hints are barely understood now. Twenty years hence all that is not sheer nonsense will be a complete mystery. It is didactic and classical—dwelling chiefly on the Constitution and consisting mainly of old general views, expressed in language good enough, but giving no definite idea of his views of the questions before the country or his course in reference to them. It is said an extra session will be called. It is intended to "relieve" the distresses of the times by some political nostrums of which a National Bank will be the more prominent. They will inevitably fail and with them will fall their projections. Time and industry—the outgrowing of our heavy State and individual debts, with a pretty heavy contribution in the shape of taxes to pay off the former, are the only remedies.

Columbia 25 March [1841]

Between company and business, newspapers and correspondence, I found my time so occupied that I have but little leisure for a Journal. Not that I have not many hours every day which might be so devoted, but they are generally passed in that listless indolence generated by previous excitement. Until yesterday I have dined out or had company to dinner ever since I returned, and yesterday our three youngest children were christened in church. I have however something more important than usual to say. Whitmore has resigned his commission of Brigadier over a month ago, a new election has been ordered for the 8th of May, and my name has been announced without any opposition as yet. I have also through M[errick] E[zra] Carn Esq of Walterboro, a warm friend of mine, received propositions from my late opponents to become a candidate for Governor and receive a unanimous vote at the next election. Whether they desire me to become their candidate and desert my own party, or whether they only desire to come in or at most write on a joint nomination, I do not yet know and have written to require an explicit explanation. Of course I shall treat with scorn any proposition to desert my friends or any arrangement for a pacification which does not embrace my friends as well as myself. This reminds me that I once heard Mr. [John C.] Calhoun say that after his rupture with Gen. Jackson overtures were made to him for a reconciliation and every thing adjusted as between themselves. When it was asked what was to be done with Gen. J's friends meaning Mr. Van Buren, Crawford etc., Mr. C. replied "They must be left to my mercy." This broke off the treaty and it never was renewed, though this occurred in the second year of Jackson's first term. He [Jackson] would have been a villian [sic] to have left his friends in this situation, though there was little doubt that Mr. C. would have dealt liberally with them. It is one of the many instances in which Mr. C. exhibited his want of tact and judgment by demanding such a thing.

Politics and Finances remain pretty much as heretofore. The President has a number of changes, but has not yet begun that general sweep which he will no doubt make. An Extra Session is called for 31 May for the especial purpose of mending the times. It will fail, I have no doubt, and break down the party now in power.

[Columbia] 26 March [1841]

I have rec^d from my friend J. M. Walker in Charleston the first reply to my letter informing him of [Albert] Rhett's propositions [concerning the 1842 campaign for governor]. He slashes it right and left. And appears to have jumped to the conclusion that I am disposed to accept of the terms and leave him and Magrath in the lurch. This is very unjust to me, and arises partly from his not knowing me, but mainly from his being brought up in the Charleston school of politics where all are selfish, intriguing, and treacherous. Walker was an open, active, and sincere supporter of mine in the recent election. Magrath also professed to be so at first, but being a candidate for Atty. Gen. played the sneak, and until he was beaten himself did not even *assure* Walker or me that I sh^d receive his vote. Even after the Election his vote was claimed by the Regency, and was doubted by my friends. Many of them are yet doubtful of him. But the Rhett's and Elmore's have incurred his lasting animosity by their violent and successful opposition to him. He now goes for *revenge*—or *something* for *himself.* [Ker] Boyce pledged himself to go for me, and could have carried Charleston, but ultimately came out for [John] Richardson in the papers, and was followed by all Charleston save W & M., and this in fact settled the question. What then do I owe Charleston? *Nothing.* What reliance can be placed on it in another contest? Almost none. Walker alone can be fully depended on. And Magrath—provided his wrath be not appeased. Charleston must not then be counted on for much in the [gubernatorial] war, particularly if it be an open one. She will always follow and drop quietly into the majority. I must not however permit these young men to suppose that my personal advancement would induce me to succumb to the Regency and abandon my principles and position. This will be hard to do owing to their Charleston education and because too, I sometimes suspect, they have views of their own for which they wish to use me, and are therefore very suspicious that I design the same thing. Such is public life in this country. The truth is we must change our tactics to defeat this Regency. We have been most signally defeated in attempting to storm this front. We must now turn their flank. I will be guilty of no treachery, but outmaneuvre them if I can. It is somewhat strange that while Walker seems to think I have gone over and indirectly denounces it, Carn has advised me to do so, and Dr. Laborde, who has seen every thing, expresses great apprehension that I have not yielded enough in my reply to Rhett. I shall calmly wait for developments and act accordingly.

[Columbia] 27 March [1841]

I received information to-day that my old residence at Silver Bluff was burnt down on the morning of the 17th inst. It was not the one built by myself, but the one begun by M. Kinne, improved by old Mr. Fitzsimons and finished by Paul Fitzsimons for my wife. It was a snug and comfortable dwelling house where I have passed many happy hours. We lived there for five winters after we were first married, and our son Christopher was born there. Old Mr. Fitzsimons died in the house. And my mother has occupied it now for five years. Alas, it is gone with all its associations. I have felt all day as if I had lost a very dear friend. I had allowed Mr. Hankinson to occupy it since I left there and mother had moved to my house. He had been unfortunate and was without a home. He is so again. I am sorry for him, as much for the loss of the House.

Silverton 30 March [1841]

At my old home again, but rather dull. I left Columbia on Sunday (28) and Barnwell this morning. I brought over my servant Joe to see his wife who is at the Bluff and also to learn him to drive. Last night he overfed my horses, and, not knowing it, I left Barnwell at 10 o'clock, and the bridges on the direct road having been carried away by the late flood I came round by Tyler's bridge some 10 miles out of the way. The drive was too much for my overfed horses, and the best and freest of them was seized with colic on the road 5 miles below here and died. Poor fellow, he has been the companion of all my wanderings for more than 3 years, and I could have wept when he expired. Thank God however, all are well and cheerful here. I am dull however for this is rather a serious loss. Times are hard. I owe but little, and nothing that is due, but having launched out on a new theatre [at the capital] and when my style of living must necessarily be very expensive, I feel some anxiety about it. I have been economizing closely to finish my establishment without going in debt, and I regret I am bare of money, while all for whom I feel an interest in the world are from the pressure of the times bare also. I feel therefore, more than perhaps I ever did in my life, the want of money now and the absolute necessity of rigid economy for the future. At this moment, the loss of my [old] house, the loss of my horses (for I must get another pair) joined to all the rest came heavily. I feel too that I must use more personal industry and embark in some enterprise to increase my property. If health is only granted me I hope, however, all will yet be well. I left home unhappy, [my son] Willie was sick, [my mother-in-law] Mrs. Fitzsimons was sick, and my wife quite gloomy. Nothing but necessity could have brought me off. I had to attend Barnwell Court or abandon my citizenship [there], and being there I wished to see how all were up here, and here I am—on foot.

I slept with [William Gilmore] Simms (the author) last night. Such was the squeeze at Brown's. He is a good fellow. He has a strong active mind and has gathered much information. A most incessant talker and talks pretty well. He is not however refined in manners or sentiment. That is, he has not the delicacy of a thorough bred man. The worst trait he has, is, I think, a disposition to disparage his literary rivals, and, in fact, most others. It is the defect of his early education I trust and nothing more.

Silver Bluff 31st March [1841]

The gloominess which I felt on my first arrival here before, and again last night, haunts me to-day. Every face I see, every place I visit on the plantation seems to bring up a melancholy reminiscence. My residence here, tho' so lately terminated and possibly soon to be renewed, seems somehow to have already taken its place among "the things that were" and its associations belong apparently to "the olden time." This is strange. But so it is. The things come more from my nature, I imagine, than from the character of the change. The change has been great. My house at the Hill [Siverton] is totally altered within. That at the old place gone. One of my oldest slaves (old Johnny) is no more and now my faithful steed gone too, and my long accustomed match, whose power I had so often tested and could so well calculate, broken up forever. Add to this what I glanced at last night, that [although] I feel uneasy about the future in a pecuniary point of view, I do not fear serious embarrassment. I can live within my income. I do not expect to expend more than $5 or at most $6,000 a year even in Columbia, and my income can scarcely ever fall short of that. But I have six children. They are all to be not only educated but provided for. It is necessary therefore that I should be adding something to my property. I must do so. But how, is the perplexing question. This is a miserably poor place. I have always known it and long since formed the determination to dispose of it. I have had it all, first and last, in the market and made some sales. For most of which I have not been paid and shall probably be compelled to take back the property sooner or later. I have hung on here partly because I disliked to leave it to go to [something] new—partly because I did not wish to remove from my native state and carry a family into the semi-barbarous west. Nor did I likely [wish] altogether to have a large interest there in the hands of a mere agent and [be] compelled to go backwards and forward every year. Mrs. Hammond was much opposed to this also. I have been partly detained here too by political prospects. First to go to Congress, next to be Governor, both of which I regarded as laying in a stock of reputation which might be of some source to my children, giving or passing to them under any circumstances a certain rank in society. I fear however that my health, which induced at once a want of nerve for a great enterprise and a rational objection to embark on any [venture] which my sudden death might make embarrassing to my family, has had more influence in the matter than any other cause. But for this I might have broken over all obstacles or perhaps combined many objects in my career. At this time I feel more deeply than usual the necessity of making some movement, and I think the times are favourable, for property of all kinds is depressed. I think I can purchase the negroes of the Estate of [Paul] Fitzsimons [his recently deceased brother-in-law] at $400 round, and it is the finest gang perhaps in the world, and [I can] get them on the most accommodating terms. But where should I place them? These negroes with my own would give me 200 full hands, and I have not open land here enough for my own. By taking back the Lower Bluff from Ardis, which has 300 acres cleared, and buying the Red House [property], which has 125 or 30 [acres], and opening the marsh, which has about 250 more, and clearing 1000 more in all, which I might do in a couple of years, I might work most of them here and hire out or sell the remainder. In this way, I think, I could pay for them in 10 years should cotton not go below 8 cents, but this I fear is too high a calculation for the next 10 years. Should it go below that point, I might sell them nevertheless and clear myself, unless a war should intervene, which is now much talked of. Under these circumstances I have a strong inclination to make the venture. Still, I fear to rely on this for a cotton country, and to fix myself irrevocably here might be ruinous. My only alternatives are to buy in the west and place some of my force there, which would be rather a slow business, or to buy these negroes and [place them] in the west also, which would be a heavy undertaking. All these things perplex me. At one time I resolve on one thing, at another on something else, and I fear that I shall at last do nothing. The political prospects still ahead of me add much to the complexity and perplexity of views. Had I passed through the office of Governor, or lost it forever, I think I should be done with politics and have that out of my way. But the shortest time that can settle that question will be two years, if I succeed, which is too much of life for me to lose now.

[Silver Bluff] 3 April [1841]

I went yesterday to Morriss Bridge on Hollow Creek to see old Jacob, the Patriarch of this region. I was surprised to learn that he was a son of old Cofe. Old Cofe was an old negro, formerly owned (so he told me once) by James Boone of Virginia, a brother of the celebrated pioneer, Daniel Boone. He came here long before the Revolution, and was old George Galphin's miller here at my mills. He said that 3 mills were burned down during his time here. He [Cofe] died on the "cold Saturday" in Feb. 1833, over 100 years old. He lived in a house of Colvin's about a mile above the mills over the Creek. Jacob was born and raised at the mill and is now near 80, he says 85. He says his old master (George Galphin) ran 8 saws and 2 sets of stones on this stream before the Revolution and sold his lumber in Savannah at $8 pr. M. He had 3 stones at the Bluff, and on any day 100 Indians with loads on their horses might be seen. Galphin was a famous Indian Trader. Jacob remembers a great deal of the Revolution. He was a great Whig and told me a number of incidents chiefly of Jim McCoy the Plunderer. Jacob called him a Whig and knew him and his father and brothers well. Tradition says he was a Tory. He no doubt plundered and murdered both. He was tall, light haired, grey-blue eyed, and very active. He lived in an old field on this side the Creek about a quarter of a mile below the mill, part of which I planted in cotton today. There he killed his wife. He left home in the morning for Steel Creek. That night a rifle was put through a crack at the head of her bed and her brains blowed out. His rifle patch was found on the bed, tradition says. He was sent for next day, came home, and cooly attributed the murder to Joseph Ambrose, a Tory who ranged on Horse Creek. He also decoyed one Murdock from the Red House, where old John Newman lived, and asked him to ride with him. When they got on the dam here, he shot him dead. John Black was one of his men. Paddy Carr, an Irish boy named by old Galphin, was a very staunch Whig and became a Colonel. John Newman himself was killed by a Tory named Bill Conway who lay in wait for him, as he, old Galphin, and P. Carr were returned from a muster at Cracker's Neck where Newman had rec'd a Commission that day. At the first hail [of gunfire] Galphin and Carr put spurs to their horses and fled. Newman was on a mare, subject to what is called studs, who refused to move. He was shot dead. His brother Alex. Newman came up soon after and was so shocked that he suffered himself to be taken. In the retreat of the Tories they shot him in the back and left him for dead, but the ball had probably rolled out of the gun as nothing but the wad struck him and he survived. . . . I must see the old chronicler again. He was long a miller here and says these mills were established "long before he was thought of." They were however probably erected about 1760—scarcely before 1755. At the close of this war McCoy established himself below on the river— probably at McCoy's Bluff—and plundered all the boats that passed.

Columbia 9 April [1841]

Gen. Harrison died on the 4th inst. Just one month President. This may be an important event tho' Vice Pres. John Tyler will be the President for the next 4 years. He has been a nullifier and strict constructionist and voted against the renewal of the U.S. Bank Charter in 1832, when it passed Congress and was vetoed by Jackson. He is however a weak man, though not without talent. [Senator William Campbell] Preston had, when I was at Washington, almost unlimited influence over him. Perhaps he may have now. I fear he [Tyler] will fall into all the plans of the Whig Party and become their mere tool. He may on the other hand think of setting up for himself and running for the next term, which will disappoint all the schemes of Clay and Webster and break up the old Whig Party. He may also revert to the principles of his early faith and endeavour to administer the Gov. on true republican principles. I have not much faith in that however. All become corrupted by power. Jefferson soon became as great a Latitudinarian as Adams.

Preston is here. I have not seen him. He is non-committal on the Bank. No doubt intends to vote for it. He has also been paltering with his friends about taking office. Pretending to them here that he would not have it and seeking it at Washington. He denies the report that he and [Waddy] Thompson have split. I know that Thompson has no good feeling for him. He depreciates him to me when ever we meet. He is a spite-ful, jealous, and deceitful fellow, however is Thompson. But he would not feign enmity, friendship he might and especially to Preston's face.

[Columbia] 28 April [1841]

I have no excuse to plead for having so long neglected my Journal but sheer laziness. I have, it is true, had a good deal of employment about the house, chiefly in hanging my engravings, and there has been another round of parties, but I have had hours every day that I might have written and much to write about. The approach of warm weather has made me listless and drowsy. I cannot sit down an hour without falling asleep and I have some how a great repugnance to taking a pen in hand at all. Yet my apparent health is very good. The matters now of the most general political interest, are first the course [President] Tyler will pursue. 2. The U.S. Bank, 3. The extra session [of Congress], and [4.] the old matter of the hard times. The Whigs profess to have great confidence in Tyler and say he will do precisely as Harrison would have done. The Democrats have shown that he [Tyler] has always been warmly opposed to a Bank and to all the leading measures proposed by the Whig leaders. If he goes now for these measures he repudiates the opinions of his past life and destroys every chance for his re-election, as one of their tenets now is to have one term Presidents until Clay and Webster can be gratified at least. I have my fears. He is not a very firm man, I fear. He will hardly be bold enough to break form, party trammels. In all probability he is irrevocably pledged already. On the 4th inst. an investigating committee appointed by the stockholders of the U.S. Bank made a report showing that the most enormous frauds had been for years back constantly perpetrated by the officers and directors and other particular friends. The charges fall heavy on the late [bank] President, N[icholas] Biddle, who has replied by several letters which, while they do not exculpate him at all, prove clearly that there were many others nearly as great rascals as himself, and particularly that the Chairman of the investigating committee was one of them. The Bank shares are now worth about $20, this being their supposed intrinsic value. This catastrophe cannot help having a great effect on the Bk. question. The friends of a U.S. Bk. all now declare that they never had any confidence in the U.S. Bk. of Pennsylvania and that it was altogether a different thing from a Bk. of the U.S. The only difference was that it did not have the use of $7 or 8,000,000 of the public money. [Senator William Campbell] Preston has written in answer to some queries . . . a non-committal letter on the Bk., saying that he shall be governed by circumstances in his vote. Friend and foe seem to condemn its want of candour, and doubtless many who have long found out their mistakes in going with him will take this opportunity to drop off. He looks like a man at the end of his row, and I fear he is. I begin to pity him sincerely. I fear he cannot get a mission or anything else from the administration—what a termination of his career! Such is political life. Raules has been turned out of our Post Office now, and Gladden put in. Johnson, a kinsman of Preston, was always regarded a prominent candidate, but the party here would not allow Preston to have him appointed.

I have heard nothing farther of the Rhett affair [offering Hammond the governorship]. [Ex] Gov. [Pierce Mason] Butler was here yesterday and said a great deal, but I cannot place implicit reliance on any thing he says. We have had a most extraordinary spring, floods of rain, then dry and frequently very cold. It is now dripping easterly weather and we have had a fire all day.

[Columbia] 8 May [1841]

This is the day appointed for the Election of Brig. Gen. in the 3rd Brig., and as I have heard of no opposition to me it is probable that I shall be elected. If so, I set out on my reviews on Thursday next.

Columbia is still very lively. The appeal Court opened its session on Monday. On Tuesday night [Wade] Hampton gave a large party and to-day he gives a dinner. Last night B. F. Taylor gave a party and the day before yesterday I had the Judge etc. to dine with me. Politics are not much discussed. [John] Preston, for whom I have a growing disgust and dislike, did broach them occasionally. He is a proud, vain, unfeeling man, without judgement, and I fear without much principle. His talent consists in a good memory, a fair portion of observation though without judgement to make a just use of its results, a flowing manner, and very ready command of language. His legal education has taught him varnish well, and to link together a chain of plausibilities, but it is clear to an observer that he never seems intent on truth, and that his *heart* has nothing to do with what he says. Such a man must be a charlatan and mountebank, which he eminently is. I invited Wardlaw and Burt, my recent opponents, to my dinner. It was not pleasant, but some of my warmest friends in the late contest advised it, and I thought I would not appear wanting in generous courtesy. Bonham and Carroll are here now, the latter came after my dinner. I am showing them great attention because they risked more to serve me than any others. I fear they think it is for the future and not the past that I am doing it. These things sometimes make me feel like swearing off forever and ever from politics, and then I should be understood and appreciated in private life. Yet this would be selfish and appear whimsical, so I must take the chances. In general politics, no change. [James] Hamilton has effected a loan for Texas in Paris. For this he gets $250,000. I endorsed his paper for $12,500 last Feb. year knowing then that he could not or barely could pay his debts. I thought him a noble fellow. He had done me many little kindnesses, and I felt like risking something for him. He will now pay off I trust.

[Columbia] 9 May [1841]

Dined with Hampton yesterday. Judge [Andrew Pickens] Butler as usual very boisterous. He enacts broad farce with much success. He is abstemious in selecting a butt and most unsparing in pushing an advantage. But he cannot take a retort. It either cuts him down completely or provokes a rude reply, which destroys good fellowship. But give him the stage, and [he will] give you an exhibition that will make your sides crack. His vein is ridicule. This, added to a pretty good fund of common sense and a lofty tho' very undignified manner, has carried him along with but little information and no powers of rhetoric or logic. He has the reputation of being a highminded and honorable man. He is as much so as a man of very great selfishness and very little real feeling can be. He puts on much of it, I do not doubt. His Brother Gov. [Pierce Mason] Butler was not at H[ampton's] nor with me. In fact I have seen him at but one dinner party this spring and winter. He is well known now to be a rascal in every way and no one can venture to endorse for him by bringing him forward. What a fule is he. He too has been an extraordinary actor. Of a different vein however. Not so farcical, but still with a mixture of humour. He is now a cynic—as the Judge is inclined to be and would be with much less provocation. Butler made Judge Evans somewhat his butt at H's, who bore it like a sensible good natured man as he is, and Judge O'Neale, who met every thing with his deceitful smiles, drinking cold water and with ultra decency hanging heavy on the party. Judge Dunkin with solemn phiz. laughed but said nothing, and Burt was ditto, Wardlaw do. and Col. Goodwyn who was gravity itself. Butler's buffoonery aided by Preston's lighter and more delicate farce was all that relieved us and did so pretty effectively. There was a new story of Judge [Richard] Gantt who furnishes many at every circuit. Charging the Grand Jury at Spartanburgh he directed the most of his remarks as usual to temperance. Among other things he said—"Many seem to think these drunken brawls and revels paradise itself. What a notion they must have of heaven! Could one of you gentlemen be instantly translated to that abode of bliss what would you think— how shocked you would be, were you there to see St. Paul astride of a whiskey barrel, with St. Peter retailing it by the half pint, and Washington, the Father of his Country, cavorting about like a Court House bully."

[Columbia] 12 May [1841]

Wearing out life in a round of frivolities. Eating, drinking and sitting up until I cannot compose myself to any thing. My head falls or I go to sleep over my books, and any exercise worries me dreadfully. Yet looking better than usual. Tired of it—of every body, and anxious to get to myself and in the woods again. The Gov. [Richardson] left here to-day. Called on him. He returned it. Quite friendly, but a poor shoat. Expect to go to Orangeburg to-morrow to join my Brigade.

II

*Sometimes I think. . . I should part with my plantations
and keep around me as few things that have life as possible.*

---

20 MAY 1841 — 30 MARCH 1842

Gillisonville 20 May [1841]

Thus far on the Review of my Brigade. The Gov[ernor John Richardson],
Adjt. Gen. Cantey, Brig. Major Schmidt, and Aid-de-Camp Lt. Col.
McPherson form our party. At Orangeburg we had a fine parade, at Walterboro a miserable one. I praised the one and reprehended the other accordingly. Last night we quartered with McPherson and perpetrated the
most horrible debauch in the way of drinking that I ever was engaged [in].
It has exhausted me completely and I fear I shall be broken down before I
reach home. I am so already, in fact. The Gov. and myself get on very
well. He seems very amiable—a snake in the grass however. Cantey is
apparently a good-natured, but in fact a coarse ill tempered man, who[se]
rough drinking manners have entirely disgusted me. I have long known
him, but those latter traits in his character I did not know. He is electioneering for the office he now holds by appointment and for which he is
totally unfit. The family mansion of the McPhersons is a miserable affair—small, rambling, unfinished, dilapidated. The yard and garden grown
up in weeds and briars, and only China trees in the yard. The accommo-
dations are on the same style. Yet they are rich. But stupid, and too lazy
to be even decently comfortable, wasting their wealth in senseless riot and
equally senseless anticipation of their revenue. . . .

21st May [1841]

The Review is over and both the Gov. and myself have lauded the perfor-
mance—full as much as it deserved. I never felt more like a fool. In fact

57

the debauch Brew too has addled my brains. I wish I was at home. I want rest—fresh air and cool water. No news politically yet. [Etienne] Lartigue, the Colonel here, has an idea of opposing Cantey for the office of Adj.ᵗ Gen.¹ I have rather dissuaded him believing that Cantey will beat him. Yet I have affixed him my support if he runs. He is the best qualified by far, I think. [Robert Barnwell] Rhett and the Gov. are now in close consultation.

I think if I were well I should enjoy my trip. There is something in the solemn gloom of these swamps which strikes me more than any other kind of landscape. Even the still, dead, black water seems to consort with the sluggishness of my spirit. I have seen some good land down here, but it is in small bodies cut up with swamps. The good is also rare. It is mostly a cold, pipe clay land, too dry and hard or too soft and wet. The hoe culture has worn it out and what is worse it is almost every where covered with nutgrass. It is also miserably sickly. It sells cheap also. Ten dollars is considered very high, and good places—that is comparatively good—may be attained at $1 per acre. This trip has destroyed all my confidence in myself. There is nothing that I can do as it should be done. I can bear no fatigue and therefore am debarred from being a man of action. I cannot be a man of intellect for an hour's reading knocks me up completely. I can only drag on then, a little here, a little there; when with a sound constitution I verily believe I should have been a great man, and I am sure I should have been a happy one—I cannot believe that even such as I am I can last long.

Silver Bluff 27th May [1841]

My trip, which has been a very worrying one, has at last terminated, so far, more unpleasantly than I even promised. Here I am to-day feeling, I believe, better than I have yet, while the Review is going on at Ashley's, which I have deserted on account of health. For the last two nights I have scarcely closed my eyes because of the most extreme pain in my hips, thighs and back, occasioned by cold or a regular rheumatic affection. This morning I left Ashley's in a heavy shower and in torture. I had not gone far before my pains left me and the showers ceased, and it is now fine weather, cool and cloudy. This is provoking. It is particularly so, after all I have endured to get through the reviews, to close it in this manner. The fact is I have left the impression on all the party that I am badly hypped, and I fear they think me unfit for any thing. Such is my opinion of myself at any rate, and I feel like giving up. Oh that I were a sound man! The

night we left Gillisonville we passed with T. H. Colcock at Mc-
Phersonville. The next day we dined with McBryde and staid all night at
John Platt's. The officers drill was the next day (24th) at Buford's Bridge
and the day after, the Review there. I passed the intermediate night at old
Mr. Ayre's, and the Gov. at his son Dr. Ayre's. After the Review we came
to Barnwell and the next day to Ashley's. Rhett said nothing to me about
politics at Gillisonville, and throughout the trip the Gov. has been most
cautious in his intercourse with me. He seems desirous to impress me with
the idea that he had no ambition, that his nature was to be modest and
retiring, and that he took a part in public affairs with reluctance. I was not
deceived. He is playing now for higher honors—the Senate of the U.S.
The impression he has made has not been bad and his speeches, which
was [sic] all flower, were such as were calculated to take with the crowd.
In the main they were written. Mine were all of a business kind relating
to military affairs and criticism on the performances. I gave him no intimation of my views and in fact did not speak of myself except in reference
to health. So far as I did say any thing it was to produce the impression
that I went for money and took honors only as incidents, and this is true.
Most heartily do I wish that I were now comfortably settled in some western wild, surrounded by rich lands, looking forward to settling my children
around me, and amusing myself solely with the gun and rod. I should be
far happier and am only deterred from it by the fear that death would
overtake me in such a wilderness before my children would be large enough
to take charge of one another.

[Silver Bluff] 31st May [1841]

I have felt so well since I came here as to be wholly ashamed of my late
complaints. Is it the air? The occupation? Or removal from constraint and
excitement? Alas! I am always so. A great hero when I think of what I
could do, and a great failure when actually called on, wearied and worn
down to apathy and stupidity by the least necessary exertion. I have been
reading here a great deal, but light. I am half inclined never to read again
but for mere amusement. It is a mere pretence, no more, to aim at any
thing more. It makes me turn aside from many an entertaining book,
while it does not force me to do better. I pass the time in resolving to do
well, but doing nothing.

[Columbia] 14 June [1841]

It has been so dreadful hot that I have not been able to write or even think. Important matters are however in progress. First as to myself, I have been just elected a Director of the Br[anch] Bank here. . . . It is a post of much responsibility and no profit, and I only accept it to learn something of the way of business.

[President] Tyler's message left all parties in the dark. It is beginning however to be imputed that he will veto a bank, at least such an one as may be carried, and that he and Clay will split. I think myself it is only an affectation of independence to which he has been put up by Preston and that he will soon take the bit from Clay.

[Columbia] 20 June [1841]

I rec^d a letter a day or two ago from my friend Carn of Walterboro, containing A.S. Rhett's reply to my letter written to C., sometime early in March, in answer to his communication about the next Gov. R[hett], after taking near 3 months to chew on it, writes, as if by impulse, and affects to be offended that he sh^d be suspected, and a disclaimer of any improper views [be] required, and breaks off the negociation. I am glad of it, I never liked it. The truth is however that there was no impulse about it. The Union men have no doubt made a difficulty. They would prefer Judge Johnson, tho' a Whig, because an Union man. I have heard that [Benjamin F.] Perry and some others have already spoken of him in that way, and that they will take *any one* rather than me. Another reason of Rhett's is that his brother, [Robert Barnwell Rhett], it is said, is no longer a candidate for the Senate. They do not therefore care now to conciliate me so much. I shall keep right on and leave the consequences to themselves.

At this moment I am much engaged in writing my oration for the Agricultural Soc[iety] Ann[ual] M[eeting] Dec. next and in trying to adjust the quarrel of [Preston] Brooks and [Louis] Wigfall. They have fought once and twice settled. But Wigfall rejects the last settlement. There has been much carelessness and more folly in the management of the whole affair, and Wigfall is a fool who has a monomania about fighting, tho' a nervous and excitable man. The chance for a settlement is slender, but I have done every thing to make it available and have a ray of hope. One must die if they fight.

[Columbia] 23 June [1841]

Our wedding day. Ten years married. It seems like yesterday in one respect, and like a century ago in another. The relations it created all seem now to me stale, while those it dissolved or revolutionized seem scarcely ever to have existed. The period has been marked with good and bad as all life's way is chequered. The good has greatly predominated however. We have had seven children. Six are yet alive and bid fair to live. God grant we may be able to do our duty by them and spare us to that end, if no others.

[Columbia] 24 June [1841]

I am a good deal worried by this Brooks and Wigfall matter. Their quarrels first broke out in the [1840] Election for Gov., tho' I believe the causes were at work before. I have therefore from the first aimed at peace and peace only, because I could not under any circumstances appear to foment a quarrel partly my own. I expect however that I shall meet the usual fate of peacemakers. I drew up a paper to the effect that neither of them is right to demand further satisfaction of the other and either would be justified in declining a challenge. This of course put the challenger [Wigfall] in an awkward position as it was signed by Cols. Gregg, Chappell, McCord, Stark, Hopkins, and Hampton, and Messrs. Preston, A. S. Johnston, W. F. De Saussure, and B. F. Taylor and myself. Of course Wigfall throws all the blame on me and thinks that in fact my counsel has occasioned all the difficulties to him. In this I fear, [Pierce Mason] Butler, who is willing to throw blame on any one and foment any quarrel, has, I have no doubt, said much to induce him to believe. On the other hand, as I have refused to give any advice or take any part in any thing tending to make a fight necessary, I fear Brooks and his friends have thought that I had come short of that thorough support they had a right to expect of me, and this too Butler will do all he can to fix firmly in them. Not that he dislikes me or would willfully do me special injury, but because he delights in setting people by the ears and by lying insinuations to keep up constant warfare. He is also a fool and a bungler who mismanages every thing. His loose way of doing every thing, his prevarication and deception have been the sole occasion of the present difficulties: A prompt, direct and firm man would have arranged it all last fall soon after the last fight. He is a bad man, who has been very intimate with us all and who forces himself so upon us that we cannot absolutely banish him from Society, tho' he is partially excluded. I wish he would go away. He has now gone up to Edgefield and so has Wigfall.

[Columbia] 28 June [1841]

. . . . There is a great rage for building fine houses here now. I believe I set the example. [John] Manning [another brother-in-law of Wade Hampton II] has recently put up a palace that has cost him probably $50,000 on a parkle-berry hill at the edge of the Santee Swamp some 40 miles below. Gen. [James Hopkins] Adams is just finishing a fine house in the fork. Internally, it is on the same plan as mine nearly, with piazzas (double) before and behind. It is built by a negro (Bill Fisher) expressly to surpass mine and tricked off outwardly with all sorts of gingerbread work, which makes it in my eye quite ridiculous. John Preston has made several demonstrations but has not yet determined to build, while Hampton is most absurdly prepared to expend $20,000, not a dollar of which he can afford, in mak[ing] additions to Millwood. B. F. Taylor also intends to build in town, and several new houses are going up. The longer I stay in my house the better I like it for the comforts it affords. It is not, however, the house I would build had I to do it over. It is too showy and impressive. The whole cost of the Establishment, every thing included, is $30,000, of which sum $5,000 has been paid for furniture. It is well built of good material and exceedingly comfortable. Too expensive for my fortune, as I can never dispose of it at that figure or near it. Still I do not think there is a greater comfort than a fine house to live in, and I will try it a while. If I find I cannot stand it, I will pull up stakes and away to the Westward, to the wilderness. I am mainly disappointed here in schools, but that, I hope, we shall remedy before long.

Silver Bluff 3rd July [1841]

We had rather a sorry celebration of the 4th July (to-morrow is Sunday) to-day. C. Hay Esq of Barnwell made us a very respectable speech, and we had a Barbecue—all cold water and no toasts. Have come over here to bring my older boys Harry, Kit, Spann, and Willie and return soon for the rest of my family for the summer here. Feel dull and restless and dissatisfied. These pages will prove me often so. The truth is I seldom write when in good spirits, at least here. Every day I look forward to the future with more anxiety. I have a family running up to an expensive age and have lately set up a fine establishment in Columbia, while cotton is falling, falling never to rise again, and nothing else can be produced by planting on the absentee system. To raise stock and provisions for market requires unremitted personal attention, and even already I see many bad fruits arising from my absence. Yet I cannot return to live here [at Silver Bluff]. I have passed nearly 10 years off and on, 7 of them almost wholly here, among the most ignorant, vulgar, and, I may add, most narrow minded set of people in the world. There is not a soul to whom I can converse of anything save neighborhood news and crops. Even about the latter they know nothing except of corn. I cannot tame any of them and give them art. But I cannot sell my land here and am forced to keep my chief interest among them, while I am equally compelled to reside chiefly elsewhere. The present prospects are, however, that I shall not be able to keep up my establishment in Columbia. I certainly cannot lay up any thing if I do. My houses and lots there have cost me $30,000. I cannot sell out for $20,000. I began to build 2 years too soon. I could have saved perhaps 20 pr. ct. by postponing it until now, and if I had the $30,000 invested in 75 negroes they could give me an additional income of $3000. These things grieve me much. I am full of anxiety about my dear children. I wish to place them above the fear of poverty, but I have too many to provide well for. They must work. Poor dear creatures, inheriting the same wretched constitution that a malign fate has imposed on me and all my blood. They cannot undergo much labour or anxiety I fear. It wrings my heart to think of them, and I grudge myself every dollar that I spend. Every day I feel more and more that the only way to be independent is to have money and who can be happy without independence. I regret my extravagance in building so fine a house, in fact, in going to Columbia at all. Yet I could not live here [at Silver Bluff]. I did not know where else to go. And I have not the resolution to deny the present as much as I ought. Forgive me my dear children if I am using what, I would to God, I could reserve for you. I want the robust health to work as I ought or to live as economically as I sh^d. Yet I am trying to give you a respectable name. This may be of some service to you, or it may be a stumbling block fostering pride and preventing enterprise and industry. If my life is spared I will try to train you in better principles and opinions. I am not deceived, however, into the belief that a name will amount to any more than a nominal advantage. It will introduce you to the best Society and open your way to any station you may merit. Nor do I place any reliance upon any friendships I may secure as arriving to any substantial advantage to you. They may help you along if you shew yourself worthy, but if you do not you will never hear of them, and should misfortune or difficulty attend you they will be no more to you than strangers. The only thing you can rely on next to God and yourselves is money. I wish I could make money for you, which I shall try to do. I wish I may be spared to help to make you what you should be. And oh that you may be able to put a confident trust in God. There is no blessing like this. "There's nothing true, but heaven." I feel too much the want of a firm hope and trust in the future beyond the grave myself. May God in his mercy yet sweep away the cloud from me and from all of you.

I have however some ground for self-congratulation. After nearly 4 years of struggling I have succeeded in recovering for the heirs of my Grandfather, James Spann, $103,733.04 from the Exec[utors] of my Grand uncle John Fox, but for the obstinacy of one person we should have got $180 in. Of these heirs mother is one, and her share will be about $20,000. This will make her comfortable and relieve me of all expense for her family hereafter. They have cost me $10,000, not counting interest, since 1831. I have, thank God, done my duty to them and it is a glorious feeling to me. Yet one—my Brother John, just returned from Philadelphia whose education has cost me near $4,000, has already rejected all further counsel from me. Poor fellow he lies in the other room half dead with anger and disease. He is of my tainted blood—the worst perhaps of us. A stomach like an ulcer—a brain of fire. I pity him from the bottom of my heart. Yet I am compelled for his good to turn a cold eye on him and force on him some of those bitter lessons which, sick or well, he must learn and cannot learn at a better time. He must curb his temper and take the world as the world is—I know he cannot wile and shall not press him too far, yet far enough to do good I hope.

Columbia 11 July [1841]

The news this morning is that Mr. Clay's long proposed Bill to distribute the proceeds of the public lands [sales] among the States has passed the House 116 to 108. It is the worst measure that has been proposed since the establishment of our Gov., and nothing but the desperate financial conditions of the States could obtain the least approval of it. It is the commencement of a system of funding State debts and thus destroying their independence by making them pensioners of the Fed. Gov. while it renders protective tariffs and high taxes of every kind necessary to maintain it. Thus striking a fatal blow at the Constitution and ruining the Agricultural sections of the Union. What a monstrous idea to collect money for the sole purpose of giving it away. Mr. Clay is the basest politician our country has yet produced. I hope SoCa will not touch a dollar of the money.

[Columbia] 17 July [1841]

The times are daily waxing harder, and the prospects ahead are gloomy for Planters. I feel as though I am wickedly wasting my energies here and am smitten with a desire to devote them to money making in some way. The Law offers small gains and too laborious and exclusive an occupation for my health and other interests. Of trade I know nothing and fear there is a poor opening here. I sometimes think of turning broker or Editor, but both these occupations a[re] exciting, and rather lower than elevate one's rank. Were this question of Gov. settled I would not mind the rank and rather think I should try brokerage. I must do something. By the by, I begin to think Pickens is making an effort to undermine me. He wrote to ask me to "let him be Gov." and go to Congress myself. I declined Congress and said I could say nothing about Gov., it being in the hands of others. I should not be surprised if the men who have attempted to cajole me have, after my repulse, sought him. If he offers [to run for Governor] at *their* instance, I shall take strong ground against him. Alas what a world this is. I do not think there is any class so base as politicians.

[Columbia] 21 July [1841]

I have just had a long conversation with Col. [Robert] Goodwyn, who has had one with Rhett (now up here, A.S.R. [Albert S. Rhett]) in reference to the Gov. election. He says that Rhett did not intend to propose a nomination to me by those opposed to me to the exclusion of my friends, but a nomination by the Democratic Party, to which we all belong. If so the matter is a very different one, and to such an arrangement, I told Goodwyn, I had no objection, nor had my friends. Rhett says it is a suggestion of Calhoun's and intended to nominate me. If I was sure Calhoun did propose it, I would write to him for I have given him reason to think me unfriendly to him of late, which I really am not. Pickens, I have no doubt, has taken advantage of this to play on him, that is if what is said of P's pretensions is true.

[Columbia] 29 July [1841]

I finished writing my Agricultural Address for the Anniversary of the State Society yesterday. It is no great thing. The subject is difficult to handle. To say any thing original is hardly possible. To condense into a reasonable space all that one has to say is a troublesome task. I have made some rather startling calculations as to the fate of cotton planting in this State. Maj. Twiggs was here last week and rode over Hampton's plantation with us. He was delighted. It is indeed fine. But Hampton is getting ruined on it, and I am trying to persuade him to go to Texas with me. Day before yesterday Rhett and some others dined with me. To-day I met him again at Manning's. Not one word about the Gov. election or any thing like it. Brooks and Wigfall have settled their affair themselves. After W. found B. intended to make no excuse but accept his challenge, he was very easily satisfied. Anxious to get away from Columbia. Nothing to do and tired of the round of pleasure.

[Columbia] 1 August [1841]

Our news this morning is that the Bank Bill has passed the Senate with an amendment permitting the States to reject branches, if done at their first Session etc. It secured Preston's vote and will be approved by Tyler, neither of whom have nerve to oppose the Whig Party. I never thought they had. Virginia was against it. Had a long discussion yesterday with Gen Adams on the doctrine of "Repeal" [of the Subtreasury Act]. He is a young man of much ardour and fluency, full of railing and broad assertion, but without information, talent, or firmness—moral, I mean. He has however a fine verbal memory and has been moved into influence by the ardent support of a large and wealthy family. It is folly to dispute with him and with all such men. We are on excellent terms. The argument in favor of repeal is conclusive to me. The policy of doing so very doubtful. I [am] not sorry however that the point has been made.

At this day and date I am in very serious thought about my private affairs. The debts due me will more than pay all I owe, and I think I cannot be worth less than $130,000 besides. It is not all active capital, but about $80,000 is and will yield me an ample support for life. But I am accumulating nothing and see little chance of ever doing it. If my negroes increased it would be doing something for my children, but they do not, but rather the contrary. If my land was ordinarily rich, I could lay up something, but it is poor and nearly exhausted. At the same time the railroad has broken up steam boat navigation and cut me out of about $2500 pr. an. on the sale of wood. Under all those circumstances I am satisfied I ought to immigrate to Texas or Louisiana where alone cotton is profitable. But the obstacles. First, I cannot dispose of my real estate here, worth $60 or 70,000, at hardly any time. Perhaps I might sell enough to buy and start in the west. Then my wife's family are all here and her mother alive. Mine I could get to go with me, but not hers, which I am trying to do. Without some such arrangement, besides the unpleasantness, I should have no one to take care of my family and property in case of death, and in those circumstances they would lose all perhaps or live very uncomfortably at best. Third, my children are all small and want schools. Fourth, I live very happily here and dread a change, tho' rich land and fine hunting and fishing will make up for much of society. Lastly, I am held here by political prospects. If I am nominated for Gov. next winter it will be three years before I can leave the State. In that time, changes will in human probability take place in our family connections that may remove obstacles [Hammond anticipates his mother-in-law's death], and my children will be better grown. On the whole I think I will wait the events of the winter and shape my course accordingly and, if I can, go out to the west in January to take a survey. In three years if I live and am in tolerable health I think I will emigrate *any how*. This will prevent me perhaps from going into my project of reclaiming the Marsh. It will be expensive and after all uncertain. But the worst and decisive feature is that my negroes do not increase here. This is insupportable.

Silver Bluff 4 August [1841]

Reached here this evening with all my family to spend the remainder of the warm [weather]. I thought I had left nothing undone or unsaid behind me. Yet I find I have done much of both. I have a great many things to say to almost every one of my friends and have omitted to do several little things which annoy me exceedingly. I fear I am eminently one of those who are wise after the event. I never did any thing no matter with how much previous preparations that I could not do twice as well immediately after. I would not deny my instincts or pronounce myself deficit in self-possession for I have some reputation for both, but reflection is very necessary for me and, what is the worst of it, I can reflect so much better after than before the event. The truth is I am deficient in invention and cannot judge by anticipation. I am here. It was time for me to tear myself from Columbia for I was beset by temptations there of no ordinary character. I have found resistance a herculean task. Thank God I have resisted and hope I may, but it is wiser to be thankful for being out of the way of temptation. Alas, should I fall, how little would the world know and appreciate my struggles. So doubtless is it with all sinners. Could the heart be looked into how often would we pity even more than we condemned the greatest of them. They have had their bitter wrestlings with the tempter, have resolved and re-resolved, have shunned, have run from, have summoned pride, honor, horror of the world's reproach, and prayed and prayed again, but fell at last. The world condemns and punishes without remorse. The fault perhaps is that those who stand are not adequately rewarded. Virtue in this world is too often profitless and how few are able fully to appreciate and thoroughly confide in the reward promised to it hereafter.

Restless and unhappy. Soothing these barrens and forming a thousand schemes to escape from them. I have been for 8 years doing the same thing. Will I ever effect anything. I fear not. One obstacle after another presents itself, and in moments of vacillation I increase them myself most seriously. There is evidently a crisis approaching with me. This year will probably fix my destiny for life.

[Silver Bluff] 13 Aug. [1841]

Rec^d a letter from Mr. Calhoun a few days ago in which he says "I do hope that the unanimity with wh[ich] you will be elected at the next election will more than compensate for the loss of time." The letter was in answer to one which I wrote myself in which I intimated that I cared little for my recent defeat. I wrote because I believed there were some disposed to make a great deal out of my occasional remarks to the effect that I was not the blind follower of any man and to poison his mind with the belief that I was very hostile to him. My object was to show that I was not. I did not altogether like to write at all for it looked a little like seeking his good opinion, tho' such an inference was not at all necessary considering our relations hitherto. Yesterday I got a letter from [Clark in] Columbia that Rhett (A[lbert] S.) and Wigfall had held a midnight revel and caucus at [John] Manning's last week and that next day Rhett, Manning, B. T. Elmore, and Goodwyn were closeted for 3 hours. In a day or two Goodwyn let it out that my friends were playing the devil with me by declaring that they intended to run me for Gov. whether or no the next time and in defiance of my late opponents and that I would have opposition if run in such a spirit. The truth is B[enjamin T.] Elmore is most anxious to run again himself, and having, he thinks, a right to the Union vote for having supported Richardson and to the Dem. vote for having been defeated by the Whigs in Columbia he believes he can be elected. Of course he will foster any such reports as these against me. Wigfall and Manning I regard as the most bitter enemies after B. T. E. that I have in the world and the most unprincipled men of their age that I ever knew. Rhett is a mountebank and weathercock, and Goodwyn so stupid, so full of bitter passion that he may be moved any and every way. I am at some loss to know whether to let this thing pass or to send Goodwyn a contradiction saying that my friends have determined to await the action of the other party before they determine on their course.

The Senate's Bank Bill has passed the House by a majority of 31. The President has not yet signed it, but I shall not believe that he will veto it until he does so.

We have constant rains and a fresh which has destroyed 1500 bushels of corn for me. It has also spread havoc in the Island generally.

[Silver Bluff] 19 Aug. [1841]

My friend Clark writes me that this caucus mentioned in his last [letter] had met again with closed doors and the result of it was a determination to run Judge [Daniel Elliott] Huger for Gov. In this caucus was Goodwyn, who assured me of my election when I last spoke with him, and Rhett, who wrote to Carn that he would not vote for an *Union man* for Gov. next time. Huger was the head of the Union Party. So much for the faith of politicians. Manning opposed this move. Not for love of me I imagine, but because to elect another Union man Gov. would be to crush his uncle's [John P. Richardson] budding prospects for the Senate. At least such is my view. I hope I may discover that his motives are more friendly to me. I don't think Huger will agree to take the place. He refused very positively at the last election when I offered to decline in his favour. And even if he should run, I think it likely some may kick against another Union Gov. now. It will strengthen us and weaken the opposition that [sic] not enough, I believe, to insure our success, and I will not consent to run against him without much stronger assurances than I now have. He is not however of the Regency precisely and stands very high as a man of character and talent. He has been a prominent politician now for near 40 years—at least for as long a period as my life. It is on this account the Regency have selected him, believing that they will not be able to beat me with any of their hacks. It is regarded in that point of view a compliment.

[Silver Bluff] 22 August [1841]

I am searching for marl and strong once more in the notion of living and dying in Carolina. The marl is yet a distant prospect tho' I design an experiment, and have for some time done so this fall. But the late fresh has made a revelation which I take great shame to myself for not having made long ago. It was a smart fresh, rather high. Eleven feet below the May fresh of '40, and six and a half below the great August fresh of '31 and others of that sort, but still such a fresh as does not come every year and not once in two or three in crop time. Yet it wanted 3 feet of being on my river swamp land behind the Marsh. I am sure I could make cotton there 4 out [of] 5 perhaps 7 out of 8 years without a dam, and with a dam of five feet I could not lose a crop once in 30 years. I think I have 500 acres of this land that lies convenient and perhaps there may be 700, and, I believe, it will yield me at least 350 lbs of clean cotton pr. acre for 20 years. I shall of course examine it more closely, and if I find it as I expect I shall go at it might and main. Five Hundred acres of such land will keep me here. I can then make five hundred bales of cotton and some 500,000 bushels of corn to sell with my present force. But if I can get this foothold, I will attack the great marsh in the rear. Clear and drain and come in upon it where cotton will not grow, I will try rice and now find I can flood it from a creek about a mile above better than I can from Hollow Creek. If not rice, grass may be grown, I know, and I picture myself a lively stock flanked by a rich cotton plantation, while down below I shall have corn and grain. If marl can be had I will in time improve this place to the utmost extent and leave a rich inheritance to my children. These are pleasant prospects. God grant they are not fanciful and that I may live and have the perseverance to realize them. I wish now often and often that I was living at Aiken instead of Columbia, where I could be near my place winter and summer and in the world too. I must sell in Columbia anyhow. But I fear it will be a troublesome job.

I went up to Augusta yesterday and there found Tyler's message vetoing the Bank Bill. It has produced a great sensation, but what *effect*, it is hard to say. Some bank men say they were indifferent to this bank as proposed, particularly to its location at Washington, and that the stock would not have been taken. The message is on the whole a manly one, though not developing the Pres. views fully. He refers to his speeches etc., heretofore, for them. He seems evidently, however, to think that a bank, not having power to branch without the consent of the States, deprived also of the power to discount, but limited pretty much to the business of exchange, would be both Constitutional and expedient. Whether he wishes a great

Brokerage Incorporation or Sub-treasury with individual stockholders to do exchange in their own and the public money, I don't know. In fact these would be pretty near the same thing and the only explanation of his views. The addition of individual interest would make the Sub-treasury scheme a worse one, any would almost admit. We shall hear more in a day or two.

. . . .[Silver Bluff] 28 Aug. [1841]

I am really persecuted with the idea of writing a novel, a drama or something of the kind. It has occasionally annoyed me all my life; but sometimes it gets such possession of me as to worry me exceedingly. I doubt very much whether I could do such a thing even decently. I want patience, and, I may say, time for any long continued literary effort of any sort. When here, I am removed from books and from the actual work too much, and also too much engaged in my plantation and in business. When in Columbia, I am constantly drawn away by the same or other occupations, and when there with nothing else to do, the want of any *real* business soon debases my mind into a sort of dreamy hum-drum state which makes it almost incapable of doing anything. It is therefore next to impossible for me to write a book even if I were competent. But I doubt my powers of description, of story telling, of invention, and I feel that I have not been a sufficiently close observer of the world in its little ways and incidents. The great points of human character have been forced on my consideration, and I have reflected much upon the workings of the human heart. But even if I could convey my ideas of these things fully, they could not make up for the want of minute practical knowledge of the ways of action in the innumerable variety of positions in which men and women must be exhibited in these works. I wish I could get [rid] of the idea finally, but I doubt if I ever shall until I write and fail, that I think will cure me.

[Silver Bluff] 29 Aug. [1841]

Greatly distressed by sickness. I have three patients very sick at the plantation and two here [at Silverton] besides many lighter cases, and no doctor. There is but one better than myself in reach, Dr. Galphin of Beach Island. Sent for him to-day but he did not come. Drunk I fear. I know nothing so provoking as to send for a physician and fail to get him when he is the only one. My ill-starred brother John [Fox Hammond] whom I

71

have educated and just graduated at the Medical University of Philadelphia has taken himself off to Summer Hill. He went before I came over, in a pouting fit. Poor child he is one of the Stricken. Dyspeptic, dreadfully dyspeptic. Ambitious, sensitive, and full of talent. He cannot bear anything, not even the most ordinary contact and contradiction of Society. Flies from advice. Becomes frantic at rebuke. Yet the terrible lassitude of his disease which destroys all enterprise, exposes him continually to both. I thought I had some right to speak freely to him, but he soon put me at defiance too, and so we stand. I do not know what is to become of him, poor fellow. Had he remained here he might have had a good deal of practice if he desired it, and I think it would have drawn his attention from himself and made him cheerful. I think my own anxiety now is doubled by the use of tobacco, a small chew of which I find myself constantly slipping into my mouth.

. . . .[Silver Bluff] 4 Sept. [1841]

Have had several days of anxiety and fatigue among my sick people. The Overseer and his family are down and several others very sick. To-day however has been the most painful of all. A valuable [slave] woman was taken in labour yesterday and last night it was ascertained that the presentation was wrong. Dr. Foreman was sent for who called in Dr. Bradford. There was also a spasmodic contraction of the womb. Three pounds of blood were taken without producing any relaxation. She was then steamed without effect and Lobelia given to nauseate. Finally she was put in a warm bath. Relaxation to syncope took place, the child was turned, but she never rallied sufficiently to bring it forth. The bloodletting had exhausted nature. The pain and the steam had its effect and I am not sure the Lobelia might not have increased or perhaps produced the spasm tho' the parts were perfectly rigid before. The bleeding I think mainly deprived her of the strength for re-action. In spite of every stimulant she died. She was a good creature as ever lived. Her child had been dead several days.

[Silver Bluff] 5 Sept. [1841]

Another death to-day. It happened up here. A child near 3 years old who for 8 months I have had up here. It died of dropsy in its sleep. The end of rickets. This the 4th instance since I came over and two deaths, stillborn children. It is the 9th this year exclusive of stillbirths which have been 3 in all. It is, exclusive of such births, the 78th death among my negroes in a little less than ten years. Which is more than half the number [of deaths] I had ten years ago and rather more. It is nearly half I have now. There have been only 72 births in that time. One would think from this statement that I was a monster of inhumanity. Yet this one subject has caused me more anxiety and suffering than any other of my life. I have adopted every possible measure to promote health and save life, but all in vain it seems. Every thing dies, not only people, but mules, horses, cattle, hogs— life seems here to be the mere sport of some capricious destiny. Whether it is a judgement on me or on the place I know not. No one has ever prospered here since old Galphin died. His son, Goodwyn and Ransey, McKinne, and Mr. Fitzsimons [Hammond's father-in-law] all failed or died [here]. Yet it may be my fortune. I am reputed fortunate, yet, except in one single event of my life, ill-luck has pursued me at every turn. And were it not that I might appear ungrateful for that one, I should esteem myself one of the most unfortunate of men. I sometimes think I see in these deaths the finger of God pointing to me to go elsewhere. Sometimes I think it means that I should part with my plantations and keep around me as few things that have life as possible. Sometimes I think it marks the deliberate design of heaven to prevent me from accumulating wealth and to keep down that pride which might in such an event fill my heart. Yet I feel conscious that I am not one of those who are elated with prosperity, and, as far as human views can extend, I feel justified in saying that I have ever duly acknowledged in my inward and outward man all the goodness of God to me. If I have not, then my standard is erroneous. I have in this respect come up to what I *thought* right, and still think so, yet I may have fallen far short of the reality. God only knows. If these unheard of deaths occurred but once or twice I should think they were judgments, but would fate pursue one so for 10 years? Nor is the place sickly. It is as healthy as the neighborhood, more healthy I believe. This is a most painful theme. It dwells in my mind much and embitters my life. I must seek some change. *Must*. I should have done so long ago, but for a series of events which I can hardly recall. A mixture of political motives and personal bad health. Let my health revive and politics will not long keep me here. I wish I was only clear of my Columbia property. I do not feel like I ever wished to go there again.

[Silver Bluff] 10 Sept. [1841]

. . . .I give it up. I shall probably never be Gov. To attain it, unless some accident should throw it in my way, I should have to [go] into the Legislature and fight my way up again. That I never can do, no not to be

President. I did wish to be Gov. not for the sake of the pomp for it would have been an anxious, irksome, and expensive duty, but it might have benefitted my children one day. I could have got it by stooping a little. Possibly I have been too stiff. The honor would have been the same to my children, when the means would have been unknown. But I could not reconcile it to my feelings, to yield in such a matter for my own gain. And I should have been afraid to meet my friends after any abandonment of my faith to them. Yet they would have been more benefitted by the union of the party than injured. It would have brought them into the fold. Most of them I now apprehend, instead of appreciating my self sacrifice, will abandon me as unavailable. Walker has not scrupled to take an active and ruinous part without asking my approbation, notwithstanding I did his. Trotti, Quattlebaum, Bonham, Carroll and some few will stand by me, but not enough. We shall see. I shall remain quiet. Neither press on nor withdraw until December. Does not this again look like the hand of Providence cutting this tie which bound me to remain here [in South Carolina]?

[Franklin] Elmore owes the Bank largely on negroes mortgaged in Alabama. Rhett owes $70,000 on which he does not pay interest.

Sickness increasing, upwards of 20 patients at plantation, none of them dangerous I think.

[Silver Bluff] 18 Sept. [1841]

I have had a terrible week overseeing 20 patients and having now upwards of 30 on the sick and invalid list, some serious ones. No death among these last as yet. Am myself feverish, languid, dull. A big fresh to-day also sweeping off 1000 bushels of corn and some 200 bags of cotton. I am worried and wearied too far for complaint. I feel subdued and like giving up. If I were clear of my Columbia establishment I think I could now make up my mind to give up every aspiration of life, beyond being a simple, plain, country farmer and devote myself to twaddle for the balance of my life. Fate seems to have decreed it. I am crossed every where. If I aim at anything I never get it, if I get it at all, until the delay and the effort have deprived it of all relish. I believe all those who lead ambitious lives feel this, and it is the reason they are never contented when they have achieved anything. They feel they ought to have more for what they have done, and then in their struggles they have made enemies whom they wish further to mortify. Perhaps it is the same thing with those who devote themselves to money, and with all mankind. Nothing satisfies. But

I half believe I have hit the secret of it, and that if one could at once have what they wanted to a reasonable extent and without much trouble, they would be more grateful and contented. What a terrible thing ambition is. If I were called on to mix a chalice of the bitterest human misery I would have but three elements, ambition, talent, poverty. From these come first ill-health, which taints every thing and deepens disappointment, misanthropy, and the pang of premature and cheerless death. I shall try to keep my boys from ambition and that is another reason why I feel like settling down a common farmer and making them the same after me.

[Silver Bluff] 21 Sept. [1841]

. . . .We have had another fresh nearly equal to that of last March which has covered all the swamp corn. My apparent loss is about 1500 bu[shels] and some 2 or 3 bags of cotton. I may however save some corn.

My sick are all better and mostly crawling about. Some 20 odd are however dehors the field. Another little child dying up here to-night. Never saw the like.

[Silver Bluff] 27 Sept. [1841]

My factors in Liverpool Messrs. Molyneux, Witherby and Co. have failed for £400,000. I lose nothing, being some £10 in debt to them. The times are becoming awful. They have long been distressing and growing worse and I think a[re] destined to become much worse still. Cotton will come down to 6 cents [per pound], and to cap the climax there is a very fair prospect of a war with England. I am not much involved and can suffer but little comparatively by any times. I am on my friend Hamilton's paper for $12,500, however, which makes me a little uneasy. Unless he makes the Texas Loan, he must fail and not pay more than 50¢ on the 100¢ of his debts. If any can be considered confidential mine is one purely so, and I may fare better. He is a noble fellow. I hope he will succeed in his loan and come out well at last.

Sickness has abated on my plantation but there is a great deal in the neighbourhood yet, and we have still the worst three weeks of the year before us.

I have no heart for politics and no news. Gov. [Pierce Mason] Butler has been appointed an Indian Agent and we shall get rid of him at last.

These are times for taking in every sail and putting the helm hard down. I feel like it and dread returning to Columbia.

[Silver Bluff] 6 Oct. [1841]

Wrote a letter yesterday to P. M. Butler declining to go his security for $5,000. He wishes to buy goods to trade to Santa Fe and offers to assign me a Bond on the Elmore's for $7000 as security. I regard him as a swindler and would have nothing with it. I told him I could not become responsible for any one in these times further than I had done already. He will be very hurt and very angry and do me all the injury he can. This he has been doing secretly for two years past.

I have not yet mentioned here that B. T. Elmore is dead. He died of congestive fever on the 18 Sept. I really bore no malice towards and always was ready to acknowledge that he possessed estimable qualities. He was I believe the most bitter and most active enemy I had. His death will do much towards harmonizing of politics in Columbia. He was the main prop of that Blackguard Pemberton and also countenanced Myers. He was the connecting link between what is genteel and vulgar of the Democratic Party in Richland [District].

There is a pretty strong prospect of war. [Alexander] McLeod was tried last week. [The *Caroline*, a supply ship for a filibustering expedition into Canada was sunk on the American side of the Niagara River by a Canadian raiding party in December 1837. McLeod, a Canadian deputy sheriff suspected of leading the raid, was later seized in the United States and charged with murder.] One of our vessels has shot a ball into one of the English Steamers (war) on the lakes and the Canadians have kidnapped a refugee on our side of the line. In spite of every thing they will come to blows on the frontier and after that in the excited state of the two countries, war will be inevitable. I am not averse. I do not like the English. They want a drubbing. The event will be fatal to her. If she escapes a revolution at home and a dismemberment of her Empire abroad, she must lose her manufacturing ascendancy. The U.S. and the Continent will in a 3 years war not only get entire possession of the Home markets, but learn to compete with her abroad.

[Silver Bluff] 12 Oct. [1841]

Gen. Bonham came to see me 3 days ago. Has been in the Reviews with the Gov. Found him very close about politics. He evidently does not favour the proposal to unite all parties on me [for governor] next Session. He has perhaps no hopes that I will ever support him. Besides Wigfall has his ear and he is bitter and unscrupulous, and, intending to offer for Solicitor in his circuit, wishes to keep parties divided, for Bonham *and my friends* are his opponents. Bonham, Carroll and others have been unguarded in their expressions, and he has reported everything no doubt in exaggerated colours. . . . No letter from Calhoun since I wrote him of this intrigue to start opposition to me. He will risk nothing for my sake. No politician will. My young friends will, but I will not allow them. No letter from Pickens lately. S[ampson] H. Butler writes me that he is decidedly in my favour now. Still I have very little expectation that I will be nominated next winter. They will probably discover, what is true, that I can make no head against them and put me at defiance. So goes the world and especially the world of politics.

Meanwhile I am in great affliction. Old Mrs. Jones has been very sick, and crowded as we are here, one of my children (Paul) and his nurse have been sleeping in her room until both have got the fever and pretty seriously. Besides a friend in Savannah sent me a present of a barrel of oysters which were opened in the yard yesterday. The weather has been hot; they were stale and since last night there have been three cases of very violent Cholera among the servants, two of rather mild [cases], and Christopher and Spann and Mrs. H[ammond] have all been attacked. All are now down except Mrs. H, Christopher, and one of the mild cases, and we are all worn out with nursing for there are few of us left to do it. The weather is very warm and sickly. What is going on at the plantation to-day I don't know, several were sick yesterday.

[Silver Bluff] 13th Oct. [1841]

[Samuel Wilds] Trotti writes me that he is out for Congress against C.R. Carroll. [Congressman Sampson H.] Butler is expected to resign. I hardly think he will. I shall go for Trotti. Carroll is a doubtful and forced friend. His brother, B.R. Carroll, is a candidate for treasurer against my friend Mr. Hayne and has had the impudence to write to me to solicit my support, after voting against me last year and doing all he could. He has taken a new course with the Members of the Leg. and written to demand of them to say whether they will vote for him or not. Thus holding a poll before the meeting of the Legislature.

The trial of McLeod is going on. A number of witnesses have sworn that they saw him go in the Boats to attack the Caroline and heard him brag of it afterwards. On the other [hand] all on the boats, officers and men, or a selection of them, declare he was not there. The bondsmen have no doubt suborned witnesses. I believe the English and that he will be acquitted, tho' I am ready to hang him if guilty.

[Silver Bluff] 19 Oct. [1841]

McLeod is acquitted. Carroll writes me a very fulsome letter of flattery, which I must answer by candidly telling him I cannot go for him. Applications for money from all sides. Went down to Shell Bluff yesterday in search of marl. Very interesting trip. [Interlineation: 1901. We went in a batteaux, Father and I—Daniel Hornsby a slave paddling. Slept with Father that night at his office at the old Quarters near the mill. E.S.H.]

[Silver Bluff] 28 Oct. [1841]

Wrote to Carroll that I should go for Trotti, to which he replies very well and says he is sorry for Trotti. It seems to me T. must beat him badly. [Trotti won.] Have lost another negro child. Twelve deaths this year. I think on a rich place I could get along with even this. Or on a poor one with health. But no human energy or ingenuity can enable one to succeed on a place at once poor and sickly. Unless the marling makes a very great alteration I cannot stand it. This is my last hope.

[Silver Bluff] 2 Nov. [1841]

Returned from Barnwell Court to-day and have much to write but no heart for it. Have lost another negro child. Did ever one poor mortal have so many deaths around him. For ten years I have been working hard, overwhelmed with anxiety and care and all I have made has been regularly swept off by death. Other people consider the shower of increase [of slaves] one of the greatest sources of profit to them. If they can make out to pay their way, they expect to accumulate at a fair rate by course of nature. But a cruel fate overwhelms me by making this a source of ruin and takes all my earnings to repair the havoc of life. Great God what have I done. Never was a man so cursed! Never has death been so busy in any spot of earth. No not in New Orleans or Madras. Thirteen deaths and 3 still births in 10 months in a population of 160 [slaves] is unparalleled. Ten percent. Good heavens they have been decimated. And so it has been for 10 long years. Every one I have hoped the scourge would cease. But I am now hopeless. It takes away my heart. It crushes me to the earth to see every thing of mine so blasted around me. Negroes, cattle, mules, hogs, every thing that has life around me seems to labour under some fated malediction. They are all more than decimated annually save the negroes, and twice they have been, and always scourged. I cannot stand up against fate and I feel like doing any thing to get rid of any thing that has life around me.

[Silver Bluff] 5 Nov. [1841]

It is just ten years to-day since I took formal possession of this place [Silver Bluff Plantation]. My family which then consisted of my wife only, did not however come over until a month later. They have been ten years of great and almost incessant change, and I scarcely know how to compare my feelings now with what they were then. I was then very ambitious. It was the predominant passion, tho' I was not ignorant of the value of money nor careless of acquiring it. Now money is my main object, and ambition perhaps less than a secondary passion. I have seen enough to satisfy me that were I gifted with genius, nature has denied me the physical constitution necessary for a long and arduous career in public, and that even if I had both, success would then depend more on good fortune and the turn of circumstances than any thing I could do. To devote myself then to such a course would be folly. I only look to such honors as events may put in my way and shall never risk much for them. I think it more rational to take my share of the passing pleasures of society and endeavour [to] extract something of happiness from all than to place every thing on any single chance, tho' if on any one, on money for the sake of those who are to come after me and the comfort of feeling that they will be comfortable.

The first year after I came here, besides my business, there was the Nullification contest in which I took an active part. This engaged me until the summer of 1833. In the next winter came the canvass for Congress and the election [to the House of Representatives] in the fall of 1834. In that of 1835 I went to Congress, full of ambition. During all these years my health was bad and a large portion of my time was lived in morbid moping. A few months at Washington broke it down. I left there in April or May and in July 1836 sailed for Europe. I returned here in November 1837, in worse health than I went away. In the spring of 1838 I went to Florida and in the fall I purchased a lot in Columbia. Building there was my hobby for a year. I then bought a small place in Fairfield. In a few months, early in 1840, I was brought forward as a candidate for Governor. I could repeatedly have gone to Congress in the meantime. [Franklin] Elmore offered to resign when I first came home from Europe and when he did resign in the spring of 1839, I was much pressed to go but refused. I also refused to go to the Legislature. In the canvass for Governor I was beaten by the force of circumstances. There was a party move and personal considerations had no weight. Had the election been with the people I should have gained it all allowed. But an intrigue to unite the two old parties who had been divided by Nullification defeated me. In the meantime I sold out my Fairfield place and in February last moved over to Columbia. Since then the foregoing pages record most that I have done and much that I have felt and thought.

And all this time how prospers my pecuniary affairs. Not much. My expenses have been enormous. My family has increased largely in the course of nature. We have had seven children one of whom was born in Rome and died near Valenciennes in France. My negroes have *decreased* in the *course of nature* and in spite of every exertion man could make, just 9. I have had 73 births and 82 deaths. I have purchased some 20 odd. I have sold some of my land here, but improved the rest so as to make it about as valuable as it was when I came here. Altogether my property here is probably worth more than it then was. It was then estimated at $80,000 and was probably worth more. I think it is now worth $100,000. I have besides my house and lot and furniture in Columbia which has cost me about $40,000 and is worth I think at least $25,000 now. My debts and credits would balance rather in my favour. Thus I have increased my property at least 50 pr. ct. in ten years. But they have been ten fine years for a planter and I should have doubled it. At one time when property was high, two or three years ago, I thought myself worth double. But now when it has fallen to nearly the prices of 1831 I count on only 50 pr. ct. It has not been doing well. I have as an excuse that these have also been ten years of heavy expense. But on the other hand they have been 10 [years] of the prime of life, and worse far, they have placed me in no better way to make money than I was at the start, and laid the foundation of much heavier expenses for the future, in a large family and a large establishment in Columbia. These call for renewed efforts. I am prepared to make them and make many sacrifices, but that Providence, which for some wise purpose blasts every thing round me and forbids all increase of life, discourages, almost overwhelms. But for this I should be content and happy. But this worm gnaws forever at my heart, and cankers every thing. Gracious heaven have mercy on me and mine! With ordinary good fortune I should have had 40 negroes more than I have. A good portion for a child, more than I ever expect to give one. Here then and here alone is a source of loss which no toil or foresight can repair. Fastened on me directly by the hand of God and shewing clearly that I am not laboring with his blessing. Who can stand up against him, when without him we can do nothing. The bitter thought mingles with every draught of life and destroys all real pleasure. My dear children, I have never ceased to labor for you, but for my sins, heaven refuses to bless my labors and cuts you off from wealth. May you be the better for it. Perhaps you will be. And perhaps for this very purpose this is designed, and what to me seems a curse, may to you be and appear a blessing. God is all wise and all good. He works his ends through means which we mostly are not able to comprehend or appreciate and doubtless whatever is, is for the best. Still I shall struggle on and will not believe that what appears evil is really good or desist from doing my part because what seems to me beneficial to you, might prove a curse. If it is my punishment, I will make it more ample by feeling and believing and struggling against it. If it is your blessing, it will be doubly so I hope by my suffering and atonement.

[Silver Bluff] 13 Nov. [1841]

I have never labored so hard any week of my life as this last. I have made one trip over into Burke some 12 miles from this Bluff and then to Shell Bluff in my boat and a canoe. I have succeeded in purchasing for one year for $100 the privilege of getting marl at Shell Bluff and have already hauled out one boat load of about 800 bushels on my land. A second is on the way by to-night. But I delayed, I fear, in consequence of the bank's falling in on two of my hands. They are not however seriously hurt, and, I trust, I may regard their escape with slight injury as a fortunate omen. I will not believe that fate is pursuing me here until I have other testimony. I have cut down my wharf to receive the Boat and hope to make two trips in the week, but am doubtful. I shall put in 18 hands and six carts and hope to marl at 200 bushels to the acre at least as much as I can clear. My expectation is to make all my marled land bring $225 to 250 average *permanently*. If I succeed in this I shall be satisfied, though the books promise a great deal more. If I can get 800 or 1000 acres marled to this point, I shall be contented here. Two years will fully test this experiment, and if it fails I have no hope left but emigration.

The labors of the week have driven politics entirely out of my mind, and every thing else but marl, marl. I am however melancholy just now, owing more I think to fatigue and segars than to any other cause.

[Silver Bluff] 15 Nov. [1841]

Thirty four years old to-day. Dined with mother and family on a 7 year old Gobbler. John going to Florida and looks dull. Overwhelmed with business. No time to say much or write or think. Preparing to leave for Columbia to-morrow.

Columbia 28 Nov. [1841]

Delivered the Anniversary Oration of the State Agricultural Society on the 25 inst. Never have I been more highly complimented. It was universally said it would prevent any opposition to me for Gov. So many say now. I do not think so. Ability enough has always been conceded to me. This impression will soon wear off. There seems no abatement of hostility on the part of the Regency. They fear and hate me. Maj. McWillie of Camden is spoken of as a [gubernatorial] candidate—another ultra-union man of the Richardson clique and connection. He can't succeed. So many rumors are afloat that I hardly know what to think.

Was elected a Trustee of [South Carolina] College on the 24th. Met them for the first time on 26 and made a speech in favour of making Dr. Henry Pres. of the College. He is opposed by Col. [James] Gregg, who is as rough as a bear in manners and ignorant as a man can decently be. O'Neale (Judge) said ignorance was no objection. Dr. Henry, not the best in the world, but infinitely above Gregg or O'Neale. [Gregg, a strong candidate for the presidency of the college and a son-in-law of Jonathan Maxcy, a former president of the college, withdrew his name from consideration.]

[Columbia] 11 Dec. [1841]

Four deer at once at my house for sale to-day. Last week there were eleven in town in one day. Prices from $5 to $10.

[Columbia] 14 Dec. [1841]

Mrs. Fitzsimons, my wife's mother, died at my house at 6 o'clock this evening in her 70 year. She was the most perfect woman I ever knew. She thought only of doing good for others, never for herself. She has been gradually giving way for 18 months and has been in bed almost ever since I came over. Her remains to the family graveyard near Augusta to-morrow.

[Columbia] 15 Dec. [1841]

Political intrigue is very rife. I have neither time nor patience to detail it. Yesterday morning it was announced that Gen. [George] McDuffie had consented to accept the nomination for Gov. In the course of the day, he denied it at the instigation of my friends. The object was to get him out of the way for the Senate next year. To-day the Regency have been making proposals to me. They affect to believe that I am not for placing severe restraints on the power of granting corporations in the Legislature, because most of my friends and I myself have opposed a proposition to take it away altogether, or virtually doing so. I have stated my opinions fairly, they can do as they like. To-day will decide.

We had a grand military display under the auspices of the Governor last week in which I acted a part. It was a pageant, theatrical as every thing he does is, and saved from being ridiculous only by those who consented to act in it, such as McDuffie and myself, with several other generals out of this Division. Our object was to assist in carrying the military bill for the revival of encampments and the militia system which was organized after the nullification crisis and broken down last year. In this we have succeeded. And the better because Richardson was no military man and not the object of envy among the military or suspicion among the civilians.

[Columbia] 16 Dec. [1841]

Last night Elmore came to me with fresh propositions to know if I were in favour of a law to compel the Banks to make monthly returns and have them published, even if the court decided that suspension was not a forfeiture. His object was to commit me to some new proposition not yet developed, for he denied that he meant to affirm the power of the Legislature to overrule the Court. Not understanding his question (in his sense) or his aim, I told him I had no opinion and could not form one and that, in fact, I would answer no more questions having any connection with the Gov. election. To-day the Regency had a caucus. Elmore, J[ames] and A[lbert] Rhett, Burt and McWillie, Fair, Davie and perhaps others called in. The Gov. among them. Henry there too. They at last agreed to surrender the hatchet, start no opposition, and support me. They have been driven to this by sheer necessity for we have broken them to pieces. This however I do not say to them, tho' they rather hang their heads and look conquered. Affecting however to have been very magnanimous in the extreme. The machinery they had put in motion to govern the State has all gone to pieces. A very strong feeling exists ag^t. a caucus and now that there is to be no opposition, the difficulty is how to bring out my nomination without having the appearance of a caucus tho' there has been none, for I had no original friend in any of their Conferences.

Elmore and the Gov. have sworn eternal enmity to [Senator George] McDuffie, it is said, because he would not be used as a tool to put me down. It is clear I am a bitter pill to them. Yet I shall not treat them harshly.

Boyce I believe is not altogether satisfied that there is no contest. He wanted a fight. He has his own views. He looks to the office of Gov. but with no chance of success at any future period whatever I think.

The session of the Legislature closes to-night.

[Columbia] 19th Dec. [1841]

I find that Manning, young [Maxcy] Gregg and J[ames] Chesnut of Camden were in the Regency Conference on the 16 inst.

Elmore and Rhett are here yet. They have the air of men beaten and disappointed, at least with me.

An appeal has been made to the Democratic Party in favour of the [Charleston] Mercury which is failing fast. Yesterday the Governor called for help from me. R & E were present. I gave $100 which was as much as any did. The paper has for 2 years opposed me directly and indirectly in every way. It has now taken my bounty and cannot bark at me more.

[Although supposedly "lonely and beaten in spirit" after having lost the governorship in 1840, Hammond recorded in his diary in 1841 that he had been elected brigadier general of the South Carolina militia, named a director of the Columbia branch of the Bank of the State of South Carolina, and chosen a trustee of South Carolina College, his alma mater.]

[Columbia] 16 Jan. 1842

The Mercury has not yet nominated me. The understanding was so general here however that I do not think it material except as showing that Rhett and Co have not performed their promise to the letter for which there must be some reason. Probably the pill is bitter. Possibly there may be some reason that I cannot divine and which would be satisfactory. State politics are at rest. All are looking to Washington where the members of the House are squabbling like school boys in a debating society to the disgrace of themselves and the country. Some five or six including Ex-President Adams ought to be expelled. It is the only remedy and unless soon applied will bring Congress into utter contempt.

Never been such hard times. The U.S. Treasury is literally *empty*, drafts are dishonored daily and they can't pay the members even. The loan authorized last Session cannot be raised and they cannot agree to issue treasury notes which are themselves below par considerably. Stocks of all kinds are down to nothing and negroes falling rapidly. Prime fellows are now $600 and soon will be $500, for times are getting harder and will continue to do so. Hampton sold 100 bags of cotton here at 5¢ the other day and I sold 34 in Savannah at 5.5/8 myself. I don't know what is to be done.

[Columbia] 25 Jan. [1842]

Nothing yet from the Mercury on the subject of the Gov. Election. Can't account for it. Nothing of public importance going on. Domestic quarrels and private distresses in abundance. Being supposed to be without employment here, I have my hands full of other people's business (Catty [Hammond's young daughter] in my arms blots this with her pen). Really am pressed for time. Find much of what I might employ taken up in smoking segars.

[Columbia] 18 Feb. [1842]

I have been to Silver Bluff and Augusta. Marling at one place and squabbling at the other with the Lawyers I employed to conduct the Spann vs. Fox case. They are cormorants, who [are] not satisfied with an enormous fee but want more. The Judge's son claims about 8 times as much as I think would be a liberal fee, and the Judge, who has been with us, is now holding up his opinion on a motion for a new trial until his son can bring me to terms. I am [not] risking any thing by refusing to say what I will do. Very anxious to hear the decision. Shall not for a month I fear.

Expect to go to Charleston to-morrow, mainly to see how Gen. Hamilton stands. I am his endorser for $12,500, and it is supposed he is broke, and many think him a knave. He has been near two years in Europe endeavouring to negociate a loan in Texas for which he is to get $250,000. He has failed utterly and we have just heard has gone via the West Indies to Texas. He is a sanguine, energetic man who deceives himself and is quite wild, I fear, in his speculations. I am very uneasy about it. The races will take place next week also, and I have sundry little matters to attend. Times are getting harder and harder and every body going to the dogs. Have to be careful myself and wish every day that I were out of this big house in a snug bower, not shut up however at Silver Bluff among the semi-barbarians there.

The Charleston Mercury nominated me [for governor] in a very respectable manner on the 10 inst. and the Carolinian has responded. The Courier and other papers silent as yet. The Courier intentionally so, I have no doubt. With ordinary prudence I shall escape opposition.

Have become a great smoker which makes me nervous, impatient, and unfit for study etc.

[Columbia] 6 March [1842]

Returned from Charleston on the 1st inst., where I had been a week or more. I went down to inquire into Gen. Hamilton's affairs. Two years ago, just now, Gen. McDuffie and myself became his sureties for $25,000 between us. We found him stuck in the mud in Charleston and unable to proceed to Europe to procure a loan for Texas, for doing which he was to receive $250,000. We offered to give him a wing if it would avail any thing. He accepted and showed us his affairs, representing his property at $500,000 and his debts at $300,000. I was of the opinion they would at least balance. The failure of the U.S. Bk. and the repudiation of Mississippi State Bonds knocked his project on the head. He has hung on, hoping against hope, and returned to Texas, avoiding Charleston, to see his Loan Bill repealed and his last hope prostrated. So far he was to be pitied. But what was my surprise to find that instead of $300,000 his joint and individual liabilities could not have been less than $700,000 at the very time we signed his paper, relying on his honor that he could save us. Had he succeeded with a Texas loan he could not have paid his debts with his property and profits. During his absence he has pledged bonds of the James River and Kenawha [Canal] Company, who employed him to make a loan, toward $80,000, he says for the Gov. of Texas. Thus he returns Bankrupt not only in fortune, but character also. What a fall. I cannot now believe that he ever intended to deceive or defraud any one, but he was so vision-ary, so sanguine, so reckless of involving himself and others, that it amounts to a crime and shows there is something wanting in him. He has been familiarly known as the "Bayard of the South" heretofore. What a lesson is his fall to the daring schemer and headlong speculator, such characters as are but too rife in this country. My loss I shall feel seriously through life. Poor [James L.] Petigru who shared his speculations will lose the hard earnings of 30 years of eminent success at the Bar and at 52 is turned out of house and home, penniless and $15 or 20,000 in debt on his own score, being quadruple that behind him in his speculations with Hamilton. Hampton loses $30,000 which with his other liabilities nearly or quite *ruins him*.

Never were such times seen. Gangs of negroes may be had at $250 round for cash, $300 credit. Prime fellow $500 and sometimes less. The Banks are pressing cruelly. They have to ruin the community or be ru-ined. The strongest men and houses are failing—and the worst has not come yet.

I met Lord Morpeth, eldest son of the Earl of Carlisle, in Charleston. He is 40 years old with a high reputation in England, having been long in Parliament and Sec[retary] for Ireland under the Whigs. He was very cautious in his conversation, but seemed quite social. I saw a great deal of him and during an Excursion of two days up the Cooper River was all the time with him and mostly by ourselves. I did all I could to give him a favourable idea of our slave institutions, our jealousy of British influence in Cuba, and our resolution to resist it etc. etc.

I found the prospect of my being the next Gov. gave me much greater currency in Charleston than heretofore. I was invited every where. All seem agreed that I am to have no opposition. But this loss by Hamilton annoys me more than all these honors can alleviate. I lose my money, my confidence in human nature, and some of my reputation for sagacity. Alas, I know I have much less than I have credit for, even now. I was not born to make money, my health denies me a high flight in the regions of renown. I will endeavour to be contented with my mediocrity in all things and shall henceforth try not to sink below that at least.

[Columbia] 16 March [1842]

Hamilton has returned full of hope and spirits, as he says. Threatens to pay every thing in 7 years. Poor fellow. I am glad he has even the temporary happiness of self-delusion. In a few months, I fear, he will find every hope has faded one by one. He has destroyed all confidence in his judgement, and much in his integrity and will soon discover that all his power is gone. He has vast schemes about making money in Texas and some of them good, if he can do anything like he says. He proposes to Hampton to join him, and I am so far in favour of it that I should be glad to see him send 200 negroes to that country. It will, I fear, be all he will save out of his fortune when he is wound up, which he will be in 3 years.

Calhoun has made a great speech on Clay's proposition to abolish the Veto. It is nothing new to us who have so thoroughly discussed the Constitution here, but it is novel and striking elsewhere. Ex-Pres. Van Buren is looked for here daily. He is on an Electioneering tour.

[Columbia] 21 March [1842]

There is a great excitement getting up at this time in consequence of the news from England that the British Gov. refuses peremptorily to give up the mutineers of the Creole. This was a vessel which sailed from Richmond to New Orleans in Oct. last with 136 slaves. 19 of them rose, killed one man, took the ship and went into Nassau. The Authorities seized the mutineers and let the other slaves go free. The B[ritish] Gov. now order them all to be released, refusing our demand for them on the ground that the law of nations does not require one nation to give up the criminals of another. In this they undoubtedly are correct. Another question is whether it be not a case of piracy. This is our ground. If so the British have the right to try them for it and should do so. The true ground is not mentioned very prominently viz. that slaves *are property* and that we have a right to claim them as such. England will go to war before she will concede this principle, and the rest of the world will sustain her. I do not care to see a war made on such a ground. There are however other causes— The Boundary question, the search of our vessels on the African coast, the Caroline, etc. All these added to this have produced much excitement and we are apparently on the eve of a conflict with England. All parts of them seem ready for it. I am dubious of the event. We should suffer much. England I believe more. With such a stupid imbecile as [John] Tyler at the head of Affairs and such an unprincipled and cowardly Sec. of State as [Daniel] Webster we should fare badly for a time. They are bent on peace. Webster is in the pay of the great English Bankers, the Barings, the head of which House, Lord Ashburton, is now on his way as a Special Ambassador to this Country. [The dispute over the Creole affair led to negotiations between Secretary of State Daniel Webster and British Minister Lord Ashburton, resulting in a treaty of extradition in 1842 for certain high crimes. The extradition treaty accompanied the better-known Webster-Ashburton Treaty of 1842, which settled the Northeast boundary question.] There is also great excitement on account of Mexico. She lately captured an expedition of Texians at Santa Fe. Among them were some Americans with Regular Passports and some Englishmen provided in the same way. On their arrival at Mexico the English were released on the demand of the British Minister, but the Americans are compelled to work in the streets. If Tyler had any spirit he would send a squadron to Vera Cruz and blow up the city if the Americans were not released. He probably excuses himself on the ground that it may be somewhat difficult to do and that he has no money. The fact is the Gov. has not cash enough by three millions to meet the exigencies of the service for the next quarter—that is the ordinary service of the country.

I begin to think Hamilton a knave and that he has a reserve somewhere.

We have thus far had the dryest, warmest, and most forward month of March I ever knew.

[Columbia] 24 March [1842]

I feel a good deal worried by a turn in this Hamilton business to which I may have made some allusion before. McDuffie, T. Pinckney, P. McRae and myself guaranteed the payment of a bond of H[amilton]'s for $5,000 *each*, in all $20,000. It was discounted by the Bk of the State 1st March 1840 and payable 1st March following. It was not until last Dec., nearly 10 months after it was due, that I knew (or any of us knew I believe) where the bond was. We then for the first time rec^d notice that we were held responsible. Had we been notified when it became due we might have recovered a judgment in attachment before H's return and probably saved ourselves. McRae is crazy. I suggested to Pinckney and McDuffie that we might perhaps avail ourselves of the laches of the Bk to avoid payment. To my astonishment they both—after communicating I presume—say that they do not think it honorable to take any advantage of this laches and are making quite a flourish of their indifference to the loss etc. This is all humbug and acting. Yet it will take with the ignorant in these matters and at my expense. I think it a prostitution of honor to talk of it in this connection. It was and is a mere matter of business, and, as we derived no benefit and expected to derive none, we have the right, if we can legally, to throw the whole loss on those who entered into it for profit sake and without any personal communication or request on our part. Men of sense and candour and all business men will agree with me, but the others make a greater shew and will prejudice some men against me as a person not governed by the highest notions of *honor*. I regard their conduct as mere Quixotism. I believe however they are both more influenced by the conviction that the defence will be unavailable than any feeling of honor in the matter. I fear myself the defence will not avail and do not expect to make it, yet I am worried to think that the thing has taken such a turn and these hypocrites or greenhorns should desert me thus. Not much however will ever be said about it I imagine. Still it worries me to suppose that any man thinks me a whit below the most elevated ideas of honor. I have written McDuffie a very free letter about it.

The latest news is an invasion of Texas by Gen. Arista with 10 or 15,000 men. It came this morning. In Jan. Gen. Hamilton wrote to Santa Anna offering him $5 million for a recognition of Texian Independence and a Boundary and $200,000 *secret service* money—alias *bribe*—Santa Anna replied thro' the papers rejecting it with scorn and insult. I thought H. would suffer. But yesterday morning came his reply and a most triumphant one it was.

We look for Van Buren and Paulding here on Saturday, day after tomorrow.

P.S. To show the *animus* of McDuffie in this matter it should be stated that when I arrived in Charleston I rec^d a letter from him, suggesting that we should levy upon the *trust Estate of H[amilton]'s wife*, and if *there should be any flaw on the deed thus save ourselves*. He gave as a reason why this should be done that probably the idea had not occurred to others!

[Columbia] 30 March [1842]

Mr. Van Buren, his son the Major, and Mr. Paulding came up from below on the 28th and left this morning. He was Col. Hampton's guest, dined with him on the 28th and with me yesterday. [Van Buren's son, Abram, married in 1838 Angelica Singleton, the daughter of Col. Richard Singleton of Home Place near Stateburg, S.C., a close friend of Wade Hampton II.] He made himself agreeable of course, being a man of the

world and free and easy in his manners. Perhaps a little too much so for
one who has held his exalted office. He would have filled the idea better
had he been a little more reserved and dignified. He gave us many interesting anecdotes of Burr, Hamilton, Monroe and others last night. He
appears to take but little interest in any thing but politics. He has no
literature, no taste I infer. He has made politics his profession. Even in
that he appears to take no scientific or historical views. He dwells mainly
on contemporary matters—men and the measures of the day. And seems
to think more about what is and will be than about what should be. He
seemed to me like an old acquaintance at once, but that was my fault. I
am too apt to make myself at ease with every one at once. It has some
advantages to do [so] and some disadvantages. Paulding is a good, sensible,
dry old fellow, somewhat slow and prosy. I am inclined to think Van
Buren will be the next President. He certainly aims by this pilgrimage to
the Hermitage [Ex-President Andrew Jackson's home in Tennessee] to put
himself quietly but effectually in the field, but calling the attention to
himself and his movements as connected with the Presidency.

Fine, dry weather. I am privately informed that the Judge intends to
refuse a new trial in the case of Spann vs. Fox which I have been con-
ducting for more than 4 years. We have a verdict now of over $100,000.

III

I write these pages to vent my feelings.

---

26 APRIL 1842 — 19 DECEMBER 1842

[Columbia] 26 April [1842]

We had Mr. [Andrew] Stevenson, Ex-minister to England, [1836–1841], with us last week. There is some coolness between him and Hampton, and he did not receive as much attention as he might have done. I gave him a dinner for he was polite to me in London and invited me to dinner there. It chanced to be a good one as I had several vegetables much earlier than usual and some tropical fruit (by accident), among it a fine water-melon from Havanna. Stevenson is a very vain, flippant man of fine person and easy manners. He has some talent, is an observer of character and expresses himself well. But he has succeeded mainly by impudence and importunity, and having run his career will probably retire at 53 in fine health without money, without any solid reputation, and with few real friends. His predominant trait is vanity—prurient ridiculous vanity. [After his diplomatic career ended, Stevenson became rector of the University of Virginia and died in 1857 at the age of seventy-two.]

[Columbia] 29th [April 1842]

I hear nothing of or from Hamilton. I believe he is somewhere in Georgia or it may be in Texas. He does not act with the openness of an honest man. But then he is much harassed, I have no doubt. He does not in this extremity show real greatness of mind. I fear he lacks it more than I have thought. He should not abandon his friends to pay his debts without a frank exposure of his situation every way. I fear he is not what he should be.

There is a lady figuring here in our Society—a wife of one of our Professors, Dr. Ellet—who is just now the theme of much remark. She [Elizabeth Lummis Ellet] is middle-aged, small, handsome. She has a turn for languages and reads not only French, but German and Italian, and maybe Spanish. She has read much and written a number of works which are translations and compilations pretty well done, but without an original idea or profound remark. Yet she has attempted to criticise Schiller. She has been here now 7 or 8 years. Several years ago an intimacy between herself and Col. D. J. McCord was much of town talk. It passed off and she joined the Presbyterian Church. This Spring she is again seen at all the parties. Her manners, which affecting simplicity are childish yet passionless, are wanting in even ordinary female dignity and expose her advances which would be highly impertinent to other women. I sometimes doubt whether she is a fool or a strumpet. She seems exceedingly well disposed to me, but I do not wish to become notorious and rather avoid her. Col. H[ampton] is just now prime favourite.

[Columbia] May 15 [1842]

Looking at the last paragraph induces me to say that this Lady has recently amused the town with an account of a Pic Nic which has been circulating in manuscript. She passes it off for a humourous and witty brochure. It amounts to a coarse lampoon in which I figure largely. Were a man the author I should feel inclined to horsewhip him and I shall certainly cut her.

By accounts from abroad some 10 days ago we learn that the English have been terribly cut up in India. This will probably secure peace to us.

My Brothers have both paid us a visit recently. Marcellus left us last night. He is a fine manly fellow of whom I feel proud in every way. John is odd. I feel uneasy about him. I am getting too lazy and worthless for any thing.

Bye the bye we have had Appeal Court here and meetings of the Trustees in which I have taken an active part. It is proposed to change the Steward at the College to a Bursar. I have it in a charge to report on it. It would be singular that I should be mainly instrumental in abolishing an office which my Father held five years, and in which he made all he ever did make, or nearly all.

Looking forward to the Encampment of my Regiment next week, which I dread.

[Columbia] 18 May [1842]

Dr. Moore of Union, who was elected Cashier of the Branch Bank here [of the Bank of the State of South Carolina] a year ago, being incompetent to discharge his duties, has after a great many efforts to shuffle them off on others, has given notice that he will resign on the first of August, and yesterday I carried thro' the Branch resolutions dividing the duties among the remaining four officers so as to save one officer and $1200 pr. an. to the Bank. The officers have now very little to do.

[Columbia] 10 June [1842]

Held the Encampment of my Brigade at Barnwell C.H. from 25 to 28 ult. Went off remarkably well. The Gov. was there and at first desired to make a gala show of the whole matter with himself the principal personage. I resisted and he withdrew pretty much from the business of the Camp tho' his tent was pitched near the lines. The Adj. Gen. did little, knowing little. All ended well however in regard to the Encampment. The officers and men improved, there was no jarring, gaming, or drinking. The Maj. Gen. was absent and the Gov. shrinking from responsibility of ordering a court Martial, ordered a Court of Inquiry, me presiding, to judge of his excuse. We determined that we had no authority legally to do so. The Gov. was mortified and intends to stir the question of his power to call courts all over the State. In the mean time he is giving a false colouring to our decision, assuming that we excused Edwards, and yet keeps the decision a secret. Something may yet grow out of this. The Court feels indignant and all perceive Richardson to be an unprincipled knave.

The Directors of the Mother Bank are acting very treacherous towards the Branch here and prove the folly of expecting managers of a State Institution to be governed by any other views than a mere regard for their own personal interests. Some two years ago they made a miserable Jew here, named Mordecai, a Director of this branch. Every other member of the board shrinks from contact with him and the Town regards it as an outrage. They sent for [Robert] Goodwyn, our President, last week, on the eve of re-electing Directors, to consult with him, and he denounced this man. They said he should not be re-elected. Yet on Monday re-elected him. The secret is that his Brother [Moses Cohen Mordecai] is a man of force and influence in Charleston and Director of the R.R. Bank where our Directors probably have accounts themselves. After requesting us to organize this Branch with four officers, which we did, making a saving of $1200 in salaries, they now propose to electing 5 as before and lowering the salaries of all. The object is to bring in old Saxon, an uncle of Elmore's, who has gone the rounds of the State offices until the public are sick and disgusted with him.

It is contemplated to open our rail road to this place on the 28 inst. and to have a grand celebration of the event with a Barbecue, etc. etc.

Late news from abroad shows no great change in affairs. Cotton seems to have touched bottom in price without any prospect of a material rise just now, if ever. The credit of the U. S. is utterly prostrate and no one abroad or at home will subscribe to the late loan. Old Hamburg has been nearly destroyed by fire, France has pretty certainly refused to ratify the Treaty yielding the right to England to search all vessels suspected of carrying slaves. This will break it up.

Pickens writes me rather despondingly of Mr. Calhoun's prospects. He says they are stacking the cards against him. I sincerely wish he could be made President. His prospects seem better now than they ever did, but I never have had any confidence in them. He is too anxious and foolishly thrusts himself into every little issue, making enemies and losing friends. He is a mere child in the ordinary affairs of common life. He sees great principles and truths clearly and presses them ably, but does so in season and out of season, thereby insuring their defeat and his own.

[Columbia] 13 June [1842]

I believe I have heretofore mentioned that Mr. Calhoun sent me a copy of one of his speeches in February and requested me to call attention to it in the papers. I did so in the Carolinian. Since then I have heard nothing from him. Whether I was too sparing in my praise I cannot say. Or it may be that my having dined Mr. Van Buren has excited his jealousy. Hampton mentioned to V. B. that I stood on my own hook and was independent of Calhoun. Could V.B. have repeated this to foment jealousy. The fact is Mr. C has not found me tractable enough. I have always had my own opinions and maintained them, and this he does not like. He cannot bear contradiction. He thinks any difference of opinion from him proves a man hostile and is ready to open his batteries on him. Hence again his want of able friends. He drives off every man who has ability and spirit to think for himself.

Have I mentioned that Judge Schley gave his final opinion settling the Spann and Fox case in our favour. It was given the last week in last month. The verdict was $103,733.14. Of this 22 pr ct goes to the lawyers and some other expenses leaving to each heir about $20,000 and int[erest] since last July. I employed Schley's son as assistant counsel and offered him $1000 fee when over last. He rejected it and intends to bring suit for $7000. I am amazed at the tone of this Georgia Bar. Not a lawyer but will squabble about a fee and resort to any means to extort from his client.

[Columbia] 21 June [1842]

The rail road cars are beginning to come into town, we now get an Charleston mail by 5 o'clock. On the 28th we are to have a great Barbecue in honor of the completion of the road. I am on the Committee of Arrangements. But I cannot bring my mind to bear on the subject. I take no interest. I am sick of Society. At least of those I am thrown with. They are excellent people but have neither intellect nor information, I learn nothing. I convey but little and feel no incitement to think or read. Time passes in the discussion of commonplaces, smoking, drinking and Backgammon. College too far off. The Professors are busy and I am little with them. Not enough to do me any good. In such Society as this I cannot long sustain my self. I lose my interest. I feel myself depreciating and must soon depreciate in the opinion of others. I must go back to the woods and *act* and *think*. Nothing can be worse than to fritter oneself away as I am doing.

[Columbia] 25 June 1842

Dined with John S. Preston (brother of the Senator) to-day. A small party given to Wm. H. Taylor of Alabama on a visit here now. Dr. Gibbes was asked what he would be helped to. "As I go for the destruction of the Quacks" said he "I will take some of the Duck"—"Why Doctor," said Preston "I did not take you for such a cannibal as to devour your own kind."

[Columbia] 28 June [1842]

This is the day of the celebration of the opening of the R[ail] Road. It is to be a much larger affair than I expected. Three hundred persons came up from Charleston yesterday, among them an uniform Company. As many more are expected to-day. The surrounding Country furnishes a full quota. I am very sick of it and wish I was at Silver Bluff. I have a dull pain in my right side. It is my liver thumping my ribs. Of course I do not feel the better elsewhere. I expect to take no part but must be there. I hate a crowd. But 2000 persons at 4 o'clock and the Ther. 90° in the shade, it is awful to think of.

Evening

The celebration is over and no body hurt. The cars arrived about 3 o'clock. The Intendant Myers addressed the President of the Road, Col. Gadsden in a most ridiculous strain of commonplace and flattery, dragging [in] some very unnecessary remarks about nullification. Gadsden replied in better taste but feebly. Gen. Schnierle, Mayor of Charleston, who with all the Aldermen was present, responded at the table to the toast to Charleston in a very respectable manner. That and another were the only set toasts. The volunteers will all appear in the papers to-morrow. They were very properly omitted at the dinner. Baker the *cuisiner* made the best speech. When all had nearly finished, he mounted the table and requested the waiters to bring back the empty dishes as there was 1500 lbs of meat yet untouched. The dishes or rather trays were then full. The crowd was immense. Probably not less than 3000 persons in all, women, children and negroes included. Perhaps more, about 800 came from Charleston. I do not think I ever saw so many persons assembled together. So the Rail Road is finished.

I cut no figure. It was expected by many that I would speak and appeals were made to me to do so. But I would as soon have stood on the Seashore and harangued the waves. Nothing could be heard, save the cannon, by all.

Silver Bluff 7 July [1842]

[President] Tyler is the Napoleon of *vetoes*. The news reached us a few days ago that he had vetoed the "Little Tariff Bill" as it is called postponing the Consummation of the Compromise Act and also the Distribution until the 1st Aug. The amount of it is that he will consent to no Tariff, except for revenue and such incidental protection as discrimination will give, and to no increase of duties beyond 20 pr ct. without a repeal of the Distribution Act. Honor to the man who has killed the Bank, the Tariff and the Distribution. If he had capacity I would vote for him for the Presidency. Perhaps he may have. I have regarded him as weak and vacillating, notwithstanding the wisdom and boldness of his course with regard to these measures.

My Brother [Marcellus], after a few weeks courtship, is about to marry Miss Harriet Davis of Georgia. A young lady of good family and handsome fortune and most excellent and amiable character. The wedding is fixed for Tuesday next. I am delighted with it.

[Silver Bluff] 8 July [1842]

The papers contain a statement of the James River and Kenawha [Canal] Company of Virginia to the effect that he [Hamilton] has completely satisfied them about the $80,000 which they charged him last winter with embezzling, and they have reappointed him their agent in Europe. I don't understand it. He has either sacraficed all of us here to secure them, or has humbugged them also, as he has done us. I fear the latter and that there will be another bust up. It is however a good omen to something like a restoration of his credit.

[Silver Bluff] 13 July [1842]

My Brother was married last night to Harriet Davis at Summer Hill. The union seems to be very agreeable on all sides. They are both amiable and intelligent. Their prospects for happiness seem to be as fair as any young couple's could be. I trust sincerely they may be realized—auspice finero!

[Silver Bluff] 18 July [1842]

The most impudent class on earth are the clergy. Because they [are] tolerated in denouncing us from the pulpit and damning our souls, they feel privileged to take any liberty whatever. There is one who having lost his voice became Editor of the Temperance Advocate in Columbia and out of compassion was elected Treasurer Session before the last. I have had a mere bowing acquaintance with him for many years about Columbia but nothing more. Last Spring he came and solicited from me the situation of Private Secretary to the next Governor. I put him off by saying I should not presume to promise the office in the most distant manner until I should (if ever I did) have the right to dispose of it. A month or two later he asked me to endorse his note for $2500. I was taken all aback. He promised to make me secure by mortgage. There was no resisting him as I had just offered (too generously) to endorse the note of a friend whose printing press was burnt in the great fire, and I consented if secured. I asked afterwards for a Confession of Judgement, which I thought had disgusted him, for I heard no more until to-day he writes me again proposing a mortgage and wants me to send over a note instanter. I cannot now avoid it without a disturbance. I wish I had kicked him out of my house when he asked for the Secretaryship.

My Brother M[arcellus] and his wife passed two days with us last week. They seem happy and behaved decently. They go north to-morrow.

[Silver Bluff] 19 July [1842]
Died this morning nearly 61 years old my half Uncle, Sterling Edward Turner. He, the son and only child of Capt. Sterling Turner, who with his command was perfidiously massacred, after a gallant resistance and honorable capitulation near the Ridge, in 1781 by the notorious Tory Cunningham. He [Capt. Turner] was my Grand-mother's first husband and left my half Uncle only two weeks old at his death. Uncle T[urner] removed with my Grandfather to Augusta and afterwards became a clerk for my Grand-Uncle [John] Fox. He was a steady, active, honest, intelligent, and daring lad with a strong predilection for the sea. He was sent to Charleston and placed in the counting [house] of a Mr. Williamson, I think, from whom he escaped and took to the seas. He traded to Africa and, I regret to say, was engaged in the slave trade. [interlineated in another hand: No proof whatever—circumstantial only] He married in Charleston but was rarely there and finally in 18—left and was heard of no more. He was given up for dead. I grew up and heard of him as a wanderer of a bold and noble character and always regarded him as lost. His miniature used to hang over my Grandmother's mantle piece in Columbia and often have I gazed at it for hours and longed to see him whose romantic life had filled me with enthusiastic love for him. When my Grandmother died in 1827 he had not been seen for years. Now and then an uncertain rumour reached us that some Sea Captain named Turner had been seen at the Brazils or Cape Verde Islands. Suddenly in February

1829 he dropped down upon us. I hastened over from Columbia, where I was practising law, and found a short, thick, old sea dog with a weather-beaten but manly face, scarcely presenting a trace of that miniature over the mantle piece. He seemed very happy to see us. Uncle Spann's and Uncle Whitner's families only being here then. He was costive however of his own affairs, and we concluded he had not prospered. In fact he spoke of heavy losses and intimated that between the disasters of the seas and the treachery of those in whom he had confided, he had amassed but little after all his hardships. And this it was we inferred that had kept him from coming back. He was proud and he would not return without a fortune. He said, however, that he would return to Africa, close his business, gather what he had, and come back to close his days among us. He took a fancy to me and wrote to me from Philadelphia and afterwards from Rio Muney [sic]. His letters however ceased, and I again thought he had given us up or was dead. In the Summer of 1833 I got a letter from him written by another hand. He had been stricken with palsy. He desired me to send for him, and some one to settle his affairs. I despatched a young man (Thomas Hobby) in the fall, who went to Liberia and returned with no other tidings than that he was probably alive and somewhere on the coast. In September of the next year he was landed at some little town in Maine. I wrote to Mr. A. Latimer, who was at the North, and then [sent] same to go to him and send him on to Charleston. About the 24 October he arrived at the Bluff on a crutch and could hardly make himself understood. I was then at Mr. Ardis' house near here. I kept him there a short time and sent him to Mother to be convenient to medical assistance. She was living at Fox's brick house then. He became attached to her fortunes and has since gone the rounds with her, to West Hill, my old House, Here, to Ardis, once again in possession of the family, and has finally closed his life there by a singular coincidence. Last week this time he was as well as usual, having been now for several years confined to his bed and almost unable to artic-ulate at all. During all his sojourns here he has been as it were dead to us. Extremely deaf he could scarcely be made to comprehend any thing, while he has never been able to relate any thing connectedly, in fact hardly [able to] connect two sentences from the first. Disease had prostrated his nervous energies and he feared to die. But he was still a reckless disbeliever in all religion and even in a future State. In his days of action it is prob-able that he neither believed nor feared God or Devil. Peace to his re-mains. He has solved the Great Mystery and knows now what is True and what is Untrue. He was at all times a generous and gallant fellow and no doubt has in those distant regions and in those boisterous seas where his life was mainly passed performed many a noble deed of which we shall never hear. But God knows them and knew his heart and knew his nature and will do justice in mercy unto his soul.

During his helpless illness on the African Coast he was stripped in that lawless region of every thing.

[Silver Bluff] 20 July [1842]

Mother and me went up to bury Uncle Turner. Met there Mr. and Mrs. McGehee and Cousin Augusta. John had left. He was placed by the side of his mother in the Presbyterian Grave Yard [interlineated in another hand: Augusta Cemetery]. For 30 years they had not been so near together, and when she was placed there he was thought to have long been under the sod or the sea. Strange world.

[Silver Bluff] 27 July [1842]

Two deaths among my negroes since the 25th. My plantation is probably as sickly as any in the world. I seldom have high grades of bilious fever and do not often lose a grown negro unless it be an old one. But consumption, scrofula, Dropsy, phthisis, rheumatism etc. are rife and my little children drop off like young turkies. I think it is owing mainly to the [slave] Settlement being on the mill pond, and I have resolved to move it to my old place up the Creek, which I believe to be nearly as healthy as up here. It was selected for a summer retreat by Barna McKinne in 1817 or 18. Old Mr. Charles Goodwyn and after him Mrs. Ramsay had long lived within a few hundred yards. Mr. Fitzsimons died there in July 1825 but his illness was contracted at old home. It has always proved healthy. I have several times remained there until the last of July. Mother passed a whole summer there. Last year I allowed Mr. Ben Hankinson to live there and he burnt down the dwelling house, accidentally of course. I shall build it up again and remove my negro houses from below. In fact I have pretty fully resolved on it.

[Silver Bluff] 5 Aug. [1842]

Another heavy loss, my favourite mare. The best animal I ever owned. I had just matched her and thought I had the best match I ever had. It is ever thus. I have lost 89 negroes and at least 50 mules and horses in 11 years. Several of the horses, blooded mares, costing me $1000 to 1500. I cannot but think that all this is intended to prevent me from becoming avaricious by shewing me that it is impossible for me ever to be rich. After 11 years of arduous toil and much reputed success, I have not increased my fortune a dollar. Something has always intervened. By the time I had begun to realize any thing, property had become very high. I turned my attention to race horses and invested thousands and lost pretty largely. Then came Congress, building this house here. The loss of $7500 in Texas land and $5000 by a Steam Boat being blown up with my cotton on it, and my European tour. On my return I commenced my Columbia House, where I have sunk $30,000, and add to all this negroes, mules, every thing dying around me. I once desired to make a large fortune. I have always felt anxious to leave my children at least independent of the world. But step by step Providence has followed and thwarted me. And now, when property is low and I have command of money in consequence of the Verdict against Fox's Estate, comes this debt of Hamilton's to cramp and crush me. What shall I do? I must endeavour to content myself with crawling along and doing the best I can. Were it not for this Governor's business, I would return to the practice of law or embark on some speculation. But that which is another heavy charge and now fetters me completely, will prevent me forever from pursuing any plan of making money which is beneath such a dignity. I must give [up] the idea of getting any richer than I am. I do give it up. I will endeavour to improve the health of my ne-groes, improve my lands, pay my debts and live snug, aspiring only to educate my boys and give them a small start.

[Silver Bluff] 6 Aug. [1842]

Can't rouse myself to take an interest in any thing beyond my money affairs. I find that I have money enough owing to me and bank stock, to-gether to pay all I owe including Hamilton's whole debt. I can borrow now from mother and Dr. Spann's Estate about $30,000. Shall I take this, pay off $8,000 that will be due in January, and invest the balance in negroes. Prime fellows can be had at $400 to 450 and women at $350 to 400. They are still falling and will not be higher for several years perhaps. But they will probably be worth double this before I shall be called on to pay. The difficulty is that though I could use these negroes now, it would be chiefly in making improvements which would not immediately pay a profit, and which I can work along though, I believe, with my own hands.

And when these improvements are made, I shall not have more land open than I can tend with the negroes I now have. The fact is I don't *really* *want* more negroes than I now own unless I conclude to attack the marsh, which I dread. I can nevertheless support myself and pay the interest on this money. Shall I then buy for the chance of a rise and to improve more rapidly? This is the question.

[Silver Bluff] 19 Aug. [1842]

The weather, the blight which has been ruining my cotton and tobacco have made me quite a savage for this fortnight. Since then we have rec^d news of the Death of the Duke of Orleans, Louis Phillipe's Eldest Son, who leaves a son 4 years old. The prospects are of a Regency in France after Louis Phillipe's time and another Revolution. I rather doubt the latter. Sympathy for the Infant will probably be stronger with the French than love for a King would be.

Tyler has vetoed another Tariff and avowed that he will not sanction any one, without the act for distribution of the proceeds of the Public Lands is repealed. The Whigs are dreadfully enraged and besides that getting beat every where. They threaten to adjourn without adjusting the Tariff which will leave us a Tariff of 20 pr. ct. ad valorem under the Compromise Act [of 1833].

On the 12th inst. Mother bought from Mr. Ardis my old place near here, which I had sold him, and on the same day poor Paul [their sixth son, born in 1838] fell out of the back Piazza and broke his thigh. He is now doing well.

[Silver Bluff] 20 Aug. [1842]

I am giving myself up wholly to my plantation business and neither mingling personally with the world or even keeping up much correspondence with my friends. It may seem bad policy thus to appear to withdraw myself at this moment, yet I see nothing that I can do either to benefit the country or myself, and I know not what to write about. There is no serious opposition to me that I know of, and to write always of myself and the coming [gubernatorial] election would probably be as tiresome to others as to me. Still an artful man—perhaps a wise one—would no doubt find something agreeable to say and keep himself in the eye of the public and the remembrance of his friends. It does not however suit my humour or my private interest. I answer all letters however as kindly as possible and can do no more just now.

My cotton fields in the meantime are a sorry sight. The rust has seized on at least half my cotton and cut off its further growth besides injuring the immature boles. I calculate on a loss of at least 25 pr ct on my whole crop, if not more. This falls heavy now amid so many other disasters and when every body else is making a large crop and the price will be reduced to nothing or next to it. In the mean time I push on my projects of improvement. Marling, making straw for manuring, and preparing to move my [slave] settlement. I feel as though I am working in the dark against fate. But is not man always [so] doing. I will be industrious and act as judiciously as I can and leave the result to Providence. I can do no more here again. If I knew what I could do more or better, of course I would do it.

I am a little moody too, I fear. My mind does not work clear. Tobacco muddies it and this gangrened stomach of mine and these shattered nerves.

[Silver Bluff] 22 Aug. [1842]

The knavishness of the world is becoming intolerable. Whether the times make men worse really, or I am only finding them out, I don't know, but it amounts to this—you can give no man a chance to impose on you but what he will immediately take advantage of it. I made the remark the other day in the case of some brick purchased in Augusta. They turned out on arriving to be only 2 instead of 3 inches thick. Who would have anticipated an imposition like that. But to-day I have an illustration which grieves me much. I requested my friend, J. M. Walker Esq in Charleston, a short time ago to have me appointed Trustee for Mrs. Latimer. He sent me back a formal opinion stating that the thing could not be done. I then enquired his opinion of the strength of my defence in the case of the Bank against me as Hamilton's Guarantee. I sent him a blank check and requested him to pay himself for his opinion in Mrs. Latimer's matter and to take $50 as a retainer in my case. At the same time making some additional enquires in Mrs. L's case. The result was another formal opinion about the Trusteeship showing how it could be done and a receipt for *An Hundred Dollars* for professional services for her. *Fifty dollars* for each opinion. The latter being merely explanatory and the first never really asked! Any lawyer would have been glad to get $20 for the whole affair I should have supposed. He could not resist the temptation of the *blank check*. In short he is not to [be] trusted with money uncounted. I am shocked to think so. I feel anxious to tell him so. Yet it would be very improvident. He will be a member of the next Legislature and can do me serious injury. He knows this. I had better therefore pocket the loss myself. But before my case comes up I will know his fee. In the mean time I cannot have anything more to do with him than I can help, and if he asks an explanation he shall have it. What a fool. My good opinion of him might be worth thousands to him. He has served me politically, and I aimed to pay him liberally in my own case. But I did not expect to be charged for these services, especially as he has already sought my support and obtained the promise of it for the Office of Attorney General. I have for some time thought him the only reliable political friend I had in Charleston. And he turns out thus.

I have been quite unwell all day and yesterday too. I have made an attempt to leave off tobacco and coffee. Whether it is this, or the bad feelings, which induced the attempt, are growing worse of themselves I don't know. But I have headache, listlessness, and irritability all to a horrible excess. A cup of coffec and a segar has relieved me a little.

It is said they talk familiarly of a dissolution of the Union at Washington. Things are in a bad state, but I see nothing that looks like a dissolution. Each section is divided. The Whigs have ruined themselves and stopped the wheels of Gov[ernment]. . . . They are a desperate party.

[Silver Bluff] 25 Aug. [1842]

Now of my luck. My old Grist Mill which has long been a wreck, but which I hoped would last until frost, when I intended to take it down and convert the place into a wasteway, having already built a new one—gave way last night. It has made a terrible gash of 90 feet in the dam and if the pond continues down will breed a pestilence. It so happened that last night I took a large dose of blue pill and was afraid to go out. I thought the overseer knew all about mill dams and endeavoured to keep myself quiet. But hearing about dinner time that he was attempting to stop water today, I hastened down and arrived just in time to see the effects of his folly. Another blow up—10 feet more of dam gone and the whole day lost. This is pleasant.

[Silver Bluff] 30 Aug. [1842]

I write these pages to vent my feelings. They are not intended for any human eye and I hope to destroy them before I die. Did any one see them they would set me down as morbidly discontented, and such would be the response I should meet was I to say to any one what I write here. I am generally regarded as an example of a "fortunate man" and one who ought to be happy. Alas how falsely the world judges. I have had my successes, but they are all dashed with troubles. And when I have been fortunate once, I have had a myriad [of] small but annoying reverses. Since I have been a planter I have been rendered miserable by the constant unvarying succession of death after death among my people. No, I have not been able to enjoy a single blessing of life for more than a moment. Death in some shape or other soon clouded it over. I am now beginning to think that I have commenced the downhill of life seriously and permanently. My condition is vastly changed from what it was 2 years ago. Then I was uneasy for fear I should not be able to add to my property, which I knew to be too small to divide among my children and make them easy. Now I do not expect to be able to keep what I have. The times, this debt of Hamilton's, my increased expenses, the prospect of still increasing them should I be made Gov., and the daily visitations of Providence upon me fill me with gloomy despondency and make my heart sink. I could fight the world, I could still stand up against man, but God seems to be against me, and for 10 years his hands, among some blessings, have continued increasingly to scatter these darts of death which have destroyed and are daily destroying my substance. I have been over here nearly 2 months. During that time my crop has withered up before my eyes while all around have been comparatively spared. By the death of my fine mare all my arrangements for moving about and for my family's comfort in that way have been destroyed. One of my sons [Paul] has broken his thigh. Many of my neighbors have showed themselves inimical, to whom I have done nothing but favours. My mill dam has given way at a most critical period. I could bear up against all these things better than I can against the old curse and scourge of death. Two of my negroes both valuable, one very much so. And to-day, just as I began to draw breath after the disaster of my dam, I find the Doctor at my plantation who pronounces a fine little boy, 7 years old, who was taken sick only day before yesterday, as hopeless (he is probably dead now) and another, about 12 years old, very ill with this terrible congestive fever. Such a series of severe misfortunes have never befallen me before in so short a time of so varied a nature. They thicken and forebode worse. I do not know what that can be unless my own sickness and death shall end the scene as sometimes I think it will soon. There is no human being with whom I can divide my sorrows. My wife only sees the one stroke, and, tho' she feels it, has no art of administering any real comfort, and, as for the rest, it seems to me every one actually enjoys it. For I am pursued by "Envy, hatred and all uncharitableness." I feel like one hunted down by the jealousy of the world and that every man's hand is against me. I see no *real, sensible, appreciating* sympathy any where. For a mere exclamation of sorrow, which those round me only give and then dismiss the matter, is a mockery, and I avoid it—I reprove it. If God would only allow my negroes to live and thrive and give me reasonable health, I could stand the rest and fight it out with the world. But this he will not do. I am about to remove them for health. But when I see the ha[n]d of fate so distinctly marking them out for victims, I do so without hope of any advantage in that respect and without spirit. I wish I knew what to do. Which way to turn. What to resort to, but alas I am utterly in the dark. If my negroes increased as they ought, I should feel that I had a fund growing for my children, and I would cheerfully apply myself to every labor of improvement or retrenchment to keep even with the world. But why be industrious when the fruits are struck down so by death. Why deny myself the use of a few dollars when the remorseless tomb is swallowing hundreds and thousands for me monthly? Thus the thing works. This is what makes my heart fail me. I know I am very wicked and unworthy. But I see men more so who flourish and men less so who do not. That seems to have nothing to do with human affairs.

Dr. [R. C.] Fowke of Aiken staid here last night. He is a clever man and a good physician, they say. He wants me to promise him to turn out the Port Physician in Charleston when I am Gov. and place him there. Bellinger backs him modestly and asks me to do so if I can. I would do any thing I could for Bellinger and must for Dr. F., but I know nothing of the present Port Physician, and I cannot bring the State about my ears by a sweeping out of the offices. I must inquire into the matter before I promise or act. I will turn out nobody without a better reason than merely to put in another. But I am not Gov. yet and do not allow myself to regard it as certain I shall be, even if I live. I wish often that I had nothing to do with it. And I have made many sacrafices for it and will go on now if I am able. Perhaps it may avail my children someday as much as money.

[Silver Bluff] 10 Sept. [1842]

Misfortunes, it is said, never come alone. Mine certainly thicken on me. Yet, may it not be that we are ourselves the occasion of these repetitions of the strokes of fortune. The first blow disturbs our serenity, disorganizes our nerves, excites our passions. We no longer think rightly, see clearly, or act judiciously. We blunder on in the dark and are sure to stumble time and again. This has been my thing always. Yet the consciousness of it has never saved me a moment. I have felt all this summer like one fated (indeed it is a familiar and common feeling with me and has been from my earliest years) and have again and again resolved so to act as to avoid my share of the bringing on of trouble. Yet it has been in vain. I am now engaged in one of the most unpleasant controversies I ever had. It is with my neighbor Mr. John Ransey. A few days after my arrival here in 1831, Ransey ordered some of my negroes from a piece of land where they were cutting wood, claiming it for his. I sent them back and wrote him a sharp note. We met and agreed to have the land run and let the Surveyor decide. It was done so, and I gained nearly all of it that was worth any thing. After that he asked me to [give] permission to dig a canal around my dam to raft his lumber to the river. He had previously been compelled to haul it at an expense of probably $2 pr. m., as permission had always been refused. To raft down the creek was not worth more than 25¢. I granted the privilege to him and Mr. Burgess, now dead. They dug out the canal, fixed locks, etc. The terms of our agreement were that so long as they acted properly towards me and did me no injury, I would allow them to use the canal, but I never at any moment dreamed of such a thing as to part with my right to shut it up. I have never interfered with them, tho' at times the travelling of the negroes backwards and forwards has been a great nuisance to me. Ransey in the mean time has been remarkably friendly to me, and I have allowed him every privilege on my plantation that he deserved. He is a very selfish man and a passionate one, caring little for any one, but I thought him honest and honorable and a warm friend of mine. A few years ago he purchased from Hale the plantation immediately opposite to the Bluff on the other side of the river, and I went his security for the payment. He has recently purchased the Red House Tract. That is last Spring. When Mr. Dixon came to oversee here, during the March fresh of 1841, some difficulty occurred between him and Ransey about a negro of Ransey's who took off my flat during the fresh. I tried to have it reconciled and rather took Ransey's part against my overseer for I did not wish to lose a friend about such a matter. Since then I have thought Ransey rather shy of me, but took no notice of it. The other day when my dam broke he took that occasion to draw off his upper mill-pond. I was perfectly astonished at such a gratuitous act of malice and hostility. I made such inquiries as fully satisfied me that it was done on purpose and then I said publicly that unless he gave me satisfaction, I would shut up the canal. He soon heard of it but did not come to make any apology, and I did not see him. The other day he told my overseer I could not stop him as he had been using the slope for 10 years. Thus converting into a right what he had begged of me as a favor. I immediately sent Mr. B. Syms to him with a lease and renunciation of the right of way for him to sign, and gave him notice that unless he signed it I would destroy the canal. He refused to do so. I shall therefore close the canal as soon as I have leisure and find it convenient. I feel, too, very much like inflicting personal chastisement on Ransey. The only thing that deters me is the prospect of the Governorship. This ties my hands and enjoins upon me not to get into an affray. I shall therefore confine myself strictly to the defensive. I suppose there will certainly be a law suit. I don't think 10 years use will give a right of way.

It is very sickly again in the plantation—a number of my present hands down and *very sick* many of them.

. . .

I do not think she is *virtuous*, but she is not *accessible*. It is not because she has *principle*, but because she wants *heart*. She can never forget herself long enough to yield up any thing to a passion for another. In secret she doubtless contemplates forbidden pleasures, longs for them and perhaps resolves to have them. Could she be actually invaded at such a moment she would certainly yield. But when the sensual excitement subsides and she comes out from her closet to the world, pride and self-esteem resume their sway, and she becomes *case-hardened*, though *rotten* within. She even shrinks back stiff and formal from him whose charms her imagination gloats on in her privacy. Alas that those only are frail who have warm hearts and generous souls. Yet so it is.

[Silver Bluff] 11 Sept. [1842]

Congress adjourned some 10 days ago after passing a very oppressive [higher] tariff, which Tyler signed. He had in his previous vetoes laid his whole objections on the Distribution Clause, and, this being omitted, he had no alternative but to sign a bill as bad as the one he once supported So.Ca. on Nullifying. Mr. Calhoun is evidently in the ascendant. Stewart, Benton, Buchanan are all evidently broken down. I think Van Buren is also. I anticipate that the Van Buren and Benton faction will try to rally on [Richard M.] Johnson [vice president with Van Buren], but they cannot. It seems to me Calhoun must be the man unless he kicks over the pail, of which there is much danger. The Whigs will be beaten hollow and Tyler dropped between two stools. Calhoun's support of the late British Treaty will strengthen him very much.

[Silver Bluff] 17 Sept. [1842]

I rec^d to-day a long, coarse, and insolent letter from my neighbor Ransey in which he says that he will, notwithstanding my prohibition, pass through my fields whenever he thinks proper. The delusions of an intense self-esteem are wonderful. This man did me a dirty trick which I denounced. The thing looked so bad on him that he affected to be and no doubt thought himself seriously wronged by my exposure. He now declares that I had as well try to stop him from going to his mills as going to the Bluff, claiming a right on account of a privilege which he has found convenient. The matter however is like to be very serious if he presents. I shall stand strictly on the defensive, close my gates, fill up the canal etc. The law will be open to him, he can recur to it. If he prefers violence, I have no alternative. I must defend my property at every hazard. The man who claims such free use of it may soon claim it all and will certainly degrade and disgrace me if I submit to him. Yet I have every motive to avoid any violence or bloodshed. If I do not desire to be hurt or killed myself, seriously to hurt or to kill him will blast my present prospects most effectually. Besides this, I have every ordinary motive for avoiding a personal conflict. But if it must come, I must meet it.

My Brother Lt. H. came back day before yesterday. [interlineated in another hand: from his Northern bridal trip.]

[Silver Bluff] 24 Sept. [1842]

Dull and low spirited, as I have been, for the most part, all summer. Have been quite ill. Serious and somewhat alarming attack of dyspepsia. Still confined to the house. Sick in mind and body. It is arranged to refer the questions at issue between Ransey and me to Patterson and Bellinger to decide according to law. I have got certificates from 7 of the neighbours and dispatched them with my argument to Barnwell to-day. For the present this unpleasant matter is over. But there is no end to such things. We have just ascertained that poor Paul will be a cripple after all. The bandage put on by my brother [John] became loose when it dried. I did not know that any serious consequences would follow, and he did not come down. The result is that the bone has lapped or is crooked. The leg is an inch shorter. Poor, poor fellow. This is heartrending and worse than all my other troubles. It is impossible to use any appliances now. He will not keep still, and I fear absolute confinement will endanger his life, and the benefit is doubtful. His excessive restlessness has been one of the chief causes of the disaster. Yet this was chiefly in his sleep, for the patience and fortitude that the dear little fellow has shown could not be easily surpassed. All my cotton is in full blow at the plantation. One third and more of my force sick or convalescent. In fact not over half engaged in picking. More than half my whole crop at this moment in full bloom, and the September storm just set in last night. My new screw has also failed entirely, after packing 20 bales!! Alas! Alas! These are small troubles yet they overset my poor mind. Let us see: grievously sick myself, negroes very sickly, crop short and getting ruined, screw failed in the midst of the press, serious quarrels with my neighbours, and to crown all, a child crippled for life. This is a sad list of misfortunes. One of my neighbours old Mr. Foreman has shewn the cloven foot in this matter and I shall break with him next.

Marcellus and his wife went up to-day.

[Silver Bluff] Sept. 30 [1842]

I propose going to Barnwell to-morrow, when I expect to meet Ransey on Monday and to have our controversy decided in some way. He goes armed I am informed, and of course I shall not neglect due precaution. He is very hasty—perhaps brave. I am hasty myself. I can't say that I feel any presentiments, but the extremely weak state of my nerves and my present ill-health make me feel quite unpleasant at the idea of separating from my family. I fear more, debility and nervous prostration, than Ransey's weapons. Yet a collision is by no means impossible. First and last it is rather probable. It may be that there will be a catastrophe to close the series of disasters I have experienced this wretched summer. Next to being killed, I should esteem it the greatest misfortune, that could befall me, personally to kill a man, and just now especially. I have often observed it, as among the mysterious ways of Providence to take off an individual just at the moment, when it seemed to all human calculation, that he would be most wanted. Besides that, I appear about to crown my public career by an elevation that will do me great honor, my life is of more importance at this time to my family than it ever has been before. I am just entering upon a series of operations which, I think, must be of immense benefit to them, if I can be spared 5 years to carry them out. And these are the most difficult times possible for such a change of affairs to them, as would ensue. It may be that it will suit the inscrutable designs of Providence to remove me from the scene, as so many others are removed, in the crisis of life. Of course I sincerely trust not. Yet life is made often a burden to me by my health and at best is but half-living to me, and sometimes I look forward to the repose of death as a blessed item. I know I am a sinner and but ill-prepared to die. Yet I have a tolerable clear conscience. I can truly say I have at least *endeavoured* to do unto all men as I wished them to do unto me, and this I hope may compensate for many faults. I have never deceived, defrauded, betrayed, failed, or proved ungrateful to any *man*. Whatever I may have done to God. And for all my omissions and commissions I ask his merciful forgiveness. Head too full to write or even think.

[Silver Bluff] Oct. 6 [1842]

I thought yesterday for several hours that my time was come or nearly so. I came down to tea however, have felt unusually well a part of this morning and have read several hours. Such are the nerves, such are mine. I am however not so well now as I have been [earlier] to-day. Literally, I have no idea what an hour may at any time bring forth. Apoplexy and paralysis are hourly before my eyes. On the 1st inst., I went to Barnwell to meet Ransey and to buy negroes on the 3rd. Ransey did not come, but I ascertained that by the advice of Patterson he gave up the slope. To save an expensive law suit, I left propositions about a road on the line between us, and, not to appear illiberal, agreed to let him have the Slope for 5 years at a nominal rent. My head however turned to a pumpkin before the sale came on, on the 3rd, and I brought it home as fast as I could that night. I'm a pretty fellow to be attempting speculations, who am never certain of surviving a trip to the Back House.

[Silver Bluff] 9th [Oct. 1842]

I have felt better for 2 or 3 days. I attribute it to my having taken no medicine and to my changing my hot water tea, morning and night, to mere milk and water, half and half. My nerves are much relieved, and, barring occasional fulness in the head, I feel quite well. But I have no confidence in my being able to do *any thing* requiring action. I mean bodily action, for my mind is, and through all my diseases has been, as clear and active as ever. My memory however is not good and has for years been growing more and more treacherous.

Ransey has refused my offer of compromise and threatens to indict me if I stop him, which I must do. I do not however like to have an indictment hanging over me while a candidate for the Executive chair. Should opposition spring up, a great handle will be made of it. I shall therefore remain quiet until after Court probably.

My workman Foster, who first suggested the idea of moving my [slave] houses on wheels, has deserted me. He made the wheels and got his pay and then on a very trifling ground took himself off. The expense has been some $100 to me, and the loss of my carpenters, a month. I believe I shall not attempt the thing, believing it likely to fail and nearly as troublesome as the other plan after all. But Foster has outwitted me completely—a cunning knave.

Had a long and confidential letter from Mr. Calhoun. He seems in excellent spirits about his presidential prospects.

[Silver Bluff] Nov. 12 [1842]

The cold weather has braced me up, and for several weeks I have been attending to my business actively. Much has passed that I should have been glad to have a memoranda of, but when I am well I am too much engaged with the active affairs of life and have too much necessary writing to do to keep a diary. I think I shall close this for I find I seldom write any thing except when in ill-health, or ill-tempered, or influenced by some peculiar feelings. In short, I write here precisely when I should not write, and therefore I ought to give it up altogether. I will only say now that the season has been very uncommon, the first killing frost occurred yesterday. Pippins etc. were injured before. We are now in the bustle of preparation to move over to Columbia.

[Silver Bluff] Nov. 15 [1842]

This is my Birthday. I am Thirty Five years old to-day. In the prime of Life now. My family left for Columbia yesterday morning, and I came down to the plantation. This morning when I first opened my door to look out, I found the overseer there with my riding horse preparing to bleed him. He had the colic. He was bled and drenched, seemed better, and then was sent to the stable. After breakfast I walked down to where they were preparing to rebuild my screw, which has entirely given out. All day yesterday they were trying in vain to get a suitable tree from the swamp and this morning set out with a new team. Soon after I got down, the Carry Log came up broken. It was mended and set again. The log was brought to within 50 yards of the spot when one of the chains broke and dropped it. The devil seems to be in it. I came back and found the old man at the stable, whom I had ordered to *watch* my horse, had taken him to the pond and *washed* him all over, and I had to stop by my blacksmith to have him rubbed dry. Returned to the house, I steamed a sick negro, and before I finished, it commenced to rain, and it has rained steadily and heavily ever since. A glorious commencement of a new year, and a new lustrum to me!! God forbid it, such to be prophetic of those that are to come after it. I have never had such a four months of trouble, anxiety, and disappointment as the last, and my plantation never was in such confusion as at this moment. And I must leave, with the prospect of paying it but flying visits, for two years. And yet never have I had such extensive and important schemes of improvement on hand before. God help me and mine. I am a wicked sinner I know, and feel and deserve much chastisement. May a merciful Creator deal lightly with me and forgive weaknesses and blindness.

[Silver Bluff] Nov. 16 [1842]

I met Capt. Ransey at the River to-day for the first time since our difficulties became serious. I commenced a conversation with him, and he stated that as soon as he could fix his landing at the river on his land, which he should set about immediately, he would abandon the use of my roads and slope. This being all I desired, I told him I should not disturb him in this use of them, until he could do so or at least until the 1st Jany. I think he will then withdraw and never trouble me any more. I am glad to get over this difficulty, so much to my satisfaction, without any violent attack. I have temporized for sometime back in the expectation that such would be the result, but had announced some short time ago that the matter must be settled before I left here and offered him better terms than these, which he declined then. He still speaks of having rights, which I told him were of no consequence to me so he did not attempt to enforce them. And yet speaks of suing me for a small strip of land which he claims.

Columbia 8th Dec. 1842

It is one o'clock and the Election for Governor is going on. Not without some doubts as to the result. A mine has suddenly been sprung within the last 24 hours, the extent of which can only be ascertained by the Ballot. When I came over I determined to throw myself upon the highest ground I could and therefore declined calling on any member of the Legislature. This gave offence to some who expected that I would electioneer with them, as candidates for minor offices do, and they were the more offended because there has been much electioneering for several offices, among them that of Secretary of State. Many of the new [Legislative] members never saw me and were averse to voting for a person they never saw. A few persons personally hostile to me and others who I may not have been as flatteringly polite to as their vanity required, took advantage of these things and began to beat up opposition. It was reported that I was the nominee of the Rhetts mainly because they were supporting me in good faith. That I was a caucus candidate, tho' not one of my original friends were in the caucus alluded to, and that the last Legislature should not be allowed to elect two Governors by nominating a candidate, tho' such a thing has been nearly always done. I was aware of all these things and a little apprehensive, but disliked to create alarm and make a requisition on my friends, which they might deem unnecessary. The malcontents had called, I knew, on McWillie to offer and had been repulsed. They did the same on Aiken with like success. I hardly thought they would get a decent candidate. But yesterday morning it was reported that Col. R[obert] F. W. Al[l]ston would be their candidate. When asked about it he said he would not run. But the truth is, he put aside the crown in such a manner that it will be tendered him, to the extent these men can do it. Since this has come out, my friends have been very active, but the worst of it is that, under the peculiar circumstances, any thing like an effort to push and force my claims will do me injury. A few quiet comments a few days ago would have done much more service. I have been urging, as far as delicacy would permit, the bringing on of the Election for several days, but could not get up the right feeling without betraying too much anxiety. Yesterday the malcontents could not have made head. Last night they had a caucus, and the result will not be known until the votes are counted. It is supposed there are about 50 of them. A trifle might swell these to 80 or reduce them to 20. The former would probably elect. Should Al[l]ston be elected under the circumstances, success may give eclat to the manoeuvre. Should he be beaten, it will, I think, do him great injury to have been made the tool of such a party. There is no one who has much pretensions to being a gentleman in the affair. An hour will show.

Evening

The Election is over. Hammond 83, Al[l]ston 76, Hennigan 1, Blank 1. As close as my strongest apprehensions. The anti-Rhett and anti-caucus feeling was the avowed cause of this, but all the other causes I have enumerated had their influence. I think it not improbable that there may be a re-action, which will cause a feeling of indignation against all engaged in this conspiracy. Such is the feeling of all my friends at least. At an early hour this morning it is thought I would have been beaten. By to-morrow the opposition would have fallen off to its original weakness. The leaders of it were Bill Myers, a notorious blackguard, who has crept into the Legislature from this District on the *democratic* excitement, W^m. H. Gist, a bladder and blatherer from Union, and L. T. Wigfall, the Edgefield bravo. F. J. Moses of Sumter, a jew, A. D. Sims of Darlington, a sot, were also leaders, and G. W. Dargan of Pedee very active. Nearly all Pedee went into it. I am endeavouring to collect the names of those who voted against me.

[Columbia] 19 Dec. [1842]

There have been two United Senators elected this Session. One to fill Col. [William Campbell] Preston's place and one to fill Mr. Calhoun's, both of whom resigned. Gen. [George] McDuffie was elected almost unanimously for the first vacancy, and on Thursday last (15th) Judge [Daniel] Huger was elected to the second. Messrs. Rhett, Pickens, and Davie also ran. Pickens highest vote was 30, Davie 29, and both fell off on the second ballot. On the third, Huger received 82 and Rhett 71 votes. This is the *denouement* of the plot formed here 3 years ago by the Rhetts and Richardson to rule the state and has ended now in the prostration of both and by each other's means. The first fruit was to elect Richardson with the Rhetts aid over me. They, the Rhetts, assisting a Union man to beat a nullifier in the expectation of receiving the eternal support of the Union Party. The end is to beat the Rhetts themselves by a Union man, [Robert Barnwell Rhett sought to be elected to the Senate but was defeated by the Unionist, Huger] who had first strangled Richardson and then obtained his aid against the Rhetts. The Rhetts committed two errors, first in trusting the Union Party, and secondly, in trusting Richardson, and of both they are now heartily convinced. Richardson and the Union Party immediately attempted to absorb all the offices instead of remunerating the Rhetts for the victory they had gained for them. The Rhetts saw this a year ago. Split off and fell back on me. Richardson sunk of his own weight as soon as they left him, but still was fool enough to think of running for Senator, until Huger's friends choked him off. He has gone into utter retirement, and the Rhetts are overwhelmed. I feel sorry for them now. They have supported me in good faith, and in the Senators' election most of my friends went for them. I shall act fairly and kindly to them but take care not to link my fate with theirs. They have talent and energy, but are incredibly indiscreet. Elmore goes down with them.

Retribution seems to have overtaken all the parties to the plot of 1839–40. I am satisfied and only wish I were well through my term of office [as governor of South Carolina].

[Having achieved the prize, Hammond abandoned writing in his diary for over a year, from December 1842 to January 1844.]

IV

The crisis of my fate personally and politically has arrived.

---

31 JANUARY 1844 – 19 FEBRUARY 1846

Silver Bluff 31 Jan. 1844

The Legislature met in November at the usual period, and I sent in my annual [Gubernatorial] message. It was well received, and I was complimented by all parties for its style and ability. The measures recommended were new and startling. The first was to reduce the Public Debt at the rate of $500,000 a year by calling in the funds of the Bank of the State and purchasing stock. This met with great opposition from all connected with the Bank in any way—officers and Debtors. The President [of the bank, Franklin Elmore] was directly called on to answer this part of the message by the House—an unusual and unparliamentary measure. He delayed his Report as long as possible to smother debate and only introduced it five or six days before the close of the Session. Of course every thing was put off to await it—a cunning movement of the Bank men. It was found that most of the Young men and a few of the Staunchest old men—particularly in the Senate—concurred in my views, and the Bank party became exceedingly alarmed. When the President's report came in, it contained nothing new to me or any of those well acquainted with the subject. I could have answered every part of it, but forebore to make any communication about it. In the mean time the committee of Ways and Means reported. [Christopher G.] Memminger, the Chairman, a man of great talent, well acquainted with the subject, and agreeing thoroughly with me, but wanting in the nerve to carry out his opinions, was tampered with by Elmore (President) his particular friend and brought in a most singular report. Building on some equivocal and oracular expressions of the Annual Bank Report, he represented that it was the wish of the Bank itself to cancel the State

118

Stock it then held by franchise. A resolution approving this course—which I had emphatically recommended—and applauding the Bank was added. Another declared it the definitively settled policy of the State that the Funds of the Bank should be applied to the extinguishment of the debt, and another charged the President and Directors with the responsibility of carrying out this policy etc. etc. All this was in precise conformity with my views—but all was claimed—to surprise and amusement of every sensible person, as the policy of the Bank. The Report resolutions passed unanimously—a bill was framed "requiring" the bank to cancel the State Stock and "authorizing" it to purchase more for the same purpose. The Bankmen made an effort in the House to strike out "require" and insert "empower." It was a test question and was lost by a considerable majority. Various attempts were made to modify the parts of the report and resolutions objectionable to the Bank men, both in the House and Senate, but all failed. The result was that the Bank was required in this year and the next to cancel their State Stock and pay the two instalments of this public debt due 1 January 1845 and 1 January 1846—in all a little over $800,000, in two years, of the Debt. We gained a complete victory, the Bank attempted to claim one. Elmore and myself were on the best terms throughout. I gave him near a month's notice of what I intended to recommend and sent him a proof sheet of that part of my message several days before the Legislature met. We treated the whole as a public question. There was little debate, none on the merits of the question in either House.

My next important measure was to consolidate all the State Offices at Columbia. This would have been a very exciting question, but it was overshadowed by the Bank question. A Bill was brought in, and, as an amendment of the Constitution was requisite, a vote of two thirds was required to pass it. It came within 3 votes of a constitutional majority in the House and would have received those in a full House.

I also recommended the establishment of Central Academies in each District. The Committee reported against it and nothing more was heard of it.

In subsequent messages, the most important measure recommended was the repeal of the Act of 1835 in relation to free persons of Colour coming into the State, or a modification of it so as to release them from imprisonment. A bill in conformity passed the House but was lost in the Senate. In this message, I conceived, for the first time in the South, a continued manifestation of sensitiveness on the Slave question.

In my annual message I also recommended the Annexation of Texas to the Union—the first thing of the sort which has emanated from any Executive in the Union. A strong resolution was passed in conformity.

I think I may say that on the whole my message and the results of the Session raised my reputation for talents and Executive ability much beyond the anticipations even of my best friends. I was repeatedly complimented in the Legislature for my judicious management of the Finances of the State committed to my charge, and every thing was done to place power and responsibility in my hands—showing a strong confidence on the part of the Legislature.

The death of Albert Rhett in the Fall deprived the Legislature of one of its ablest men and the bank of its strongest friend.

An unfortunate rupture with Hampton just before the Session terminated my relations with him and his whole family, including Manning and the Prestons. They pursued and are still pursuing me with the bitterest persecution. This event deprived me of all satisfaction at the proceedings of the Legislature and will embarrass me through life. I have been wrong in the matter—the result of impulse, not design. The truth, if known *fully*, would not seriously injure me, but *fully known* it never can be, and I have been reduced to the humiliating course of endeavoring to smother every thing. But I fear that to ruin me, Hampton—who is desperate in his fortunes—will be mad enough to ruin himself. This rupture had its effect in inducing me to remove finally from Columbia. I intended to have done so in the Summer any way, for many reasons, the strongest that my boys were learning nothing but bad habits there and would have been totally ruined by being brought up there. My interests here were suffering greatly and required my attention at the earliest moment—so I removed after the Session and reached here 1 January 1844.

[Silver Bluff] 2 July 1844

The rumours put afloat by [Wade Hampton II's brothers-in-law, John Lawrence] Manning and [John Smith] Preston have been taken up by my enemies—and by [Francis Wilkinson] Pickens, a treacherous friend, whose aim is to kill me out of his way for the Senate. They have gone all over the State and are generally believed. The effect is crushing to me and must prove serious to Hampton. I often feel like coming out with the *whole truth* and fighting my way through. But the idea of the injury I would do to those I hold dearest on earth is shocking to me, and, after all, my triumph would not be complete. Calumny can never be killed. It sometimes, but seldom dies. I yet anticipate a serious termination of the matter. I have every motive to bear and forbear, and I shall do so to the utmost.

[Silver Bluff] 7 August 1844

The expression of public sentiment on the 4th of July was decidedly favorable to me. Highly complimentary toasts were given in various quarters. I set out [as Governor] to-day for Reviews. The weather is hot and sickly, and I shall be nearly all the time in a sickly country.

A crisis in our [national] government is at hand. I do not see how the Union can stand against the resolute and successful efforts of the North to tax the South for its benefit—and their determination which is manifestly to uproot our peculiar domestic institutions. A peaceful seperation is now my only hope.

[Silver Bluff] 25 October 1844

Mr. Calhoun has at length revealed himself to me in the character so long assigned to him by all the Great Men of the Country. I have heretofore attributed their hatred of him wholly to jealousy and believed that his enemies were only their friends, who retailed their malicious aspersions of him. I have thought him a fine patriot and honest Statesman up to this period. I cannot now believe I have been deceived in him. I think he is changed. I cannot doubt that at this moment he is endeavoring to sacrafice the South—So Ca in especial and his most devoted friends on the Altar of his Ambition. An ambition the more culpable that it is so blind as to render him the dupe of every flatterer as well as every intriguer.

So Ca should have nullified the Tariff of 1842 at that time. When she accepted the compromise of 1833 it was with the distinct understanding that she would again resort to her Remedy if it was violated. In 1842 it was utterly and unscrupulously abrogated by the Tariff act of that year [raising the tariff back to the level it had been in 1832]. But we did nothing. I will candidly own, I was as supine as any. The truth was, I believed the only sure remedy was a dissolution of the Union, and I was not ready [in 1842] to propose that on account of the Tariff. I no longer believed in Nullification as a *peaceful* and *constitutional remedy*. I do not now believe in it *as such* . At that time, too, we had fair promises from the Northern Democrats, and the recent elections had given them a majority in the next Congress. And more, we were deluded into the belief that Mr. Calhoun stood a good chance for the Presidency, and could he be elected [in 1844, and] with a Democratic majority in the House, we might hope to reform the Government. Some or all of these views doubtless influenced the State, as nothing was done.

During the last Session of Congress the Tariff was brought up in both Houses and all modifications rejected. A majority of Northern Democrats voting against us.

During the Session the Treaty for Texas, made by Mr. Calhoun himself [while President Tyler's secretary of state 1844–1845], was rejected, only 16 votes for it. Benton and Wright, two leading Democrats, opposed to it. The rule of the House requiring Abolition Petitions to be at once laid on the table [also] could not be passed. And the Methodist Society dissolved into northern and southern Societies on the question of Slavery. All these things, and many others concurring, induced every reflecting man to believe that the Tariff was saddled on us forever and that there was a settled determination [in the North] to force the abolition of Slavery. Our members in Congress endeavored to get up an address by the Southern Members proposing a Southern Convention to take this matter into consideration. It failed. There was [sic] no doubt many personal reasons which prevented members from signing. The public one was that the South was not ready. Some members from the South were Whig and Tariff—all of them absorbed in the Presidential Election. The members from So. Ca. then resolved to address an united circular to their constituents, recommending State action by a Convention to meet next Spring [1845, to nullify the tariff if it had not been repealed and to demand the annexation of Texas]. Many signed it. McDuffie did, he told me. [Robert Barnwell] Rhett wrote it. ["It" became known as the Bluffton movement, an organized campaign in South Carolina among a vanguard of planters, who advocated separate state action despite John C. Calhoun's plea for moderation]. At the eleventh hour Calhoun came in and broke it up—chanting praises to the Union and to peace. Rhett came home after sending the address under his own name and rather imprudently, because unnecessarily, commenced agitation. The Mercury sustained—the Whig papers denounced, and no others took on an active part. It was soon understood that Calhoun was opposed to State action, and every body was paralyzed. After a while Rhett ceased to agitate. The Mercury became tame. Mr. Calhoun returned to So. Ca. early in this month and has silenced it altogether and every body. We are as calm as the dead sea. He has been seeking an interview with me. I shall not avoid it—but do not desire it and shall not go far for it.

I can see no reason for his course but his desire to obtain the Presidency. He is sanguine that Polk, the Democratic Candidate, will be elected. Is deluded enough to believe that he can control and succeed him and that if he was President he could cleanse the Augean Stable. Now the fate of the Texan Treaty satisfies me completely, and ought to satisfy every body, that he could effect nothing either as President de *facto* or de *jure*. It is in my opinion too late to reform the Government. But his prospects are so utterly hopeless that it is absolute absurdity to entertain the idea. The points at issue in the present canvass show that any body can create an avowedly free trade candidate if there were no other objection. It is so obvious that every body but Mr. C., and those who look through his glass, can see it. Yet he does not. A few flattering and designing Northern Democrats, who believe that by holding out these hopes to him they can keep So. Ca. and the South quiet, have completely blinded him. I have now no doubt that this was the game played in 1842, and that everything said at the North (except here and there he had an admirer) were designed, like supporting Mr. C. was designed, to prevent us from nullifying as it now is. We fell into the trap then. Mr. C. has fallen into it again, over head and ears and is straining every front to drag in this State and the South. He limits the forbearance of the State to *two years*. Why? because he thinks two years will settle the question of his succession to the Presidency. If he is to be elected, of course he will still oppose it. If he is not— he will be for doing any thing. What a reckless sporting with the vital interests of the South and the honor of So. Ca. thus to place them and use them as entirely secondary and subsidiary to his elevation to the Presidency. Yet he is to my eyes clearly guilty of it.

If So. Ca. takes no action this year on the Tariff and abolition, she is disgraced and destroyed. Two years hence, the South will be in favour of the Tariff and prepared to acquiesce in any compromise on Slavery. When Mr. C. attempts to make a rally to revenge himself for his blasted hopes, he will find that even So. Ca. cannot be brought up to the mark. Even in one year the precious time will have passed away. That period will probably be long enough to explode all Mr. C.'s present [presidential] visions— but can he [then] turn round and say to the State, now assert your rights? What fresh cause will there [be] but his disappointed ambition? All will see it, and any movement of the State will be met by open ridicule or indignant scorn.

Believing as I do, I shall meet the crisis as I think my duty requires. But I have no expectation but utter failure. The State will do nothing but what Mr. C[alhoun] wishes now. There is only one hope. If Mr. Clay is elected President, which is highly probable, Calhoun may out of hatred to him attempt at once to make war on the Federal Government and call up nullification. He may still, however, wait until our Session has passed in the vain hope of seeing some straw on the surface of affairs at which he may catch. It is clear to me that in his ambitions to be President he has forgotten or recklessly trampled on every thing else—Yet, I paid $500 a year ago to advance him to that office.

[On Hammond's thirty-seventh birthday on November 15, 1844, he recorded, "What a year of suffering," it had been. "Mind, body and estate are afflicted, deeply, awfully." He wrote, "I tremble to look forward, I shudder to look back." Birthday Prayer, HBC, SCL.]

[Silver Bluff] 17 November 1844

The crisis of my fate personally and politically has arrived. I leave here alone for Columbia in two days, to meet it [at the opening of the legislative session]. Whatever it may be. My path is dark, and I see no gleam of light before me. My only hope is that God will bear me through where I cannot perceive how I can pass of myself. I mean to act in every thing as nearly right as I am able and to stand on the defensive wholly. If I have done wrong, I do not mean to vindicate and maintain it by doing wrong again—at least not wilfully—Resting on this principle I put my trust in God, who orders all things and in whose hands I am. Of my personal difficulties so much has been said—so much has been done—they are intrinsically so serious—and a denouement is so generally expected, that I hardly see any way of escaping it. I shall however provoke nothing and will not be easily provoked. As much as I may lose by letting matters rest as they are—I shall gain nothing by stirring them. And yet could the *whole truth* be fully known, I believe few would in their hearts condemn me. No one would more than they would, my persecutors, or prosecutors I may call them.

Politically I am compelled to do what will, I have little doubt, crush me for the time and perhaps forever. In my Message which is written and in the hands of the Printer—I recommended substantial early and decisive State action. I think I have made my points strong and put them forcibly so that those opposed to them and to me will feel called on to use effective measures to put me down. Calhoun will look on me as a revolter and has, I have no doubt (for he is apprised of my views), already instructed his understrappers to hunt me down. Nearly all the old Union men—the immediate Calhoun set—and the timid old nullifiers are violently opposed to State action, and now that it is settled that Polk is elected President—*all*, will probably be for *waiting*. All but a chosen few—too few even to make a respectable rally. I shall therefore literally *stand alone* [on disunion]. I am not aware of a single man who will openly sustain me in either branch of the Legislature, nor do I know of more than one or two sympathisers. Thus politically cut off and personally vituperated my position is forlorn. Add to this that I have mortally offended the Jews by mentioning Christ in my Thanksgiving Proclamation and made the offence more heinous by a pithy letter justifying it, drawn from me by an insolent Memorial and protest signed by all the Jews in Charleston. To my letter they have made no reply but I look for an outburst of their wrath during the Session in some way or other.

Thus encompassed, how am I to escape scatheless. I may hope but cannot expect it. I must only endeavour to be prepared for the worst. He who has placed me, or suffered me to place myself, in this position will work his will, let me think, speak, or act as I may. So far as my finite ability permits, I will be prudent and leave the rest to him, firmly relying on His Mercy, if I may not appeal to His Justice. To do that would be presumptuous for I know that I have erred, and I may be in gross error that I wit not of.

I leave my poor blessing to my dear, helpless family, whatever betides me.

Columbia 21st Nov. 1844

Arrived here this evening in the Cars. Not without melancholy and misgiving feelings, yet not wanting in resolution. I have all my life had a feeling of great depression on arriving any where from a distance. Which [when] I reach home is accompanied with melancholy and gloomy apprehension of some undefined evil until I know how all are. When I approach a city or a large crowd or a strange place, this depressing sensation amounts to a nervous timidity and shrinking back that almost unmans me quite. Coming to this splendid but unfurnished and lonesome building has at all times made me miserable for a while. Strange to say never less so than now. Is the omen good or bad. Is it the secret sustaining of a Good Providence, or the presumptuous self-reliance of a desperately wicked heart. I can scarcely tell myself. I humbly trust that God has not given me over to the Devil and his Angels. I hate no fellow creature. I bear malice to no one. There is not a breathing mortal to whom I wish any evil or on whom I would voluntarily bring it of my own accord, much less for my own sake. These are my sincere sentiments sustained in my innermost heart. If I know my own feelings I have neither Envy, Hatred, Malice, or Uncharitableness in great or small things towards any human being. Not even against those who hate, revile, and persecute me. And it does seem to me that I am at this moment surrounded by more and bitterer enemies than ever man had. God forgive them and preserve me. And give me patience to endure to the end.

I met Clark at the Rail Road. He seemed far less cordial than usual. In fact few faces appear cordial to me now-a-days. Am I exacting? I think not. Am I preter-naturally suspicious? I think not, though this may be more natural. Clark excused himself from visiting me to-night on the ground of being invited out. Was in haste to do so and distant afterwards. He is nobody in himself, but a good sign of how the wind blows. He owes me money past due, this may be the solution. I think it is not. Nor was he *decidedly* distant after all. He spoke of my controversy with the Jews, and so has every one I have met to-day. It is said to be the latest topic of Charleston and Columbia and is worth noting.

I announced and set apart the 3rd day of October for Thanksgiving. In my Proclamation I invited the State to worship "God the Creator and His Son Jesus Christ the Redeemer of the World." The Jews of Charleston took great offence, announced themselves displeased at being apparently excluded, and called on me for an explanation through the public papers and by private letter. I informally answered them through Col. Pinckney, Sec. of State, in Charleston that it was an oversight. But they wanted some public notice and apology. They refused to open their Synagogues and finally about 5th inst. addressed me a long and impertinent Memorial and protest. I had declined noticing them until now. But this Memorial was signed, I presume, by every Jew in Charleston, 110 names. I answered it pretty sharply, refused to make an apology, and defended my Proclamation. I hoped the matter would end there. But they called a meeting, had a report in reply to my letter, and published the whole in yesterday's Charleston papers. My letter badly printed, which I must have corrected up here. This will be a three days talk for the public. But it has drawn on me the everlasting and malignant hostility of the whole tribe of Jews, which is very unpleasant in many ways. Their Report declares that they wish to drop the matter, and so do I. Publicly it will end here, but privately they will be thorns in my side.

[Columbia] 24 Nov. [1844]

A large proportion of the Members of the Legislature have, I understand, arrived. The immediate friends of Mr. Calhoun and *their* friends are extremely decided against State Action, and most of the rest are paralysed.

Some have called on me. None—not even Stuart of the Mercury and Gen. Bonham—are for action. *Wet-blanketed* by Calhoun & Co., Pickens has denounced the late movements in the State as Ultra, unwise, and unpatriotic. *His* object is to break down Rhett, as Calhoun's is to sell So. Ca. for his miserable chances for the Presidency. My Message will, I fear, find few or no supporters. I am not at all disappointed in the state of things. I have foreseen it ever since the Charleston meeting, in August, to repudiate Rhett. Nothing will be done. Doing nothing will be in fact going backwards, and I fear the moral influence of So. Ca. will be sacraficed forever, and with it all will be lost. A seperation of the States at no remote period is inevitable. It might now be effected peaceably and properly. A few years hence, it must take place in blood, or the South remain much as a subjugated region.

There is much interest manifested in the approaching election for Governor. [William] Aiken is the Candidate of the Union men and peace-at-all-hazards party. [Whitemarsh] Seabrook of the would-act party. [John] Buchanan and [Robert] Allston of the Independents. I fear Aiken will be elected. Of course I prefer Seabrook, but do not much care for any. All will shun my Message as fatal to their hopes if they are known to favour it. And I shall take part for no one.

[Columbia] 26th Nov. [1844]

My Message was read to-day. It has elicited many compliments for its ability and, I think I may say, is regarded as a *first rate* State Paper. The views taken on Federal Affairs are however, as I expected, loudly condemned by a majority, not approved of by many others, and backed by few, no one that I know of. Certainly no one of any influence in the Legislature. In the [state] Senate Pickens [acting as Calhoun's spokesman] immediately offered Counter Resolutions [opposing Hammond's call for Southern resistance to Northern "aggressions" and affirming instead South Carolina's confidence that Polk would act in the South's best interests on both the Texas and tariff questions] to go out with the Message, which it was thought at one time would be passed at once. They were however laid on the table with the Message and both made the order of the day for day after to-morrow. There is not the least reason to believe, and not apparently to *hope*, that any thing will be done by the Legislature. On the contrary, there is good ground to fear that they will express entire confidence in the Democratic Party and throw themselves upon it for relief in such a manner as to preclude State Action forever. I fear too that my personal unpopularity will have a decided influence to prevent an approach towards adopting my views. What a fall for So. Carolina when personal interests merely and likes and dislikes can influence her Legislation.

Some of my friends seem cordial, very cordial. Some quite shy, as tho' it might be injurious to associate with me.

[Columbia] 28th Nov. [1844]

Pickens resolutions passed the Senate to-day *unanimously*. A great triumph to him, and rather mortifying to me, I must confess. I did not expect *unanimity*. I express great indifference and feel much of it. But it is a hard hit. I rather think it is also a shock to public sentiment. Some of the Senators will rue it. They are under a Calhoun panic. In the House there is great confusion. I had the Com[mittee] on Fed[eral] Rel[ations] packed [with pro-Blufftonites]. Memminger and others saw it and wished the matter referred to a Com. of the Whole, which was done 77 to 40. My friends and new members voting indifferently. No test. A motion was made to print extra copies which was resisted, but prevailed. A bitter test, but I am in the minority. A large number of resolutions have been introduced and the debate was warm. Col. Train brought in resolutions to call a Southern Convention *which I penned myself.* I think a Southern Convention cannot be obtained. But to call it will be doing *something.* Saves the honor of the State and forms a platform for future action. No one but Fair knows my urgency. It will bother the quidnuncs. Most of the politicians of the State are pledged to go for a Southern Convention and I don't see how they will get round it.

My message elicits high encomiums from all quarters. Preston paid it an elaborate compliment before the Trustees last night. He referred to that part relating to education.

[Columbia] 29 Nov. [1844]

Although entitled to go into the House and Senate, I have thro' delicacy never done so since Gov., as the only interesting debates have been in topics suggested by my messages. The debate on my message has been going on all day to-day in the House and is adjourned for to-morrow. I get but meager accounts, every one thinking that I must be well informed. I understand, however, that the debate is very warm and new resolutions still coming in. DeSaussure, Memminger, Henry, and Seymour spoke to-day in favour of resolutions like the Senate's. Colcock and Herndon in favour of my views, Colcock's speech was said to be remarkably fine as was Stuart's yesterday on the same side. Very few seem to comprehend the real issue. And even the Senators seem few of them to be aware of what they have done. The general idea is that my Message demands instant State Action of some sort, and the resolution of this Senate and of that character only contemplate postponement. This is far from being the *real issue*. Pickens, Memminger, McWillie, Hunt and the Union Leaders generally comprehend what they are after and have a very different purpose. Altho' I am myself decidedly in favour of State Action at once, and it may be inferred from the Message, I carefully abstained from expressing it in a manner calculated to embarrass the State. But I did unequivocally express an entire want of confidence in the Democratic Party. And here it is that Pickens and Co. make the issue. They want to get back into the Fold. They want their share of the Federal Loaves and Fishes. And these resolutions are intended to destroy the isolated and independent position which So. Ca. has maintained for 20 years, warring against Consolidation, the last refuge of State Rights, and to throw her once more into the amalgam of the Union, resting all her rights and hopes on Federal Action. Could the Legislature be made to see this, as, before the debate is over, I hope it may, they would not near do it. The Unchanged Union men would do it. Pickens and the Calhoun clique would do it, but they could not get a majority in either House nor a fourth of the suffrages of the people. The truth is—as it was just now confessed to me by [Robert] Elfe, a Senator—the resolutions passed the Senate because it was thought Mr. Calhoun wished it, and for no other reason. Shameful as it is, the fact is so, that that body has acted without reflection on the subject, simply in accordance with what they suppose to be the wishes of *One man*. Thank God there is a different spirit in the House, tho' to what extent is not yet determined. I hope the best and will hope, in spite of all the despair around.

Personally I have no reason to complain. The ability of my Message is a topic in every speech, and if such compliments could soothe and quiet, I should feel no anxiety at passing events. But I feel anxious for So. Ca. I pity the deluded Senate from the bottom of my heart, and I mourn over the profligacy so apparent to me.

[Columbia] 1 Dec. [1844]

I rec^d night before last a communication, dated Charleston, from Sam[ue]l Hoar, announcing himself to be a special agent of the State of Massachusetts, sent to reside in Charleston for the protection of her citizens imprisoned under our Act of 1835, which requires that all coloured persons coming on shipboard into our ports shall be arrested and confined in Prison until the departure of the Vessel. His duty was to ascertain every case of the sort.

[Columbia] 5 Dec. [1844]

I was interrupted here on the 1st inst. and up to this moment have not been able to resume. Mr. Hoar's mission was for the purpose of instituting suits in every case where the citizens of Massachusetts were imprisoned without allegation of crime. Meaning her Coloured citizens taken up under the law. He courteously gave me notice of his arrival, and I placed his letter before the Legislature without any recommendation. The matter was in both houses referred to the Com. of Federal Relations. *After the references,* Pickens, true to his scheme of surrendering States Rights wholly, moved a reconsideration and reference to the Judiciary Com., on which Moses (old Union man) moved to lay the whole *matter on the table*— which was done. [Richard] Treville afterwards introduced spirited resolutions declaring that the State would not submit to such interference or to any decision of the U. S. Court on the subject. Which with these referred to the Com. on Fed. Rel. To-day the Com. on Fed. Rel. in the House reported a resolution that the Governor be requested to expel Mr. Hoar forthwith from the State, which after many warm speeches was carried 117 to 1.

That one was Col. Memminger. If this resolution passes the Senate I can carry out its purposes without much difficulty, if I am the Executive. Hoar however is an old friend of mine. He was in Congress with me, and I was walking with him in the Capitol when I was stricken down and he carried me into the Post Office where Dr. Linn bled and revived me, not again to resume my duties there.

I settled my a/cs with the State to-day, having spent in my two years only $7,250.00 of the $24,000.00 voted for the contingent funds. I also sent in my final message to both houses.

It is thought the Senate resolutions cannot pass the House, tho' I fear they will. The debate on the Message still continues. Opinion has settled down that it is among the ablest of our State Papers, and the discussion strengthens it. I see no demonstrations of hostility from any quarter, but am every day assured by members that they regret my ineligibility to re-election. I rejoice at it.

[John A.] Stuart of the Mercury [and brother-in-law of Robert Barnwell

Rhett] is one of the Lions. He is a man of great original genius. A wit and humorist, and very stanch. The other night he was sitting near [Henry] Pinckney, the Editor of the Mercury in 1832 and for long before, now a quidnunc, "Here," said some one, "is the old and New Mercury, father and son." Stuart drew off in apparent disgust. "There" said he pointing to Pinckney "is the Ashes: I am the Phenix."

[Columbia] 7 Dec. [1844]

I had scarcely finished the above when I was informed that the Legislature had passed a resolution, with only one negative in each House, requesting me to expel Mr. Hoar from the State and giving me unlimited power for that purpose. Col. [Preston] Brooks one of my aids came and volunteered for the service. I immediately wrote to Dr. Irving, Sheriff of Charleston District, to execute this duty, giving him full instructions and authorizing the use of force. Fearing he might resort to the Law and that Mr. Petigru, who I presumed would be his counsel, might overawe Irving, I sent down the Attorney General, Mr. Bailey, with Brooks to baffle Petigru. My orders were to let no impediment prevent his being sent off on the next Boat. I also furnished Brooks with authority for calling out the Militia in case of need. I did not apprehend that Hoar, whom I know, would go further than to require that he should be removed against his consent. But I feared a mob might be raised in the excitement. They went down in yesterday's Car. News came up on the same cars that Hoar would leave yesterday evening at the request of the Citizens of Charleston, which request he had, as we knew here, refused previously to comply with. I hope he left. My great fear was that something violent would be done, which after the matter became a State affair would have been very unbecoming. The Legislature have acted with great and proper spirit. And it is a move of vast importance. The most decided yet made by any State towards another in the Union. I am glad of it. Yesterday, resolutions were passed requesting me to forward my message (communicating Hoar's letter) and the Report and Resolutions of the Legislature to the other States. The Senate wished them to be communicated only to the Slave-holding States, but the House amended. I am sorry for it. Any drawing of the line is important. I am sure the Senate did not oil the bearings of the resolution or it would not have passed, nor would the House have amended, probably, had they considered it as so strong a move. In the whole affair the Legislature has evinced great confidence in me, which is very gratifying. Maj. Henry of Spartanburg brought in a resolution, that I—naming me—should issue a

Proclamation giving the reasons of the Legislature for their action. This is rather an absurd item, I have not heard its fate, but I presume and hope it has not passed. I am wearied of appearing before the public and of applause. My prayer now is to depart in peace.

My Letter to the Glasgow Free Church [on slavery] has appeared, and I have rec^d many warm thanks for it. Good judges think it the best thing I have done.

Dr. Henry and Col. Preston both said the other day at a dinner at the latter's (I am told) that my message was the ablest State Paper they had ever read and that the last paragraph was unsurpassed in the English language. They are Whigs. But such opinions from such persons are worth recording.

All my old friends except the Hampton Connection and Ben Taylor have been to see me and are very kind. They—many—offer *special* services. My position is *defensive* and I shall maintain it.

Even Wigfall so long and bitterly my avowed enemy has come in and declares himself warmly my friend. He, I find, betrayed Manning's confidence last winter, and first made public my quarrel with Hampton. I ought to hate him for he has done me the greatest injury, but I don't know how it is I cannot *hate* any body.

Since writing the above I have received a note from Simms saying that he had heard a full statement of my difficulties with Hampton. His author, and what he has heard, I know not. He has undoubtedly heard much falsehood. The *whole truth*, I know, has not been revealed, even to Hampton himself I imagine. But the affair, I doubt not, is again on the tapis. Envy perhaps has brought it up to soil my present popularity. Perhaps this is the forerunner of some personal movement of the Hampton clique. This was not necessary to make me unhappy. The idea of it completes my wretchedness.

[Columbia] 8th Dec. [1844]

William Aiken was yesterday elected Gov. on the 4th balloting over Seabrook, Allston, and Buchanan. The Legislature were loath to elect him, and it can find no sensible man who does not deplore it. They were forced to act in the confusion of so many ballots by Boyce, Pickens, Hampton, and such. He is an old Union man. [Ker] Boyce brought him out to strengthen himself in Charleston. Pickens went into his support to secure the Union influence for him for Senator, precisely as Rhett elected Richardson for the same purpose. He will gain about as much—possibly a little more, but can never be Senator I think. Aiken was a classmate of mine in College. He was agreed to be the greatest dunce in College and thought by many to be the most niggardly. The latter was perhaps unjust. He has improved since in every particular but is wholly incompetent to this office. He is vastly rich. His sole pretension. He is however a good fellow. Our personal relations were always kind, and are so still. I have not influenced a vote in the Election any way.

Last night came the President's message. He [Tyler] advocates "discriminating duties" alias protective tariff. On the *second* day of the Session, the House rescinded 108 to 80 the 25th rule which forbade the reference of abolition petitions or their discussion. 56 northern Democrats voted for it. And [Thomas Hart] Benton, it is said, has organized a powerful opposition to the Texas question. After this [opposition to the annexation of Texas and rescinding the "gag" rule on slavery] can our [state] Legislature vote confidence in the Democratic Party? It will be seen tomorrow.

(Copy)   (Private and confidential)

Dear Simms,

I cannot suppose your note rec^d to-night to have been dictated by any but kind feelings towards me. I do not know from what Source you have heard the "narrative" to which you allude, but I do not doubt you have heard much that is untrue and I am positively certain you have not heard the whole truth. Few besides myself can tell that. Considerations far stronger than any apprehension of consequences merely personal to me, have prevented my making explanations on the subject to *any human being*: and I trust I shall not be driven from the course I have prescribed for myself and which I have made the greatest sacrifices to pursue. The Affair is one of inexpressible delicacy; which no one *really* interested, if in his senses, could desire to moot; and which only the *basest* of enemies would agitate. For the rest it has long been my desire and purpose—expressed years ago—to retire from public life *forever*. But I do not intend to be *driven* to any measure, nor will I turn to the right or the left in consequence of any act of my past life.

Very sincerely yours,
J. H. Hammond
7 Dec.

Simms letter was immediately burnt as have all the communications I have ever rec^d on the subject.

[Columbia] 9 Dec. [1844]

Simms thinking me hurt from the tone of the above letter sent me a kind reply and said his information was doubtless exaggerated, tho' not from an enemy. I made a kindly response.

[Columbia] 10 Dec. [1844]

2 o'clock. I have just got home from the [Governor's] Inauguration. Every thing went off pretty well. Hampton, his son Christopher, and Manning were prominent spectators and from their movements I rather apprehended an attack [on my person] after the ceremony. I went with Aiken to his lodgings whither he was escorted by the Gov.'s Guards and College Cadets. Manning and C[hristopher] H[ampton] walked in the line with us. I took a glass of wine with Aiken and returned with Col. Brooks who handsomely followed the procession to escort me back, he said. We left M. and C. H. and on our way to the State House met Hampton and Rose. The latter has come up here without any apparent reason. He is Hampton's most intimate friend. Ex Gov. Richardson has been here some days also. Probably on Manning's account. He is a malignant fellow and is doubtless stirring up Strife. Another day will reveal all.

As this Journal is not for the public, I may be pardoned should it ever meet any eye but mine for its egoism to which I am about to add.

It is a common expression that I go out of my office in a "blaze of glory." I suppose it is common because several have used the same phrase to me. It has also been repeatedly said to me that no administration ever went out so popular. Numbers have expressed to me their great regret that I am not re-eligible and I am inform[ed] that the feeling is very general. It seems to be conceded that I should be elected ("by acclamation" as the phrase is) if re-eligible. My letter to the Glasgow Free Church has had quite a run. The Printer says he cannot supply the demand for it and is about to issue a pamphlet edition. Some say it is better than the Message. Even Gregg took me aside to thank me for it and many have done the same. In short my name seems to [be] established on the roll with the front men of the State, who are the front men of the Union. This would be, I own, delightful to me under other circumstances. It would be the harvest of many years of study, toil, and anxiety. But there is yet the canker in the bud. I would give it all a thousand times told to be at peace and as I was when I entered this office. Alas what are the pleasures of this world. Bitter in every draught, poison mixes with the most delicious. Oh that I had a steadfast faith in a better, an anchor cast in heaven. Why can I not? When so many believe and are happy why can I not do the same? God help me. Gracious Parent above show me the right way.

Aiken shows his weakness in being unable to conceal his excessive elation at being made Governor. There may fall out something worse than a mere exhibition of weakness. Being unable to comprehend and feel his true position, he imagines it to be a much more important one than it is and will, I fear, assume beyond his sphere. To use a vulgar expression he seems to think that he has the world in a sling. This may lead him to commit great abuses. He came into the Executive office to-day about 1/4 past 11 o'clock, 12 being the hour for qualification. The Captain of the Governor's Guards soon appeared and proposed he should return to his lodgings and be escorted down by the Company with drum and fife. This was ridiculous, but he was tickled and agreed. Went back. After the hour had expired and the Senate had gone into the House, I sent Col. Hunt, one of the Committee, after him. The Guards had not assembled and with difficulty he was brought down without them. It was not only in bad taste to attempt this parade but highly disrespectful to keep the whole Legislature waiting half an hour. He seemed to think it was nothing for a Governor to do, tho' his real good nature induced him to make many apologies to us. He may learn better. The Guards and Cadets came however and escorted him back to his lodgings, in which flummery I could not well avoid playing a part. His mind runs on the pageantry of his Station. He opened 30 dozen of Champaign the first night and had all the modus in town with him. He opened the bottles again today and evidently goes in for a show. His inaugural was decent. In one part he pledged himself that he would carry out any action of the State whatever might be its character for the redress of grievances. This alone was applauded and marks the spirit of the Legislature.

Stark called round to see me to say that he and some of my friends thought that in consequence of reports put in circulation about my leaving Columbia last year, I would do well to remain a few days more. I asked him if he had heard anything which would lead him to suppose I would be attacked. If so I would remain. He said he had not and on the contrary did not think I would. I told him that I had proposed to remain 24 hours after the inauguration to give [Hampton] a chance for a challenge or rencontre and had named for several days past to-morrow as my time of leaving. That to remain longer might evince a desire to invite a difficulty which candidly I did not wish to do. And also that I had from the first determined to act in every respect precisely as though there were no reports in circulation, as I knew well nothing I could do would put them down. That my remaining here even 24 hours was an unusual thing for Ex Gov[ernors], but I had done so to give a chance to my enemies and not to appear to fly. This was long enough for that purpose, which was all I wanted. These reasons seemed to satisfy him, and it was agreed that I should ride down the main street to-morrow between 10 and 11 o'clock, go to the State House, show myself, and go on.

[On the following morning he rode down Main Street to the Capitol. Hampton did not appear.]

Dec. 12 [1844] Silver Bluff

Left Columbia yesterday between 11 and 12 o'clock and reached here safely to-night, all well.

Perhaps I should not omit to mention a development of the late canvass for Governor which marks a change, which if not accidental and temporary, will be of much consequence to the future character of the State. It has always been considered very indelicate for any of the candidates for Gov. to take the least part in the canvass. If it ever has been done, it was by [John] Geddes and [Thomas] Bennett in 1818, but I do not know that it was. [The former was elected governor in 1818 and the latter succeeded him in 1820.] Since then, up to 1840, there had not been a contest before the Legislature for the office until 1838 between [Patrick] Noble and [Benjamin] Elmore in which both behaved well. In 1840 Richardson was charged with having left a card for every member (I don't know how truly), and I was prevailed on, much against my will, to do the same with perhaps half a dozen leading men, personal acquaintances but doubtful friends. I did not go to the State House before the election nor did R[ichardson], that I know of. In 1842 I pursued the same course and it was nearly fatal to me. Not half the members knew me by sight even, and a number of vulgar characters alleged that as a reason for not voting for me. Having no named opponent, it was perhaps extreme delicacy in me not to mingle with the members. But it was to my taste not to do it. Had I done so, no doubt I should have discovered at an early date the conspiracy against me and quashed it. I have always been a shy and sensitive person and this is a proof. I am however generally regarded as a strong example of a confident, bold, and indifferent person. The very excess of my sensitiveness has led me to assume as much as possible of the reverse in order to conceal it. To feel is severe enough to me, to let all the world see it would be overwhelming. But to state what I set about. In the late canvass Aiken and Seabrook made no disguise of their electioneering. Allston and Buchanan did less of it, at least openly, for they too are both shy sensitive men, but being members of the Senate they were always looking on, and in their way did their share. Aiken and Seabrook, however, took men by the button and made explanations. Both visited me on the subject. The former solicited my support, and the latter, intimating that he understood I was with him, came to make an explanation and inquire how others were going.

I refused on all sides to take any part and really did not influence or attempt to influence a vote. I should have voted for Seabrook only because I regarded him as the most decided man for resistance. And my inclination that way must have leaked out in some unguarded manner, as I understood afterwards it was generally supposed I preferred him. None of the candidates possessed a spark of talent, scarcely mediocre among common men, and Aiken rather below this standard even. Personally my feelings were kindest towards him as an old classmate.

If this example is to be followed and candidates for Governor are hereafter to canvass the Members of the Legislature, the office is effectually quashed. It is mainly desirable for its dignity and high tone, both of which will of course be destroyed by such a mode of seeking it. Its duties and labours however are growing more important and may sustain it after a time, but it never can possess that charm it once did, if won by personal solicitation.

After I was inaugurated Richardson took me cordially by the hand and said my administration should have his warmest support. I have never seen him from that day to this. He was in Columbia both Sessions but did not call on me. Since I came home I have heard that he said recently I was "an ornament to the State." I promised Aiken the same that Richardson did me. Moreover I left him Memoranda of all the unfinished business of the Office and advice as to his duties so far as I could with propriety. Gave some on Codification of the Governor's duties, powers, etc. furnished me by Bellinger and promised to counsel him hereafter whenever called on. In short I did all for him that I could have done for a Successor of my own appointment.

The very day after his Inauguration, the day on which most of these things passed between, he wrote a Proclamation, since published, appointing the 9th January for Thanksgiving etc. in such terms as to give up the point made by me with the Jews and start directly to censure my course.

Such a Proclamation was wholly uncalled for and unexpected, equally unusual as my reference to the Redeemer in mine, and cannot be regarded as having been done for any other purpose than palpably to disavow the precedent I had set, at the earliest possible moment. If he were a man worth being offended with, this should terminate our relations. But I have too much contempt for him to be really angry and shall then say nothing about it and act as if it had never happened. I am mistaken if the Christian community will regard it with the same complacency. However there is no telling. Most Christians are very indifferent and the best very forgiving. I never expected any essential support from them in my controversy with the Jews and knew perfectly well from the beginning that the only result of it would be to make fierce and implacable enemies of the tribe of Israel. In compensation for which I have expectedly won a good many compliments and perhaps added to my notoriety, I cannot say *fame*. I acted on principle, for the good of the State and for conscience sake; for whatever may be my religious doubts, I could not conscientiously omit the name of Jesus Christ in my public worship.

Aiken has also, I am told, granted pardons refused by me. Be it so. Let him go so.

[Silver Bluff] 22 Dec. [1844]

When I left Columbia, I told them that the Legislature would dissolve the Union if it sat three months longer. Events would happen within that period that would induce it if they were in Session, but which would have their influence [weakened] by having grown familiar before November next. Circumstances that have happened since remind me of the prediction, while they triumphantly indicate the truth and policy of my Message and must make its opponents in the Legislature feel very cheap, that is, such as *feel*, which thoroughbred politicians never do.

The rescinding of the 25 or 26 Rule of the Hs. of Reps [the "gag" rule] at Washington seemed to produce very little sensation at Columbia. The debate on the Message etc. was not resumed after it, before I left, and Col. Hunt even told me in my office that he was glad it was repealed. He averred because it would bring on the issue, but he neither expected nor wished that. He was only throwing cold water to prevent excitement at the time in the Leg. I told him the result of it would be to convert the Hs of R. into an abolition Soc[iety] and to flood our country with incendiary pamphlets in the shape of speeches reported and published in all the northern papers. To beware, for while he was waiting [on] the issue, our enemies were taking grounds that would conquer us before we could fire a single gun. These remarks and others seemed to make an impression on him. But I was apprehensive nothing would be done by the state Leg. in regard to this outrageous Act of Congress, which apart from the intrinsic merits of the 25 Rule, was a palpable overthrow of a point made and adhered to by the whole South and an abolition[ist] triumph over us. On Monday last however resolutions were presented in the [S. C.] Senate, denouncing this repeal of the [Gag] Rule as a flagrant outrage infringing on the Fed[eral] Compact, declaring that any legislation by Congress would amount to a dissolution of the Union, and requesting the Gov. to convene the Legislature in case of any such legislation. These resolutions more openly threaten dis-union than any ever passed by any State. Yet they passed the Senate *unanimously.* And who proposed them? Why Pickens. He who three weeks before denounced my violence and proposed resolutions of confidence in the Dem. Party and of relief thro' Fed. Legislation, which this same Senate also passed *unanimously.* What a change! What a complete vindication of my Message.

I have only seen the resolutions and the fact of their passing the Senate. The next mail will give more particulars. By the last [mail United States Senator George] McDuffie informed me that a Joint Letter of our delegation in Congress had been written to our Pres. of the Sen. and Speaker of the H. on this subject, but afterwards suppressed and each member was to write for himself. I regarded the suppression of the Joint Let. as a blow up of the whole affair, but I presume some communication from Congress must have caused this explosion from Pickens. Probably Calhoun has already discovered what is so manifest to every body else, that his chances for the Pres. are gone and has instigated Pickens [to change his course]. If so, I rejoice and forgive, for it is in time to save us. Nothing in my opinion but Dis-union now or very shortly can do it. Those who are for delaying this event for the sake of peace are taking the surest steps to render war inevitable. If passions are excited and the thing is done in extreme heat, it will be done in blood.

Our relations with Mexico seem approaching crisis. I cannot apprehend war. With any other Power it would be inevitable after what has happened. Calhoun will be held responsible for every thing that does occur. In all his communications about Texas he pushes the Slave Question. I approve of this in the main, tho' perhaps it is sometimes a little out of place. He does it ably but not as thoroughly as he might. His style is rather slipshod. For each year of my administration the Legislature appropriated $7,000 to the Civil and $5,000 to the Military Contingent Fund. I drew and deposited my first year's contingents amounting to $12,000. The Second year's I did not touch and left a balance at the close of my term of $4,850 in favour, having carried on the Government for two years with $7,150. During this time, besides defraying the Ordinary Contingents, I fitted up the Executive Office, which I found in a miserable condition, by purchasing a fine Book Case, a fine table, both mahogany, a dozen handsome arm-chairs, and two neat cases for the specimens collected by the Geological Surveyors. I expended over $300 for military equipments for the Military Academies, fitted up one of the Rooms in the College Library for the State Books, rebound and repaired the Records, and had new cases made for both offices of the Secretary of State, those in Charleston all new, and purchased a Sword for Com. Shubrick at $750. All these things were paid for out of these Contingent Funds and absorbed about $2.3 or less. The amount expended for ordinary purposes, and which I left nothing behind for, was only about $5,000. Some Governors have overrun the Contingent Fund. Gov. Butler did considerably.

[Silver Bluff] 26 Dec. [1844]

The [South Carolina] House after all has behaved worse than the Senate did. On the last night of the Session, Pickens' first resolutions in reply to my Message were passed by 59 to 37. His last resolutions on the 25 rule together with all other resolutions were laid on the table. And on the motion too of my particular friend and Aid[e]-de-Camp [Preston] Brooks, a mal-apropos young man of little talent, but fidgety to be doing, and always moving in the wrong time and place, just like his father before him, another particular friend, both of whose doings in my behalf have cost me no little in many ways. Pickens' resolutions on the 25 Rule were mounted by other resolutions, offered also by another particular friend of mine, W. Gilmore Simms, who has a perfect mania for resolutions and always has a set, no matter what the question. Bauskett also offered resolutions, very well written and spirited, and Stuart then condensed these two sets into two small resolves, and so the whole were smothered together. Pickens' resolutions were good enough, and, if presented to the House without riders, must have passed, I presume. But they evidently got into complete confusion, and there was no leader to extricate them. The House is full of spirit and mediocre talent, but no man to guide it. Hunt and Memminger, the two ablest members, perhaps, were both wrong and probably enjoyed the floundering. I have no private communications and conjecture these things from the papers.

So the [Gubernatorial] Message goes forth *repudiated* by both Houses. I rather anticipated this fate for it while writing it. To escape it, for I did not desire such a thing, I softened much. Perhaps it was as well, for now they have less justification. I am content to bide the issue and mistake very much if they do not turn to me for help, yet I do not intend to have any thing more to do with public matters than I cannot possibly help. I have announced my entire and final withdrawal in every way I could. Still when *drafted*, I shall not refuse to serve. But it must be a clear draft for a stated period and no rank.

My Message has been thoroughly defeated, I find, in the Boston Papers. All about Fed[eral] Rel[ations], published at large and severely censured and ridiculed of course. I don't know what is said of it in New York and at Washington. Nothing in the two papers I take thence that I have seen.

McDuffie writes to congratulate me on the "brilliant close of my administration." Holmes and Rhett has sent me most flattering eulogies. I hear nothing from Calhoun. He could burn me at the stake with good will, I do not doubt.

Rec^d this afternoon a Doc. from Calhoun, his letter to King. I presume he wishes to renew intercourse. This is his way of beginning. I have nothing to send him in return just now, and shall not write to him unless he does to me. I do not wish to discuss politics with him. Whether he designs this notice to indicate that he is willing to meet me half way and to recognize my being right in principle altho' wrong as to action, or only desires to show his magnanimity and console me for being defeated in the Legislature, I can't determine, and care little. His whole strength in this State—and he has none elsewhere—arises from the confidence our people have in his devotion to our peculiar interests. Let them once think he has sacraficed us, as I think he has, to his own ambitious views, and he is prostrated.

[Silver Bluff] 29th [Dec. 1844]

I have written to McDuffie a letter setting Mr. Calhoun's conduct in a strong and, I think, true light, of which I have kept a copy. I omitted to mention that I rec^d some days ago a letter from Barnwell in which it was proposed that I should accept a Public Barbecue from the citizens. I declined it in courteous terms on the ground that I wished to withdraw wholly from public life, and also that I did not wish to make a personal issue with the Legislature, who had disavowed my political [views], and the Governor, who had repudiated my religious sentiments.

[Silver Bluff] 8 Feb. 18[45]

I don't know whether I mentioned that Gov. Aiken issued his Proclamation, dated the very day after his Inauguration, ordering the 9th Jan. as a day of Thanksgiving. It was so worded as to please the Jews and, coming so immediately after his election and my Proclamation and at so unusual a time, was every where regarded as intended to disavow the ground I had taken. In many places the religious people disregarded it. Soon after the 9th, Pemberton noticed it in the Carolinian in severe and proper terms. Aiken immediately wrote to me disavowing all intention of opposition to me etc., which I answered accepting his apology. I think he has gained nothing by this, to which Boyce doubtless advised him. He also corrected some of my Proclamations offering rewards, by increasing them, a very indelicate thing. And he has made himself ridiculous by appointing 40 aids. He is only a fool. Good-natured and well-meaning, but a fool elated with his position and with bad advisers, likely, I fear, to do much harm in some way or other. Fools in power are the most dangerous characters. By the bye, Pemberton has sold the Carolinian, and Stuart abdicated the Editorship of the Mercury. Both stood by me manfully and may be regarded as sacraficed partly by their course and partly disgusted with others. These papers have both long been *organs* of Calhoun. See how he disperses his friends! Yeadin left the Courier some time ago, probably in consequence of his Ultraism the other way.

I have been engaged in writing a very long letter to Thos. Clarkson Esq. of England, the Patriarch of Abolition. He sent me a copy of his printed circular addressed to professing Christians in our Northern States not connected in any way with Slavery. I think my reply to him [in defense of slavery] the best thing I have written and have no objections to his publishing it. I do not care to do it myself. I do not wish to go before the public. I have written already sufficiently on this subject—and I am satisfied with my reputation just as it stands. This might hazard it, would look ambitious, and scarcely gain anything for me. So I shall not publish it, highly as I think of it.

[Silver Bluff] March 2 [1845]

[Col. A. H.] Pemberton has recently published a sort of review of my administration, lauding it. The feature he praises most in my public character is my constant effort to keep my merits from the public. This is just. That is, while Gov., I discouraged and prevented as far as I could all compliments to myself in the papers. I have been called vain and forward all my life and not a little aspiring, and such praise as this will take most persons who think they know me by surprise. The fact is my character, like that of most persons, is apparently inconsistent. Notwithstanding I have done enough to warrant the charges of self conceit and imprudence, I am at bottom, shy, modest, and very retiring. All that I have done to the contrary has been acting, done from the apparent—probably mistaken— necessity of the moment. It is likely I have often over-acted, as most do. In small matters I have put on airs and done my share of boasting, in great ones however I never have. And really felt and acted as Pemberton describes throughout my administration. Candor requires me however to state that during the greater part of it, I felt myself to be, as indeed I was, under a cloud and shrank from drawing public attention to myself, in an unusual degree. This feeling may have influenced me even more than I think, though I believe I took my stand on the subject and evaded all unnecessary display *before* these circumstances arose. I regret Pemberton's publication. It will no doubt produce the impression in some quarters that I am looking to the U. S. Senate & may draw down obloquy & a painful discussion. I do not care for newspaper praise or for any mere contemporary compliments. I care for no further honors unless the opportunity offers to render my name historical. The whole thing, too, has been badly done. The article was written for P.'s last number of the Carolinian—but omitted to Summer's (his successor) second number. Here was an apparent want of genuine heartiness in the matter, and it looks a little as if done by contract and forced in merely to comply with the bargain. Tho' well written for P. it is not very judicious in its criticisms and some expressions are introduced that give the whole thing a bad turn. He seems evidently to think he is doing a bold and unexpected thing to *praise me* and that he incurs considerable responsibility. His praise, too, is occasionally awkwardly qualified and, in some important particulars, falls short of what, I am sure he thinks, I have been led to believe was public sentiment. On the whole it does not place me in the rank to which I think myself entitled. This is not very modest in me. I would not of course say it aloud. I wish the article had not appeared and hope I shall hear no more of it.

[Silver Bluff] March 9th [1845]

Texas has been annexed by a Joint Resolution of Congress. The Constitutionality of it I think doubtful. It is an acquisition of Territory. Territory has never been hitherto acquired over a civilized people but by Conquest or Treaty. The Treaty making Power under our Constitution is the President and two thirds of the Senate. It is said Congress has power to "admit new States" but this is different from the Power to *acquire* new States. It is true Congress is not *forbidden* to *acquire*, but that is not necessary. It can only exercise *delegated* powers. It is also true that there is no reason in the nature of things why Territory might not be "acquired" in this way as well as by Treaty or Conquest. But Custom and international law has established it otherwise. And there can be no doubt that it was understood by the Authors of the Constitution that this was one of the Powers confirmed solely on the Treaty making Power. Had I voted for it in Congress it would only have been on the ground that the Constitution was a dead letter. The admission of Texas is an event of great magnitude, the greatest of the present day. It strengthens the South and the Slave interest. It, however, must contribute to lower the price of our lands, to enhance the price of negroes, and keep cotton at what it is. The *feelings* of the North may be offended, but their interests will be better served, perhaps, than ours.

It is rumoured that Mr. Calhoun was thrown overboard as the condition on which Benton and New York went for Texas. That Calhoun is out I have little doubt. It is what I have always anticipated.

Polk's inaugural has arrived, but not his Cabinet. The Inaugural means any and every thing. Nothing specific that binds, but that he is in favour of Texas and opposed to a Bank.

[Silver Bluff] 16 March [1845]

Some days ago came Polk's Cabinet. Calhoun out, no man from SoCa or of what can be said to represent SoCa in. It is said by some newspapers and letter writers that Polk has aimed to form a Cabinet without taking any of the extreme friends of Calhoun, Van Buren, or Benton. This is all a humbug given out to pacify Calhoun's friends. Every man in the Cabinet is or *has been* a full blooded Van Buren man, and they are all thorough *intriguers*. Mediocre men, like Polk, the only prospect for them to sustain themselves, and the administration, is by *management*.

Calhoun, I am well informed, fully calculated on retaining office [as

Secretary of State] until 4 days before the Inauguration. Polk has preserved a mysterious silence as to all his appointments up to the period of the Inauguration. The sole object was to prevent embarrassment from Calhoun and his friends and keep them faithful to the last. I have some accounts that Calhoun returns in great wrath. I do not think he will boil over publicly at once. But that he is deeply mortified and full of gall cannot be doubted. He has reason.

How completely my anticipations in December have been verified. The fact has long been apparent to me, that all parties in the country reject Mr. Calhoun. They fear and hate him for his superiority of mind not less than for his arbitrary will. Besides he has an unfailing tact at destroying all parties with which he is associated. This is well known to all experienced men, and he is shunned as much as possible. He destroys parties because his abilities give him prominence. He will never take counsel or concede the smallest point. He marches and countermarches all who follow him, until, after having broken from the bulk of his following, he breaks down his friends one by one and expends them in breaking down his late associates, so all ends in ruin.

My Glasgow letter has, I understand, been republished in Paris in pamphlet form with Mr. Calhoun's letter to Mr. King and extensively circulated. This is a compliment, of course unsought and therefore more to be valued.

[Silver Bluff] 20 March [1845]

I rec^d today a letter from McDuffie in which he says "I congratulate you as a friend and as a Southern man on the decided impression made in this country and in Europe by your letter to the Scotch Church. A distinguished member of the House of Deputies in France has translated it and Mr. Calhoun's letter to King, and circulated them over Europe."

He adds what is much more agreeable at this moment. "I late rec^d a letter from Genl Hamilton in which he says "I have adjusted my claim against Texas and am happy to say I will now be able to relieve every friend who has generously endorsed for me."

Mons. Jollivet has sent me several copies of his pamphlet containing my letter, Calhoun's to King, and Clay's Speech in the Senate on Abolition. Also an Essay of his own on the Slave Trade and Right of Search, and a complimentary note.

My letter is translated with spirit, but only a summary, made not I think with taste or judgement.

. . . .[Silver Bluff] 11 May [1845]

Col. A. H. Pemberton, late Editor of the Carolinian, has been with me a week. He is a man of true instincts and generous impulse—proud, enthusiastic, rather ambitious, neither well bred or well-informed but not coarse or intrusive. He has persuaded me to give for publication in the Carolinian two letters on Slavery which I have been writing to [Thomas] Clarkson [entitled Two Letters On The Subject of Slavery in The United States]. He speaks of them extravagantly. I think well of them myself, but am not confident they will be well received by the public, and have a strong repugnance to appearing before it again in any way. I have on this account resisted much importunity to publish these letters before now.

Pickens has the offer of the Ministry to England. Elmore has declined it. He is too poor and embarrassed. Calhoun first refused it, and Polk seems resolved that some of his friends shall have it. A worse appointment than Pickens could hardly be made. He is wholly inept for such a post. Particularly at this time when it is supposed a war with England on account of the Oregon territory is not unlikely. Pickens will precipitate matters and bring on a war if it can be done. He is pompous and blustering, which by no means suits the Court of St. James.

Elmore wrote me that he intended to recommend me for it, but I supposed it a mere banter and treated it accordingly. Of course it was. I don't suppose my name was ever mentioned to Polk. It would not suit me. Both my health and my private affairs forbid my embarking on public life, most especially in such a career.

[Silver Bluff] 14 May [1845]

Pickens has declined. It is probable now that some northern man will be offered the mission. [Louis McLane of Delaware who had formerly been Minister to Great Britain, 1829–31, and Secretary of State, 1833–34, accepted a second appointment as minister to England from 1845–46.]

[Silver Bluff] 15 May [1845]

I have been and am in a State of feeling hard to describe. I am more subdued in point of fact than I ever have been in my life, yet unfortunately less submissive in mind to the decrees of fate and the will of God than I supposed possible.

Having withdrawn from the world, soured, disgusted, and amid all the applause showered on me at the close of my public career, deeply wounded by the situation of my family relations, my aim was to bury all my griefs in the active pursuits of agriculture and to improve extensively my lands and my fortune if I could. I have long been thwarted in my hopes of the latter by the extraordinary mortality which has prevailed among my negroes and even my stock of all kinds. I thought however in the useful and innocent scheme of regenerating my poor soil, I could meet with no difficulties that energy and judicious care would not overcome. Soon after I came here nutgrass was found on a cut of my river fields. Hopeless of eradicating the pest, I left it alone. It spread slowly and last fall I concluded that 200 acres must be given up for cotton on account of it, and I made my calculations to ditch round it and devote it to corn. There were spots elsewhere in these fields, but I thought to dig up, ditch round, and plant these in plum trees to arrest it where it was. When however I began to break up this winter, spot after spot was found there. Soon it was discovered in my large Snow f[ield] near 3 miles off, then in first one and another field over the creek and ever[y] where. Only yesterday a new spot was found in Snow f.—in short it seems to be every where. My plan of improvement is extensive, laborious and costly. Can I continue it with the prospect of having, in a few years and before I have reaped any substantial reward, to surrender the whole place to this accursed weed? It seems to have been spread with the marl which at a cost of $10,000 (in labour) I have put on my land. How it got *in it* is wholly unaccountable. But the hand of fate seems to be in it, and it is decreed that I must still continue to destroy myself by every effort I make to advance my interest. My hopes are cut up by the roots. I have no heart to continue my improvements. This source of employment, of happiness, of making a provision for my family seems to be taken from me. God evidently has designed it. I cannot fathom his purposes. I do not know what to do. Sometimes I think my destiny is not here. He proposes me for other scenes. But I see no clue, no light to lead me elsewhere. All is darkness and I am bewildered. That I am not pleasing to him and that my ways and views do not meet his approbation is further shown in that after selecting every experiment for this year that I could believe likely to succeed here, after going to immense labour and expense to put large quantities of peat on the whole snow f[ield] and testing it also elsewhere, after trying plaster, manure, in various quantities, rice, tobacco, potatoes on a new and laborious plan, planting in various ways with different seeds, in short, after doing all that man could do, it seemed to me, when it became necessary for God to aid me, He *failed*. From 24 March to 12 May there was not rain enough to bring up any kind of seed, I had corn up before, but lost the stand by the drought. Such a scene as my plantation now presents is unparalleled to me.

Add to this that in February the [James] Hamilton Case was decided against me, and I have to raise $7,000 to pay for him, now, and it will be seen that I have cause for despair. And I do despair. Deserted by God, persecuted and robbed by man, what can I do. My spirits are gone. I have lost all cheerfulness. Gloomy, moody, I seldom smile, or speak a kind word even in my own family. I cannot read with any pleasure. I have lost my relish for the fiddle, which has been a great relief in my troubles.

I am, I believe, just in that state which carries so many men to the bottle and the faro bank. Every natural and rational source of enjoyment seems utterly closed to me. My heart is a fountain of bitterness, defiance, and desperation. I know not how to ask strength to support me from God, though I do it (without faith or hope) daily; nor can I look to man for sympathy or comfort. The only question is how long will this last? It must soon cease to exist, or I shall. One so broken in spirit as I am cannot long hold out against such heavy, repeated, crushing blows. I have thought and thought, ransacked every nook and cranny of my mind, brain, and heart for relief, until I have exhausted all. "Perdura" is my motto. But I too sadly fear I have not strength.

[Silver Bluff] 25 May [1845]

A good deal has been said about Calhoun, Elmore, and Pickens successively declining the English Mission. It is said Hamilton has done so likewise, This I am inclined to believe, though it is not officially stated. Elmore and Hamilton might have done, the others were wholly unfit for it. But why urge it on SoCa? I have heard on good authority that when Calhoun left the Cabinet, he had carried the Oregon negociation to a point that rendered war inevitable unless one party retreated. He had refused an arbitration. If this be so, it is probable that Polk wishes to hold him and his friends responsible for any backing out, or for war, as the case may be. Possibly he may be weak enough to expect to buy over the State by such a bribe. This would be ridiculous. But such is the wisdom of politicians. One might think they would see that the true way for a President to strengthen himself would be to select the most capable agents on all occasions and so conduct affairs as to gain applause and confidence from all quarters.

[Silver Bluff] 20 June [1845]

My Letters to [Thomas] Clarkson are out and have produced quite a sensation. I have received many extravagant compliments. They are publishing 5000 in pamphlet in Charleston for circulation. I think from all accounts they have considerably advanced my reputation.

[Silver Bluff] July 2 [1845]

My Clarkson Letters must have added considerably to my reputation. They are published in all the papers and many thousands in pamphlets. Walker writes me from Charleston that they are equal to any thing Calhoun ever wrote in matter and superior in manner. This is probably the opinion of his set and I know it is also of some others. If it was the general sentiment in SoCa, no higher praise could be bestowed, for Calhoun is regarded here as the non-pareil of the age.

But as usual all my fruits are full of thorns. The miserable Editor of the [Columbia South] Carolinian, A. G. Summer, to whom at his urgent request I gave the publication of the letters in his paper, announced also a pamphlet edition at $20 per hundred. This extortionate price induced proposals at once for a large pamphlet edition in Charleston. Whereupon Summer took out a *copy right*. I knew nothing of it until I rec^d a copy of his pamphlet two days ago. I was compelled to write him at once denouncing the impudence of this thing, and to the Mercury I requested a statement to be made that it was done without my knowledge and consent, against my wishes. It would otherwise be supposed I had authorized it and perhaps profited by it. I refused to accept or to circulate Summer's pamphlet and have enclosed $20 to the purchase of the Charleston edition. A meaner or more impertinent thing I never knew done. It must disgrace Summer. I regret it. It is very unpleasant every way and may end in a serious difficulty.

More than this. There is much talk of running me for the Senate. I have rec^d several letters on the subject. I do not wish to go. For the present and for five or six years, if I live, I prefer to attend to my affairs here. I must do it. But this talk will no doubt amuse my enemies. The old scandal will come up. Perhaps be brought to a head. This I in some sort anticipated if the letters should take. What can I do to avert it. I have answered all that I do not want to go to the Senate. What more can I do. It would be immodest to declare I *will not*, when it is so uncertain whether I could. I am in the hands of fate. I must meet my destiny whatever it may be.

How little do we shape it. I left Columbia in Dec. resolved on profound retirement. See me now. I would be glad to close here and hope I may be permitted, but *fear* not.

[Silver Bluff] July 3 [1845]

I am unhappy. I have acted foolishly and wrong. For some time my motto has been "Perdura." In a moment of passion I have wholly forgotten and inflicted lasting injury. Summer [editor of the *South Carolinian*] behaved meanly. It was foolish, knavish, and treacherous to me. What then? Might I not have remembered "Perdura?" Might I not have simply declined to accept his pamphlets and dissolved connection with him—that would have punished him. I could have written to authorize the Charleston publication, that would have satisfied the public. My own feelings of indignation and mortification I ought to have repressed. I should have thought of "Perdura"—my own sins, and been *charitable*. Now I have insulted him by my note to him, and exposed him by my note to the Mercury, both of which were unnecessary, and the latter in exceeding bad taste. I felt this bad taste of the matter at the time. My indignation blinded me. Could I hope the Editor of the Mercury might have good sense enough to suppress my explanation? Ah, what fools we are, creatures of impulse, led by fate. How often have I resolved never to act in a passion, yet I do it daily. And daily I seem to have less power over myself. My nerves are terribly shattered. I am a chaos of all sorts of feelings, good, bad, desponding, desperate. Hope scarcely mingles with them. I did not want to publish these letters. They have exalted my reputation, placed me at the full height of my merits, tho' I do not regard them as altogether the best thing I have done. But what is fame for me. I despise the mass. I would not turn on my heel for temporary applause. There are but two things worth living for—Love in life, immortality after death. I mean pure personal love from male as well as female, love to fill up one's yearning heart, not *admiration*. And I mean by immortality to fill a niche in History to the end of time, not to die out with the death of contemporaries. No body *loves* me, but my wife—no body will remember me who has not seen and known me! My life is a blank, all daily sorrows aggravated by my follies, arising mainly from sensibility and passion.

[Silver Bluff] July 14 [1845]

My [Glasgow & Clarkson] Letters [proslavery tracts] have increased my reputation vastly. Far beyond my expectations. [William] Harper says he has seen nothing equal to them, and he has written *ably* on the subject himself. [Langdon] Cheves, who is very costive of praises, says they are the best things he has seen for a long time and has obtained copies for circulation. Calhoun has written to enlist me in a review of Bascom's work, but, as usual with him, no particular praise. From various minor sources I have compliments. At every 4 July celebration I have been toasted once or twice. Pemberton says they have made a greater impression than anything published in his time. Dr. Davis who is very knowing (in his own opinion) says that all sorts of people "literate and illiterate" concur that I am the most "talented efficient and popular man in the State" and that it is resolved that I shall go to the Senate. Simms writes that they have placed me on such a position that I can "take the wind out of the sails of any aspirant for the Senate if I please." Brooks (Sen.) writes me that I have acquired a more enviable position than any SoCa ever had done at 40 years of age, and one that my enemies cannot deprive me of. Davis says my enemies yield their prejudices. This last is the best news of all *coming from Columbia*—if I could credit it. Of all things I should prefer to make peace there. But such pride as I know exists there can never be overcome. This anxiety of mine does not arise from any consciousness of having done wrong, but from the knowledge that appearances are against, are too delicate for proper explanation, in fact too much so for any whatever before the public. I therefore stand in the battle without arms as it were.

I mention the compliments paid because they and the other excitement on my favours now will be wholly forgotten in a few years.

I don't want to go [to] the Senate. I am not ambitious of further *office. Power* in our country no man can have, but *at home* writing on topics of deep interest with unsuspected motives, or at the head of an army.

[Silver Bluff] 18 July [1845]

Bellinger and Aldrich have paid me a visit. B[ellinger] joined the Catholic church last winter and is full of it now. It is melancholy to see an intellect like his so prostrated by bigotry. He believes implicitly every thing that has the sanction of the Church. Even modern miracles. He will listen to nothing that militates against her. His mind is perfectly closed to reason and common sense. He evidently regards the Bible as worth nothing except so far as it has the sanction of the Church. He worships Holy Mother and her alone. It is shocking. Such is human nature however. Nothing is too silly or too wicked for belief, nothing too clear and reasonable to be rejected.

[Silver Bluff] 9 Aug. [1845]

My friends say the 4th July was celebrated this year solely to toast me. The fact is I was toasted oftener than all the rest together, and nobody scarcely beside but Calhoun and McDuffie. Judge Cheves says (privately) that my letters are the best things that have been published in this country for 20 years. Calhoun is *costive*. He has no generosity, no real soul. I don't say so on account of his conduct now, but from long and intimate knowledge. After reading Bascom's book I declined reviewing it. It is a crude, undigested, and confused affair drawn out endlessly, and *very unsound*. He says the Bible is neither for nor against slavery, that it is a great evil, that the South is anxious to get rid of it, that abolition is only a question of time and expediency. I could not, the South should not, set her seal on such opinions. It would be utterly fatal to us. So I said to Mr. C[alhoun]. He has written back pressing me again. I am astonished. He has some small narrow view and object to gain for himself and would not hesitate to sacrafice me and embarrass the South to advance it. I can't see it. Probably it is so trivial (intrinsically) and so far-fetched that nobody does or can, but himself. I shall not yield. The South cannot stand a moment on the grounds Bascom assumes, and I will not assist in placing her there. . . .

[Silver Bluff] 6 Sept. [1845]

I have ascertained the secret of Mr. Calhoun's persisting in this [Bascom] matter. A Letter from him dated 7 July to the person sending him Bascom's book has just been published. It is fulsome in Compliments to Dr. Bascom and extravagant in praise of his book as "the best vindication" of the South that had "yet appeared." He gives it in all respects his *unqualified approval*. This letter was chiefly dictated by the hope of *securing* Kentucky Methodist influence. I have no doubt also that he wished to give the go by to my Letters. It may be vanity to think so, but I am convinced he is jealous of them. Very possibly some one pointed out afterwards the unsound doctrines and admissions of Dr. Bascom, and then he sought for backing. I have just rec^d a letter from him in which he at length concedes to my views, mainly as he admits, because I said the book was rather coldly received by the Methodists here. Did ever any man snatch so desperately and foolishly at straws before or move to and fro from shadows. He is dying to be President, in spite of fate.

[Silver Bluff] 14 Feb. 1846

I have been dreading a war with England ever since Polk in his Inaugural declared our title to it [Oregon] to be "clear and unquestionable", and the British Ministry and opposition united in retorting his words in reference to them. The people of both nations hate one another and the Politicians has [sic] raised this Phantom question in which neither the honor nor real interests of either nation are concerned, merely for popularity sake. Polk, Gen. Cass, and Allen of Ohio together with a host of small fry in the House, and Adams among them are riding the hobby. Calhoun has taken a noble stand. (Judge Huger resigned [from the Senate] and he [Calhoun] was elected to the Senate again last December). He at once declared himself for peace and breasted the popular current. I wrote him a very cordial letter on it and really feel as though I may have in my thoughts done injustice to him as a man of firmness and lofty purpose. If he goes through this without flinching, I shall rank his qualities far higher than I have done. He is the Ajax of the peace party. I have lately written several hasty articles on the subject in the Augusta Constitutionalist under the Signature of "Phocion," to open the eyes of the Georgia Democracy. The Governments [British and American] have both acted so indiscreetly that they are greatly entangled. The game of each has been to bully the other, neither desiring war, but only the credit of a victory. The result I fear will be war. The resolution giving notice has probably passed the House by a large majority. The Senate are debating it this week.

[Silver Bluff] 19 Feb. [1846]

The resolution to give notice has passed the House by a vote of five to one. The South divided on it and so did the North, only a few staunch Whigs from that Section going with us. The West almost en masse for it. Virginia, SoCa, and Massachusetts standing out strongest for peace. One SoCarolinian voted for the notice, James A[ugustus] Black, [a member of the House of Representatives, 1843–48] a low bred intriguer whose object is to sacrafice himself if possible for the administration that he may claim an office. He is a man of little information and less facts but shrewd and unprincipled, as was his father and all his brothers, and now are. They have all figured in politics in this State as cunning managers coming from the very lowest of the Long Cane Irish population in Abbeville and of course always throwing themselves open mouthed on the mob. J.A.B. represents Union, York, etc., where no one that is much better will offer, partly from disinclination to go to Congress and partly from fear of his low cunning and malice. He was in the army in the war, has tried all occupations, and is now without property and pretty much without character.

The notice before its passage was stripped of some of its war aspects—"Forthwith" was stricken out and the *time* is thus understood to be left to the President. It also authorized negociation. A motion was made that no further negociation should be carried on, but only 10 voted for it.

Before the passage of the Resolution, the Pres., in answer to a call from the House, laid before them parts of a fresh correspondence with our Minister in Eng[land] and the Eng. Minister here, in which an offer had been made to refer the matter to arbitration on the most liberal footing for the U. States. The offer was promptly and peremptorily rejected by our Government. This alarmed some and no doubt occasioned the modification of the Resolution. I do not like the idea of an arbitration myself, but when such ridiculous pretensions on both sides are likely to bring on war I should object to no decent mode of settling the matter, regarding it as perfectly indifferent what portion of Territory may be assigned to either.

The Senate are now debating the question of notice and will probably pass it. The Whigs fearful that the Democrats may outbid them for popularity will some of them vote for it. Some of them too do not care to see the Administration involve the country in war, forgetting that their votes will make them responsible also, and that they will share all the odium that may accrue and cannot reap any of the glory. Such is the blindness and malice of party.

The People of all Parties and the Politicians of all Parties too doggedly refuse to believe there can be any war, rapidly as we are rushing into it. They think England cannot risk her immense interest in peace for such a paltry gain as Oregon, though our interest in peace is even greater, yet we are doing it. Thus they give England more credit than ourselves for wisdom, calmness, and Christian magnanimity. So wars are ever brought on, by folly, rash committals, and cowardly calculations.

The general impression, too, is that the President has assurances of peace which he reserves from the public and communicates only to his confidential friends. This is almost impossible. He cannot be such a fool.

If it comes out that he does hold such knowledge and yet permits Congress to go on with its bullying speeches and resolutions, that he is fighting a sham battle, with the whole of our people, save a few, for his dupes, he will be utterly destroyed by ridicule, if not overwhelmed by indignation, for permitting the U. States, in fact urging it, to enact such an absurd farce.

Rhett writes me to-day from Washington that the Administration Party is greatly alarmed, and it is evident the country is neither prepared for war nor [prepared] to go into one, that Congress wd not support the President's policy, but that no danger is apprehended, and he seems to apprehend none himself. That the Adm. is alarmed is evident. Its organs are very fierce and are drumming up its supporters every where, resorting to every shift to gain votes in Congress. All this looks hopeful, and my hopes would be stronger but that I anticipate the greatest danger from the folly and recklessness of those in power. They will be carried much further than they intended. It is even now thought that Polk would not dare, after all he has said, to accept the 49°, or any Compromise, without consulting the Senate. This shews the danger of his rash movements, dictated by motives of party. How utterly disgraceful for him to shrink from his duty thus and consult the Senate before accepting or refusing a Treaty. I cannot think he will do this.

In short, rumours and speculations are rife. People will suggest any thing and believe any thing rather than anticipate such a horrible thing as war without any earthly cause. [By February 1846, because of the problems with Mexico and because the British appeared willing to make concessions, Polk had changed his hard-line policy toward England over Oregon to one of willingness to compromise.]

I close this volume which I have for five, to me, most eventful years [1841–1846] made the repository of many of my thoughts. I have not been as diligent in recording them as I might and for long periods have omitted it altogether. I began, I state[d], because I had no friend to communicate my thoughts and would place them here. Now alas my thoughts are often too bitter to trust on record any where, to whisper to any one. I am wiser and I do not think a worse man than on 6th Feb. 1841. But I have not since then found a friend, while I have lost many that, were then if not *friends*, at least might pass for them. The period has been eventful to me. I have passed through many important scenes, many trying, many agonizing ones. They are not fully depicted in these pages. Often I could not endure my own thoughts and feelings long enough to paint them here.

The Scene is changed. I am once more at Silver Bluff, anchored I trust for life. In the woods, without society once more. Struggling to recover from the pecuniary sacrafices of these five years, to find, in solitude, comforts and consolations which the world has not afforded me, to establish a peaceful home for approaching age.

James Henry Hammond at age 35 in the uniform of the governor of South Carolina (1842–44). *(Courtesy of the South Caroliniana Library)*

James Henry Hammond at age 42 as painted by William Harrison Scarborough in 1849. (*Courtesy of University Archives of the University of South Carolina*)

James Henry Hammond, United States Senator from South Carolina (photograph taken by Mathew Brady, 1858). *(Courtesy of the South Caroliniana Library)*

Redcliffe, spring 1987 (photograph taken by Bill Rouda). *(Courtesy of Clemson University)*

V

*I have aimed to make a candid statement
of facts and to tell the unvarnished truth.*

---

1 APRIL 1846 – 30 DECEMBER 1849

1846

[Hammond, in forced retirement for over a year, began a fresh new diary-volume in April 1846.]

THE CHOICE
By [John] Norris—17th Century

No; I shan't envy him whoe'er he be
That stands upon the battlements of State;
   Stand there who will for me;
   I'd rather be secure than great:
Of being so high the pleasure is but small,
But long the ruin if I chance to fall.

Let me in some sweet shade serenely lie
Happy in leisure and obscurity;
   Whilst others place their joys
   In popularity and noise,
Let my soft moments glide obscurely on
Like subterranean streams, unheard, unknown.

Thus when my days are all in silence past
A good plain countryman I'll die at last;
   Death cannot choose but be
   To him a mighty misery,
Who to the world was popularly known
And dies a stranger to himself alone.

Illi mors gravis incubat, qui notus nimis Omnibus, ignotus moritur sibi
Quoted by [Francis] Bacon, Essay on "[Of] Great Place"

[Silver Bluff, 1 April 1846]

I have been reading to-day [Robert] Gibbes' Memoir of [James] De Veaux
and I could not help weeping when I reached the catastrophe. Poor fellow.
I used to dread dying in Rome when I was there. I visited the foreign
cemetary, where he lies, and shuddered at the thought of lying there, so
far off from home and all I loved. Bury me on the highway I have been
used to travel—let me still keep company with the wayfarers I have known
or who at least tread the soil I have been nurtured on. I knew De Veaux
well. I had seen him and been in his studio in Columbia. I felt as tho' I
had found an intimate friend when I met him in Paris in the spring of
1837. He breakfasted with me often there. I went with him to his atelier
for drawing from the living model. I was curious to see a naked woman in
a crowd of men. Poor D.'s timid and sensitive nature kept him unhappy
lest my presence should draw some sarcasm from the 20 or 30 ill-looking
and worse dressed young artist[s] there, while I was disgusted to see a woman
in such a state among such men without a blush or slightest shew of
modesty. Here Deveaux gave me a copy of Vandyke's Portrait of himself,
which he had painted and which is the best thing I have seen from his
easel—tho' I have seen his "Christ and Angels." I was touched with this
attention. I had been to Italy among the real works of art and felt contempt
for the gewgawism and tawdriness of every thing I then saw in Paris. De
Veaux was full of enthusiasm, as I had once been, in regard to Paris. I
advised him to go to Italy. He thought the Louvre the very Capitol of Art,
and I could not persuade him out of it. I saw he was deficent [sic] in
drawing. He said the French School was pre-eminent for that and evidently thought himself proficient. This defect became still more apparent
to me when I saw his after pictures in this country. But it seems he only
became sensible of it the year of his death. I proposed to him if he would
go to Italy, I would advance him Fifty Pounds a year as long as he wanted
it. This I knew would be an ample support for an artist there, beyond a
mere support, he would of course depend on his own exertions in Copying
etc. He did not receive my offer as I expected, tho' I urged it earnestly. It
was very far below Hampton's Letters of unlimited credit. But I did not do
foolish things of that sort. When I got to London some months after,
Deveaux was there. We had both in the interval taken the tour through
Belgium etc. I hunted him up and found him a way up near Regents Park

somewhere, brought him to my lodgings in Jermyn Street and made him take my wife's portrait. It was a wretched failure and mortified him dreadfully, but I made him take 10 sovereigns for it. I think he left for Paris before I came from London.

I don't remember meeting De Veaux again until 1840, I think, in Columbia. Possibly I may have seen him before that. But I remember then he was from the Richardson neighbourhood [Clarendon], where he had been painting. I took great interest in his pictures, praised, and found fault. I hardly think I offended even his sensitiveness. But when I got over there [to the Columbia townhouse] with my Gallery and was anticipating great pleasure from conversing with him about my pictures and his, he was very shy. He paid me only one visit, I think, and looked hastily round. He belonged to Manning, Richardson, and Young Wade [Hampton]. He knew better than I did (for understrappers and hangers on are quick in such knowledge and act instinctively on it) how hostile these people were to me. I did not suppose the two former particularly friendly, and I had been too unable to disguise my disgust at the *puppyism* of the latter to expect any warm regard from him. But I was not aware of that bitter hostility and unappeasable jealousy which exhibited itself afterwards so ruthlessly towards me. I ought to have taken more warning from the conduct of Deveaux, Gibbes, and Sid Johns[t]on, the lacqueys of that set. De Veaux best of all and least disguised. He never mentioned his going [back] to Europe to me. But finding it out I asked him to inquire about certain people in Rome for me. About 18 months after, I rec^d a letter from him about them, but it was not in a spirit to induce an answer.

When I knew DeVeaux in Paris, London, and Columbia, his whole imagination was taken up with *colours*, and wild action. Rubens, Titian, Paul Veronese, and Salvator Rosa were his favourites. Raphael and Claude he did not like and Michael Angelo he knew nothing about. It seems that his trip to Italy gave him higher conceptions of his Art, as I had anticipated it would, and his constant regret was that it was too late. I dare say he often thought of my advice and offer in Paris, which would have sent him 4 years sooner. My opinion when I saw his paintings in Columbia was that he had reached the perfection of his genius and never would be more than a third rate portrait painter. His Christ promised something better, and after reading his Journal I have a much better opinion of his talents in every way. And if it was not, as he thought, "too late," he might have done something had he lived. But his contracted, cramped style of drawing would have been hard to cure.

Yet I wept over the Poor fellow's untimely fate, was sorry I had not done more for him.

[Silver Bluff] 10 May 1846

I have just read Capt. [John C.] Fremont's Journal of his Expeditions to Oregon and California. He is a man of the Napoleon stamp and if troublous times ensue, he will, if spared, reach the Summit. A war of any duration will find him at its close Commander-in-Chief and then—

He is I understand a South Carolinian by birth, of which I am proud. [Fremont was born in Savannah, Georgia, but did attend the College of Charleston.] Son in Law of Col. [Thomas Hart] Benton, [Senator from Missouri, 1820–1850] of which I am not proud.

[On May 11,1846, Polk requested Congress to declare war on Mexico. War was declared on May 13 with a minimum of debate.]

[Silver Bluff] 3 June 1846

Capt. Fremont is already a Lt. Colonel, appointed by the President in the New Rifle Regiment. His name as an applicant had never reached us until the appointment was officially announced.

About the same time Col. Benton makes a fierce and destructive attack on the [Polk] Administration in reference to its Oregon policy. What does this mean? [Three days later, on June 6, Britain agreed to draw the Oregon boundary at the 49° North latitude and the Senate ratified the treaty on June 12.]

[Silver Bluff] 21 Oct. 1846

Gen. [George] McDuffie's resignation of his office as U. S. Senator was formally announced by the Editor of the Carolinian about the last of August, and very soon after [Franklin] Elmore was nominated in the Mercury by Ker Boyce. The nomination was followed immediately by several communications in the Carolinian, and I believe the Charleston papers, approving, and several of the Country papers also approved Editorially. The whole movement was a counterpart of that made in favour of Gov. Richardson in 1840 and was evidently concerted. I had not before supposed Elmore desired that Station. But he visited Washington in June and no doubt both Polk and Calhoun urged him to accept. It is a total sacrafice of his pecuniary interests and involves his ruin, since he only keeps up by his control in the Bank. I presume he has his reward in view elsewhere.

Some of the Country papers however nominated me, and some of my friends are very urgent that I should run, being of the opinion that with a sufficient effort I could be elected. I have only reflected on the matter. Besides the many losses and family inconveniences of such a thing, I believe my health forbids my going to Washington. I don't think it would permit me to serve my country or myself there, and that the only result would be to hasten the catastrophe, which I do not think is at best far off. I am wearing down by degrees, and latterly with rapid ones. I do not therefore desire to go to the Senate, where if my health was robust, I would be delighted to be. If it was the general wish, and the appointment was tendered to me, I could not resist such a mark of confidence, cost what it might. But it would be folly for me to go to the Legislature and *contend* for an office that every thing considered I do not desire. Every day, whether owing to increased feebleness of health or increasing disgust at the intriguing spirit which pervades politics more and more, I grow more averse to mingling openly in public affairs. I almost regret it is so. But I cannot help it. I ought to mention that after my nomination the Carolinian came out with a list of persons who were "spoken of" for Senator. It was in the following order: Elmore, Hammond, Cheves, Rhett, O'Neale, Butler (Judge), Richardson, Davie and Barnwell. I don't know to whom I owe my nomination, nor who has "spoken of" these gentlemen. They have all been silent and so have I been. But I have written to my friends what I have expressed here.

[Silver Bluff] 25 Nov. [1846]

The [South Carolina] Legislature met day before yesterday. I have heard nothing from there as yet, but I have no doubt of Elmore's election to the [United States] Senate. Pickens will probably persist in being a candidate and perhaps Davie also. They will only expose themselves. For my own part I should scarcely know what to do were I elected. It would interfere seriously and even ruinously with all my arrangements as regards my planting interest, and I believe that if I were in Columbia and saw any prospect of such an event, I would *peremptorily* decline. I have not done so thus far because I thought it likely I should be let off by simply manifesting a reluctance to take the office, if indeed I might not be beaten with all the efforts I could make. But I do not wish by any means to be beaten. It would not mortify me much except that it would have the appearance that I was a fallen public character, to recover from which would require me to enter public life again. My friends are instructed to keep my name out of the canvass unless the tide runs too strongly in my favour to be resisted, without my giving such offence as would not be forgotten as well as establishing for myself a character for sullenness and selfishness inconsistent with patriotism. But I make no doubt it will be easy enough to get me out of the scrape and that Elmore is the Senator or will be in a few days. There is but one thing that can prevent it. The Bank has been importunate this year and will be severely handled. Elmore may either be compelled to remain in order to retrieve himself there, or may be so injured by the discussion of the Bank matter as to lose his position altogether in public estimation.

Calhoun will be delighted with Elmore's election, expecting from him complete subserviency and the most skilful services in managing his affairs for him. But he will be greatly disappointed. Elmore has a game of his own to play. Indeed several of them. He is a Bankrupt. Polk professes the warmest friendship for him. He will cultivate it at Calhoun's expense if necessary. He wants a great many things of the President, and, among others, he wants contracts for iron, which he is making in Spartanburg and in which lies his only chance of retrieving his affairs. Besides all this Elmore is himself actually looking to the Presidency. Some Boston paper has, I am told, nominated him. Of course *he* thinks there is a chance, and will do all he can to ingratiate himself with the Democratic Party. He is very adroit, but I do not doubt he and Calhoun will split in a year, at most before the close of the second Session. Calhoun is too keen, and jealous to be fooled by Elmore.

But I hardly intended to write all this. A great clamour has been made this year in Charleston and elsewhere about giving the appointment of Presidential Electors to the people. Calhoun's opinion was loudly called for before the general election, but in vain. Just before, I sent an article to the Charleston Mercury which has been well received opposing this proposition. My ground was that the People should not exercise any power. Especially should [not] directly hold any elections, which could be as well executed and managed by *responsible* agents, already chosen. That the appointment of Electors would be virtually made by self-constituted Caucuses, who would soon assume the power of choosing all the officers and managing all the affairs of the State etc. etc. See article signed "Falkland: [The Appointment of Electors," Charleston Mercury, October 6,7,1846]. Calhoun has just now come out with his views on the same side. But his argument is more abstract and obscure than usual with him. Instead of taking the high grounds of true principles and sound policy, he rests mainly on the Compromises of the Constitution of the State. This more endangers those compromises than it strengthens his cause. Besides he admits the people may elect *by District* without violating them and thus surrenders the question of electing by the people directly. On that point he gives an opinion against it very decidedly but does not press it with either ability or zeal. On the whole I think he has injured the cause, tho' should the project fail he will be looked upon as having crushed it. My hope of its failure certainly rest more on my belief that the Senators from the Parishes will be true to their interests than that the Legislature will be governed by any elevated sentiments of public policy.

Mr. C's Memphis report will also be upon the tapis. I dissent in toto from his Constitutional Doctrines. He in fact gives up the whole cause of strict constitutional construction for wh[ich] SoCa has been so long struggling, under his lead apparently. His object is to get votes in the valley of the Mississippi, in which as usual he will fail. The West does not thank him, the East scoffs at his concessions. The South, I think and trust, will reject his doctrines. His argument is the most finished specimen of wiredrawing he has yet produced. In many parts it is absurd, in others trivial, in all unsound. By his formula of construction, any power may be derived from the Constitution not positively prohibited by it. Still the fixed fact remains that one half the Union will soon be directly interested in the navigation of the Mississippi, and its commerce is almost equal to the whole coasting trade. Such powerful interests will not be controlled by constitutional scruples. The only way to save the Constitution is to make a timely concession. I have proposed to W.F. DeSaussure and J.M. Walker of our Legislature and R.B. Rhett, our Rep. in Congress, to amend the Constitution and give Congress power to remove obstruction to the navigation of the Mississippi. This will preserve the Constitution and save us from improving the Tributaries of the Miss. and ultimately all the navigable streams in the Union. I would even include the chief Tributaries up to certain points rather than not *estop* proceedings somewhere. But the Improvement of the Miss. might satisfy and would be a fair offset to the Light Houses etc. on the Coast.

[Silver Bluff] 4 Dec. [1846]

The crisis in my fate which I have long apprehended would in some way come up has at length arrived. On the evening of the 29th ult. it was understood in Columbia that Elmore would not run for the Senate. The reason assigned was that it would ruin him [financially] and all those who were dependent on him. This might have been the case. But if so it must have been foreseen long before. There were other potent reasons. 1st. A contract with the Government to make Cannon Balls which was one of the objects he had in view as Senator was accepted by Gov. only a day or two before and this point was already gained. 2nd. Colcock, who was to succeed him as President of the Bank, declared he would bring to account all who [had] taken too much money from the Bank or had kept money too long. This would have been fatal to a large number. 3rd. It was ascertained that altho' no candidate, 55 votes were already pledged to me and more were expected. This was not agreeable [to Elmore] even tho' he might be elected. Col. Hampton for the 2nd reason was, it is said, active in inducing him to decline. As soon as it was known he was out of the field I was announced by acclamation and without consulting my authorized friends, who had previously declined to run me. Col. Hampton then took his stand. He sent Torre, a lick-spittle of his, to urge my friends not to run me *now* in consequence of my quarrel with him. A few years hence that would be blown over, and I might go in without objection. This was scouted. If I had done any thing which rendered me unworthy of the [United States] Senate now, a few years would not make me more worthy. Besides what guaranty was there that the same objections would not then be brought forward. Torre and Manning then threatened that the next morning an exposition would be made that would prostrate me forever. The next day Hampton took Col. J. M. Walker and Gen. Jamison, my friends, out of the House and told them I must not be run, that my election would destroy him, that if I run one of us must fall, and asked them to read certain documents which he had placed in the hands of Col. J. S. Ashe of the [state] Senate, and after reading which, he thought they would withdraw me. These gentlemen very properly replied that they would not be agents in my destruction and that Col. H. must make his publication through his own friends. They refused to read his papers, and it was agreed that Maj. [Alfred P.] Aldrich should come over to see me and get instructions how to meet them. Nothing could have been more proper or kinder to me, and I can never cease to feel the obligation. I was greatly shocked when I learned Hampton's course. To me it indicates a degree of folly scarcely consistent with sanity. What consummate impudence to suppose that the Legislature could not act in a public matter without deciding a quarrel in which he was a party. When Aldrich left on 1st Dec. there was a strong feeling of indignation at his thus attempting to thrust a private matter dispute into a State election. The causes of our quarrel I have never revealed nor even hinted at to any one save my wife. It would have been highly dishonorable for me to have done so. Yet could the whole truth be known it is Hampton and his family who would be prostrated, while I should escape with small damage. I am persuaded that he does not know the whole truth. But in any event, his attempt to make the Legislature avenge his private wrongs, over which he has slumbered for more than 3 years and that were almost forgotten by the Community, must stamp him a base, malignant, and miserable poltroon. So all sensible and honorable men must think of him, whatever they may think of me. I was compelled to disclose all to Aldrich in order to confer fully with him. I bound him, however, not only never to reveal it, but not even to hint that I had told him. It is highly important to me that Col. Hampton should herald his own infamy. Aldrich, after learning all, concurred with me that Hampton must be demented to make this issue and would certainly withdraw it. I gave him the following reply to Hampton's documents to which his only objection was that I assumed too much blame to myself. But I desire to acknowledge my full share of guilt. It is a penance due from me. It is the true, manly and magnanimous course and sooner or later it will be so deemed. Aldrich reached Columbia on his return last night. I would give a great deal to know what has transpired there today, but there is no mail for three days. Hampton and his set will be loud-mouthed and denunciatory if they pursue the course they threaten. The Legislature may resent it as dictatorial. It is more probable they will succumb, I being absent and my friends ignorant of my defence as well as entreated by me not to involve themselves, come what may. No doubt also, facts will be highly colored against me and the most infamous lies told. Manning is capable of any thing. He is, I am persuaded, at the bottom of the whole movement, and his object is to destroy me if he can, not caring who he may destroy also to effect it. He will, if he can, drive Hampton on to desperation. Robt. W. Barnwell is the man they run. Judge [Andrew Pickens] Butler is also said to be in the fold. The latter would not, I am persuaded, aid to injure me. If I am withdrawn, I am indeed prostrated, probably forever. If I am beaten, I shall be severely but not permanently injured. If I am elected, Hampton, I think, will challenge me [to a duel]. Had he done so at first or even when I left the Executive Office two years ago, I would have received his fire without returning it. But he has waived his private right to demand satisfaction from me both by his long delay and his vile attempt to avenge himself by an appeal to the public. I do not therefore feel myself bound to meet him, much less to receive his fire. I shall not, however, make up my mind on either point until more results are known to me. I hardly think he will resort to an attempt at assassination. Yet, if after his exposition I shall be elected, he will be so utterly broken down that nothing will be too desperate for him.

Here is a copy of the writing I gave Maj. Aldrich to be used at the discretion of my friends in Columbia.

"Being informed that in consequence of my nomination before the Legislature for a distinguished office, Col. Wade Hampton has threatened to make disclosures which he avers will be destructive to my character and that he has actually placed documents in the hands of Members of the Legislature for that purpose, I feel compelled to make a response altho' I have not directly or indirectly sought this nomination. The difficulties between us have been to me the source of inexpressible pain—the more that I am conscious of having committed a great indiscretion for which I have avowed to Col. Hampton and still feel the most profound regret. Influenced by those feelings I have for more than three years endured in unbroken silence a weight of odium more galling to me who has never hitherto concealed or had occasion to reproach himself for any material transaction of his life, than any other can conceive. After such a lapse of time I was not prepared to see an affair so painful and so purely private agitated again, much less introduced into the Legislature of the State and brought to bear upon elections.

It is not my intention now to disclose the causes of the differences between Col. Hampton and myself. It is my firm intention not to make, and not by any act or expression of mine knowingly to provoke from any quarter such a disclosure. If Col. Hampton chooses to make it himself, on him let all the responsibility rest, on me such a share of condemnation as an impartial public may award. If the documents alluded to comprise, as I have been informed they probably do, a correspondence between him and me, I can only say that I must submit to the construction which the community in its indulgent justice shall be pleased to put upon it and upon my conduct. My letter was written under the most deeply excited feelings, without the remotest idea that it would ever meet the public eye, and without my preserving any copy of it, or of Col. Hampton's note to me to which I can now refer. Should the documents contain a statement of the causes of our difficulties, I shall, unless it gives a gross miscolouring of facts, abide in silence the verdict of my fellow citizens. I shall neither attempt to vindicate or excuse being assured that not having done or designed to do anything criminal, the weakness of our common human nature will prove my best advocate and that only those will cast stones who are themselves without reproach.

"J.H. Hammond"

"Silver Bluff SoCa"
"2 Dec. 1846."

I need not say that all this has made me as unhappy as any human being can be.

[Silver Bluff] 6 Dec. [1846]

I have heard nothing more from Columbia and do not expect to hear for two days more. Of course I am as anxious as possible. There is to be a parade of both Regiments at Barnwell on Monday to form a Volunteer Corps for the Mexican War under a recent requisition of a Regiment from SoCa. One was last spring formed for that purpose and called "the Hammond Guards" in honor of me. I promised to attend at Barnwell and assist to reorganize it. The fact being that since the battle of Monterey our people are not so eager to volunteer as formerly. But I cannot go. I must remain here to meet the news from Columbia. Besides in my present state of feeling I should cut but a poor figure there, and, still more I think, it would be improper, while a blasting imputation is threatening me, that I should go down there to take part in a matter where I was proposed to be thus honored.

[Silver Bluff] 9th Dec. [1846]

I have been so much engaged in writing letters that I have not found time to record the results of the Election for Senator, which came by the mail on Monday (7th). My friends report my defeat and victory. Beaten by Judge Butler for the Senate, but signally triumphing over Hampton and his set—so say all my friends, and one who was a *trimmer*. Up to Thursday Hampton and Co. were fierce. That day Pemberton was in town and returned home to write me a most feeling and painful letter. On Friday the election came on and P. added a P.S. on Saturday evening to say that "more than an entire re-action" had taken place on the receipt of my statement by Aldrich on Thursday night. It was a "terrible mortification" he says. "They are beaten" says Clark "and fear you—they *show* it." Walker and Aldrich write that I am far stronger than ever, all the others say so too. After my letter arrived, no man could be found to acknowledge he had seen Hampton's "documents" and Ashe said he was not authorized to shew them. The race was with Judge Butler. On the first ballot I rec^d 66 votes, Butler 56, Davie 32. On the last Butler got 83, just a majority. I have not seen a full Statement. There were four ballotings. Davie at last withdrew and his friends went for Butler on a pledge that B's friends would go for De Saussure for Chancellor. This logrolling defeated me: It is distinctly understood that this and the desire to make a vacancy on the Bench elected Butler. No man but Butler could have beaten me. Besides his Judgeship and his popularity, he is an Edgefield man and took there 7 votes no one else could have got. Had they been cast for me the vote on first ballot would have been 49 against 73. No doubt others voted for him who would have voted for me against any one else. For our friends are almost every where the same. There has always existed the warmest friendship between all his family and me, as well as between him and me. Under the circumstances I did not think he would have allowed himself to be used against me—the tool of a set I know he despises, and who have done him the greatest injury. His Brother [Pierce Mason Butler] when Governor, was detected in cheating *his young friends* at cards and won large sums from them. This set—not Hampton—but all the rest have been his denouncers. I am sure the Judge knows nothing of all this nor of his Brother's delinquencies, or he would not have joined to sacrafice me for much smaller errors. It has ruptured our ties. I *never* can feel any friendship or respect for him. He is a proud, ambitious man. So are some of our *best* men. I always thought him generous and magnanimous and for these qualities I loved him. I love him no longer. And from this source arises all the pain I feel in this affair. Alas! who is to be relied on? I ought not perhaps to ask this question, for a more glorious set of friends man never had than mine, with one or two exceptions, have proved in this *ordeal*. Wrapped in mystery myself, and denounced by men standing at the head of our chivalry, they have stood by me with unshaken confidence and courage—fidelity and prudence. I will name those that I owe most to so far as I yet know—Maj. A.P. Aldrich, Col. J.M. Walker, Gen. D.F. Jamison, W.G. Simms, Edmund Bellinger, Wm. Gist, J.A. Alston, Col. De Treville, E.M. Seabrook, J. Dukes, and Col. John Bauskett. These men have stood the brunt of the battle now and heretofore for me. I owe them a debt of gratitude I never can repay. There are others tho' less prominent but equally sincere—as Pemberton, Harley, Wilson etc. I will try hereafter to name all. As to Hampton, his grossness, malignancy, and poltroonery seem to be perfectly appreciated by all. His position is not such a one as can be well reached by public opinion, as he is a candidate for nothing but the servile flattery of lick-spittles, bon vivants and jockeys, and for the forbearance of the banks and his other creditors. It may be that no intimation of the real state of opinion will reach him. If it did, his pride, not his sensibility, would be so wounded that he would become desperate and probably challenge me. Such a contingency may happen and would not at all surprise me. After waiting three years to demand redress of me, I should hardly have been bound to give it, but his recent attempt to make the Legislature his avengers deprives him of all shadow of *claim* on me. Still, perhaps it would be my best course to meet him. I shall not decide the matter until it becomes necessary. I would not like to kill him. I rather pity than hate him. Besides in such an unfortunate event public opinion would re-act against me. Still I feel now no desire to expose my life to him gratuitously now, as I once might have done.

Altogether I am rejoiced as events have turned out in regard to every thing, save that Butler was the man to beat me. I really did not desire to go to Washington, believing that my health would not enable me to achieve distinction there or do much for the country, while my occupations here are both important and agreeable. I have heard that Gen. J[ames] H[opkins] Adams took an active part against me. I trust it is a mistake. He has always been a warm friend. When the quarrel between me and Hampton first took place, he and H. were at points. I had been supporting him against Manning whom he

[Several pages were removed from the Diary at this place, one of the few instances of censorship. Later accounts by Hammond of his dalliances with his nieces are however left untouched. The diary account picks up here with the Hampton family men having just become aware of Hammond's indiscretions with the young Hampton women.]

. . . .of small pocket pistols and ascertained in the course of my purchase that both J[ohn] Preston and [John] Manning [brothers-in-law of Wade Hampton] had supplied themselves the day before. Could they expect an attack from me? Such cowards as they are fear every thing and I could not but smile to myself when I found what they had done. Having however some confidence in the good feelings of J[ohn] Preston, whom I had stood by in some of his past trials, I addressed him a note requesting an interview and expressing my desire to bury this matter in oblivion and to make due atonement. I knew by the pistol purchase he was acquainted with all that had happened and also by the Camp Hunt. I knew he was acquainted with the ways of the girls, and to him I could give a full statement of every thing, which I would not do to any one nearer to Hampton. I sent the note by Clark's servant to avoid any suspicion of my wife. In my piazza I awaited the answer. I saw a servant on horseback pass backwards and forwards several times down the street. He went, I did not doubt, to William (Preston), and thus I discovered that he was in on the secret also. In an hour [John] Preston returned an answer declining to take any part— declaring that "atonement and oblivion were impossible" and announcing the termination of our relations. I now saw that all chance of reconciliation was at an end and that I must take a decided course for myself. I would gladly have met any of them in the field. But this course was out of the question. Hampton I could not harm after what I had done to his daughters, and I would not war with his understrappers. Besides, knowing their cowardly natures, I did not doubt they would refuse a challenge on the ground that I had disgraced myself, and I could not think of involving a friend in such a matter. My policy then was concealment. Profound and utter secrecy. And for this course there was the most powerful reasons. 1st. For my wife's sake, to whom I dared not say a word of the matter. 2nd. For the sake of Hampton's daughters, on whom publicity must inflict indelible disgrace. And 3rd. I was Governor of SoCarolina, and such a tale of scandal, which my position would carry over the union, would injure her character through me. I therefore resolved, come what might, never to allude to the matter to any human being and, if it should be ascertained that there was a break between Hampton and me, to decline satisfying any inquiries in regard to it. And to save my wife's feelings, as well as enable the other side to conceal also, I determined to remove finally from Columbia at the close of the [December 1843] Session, as I had arranged to do anyhow the June following. A few days after this Guignard sent me some bonds on which I was Hampton's surety, *cancelled*. I then inclosed Hampton's collaterals, deposited for my safety, to him and on a slip of paper stated my intention to remove [to Silver Bluff]. My purpose was to give him intimation of my plan that he might make his own to correspond, supposing that concealment must be equally desirable to him.

By the time the Legislature met [on November 27, 1843] it seemed generally known there was a blow up. But I heard none of the reasons that were assigned for it. Manning's unintended and *withdrawn* denunciation of me, I did not hear of until the last of February [1844] following. My best friends made no allusion to the matter before me. I saw very soon the despicable game of the other party. Notwithstanding my letter to Hampton and my announcement of my intention to leave Columbia their low and cowardly malignity led them to seek a most pitiful revenge. Their desire was to black ball me and to mortify me and mine by keeping us out of Society and all respectable persons from coming to our House. I chafed to get at them. But my reasons for concealment were paramount. I was careful in selecting guests at my dinner parties and they were well attended. Our Ball [went] brilliantly, tho' I knew they endeavoured to keep many from attending. To B. F. Taylor and W. F. De Saussure I am very grateful for carrying their families in spite of everything. My wife, ignorant of every thing, sent invitations to the whole set. To have objected to it would have rendered a disclosure necessary. To her I pretended ignorance of all causes of difficulty and made light of their not coming to see us. I told her it was all between Hampton and me and might blow over. Thus I passed this horrible Session, enduring the agonies of the damned. About the 26th Dec. [1843] we left Columbia with all our effects.

It was not until six weeks later I learned the rumours in circulation. I received the first intimation of them then, I think, and gradually heard more and more. When I learned the report that I had run away from Columbia and dared not return, I wrote over appointing a time to go there and accordingly in April passed through and remained a day or two on my route to the Orangeburg encampment. I came through there again and remained a day in September. I was resolved to go through my duties come what might. Not by any means desiring to provoke, but determined to meet any attack. I went armed and would not have submitted to the slightest personal indignity or to any public insult.

I expected almost as a matter of course either a challenge or an assault at the close of my term of Office and remained in Columbia 24 hours after the inauguration to give an opportunity, tho' by no means desiring that either should happen. For by that time I saw that bloodshed would in no way relieve me, and as yet my wife knew nothing, and I wished she never should know even the truth. Nothing was done. I left Columbia supposing that time would in its lapse bury our difficulties with ourselves and that they would certainly never be agitated again. For Hampton must, I thought, desire every thing to remain concealed and, if the causes of our quarrel were thereafter revealed, must be doubly disgraced by the injuries done to his family and his cowardly failure to revenge them. Here again I calculated without fully estimating the coarseness and fatuity of Hampton, the reckless malice of Manning, and the insensibility of the Prestons—on fools, knaves, and malignants no calculations can ever be made with safety.

How and by whom my familiarities with Hampton's daughters were disclosed [to Hampton] I have no means of ascertaining. But I must think he knows, after all, but little about it. I cannot but make this excuse. He must only have heard of what happened on the 13 April 1843, and doubtless believes that I made a gross attempt to seduce perhaps to force his daughter Catherine. I question whether he has ever said one word to the girls on the subject. It has come to him through others, probably from women, and they have given their own colouring. Yet in my letter to him I spoke of my dalliances with his Daughters, using the plural, and that they had been long continued. A man of any sense would have been led by this to probe the whole matter to the bottom. But Hampton is not such.

The charges that Hampton might *truly* bring against me are susceptible of the highest colouring, and it would doubtless be given to them not only by him but by a large portion of the public. Here was, it might be said, a systematic attempt to train up pure and innocent young girls to debauchery, commencing from their tender years, by one who should have [been] their guide and protector, who was the husband of their mother's only sister, their Father's friend, in whom every confidence was implicitly reposed. It would be forgotten that this thing commenced with one [Harriet] who, a woman at 12, was then 16 to 17 years old (in 1839–40) and who had been almost a stranger to me. The loose manners and ardent temperaments of these lovely and luscious creatures would never be known. My own morbid and solitary habits, engendered by disease, rendering me keenly alive to every excitement of which I could partake without immediate suffering, would not be taken into the account. And without a knowledge of the *antecedents*, a simple statement of the occurrence of 13 Ap[ril] 1843 would indicate a deliberate attempt to perpetrate a base crime. Yet I declare that on that night I felt no more animal excitement than I do at this moment. And worn down as I was with fatigue and full, the very moment, of anxious cares, I was almost literally incapable of sexual connection.

And how could I meet these charges? Could I make before the public the statement I have given here? If I did, I should be stamped as a most infamous betrayer of secrets that no provocation should have instigated me to lay *before the world*, even if I could prove every word I state. But I have no proof, unless I summon the young ladies themselves. Of course I would not be believed. One must reflect on all the matters more fully than I can here suggest before they can see it to the full extent how utterly powerless I have been and still am in this affair. And how all important to me, as well as to all, concealment has been. A concealment which I have borne every thing to keep up, but which I now find has never been appreciated by the stolid intellects and coarse sensibilities of my enemies.

The truth is that after all the consideration I have given to the matter, I cannot pretend to justify myself. I feel that I am worthy of great, very great condemnation. I condemn myself and can plead only in excuse my sincere contrition, and the inexpressible tortures I have already suffered. It is true David took Uriah's wife, and he was regarded as a favourite of heaven, that Caesar spared no woman, that in all ages and countries down to our present day and nation the very greatest men that have lived have been addicted to loose indulgences with women. It is the besetting sin of the strong, and of the weak also, of our race. Among us now Webster and Clay are notorious for it, and President Harrison got his wife's niece with child. This last is my case only a thousand times worse. Still I cannot conceal from myself that I *have done wrong, grievously wrong* and I *dare not vindicate it*. May God forgive me.

We are taught by our Saviour to pray that we may not be lead [sic] into temptation. Who could know as he did the strength of our desires and the weakness of our resolutions? If I have erred, as I have greatly, let the greatness of my temptation be considered. Here were four lovely creatures from the tender but precocious girl of 13 to the mature but fresh and blooming woman nearly 19 (in 1840–1), each contending for my love, claiming the greater share of it as due to her superior devotion to me, all of them rushing on every occasion into my arms and covering me with kisses, lolling on my lap, pressing their bodies almost into mine, wreathing their limbs with mine, encountering warmly every portion of my frame, and permitting my hands to stray unchecked over every part of them and to rest without the slightest shrinking from it, in the most secret and sacred regions, and all this for a period of more than two years continuously. Is it in flesh and blood to withstand this? Is there a man, with manhood in him and a heart susceptible of any emotions of tenderness, who could tear himself from such a cluster of lovely, loving, such amorous and devoted beings? Nay are there many who would have the self-control to stop where I did? Am I not after all entitled to some, the smallest portion of, credit for not going further? If there are any who *utterly* condemn me, I cannot but think theirs is the virtue of the closet, removed from temptation, incapable of realizing the extent of those by which I was beset. If there exists a record of any who have resisted equal seductions to a greater extent than I have, from which they did not free themselves by a violent effort and fly the daily importunities of it, I cannot but believe that record must be of legendary lore, and the hero of it a creature of chivalric romance. Joseph *fled. I could not.* At least I could not without encountering inconveniences and surrendering purposes which I deemed as important as the dangers I should leave behind me. In resolving to stand my ground, and to rely on my own strength, I perhaps proposed more than human power could accomplish. The result has proved that it was so in my case.

There are many reasons why [Wade] Hampton [II] and his set should take up this matter against me with more than common virulence and pursue it even to their own disgrace. Hampton is a man of strong and unconquerable prejudices. He opposed my marriage [to Hampton's sister-in-law, Catherine Fitzsimons]. I defied him and, after it, was elected to Congress not only without his aid, but against his wishes. Our cordiality never was perfect. At times it seemed so. When in Columbia he applied to me in his severest troubles, but only then. I rescued him from a cata[strophe] in Charleston in 1842 (races), I think, by arranging, not however involving myself in, his debt. I saved him afterwards from a duel with Wm Gregg with much difficulty, which I hardly think any other could have done. In 1843 (races) I sold his Gadsden place to Singleton for him, when tight pressed and in despair of selling. I also arranged his business with Moore in Augusta and secured him $8,000 there, which but for me he would have lost inevitably. These were his emergencies. In such he came to me. At other times he always assumed somewhat of a lofty air. The truth is he felt, and so did all his set, Manning, Preston, etc., my great superiority over them, and they could not ordinarily brook it. He threw away $30,000 to make his house [Millwood] finer than mine. And he was galled, and all of them were, that, besides every thing else, I beat them in *their own line*, furniture, balls, and dinner parties. All were exceedingly jealous of me. [John Laurence] Manning could not conceal it. He built his fine house in Clarendon to beat me, and he endowed a scholarship in [South Carolina] College [in 1846] because I had presented to it a lot of land. This miserable jealousy has had a great influence in all the events of our difficulties. It was this that instigated Hampton to sacrafice even his own daughters to denounce me lately in order to prevent my being elected [U. S.] Senator. He would have bursted if I had been elected. Such is the heart of man or rather such [are] the hearts of purse-proud fools, who claim positions which God has not given them the intellects to win or to hold.

In the preceding narrative I have aimed to make a *candid* statement of facts and to tell the unvarnished truth. I have also stated the colouring *against me* of which the affair is susceptible. I will now show how without any violation of truth the case may be coloured in my favour. I could with propriety make the following statement.

After many years of non intercourse between Col. Hampton and myself which extended in a great degree to our families, we were at length brought together at a period when his eldest daughter [Harriet] had reached her 16th year, and during the next two years we and our families became gradually more and more intimate, about which time I removed to Columbia and was thrown into constant communication with all his children and especially his daughters, the four eldest of who[m] were then in their 14th, 15th, 17 and 19th years. From the first I had found all of these young ladies extremely affectionate, lavish of their kisses and embraces, professing great love for me, and not only permitting but promptly responding to every species of dalliance which circumstances brought about between us. I had not long been in Columbia before I felt called on to reflect seriously upon the character of my intercourse with them and to adopt one of three courses. First, I might put an end to it by ceasing to indulge myself in toying with them. But after a few slight trials I was satisfied that this could only be effected by removing from Columbia or again opening the breach between our families. Secondly, I might, at least so I believed, have easily seduced any or all of them, and thus carried our intimacy to the end which its closeness seemed to indicate as the one *almost inevitable*. But this I could not for a moment think of doing. Thirdly, I might continue that intimacy for the present on the existing terms, and trust to time to afford an opportunity to embrace the first course suggested, and to my own self-control to avoid the second. Unfortunately I adopted this middle course. And for two years [1841–1843] I gave way to the most wanton indulgences. It would be improper to state in detail what these indulgences were. It will be sufficient to say that they extended to every thing short of direct sexual intercourse, that for two years they were carried on not with one, but indiscriminately with all of them, that they were perfectly habitual and renewed every time or very nearly every time we met at my house in Columbia, which was never less than once a week while I was there, and most usually much oftener, that they came *voluntarily* thus often to my house, and that during the whole period no one of them took the least offense, not only did not resist, but did not even attempt to check any amorous advances made by me, nay again and again made the advances themselves, so much so as often to excite my astonishment and to fill my mind with the most extraordinary suspicions as to their past experience.

At length after two years had thus elapsed about the 13 April 1843 one of them [Catherine, the next to the eldest Hampton daughter] took offence at a familiarity from me, which under the circumstances and considering all that had passed between us excited my surprise. In an instant however I fully recovered myself and decided on my course. I had never designed anything criminal and did not on this occasion, but at this first check I saw clearly and at once the full extent of my past indiscretions. I begged pardon and as I understood received it from this young lady then approaching 19 years of age. And I resolved from that time forward never more to take the slightest liberty either with her or her sisters. I remained some 7 or 8 weeks longer in Columbia before removing for the Summer and my intercourse with all these young ladies was frequent and as cordial as ever it had been, save that there was no more wanton toying between us. They were at my house as often as usual and attended a large ball there given to their Brother [Christopher Hampton] and his Bride [Mary Elizabeth McCord], while I was at Col. Hampton's a number of times. I think oftener, owing to circumstances, than was my custom. I saw nothing that [would] lead me to suppose for a moment that any difficulties would ever arise from what had heretofore passed between us, but on the contrary left Columbia under the impression that our relations had at length assumed a proper footing and [was] full of self-congratulation that such was the case. I never knew to the contrary until my return to Columbia with my family in the fall, where on the 1st Nov. 1843 I rec^d a note from Col. Hampton denouncing me in the coarsest terms. I could not for a moment doubt the grounds of it, tho' they were not stated. Whether the facts of my intercourse with his daughters had reached him through third persons, or whether they had communicated them, and if so whether they were influenced by indignation at what I had been doing without check for many years, or at which I had for the last eight weeks we were together *omitted* to do, I did not then nor do I now know or have any data on which to form a reasonable conjecture. However Col. Hampton may have been made acquainted with the facts, they were no doubt stated in the strongest form against me. This was a natural conclusion. And there was another most painful one to which I was on mature reflection forced to come, that happen what might, my inevitable part was to *endure* as *patiently* as *possible* the consequences of my own errors, since neither my own conscience nor public opinion would sustain me in seeking any satisfaction from those I had already injured; and that the most I could do would be to defend myself from any attempts to assault or cast any public indignity upon me. Hence it has been my first wish to bury the whole affair in oblivion as speedily as possible.

[Silver Bluff] 26 Dec. [1846]

Further information from Columbia leads me to suppose that altho' the course of Hampton is very generally regarded as unfair, base, and cowardly, some response in word or act is expected of me. I am not aware that my immediate friends expect or desire this, but the [h]oi polloi do. This arises in part from the natural curiosity of the public to pry into this matter and get the kernel of it, and partly because they are always anxious to witness a tragedy, whether real or fictitious. Some of my friends write me that the matter will soon be forgotten or laughed at, others that it will never be mentioned again, others that it has increased my real influence. Col. Trotti, who was here last Sunday, seemed to think I should remain perfectly quiet, and Simms writes that *patience* is still my cue. Still, some intimate that I should shew myself abroad and hint that certain characters must be silenced. Now as to taking the offensive in this matter, I must candidly confess I have a nervous horror of it. I am in the wrong. It is not to my notions either to bully or fight through. Nor do I believe that such a course would have any other effect than simply to prove my courage. That however has not, it seems, been really questioned throughout, and Hampton's course affords palpable proof that he at least fears me. I cannot call him to account. I feel no disposition to kill him. Besides it would rupture many ties yet unbroken, and in fact it would destroy me ultimately in public opinion, however lightly some may think of such a thing now. I must not take his life with any appearance of deliberation. It would injure me seriously to do it in a duel if he were even the challenger. Shall I then stoop to the understrappers to show my courage and satisfy those who have been fighting? I have no great inclination for it. Still I am balancing in my mind whether I should not seek a meeting with Col. [John] Ashe, Senator from Charleston, in whose hands Hampton placed his documents and who has said enough to entitle me either to demand satisfaction or draw a demand from him by denouncing him as a bully employed by Hampton to do his dirty work etc. Such a course would gratify the masses and probably put it out of Hampton's power to procure another substitute. As Ashe, after seeing the "Documents", has given his opinion against me, I might and possibly ought to make him responsible for this opinion. On the other hand, every one knows him to be an ass whose intellects are so narrow that his judgement is of little weight in any matter, while he is the very man to be duped by such designing poltroons as Hampton, Manning, and Wm. C. Preston, who I think advised this move and selected Ashe. It is all very like Preston. I feel a sort of contempt mingled with commiseration for Ashe, and, however others might think, I cannot *feel* that I should gain anything by chastising him. Why should I wreak my vengeance on the mere tools in this matter. There are besides other objections. Such a step must bring Hampton forward again. As matters now stand he is a convicted dastard who, not having nerve to redress his own wrongs, puts forward bullies to do it for him and calls on the Legislature of the State to avenge him in a private and most *delicate family* matter. Sooner or later the bluntest and most prejudiced mind must see them in this light, as all sensible men do already. If he is not already, he must soon be fully aware of public sentiment. Indeed I am told he is quite chop-fallen. Yet he cannot possibly extricate himself honorably now. If he were to challenge or attack me, he would gain no credit, for it would be at once seen he was driven to it by desperation. But if I bring on a difficulty with his friend on his account, I give him a chance to *retrieve himself.* He can step forward to rescue him and others, make a shew of courage in a generous cause, and, if his pride so far overcomes his fears as to enable him to go through it well, he will make an indelible impression that he was influenced in his past course towards me by other feelings than that sheer cowardice which I know has also deterred him from seeking my life. Thus by making this side issue, from which I cannot in any event gain much, I may enable Hampton to get upon his legs again. There is another objection to this course. It must end in an exposure of the whole cause of the quarrel, and, if I make the move that brings it out, the odium of the revelation will, after all I have suffered to avoid this, rest on me at last. Now I not only wish to avoid this, but it would be far the best policy for me to let the matter drop where it now is. The public knows nothing certainly. They will believe or not believe hereafter as they please. And they will disbelieve if circumstances should make me a favourite. But the whole truth once out *on authority*, there will no longer be a chance for me to avoid the stigma, such as it is, of being a roué. On the masses the impression this would make I should not so much regard, tho' far from wishing to see it. But there are female ties, yet remaining dear to me, that would be broken. Many of my wife's family, now entirely friendly, might feel called on to take part against me after such exposure, and it is certain that few ladies would visit us for a long time. All this would be extremely painful. I cannot therefore but think that profound concealment on my part is still my undoubted policy and that I ought not to hazard an exposure of this matter for any light purpose. Still I am very unhappy and dissatisfied with the state of affairs and cannot but form many projects for bringing things into a more agreeable condition. I would jump at an opportunity to settle and bury all, by fighting one or even more duels. Yet these must be thought of with great deliberation. I must not miss in my antagonists nor on the grounds on which such a meeting shall be brought about. I have been patient and long-suffering. I must bear the goad yet longer and bide my time. At the very least hear all and know certainly how men and things stand before I move.

[Silver Bluff] 5 Jany 1847

I have rec^d letters from both the Butlers. Col. [Pierce Mason] Butler is full of compliments, says I am stronger than I ever was in the State etc. etc. Senator [Andrew Pickens] Butler is very cautious. His aim is to disconnect himself from the Hampton movement and to re-establish our relations, being evidently ashamed of the manner of his election and afraid that I will oppose him. I have made a diplomatic reply, which he will feel deeply I think, in which his course towards me is contrasted both with mine towards him and my other friends to me and in which I concur with him that my enemies did not originate his nomination, meaning on my part that he was not their *first* choice, but the tool they used only because it was efficient against me. I also concur in the desire that the result will engender no *ill feeling* between us, but do not intimate a wish to re-estab-

lish our relations. I say that *at this time* it would have been very inconvenient to me to be elected. I don't wish to draw a line and make him an
open enemy, but I mean to hold myself at full liberty to *oppose him* if
circumstances require it. He has betrayed my friendship and it cannot be
renewed. As to Col. B[utler] I shall not answer his letter. I have long
thought him a scoundrel utterly devoid of principle, yet have weakly sustained him because (tho' justly) he was abandoned by most of his former
friends and out of regard to his family. He is now gone with his Regiment
to Mexico, where he will do nothing creditable to himself or the State.
[Pierce Mason Butler was killed at the Battle of Churubusco.] My information from all quarters is that there has been a great re-action in my
favour already, that my forbearance is appreciated and Hampton's baseness
comprehended. I never have doubted that the ultimate judgement of the
country would fix an indelible stigma of utter disgrace upon a man, who
not only did not resent but made *political capital* out of an attempt upon
his daughters' virtue. The very idea is horrible and would be incredible if
it had not happened. Yet I pity Hampton. He is the dupe and victim of
Manning and Preston, who would destroy him and his to prostrate me. I
can now see but one course for Hampton to pursue and that is to attack
me the first time he meets me. To challenge me would be to throw himself upon my mercy for he knows I am not bound to meet him. In his
desperation therefore he has no course left but to assault me. I hope his
fears will so far get the better of his malice that he will not do it. If he
thinks I ought to challenge or assault him as I have sometimes thought he
did, he is the most self-deluded man I ever knew. How would I be sustained in adding injury to insult by shooting him? My letters rec^d and
written about this time will give a fuller insight into affairs than I can do
here. The former are all filed in my familiar correspondence of 1846, at
least up to 1 June.

[Silver Bluff] 23 Jany [1847]

[George] McDuffie came down on the 16th inst. and remained with me
until the 21st. His health seems somewhat feebler than it did two years
ago, but unless he has an attack of inflammatory cold or something of the
sort I think he may last many years yet. His mind seems fully as clear and
vigorous as ever. He seemed extremely friendly and free in all kinds of
communication. He spoke to me of his surprise at Butler's election and
attributed it entirely to log-rolling. To others he has expressed indignation
I am told. He made no remarks about Hampton's course, and when I

mentioned it he said the votes I had got satisfied him it could not have materially affected the election. It so happened that W. G. Simms and Aldrich came up the day after McDuffie did, and Simms remained also until the 21st. Simms is collecting materials for McDuffie's biography and this was a fortunate accident for him. I drew McD. out on all occasions I could for the benefit of Simms. I conversed freely and fully with the latter about the Hampton business, and he concurs entirely in my past course and the one I propose henceforth. He entered fully into all my views and feelings in the matter. He says he was informed two years ago in Columbia by *good authority* (Col. R. H. Goodwyn) that the charge against me was that of seducing one of Col. Hampton's daughters and of going so far finally as to attempt violence. That I threw indecent pictures in her way. That the matter leaked out while H[ampton] was in Tennessee in Oct. 1843. That hearing it when he returned home, he armed himself with his gun and was on his way to shoot me when W. C. Preston interposed, shewed him how such a course would affect his family and induced him to desist and to send me the note he did, which was written by Preston. This story tallies so well with what I know that it may all be true so far as H. and others are concerned. I am of opinion however H. knew of these things before he went to Tenn. to the great Race there. I judge by his manouvre of the hunt and the girls ceasing to write me in Sept., *before* he went. Goodwyn's story is that John Preston, Manning, and young Wade could [only] with difficulty be restrained from attacking me. Yet I was with them, and W. C. P[reston] also, in friendly intercourse up to the time of H.'s return from Tenn., that for about a week before that I had been in Columbia. Who could have told all these things and for what motive? Clearly Hampton has had some confidant in this matter who has betrayed him to injure me. I do not doubt that Manning is this Traitor, and that W. C. Preston has acted the same part.

Aldrich says Members openly declared during the ballottings for the Senator that they went for a *vacancy* on *the Bench*—not for Butler or against me. And that one young man, unmarried, who did not vote for me, said that after all the fuss made no man who valued his standing could marry one of the Hampton girls. Others no doubt said or at least thought so too. [They never married.] So much for Hampton's revenge on me. I deeply regret this. I feel no joy but the sincerest remorse to have had any hand in blasting these girls whom I still love. I have faithfully and under the most trying circumstances done all in my power to avert injury from them and shall continue to do so. *I have again and again declared that I have never seduced or attempted to seduce any of them and that I believe them virtuous. I have repeated this frequently since the elections.* The effect of this if believed will be to throw me under the imputation, after my own confession, of having acted very improperly in some other matter where temptations might not have been so great and misconduct would be less likely to be overlooked. Knowing all this I have made this fresh and voluntary sacrafice to save these dear girls whom their own Father has destroyed.

[Silver Bluff] 21st Feb. 1847

I rec^d a letter a few days ago from Judge [Nathaniel] Beverly Tucker of Virginia which really afflicts me. He was a correspondent of mine when I was in Congress and renewed the correspondence with me a few months since. This letter was highly complimentary and in it he intimates a hope and expectation that I should succeed Mr. Calhoun as Leader of the State Rights Party. He speaks of anointing me for it. My partial friends in this State have often spoken to me in the same strain. But I attributed their expressions to personal regard and did not regard them as referring to any influence beyond SoCa. Have some of them met Judge Tucker, or how has he taken up this idea? His remarks prove that it exists out of the State. Now what afflicts me is my perfect conviction that I can never meet any such expectations. It is very painful to know that one *must fail*. This feeling makes me look with absolute horror on the idea of re-entering public life, and if I can, without sacraficing my present position and reputation totally, I mean to avoid it. Without adverting to any deficiency of mental powers, it is enough for me to believe that my past training has not prepared me to fill such a position as the one suggested. I have seen little of public service. I know but slightly the leading public men, and I have not been as close an observer of events and characters even as I might have been with my limited opportunities. I might however make up for much of all this by diligent study and active intercourse with the world even now. But alas, I have not the health. *I have no health*. I can barely keep myself alive by regular habits and the most careful avoidance of over fatigue, mental or physical. I cannot sit up in a chair an hour at a time unless under considerable excitement. The least irregularity in food, exercise, or sleep overcomes me completely. What a mere shell of a man I am, out of whom to make the Leader of the Forlorn Hope of our Republican Institutions? If I had the physical powers, I would not hesitate to do all in my power to prepare myself for any and every position to which I might by chance be called. And I own I should esteem the one suggested as the highest post in America. But with such a wreck of a constitution as mine is, it would be folly even to think of such a thing, and it is painful to be designated for it by any one. Whatever may be intended—and I do not doubt the idea has been suggested in the kindest feelings, if not the sincerest—I feel that it is a mocking. Even while I write now, my temples burn with a scorching heat and my hand stiffens. I have not stood on my feet to talk for some months without a constant swimming in the head, and in a few moments my voice grows husky. Shall I ever be better? I fear not. My God what a fate is mine. Stricken in the bud! Not stricken and finishing in the very germ, but when so much of the flower was expanded as to give promise at least of good fruit, that is doomed to decay ere it can be tasted. Oh that I were sound. If not to serve my country and win a name, yet only to enjoy myself in "leisure and obscurity." I could bear the mortification of failing all public expectation, if I had only health and strength to make life agreeable. Alas it is now a burden to me.

[Silver Bluff] 6 March [1847]

When my Annual Message of 1844 was read, Pickens after consultation with Mr. Calhoun introduced resolutions cut and dried to answer me expressing the greatest confidence in the Democratic Party and Mr. Polk I think his name was mentioned—He was certainly meant and the object was to keep Mr. C. on the right side of the Dem. Party at whatever cost. The resolutions passed both Houses, the Senate unanimously. I then said, "Gentlemen you will have to swallow all this in six months." I calculated then Mr. Polk would dismiss Mr. C. from the post of Secretary [of State] and then the split would take place. But Mr. C. forebore when that occurred [and returned to the Senate]. It was too purely and obviously a *personal* matter. But he nursed his wrath. In the meantime the Administration becoming thoroughly Free Trade and Anti-internal-improvement, I was cordially reconciled to it. Not so Mr. C. He divided on the Oregon affair very properly. On the Declaration of War with Mexico Mr. C. was prepared to leave the Administration, but he could not get a single follower. But the Whigs during this Session have harried Mr. Polk and raised an Anti-War Party and Mr. C. *has joined them*—abandoned and denounced the Administration and indulged his mean malignity so far as to expel Ritchie from the Senate floor, in consequence of some severe strictures of his. In this no one joined him of the Democrats, but our other Senator Butler (very reluctantly) and Yulee and Westcott, two miserable devils sent to the Senate from Florida, most disgraceful company and a very puerile affair, that of Ritchie. As to the war there is no sort of ground for supposing that the President has not acted fairly honestly and done the very best he could. It is not certain any one could have done better. It has been a most difficult and embarrassing matter from the first. At best Mr. C. has seperated on a question of *policy* from those who have vigorously and efficiently maintained the *principles* of the Free Trade and States' Rights Party. And in doing so has I think annihilated himself at last. My own opinion is that he has been influenced by his mortification at being put out of office by Polk, but more by ascertaining that he is not the favourite candidate of the Adm. for the Presidency. His malice and ambition [is] always a key to his eccentric conduct. As usual where he makes these splits he is following up with strong appeals to the Country and now he has moved on the Slavery question in a very violent speech looking far more towards dis-union than his hopes of the Presidency have heretofore allowed him to do and with a string of declamatory resolutions having the same tendency. In the Speech and resolutions I, and I presume, all Southern men will concur. The only question is whether they have been brought forward at the proper time. *Appearances* justify them, but I do not know enough of what is passing behind the scenes to judge fully. If Mr. C. has unnecessarily brought forward this matter now to press his adversaries—if for any personal purposes he is making sport of a question so vital to the South he deserves to be *Gibbetted*.

It is clear from a speech made by Mr. C. in Charleston on his way from Washington that his object has been in opposing the War to prevent Benton from getting at the head of of the army and that his object in agitating slavery is to rally the South on himself for the Presidency and carry him into the House of Representatives.

[Silver Bluff] 4th April [1847]

My present position is one of no small embarrassment and difficulty. The events of last winter disclosed that I possessed a considerable share of positive popularity in the State, and many are seeking to take advantage of it. My real friends are apparently impatient for me to come forward and take a leading part in public affairs at once. Others, whose friendship may also be relied on, desire this not solely for my sake or that of the country but to advance themselves through new party arrangements. Others again desire to use me to revenge themselves on their enemies, who are also mine, while the discontented in general are disposed to rally under me as an available Chief. The efforts of all tend to one end—the pressing me into public life and placing me at the head of a party. Now I have no desire to go into public [life] except by a general call from the State, and I will not make a move towards placing myself at the head of a party. I should say *Faction* for I do not see the basis or materials for the formation of a new principle party. I have no sort of desire to burden myself with the drudgery necessary for me to undergo in order to maintain a conspicuous political position. I have no confidence that my health would enable me to do it, I should probably fail, and I never will voluntarily undertake any thing where the chances of success are against me. If *forced* into it, I can only do my best and failure will not be dishonorable. I anticipate that my supineness will discourage my best friends and entirely disgust those who look to me solely as a Chieftain likely to lead them to victory, and that in all probability I shall be altogether dropped ere long. If so I cannot help it. It will give me pain to disappoint my friends, I shall even regret to lose the good opinion of those whose present support of me is interested. But I cannot and will not attempt any thing that duty does not demand, nor inclination prompt me, nor allow myself to be used as the tool of any set of individuals. I shall lie quiet, watch events, endeavour to discover the truth, and stick to it throughout, openly and fearlessly, as far as occasion permits or requires any expression of opinion from me. For the rest, time and circumstances must shape my destiny. My private occupations are interesting and important. In them and in them alone I look for temporal happiness. Public honors and employments I shall never allow to enter into my calculations, and if they fall to my lot, I shall rate them always as accidents and incidents. To make it a chief part, or any serious part, of the business of one's life to seek them, I hold to be the greatest of all earthly follies. The disappointment and misery attendant on such ambition is so illustrated in every page of history, and is so palpably placed before our eyes by every day's experience that I regard it as one of the strangest perversions of the human mind that so many should fail to take warning. I will not be of the number. I will not put my trust in Princes, nor in Peoples.

The Editor of the Hamburg Republican has, I find, a private pique against Hampton and his set, and, I apprehend, so have Gist and the Union [District] People. It has probably originated somehow from Hampton's connection with the Iron Works up there. I have had to act very decidedly to prevent them from harping on my quarrel with H[ampton] to such an extent as to force an open issue. I have suppressed several communications, but they are such a set of fools and so wanting in every sentiment of delicacy that I do not know how long I shall be able to restrain them.

The recent brilliant operations in Mexico have, I presumed, knocked

Mr. Calhoun and his "Air Line" of defence into a cocked hat. At least the reports are thus far brilliant and the prospect still more so, but we do not yet know the whole truth nor the end. Mr. C. is I apprehend nearly *felo de so* from his late desperate movements.

[Silver Bluff] 29 April [1847]

I rec^d a letter not long since from my gossip in Columbia, J[ames] L. C[lark], in which he stated that W. C. Preston *told him* that he had done all he could to prevent the attack on me last winter in Columbia and spoke of it with great indignation. He before stated that he knew Col. Hampton was at first opposed to it and Col. Manning had sneered at it after it was over. If all this is true then John Preston and young Wade must have set the ball in motion, two fools universally acknowledged as such. Both their wives hate me because I have always held them in contempt, and they have perhaps been the instigators. But I believe Manning had a hand in the plot and I fear W. C. Preston had also. They find the move has been unpopular and have tried to sneak out of it. Possibly I do P[reston] injustice. But I do not Manning. [The wife of Wade Hampton III was Margaret Frances Preston, the sister of John Preston. The wife of John Preston, Caroline Martha Hampton, was the sister of Wade Hampton II, and therefore the aunt of Wade Hampton III and his sisters, the young Hampton girls abused by Hammond. The mother of these girls, Ann Fitzsimons Hampton, had died some years earlier. She was the sister of Catherine Fitzsimons Hammond, James Henry's wife. The deceased wife of John Manning, Susan Frances Hampton, was also a sister of Wade Hampton II and an aunt of the girls.]

[Silver Bluff] 17 July 1847

I ought to have stated before now that I visited McDuffie at Cherry Hill [Plantation] about 25 May and met Mr. Calhoun and Col. A[rmistead] Burt there. Mr. C. seemed more resigned to his fate than I ever saw him and had apparently given up the hope of the Presidency. He seemed however a little reserved towards me about his political prospects and evidently does not regard me as one of his devoted followers. Nor do I desire he should. I cannot and will not surrender myself up to any man. I referred to the Resolutions of our Legislature in 1844, introduced by Col. Pickens as an offset to and in censure of my Message, and told Mr. C. that it was then supposed he was virtually the author of them, that I had always thought so myself, and that they passed only in consequence of this impression. He declared he never had the slightest intimation of them until he saw them in the proceedings of the Legislature and that he did not wholly approve them. He also intimated that in some things he preferred my Message. He did not specify the *parts* in either case that he approved or disapproved. The fact is there has been a great change, Polk ejected him from the Cabinet, and they are now at war. It would be very awkward for him to father Pickens' resolutions. He at the time *cordially approved*, if he did not suggest them, I do not doubt at all.

I learned from McDuffie that he was born in Aug. 1790. Came to Augusta and went into a store in 1806, went to Willington early in 1810, to College in the fall of 1811 and graduated in 1813.

I do not see why I keep this quasi-journal. It can never be of use to me or any one, and I think I shall give it up. I do not write continuously, I have not the health, leisure, or inclination to do so.

[Silver Bluff] 15 Dec. 1847

A great effort has been making during the past year to get up an excitement in favour of Rail Roads, and chiefly Rail Roads to Greenville in S. C. and Charlotte in N. C. from Columbia. Charters have heretofore been obtained and the object of the excitement has been to get Legislative Aid. In October Mr. C. G. Memminger of Charleston published a pamphlet in which he proposed that the State should issue Bonds for a million of dollars, pledging her R. Road Stock and Bonds estimated at some million three hundred thousand dollars and assuming no liability herself. This pamphlet was sent to me by Mr. Ker Boyce of Charleston, a Senator, requesting me to answer it and saying that Col. Carew, Editor of the Mercury, would be glad to publish [a reply]. Being greatly alarmed at the prospect of the State incurring fresh debts to build roads which I do not think will ever pay expenses until they have been worn out several times, I immediately set to work and wrote 12 short articles headed "The Rail Road Mania [:And Review of the Bank of the State of South Carolina"] and signed "Anti-Debt. . . ."

[Silver Bluff] 18 Dec. [1847]

The proposition for the State to subscribe to the Rail Roads has been defeated in the Senate by a very large majority. Some of the credit for this is given to Anti-Debt in Columbia. I have no doubt but the proposition would have succeeded but for Anti-Debt. It may not have created the opposition but it brought it out, rallied it, gave it a ground and reasons to stand on and meet opponents with. Before Anti-Debt came out not a man could be found who doubted that the Legislature would subscribe to these roads. The fall of cotton, and the crash in England have no doubt had much influence.

[Silver Bluff] Jan. 29th 1848

. . . .My friends flatter me that I have struck it between wind and water, and that the nos. of Anti-Debt have materially increased my reputation. I can't tell how this may be. I have no opportunity of judging. I see no body whose opinions I value, and the communications of my few correspondents are of course in set phrases. There has been no gush of public sentiment as on the publication of my Clarkson Letters. Our people are divided in opinion about Rail Roads and Banks, and those who entertain my sentiments [against railroads and banks] are generally too fearful of giving offence to come out boldly. The action of the Legislature on R. Roads was, it is agreed, much influenced by my articles. What effect those on the Bank may produce remains to be seen. But really, I feel little gratification in what I have done, save from the consciousness of having done right. I see no reward, should these articles prove ever so successful, that can fill my desires. I do not think that the State of SoCa could confer any office on me, that give[s] me as much pleasure as pain. I am most unhappy and all my unhappiness proceeds mainly from one cause—ill health, which cramps me every way. It is true I attend to my plantation and in doing so ride 4 or five hours every day. But I do nothing to my satisfaction. I am unable to look thoroughly into any thing and can at best exercise only a general supervision. Many details go wrong every day and annoy me excessively. I also eat heartily, drink wine, smoke and chew tobacco and could not pass for an invalid with any but the closest observers. Yet I am always nearly half dead, and scarcely ever make the slightest physical or intellectual exertion without great effort. I feel myself to be utterly misplaced or rather unplaced in the world. Endowed, as I am conscious of being, with both moral and intellectual qualities that would enable me to lead an army or rule a nation far better than any of those who occupy these positions in our country at least, and seeing clearly *how* I might place myself in either position, I am unable to make effort sufficient to overcome any of the obstacles in the way, and should hesitate to accept either station to-morrow, if it were offered to me. I have no confidence,

at any time, that I shall be able even to set up the next hour, and I dread
even to go to Augusta on business, for I always return exhausted and worn
out. This condition would be an unhappy one, with all the alleviation
which the world and even religion could afford. But alas I have few of the
consolations of either. My mind, fretted by the petty troubles to which by
the weakness of the body I am condemned, refuses to receive those religious impressions, which under other circumstances I think it would. And
though I cannot believe in Predestination, it often crosses my thoughts
that it is true and that being foreordained a non-elect, I have been placed
in the precise and perhaps only circumstances that could accomplish my
fate. I desire to believe, I am inclined to believe, I have tried hard to
believe. And believing, I think I should have moral strength to act up to
my creed. As it is, I aim only to do as nearly right as I can, to be perfectly
just in all things, and to do my duty to all men. My conscience requires
me to do this. But I have not a Christian's hopes nor feelings. The comforts of Religion are wholly wanting to me. As to the world, I am surrounded and hemmed in by people entirely incapable of appreciating me,
who carp at what is not in conformity with their narrow views, and have
no conception of mine. I love my family and they love me. It is my only
earthly tie. It embraces my slaves, and there to me the world ends. All
beyond is a blank. There is no one to whom I can communicate thoughts
and feelings which I experience. There is no one who can for a moment
excite the intellectual or moral, much less the spiritual part of my nature.
I have no one with whom to reason, to talk philosophy or poetry, or even
love. It is true I am surrounded by the mighty dead and hold daily converse with the great spirits who have lived before me. But these ideal feasts,
which I can share with no one living, sometimes pall, but oftener inflame
my imagination, and heighten my misery, by exciting fancies of what under different circumstances I might myself have done or said or written. I
am not a poet. I have written verses and I think poems daily, but I have
not the turn nor the patience to commit such ideas to paper. I could write,
it seems to me, immortal books, but there is no subject that with my little
library I can trace much beyond its rudiments. None of which I can take
a view at all satisfactory to myself, because everything has been treated
and, even in philosophy and poetry, one must have facts and know how
they have been handled before. Besides my affairs would constantly interrupt extensive investigation, and more than all, my health does not allow
severe and continuous study. I read many Newspapers and Reviews, I also
read many books and perhaps I pass 4 or 5 hours a day or more in reading
and writing. But I do both without system, because I have neither health,
nor books, nor any stimulant to systematic intellectual exertions.

Thus do I spend my time, in a miserable consciousness that I do not occupy the sphere I could under propitious circumstances, deterred from doing anything to lift myself up to it, from the certain knowledge that my physical powers will fail me, without the consolation of sympathy in this world, and without the hope that another world will relieve my sorrows.

The only thing I can do with any earnestness, because the only thing in any degree within my power, is to endeavour to increase my wealth and for this I am called avaricious. Yet I despise money and I despise money-making and, after all, my efforts have been not so much to make money as to make it in certain ways. Nor have I been sufficiently successful to give me much satisfaction. By some small oversight, some impulse of generosity, and a continual succession of accidents, I lose about as fast as I accumulate.

It is a long time since I have thus vented myself. I have in a measure ceased to complain. I have long felt my case to be hopeless and I will not make those around me unhappy by my repinings. I love them all, I love all the world. There is scarcely a human being against whom I harbour unkind feelings or would harm. I don't know one that I would wish to see suffer, tho' I have received from a few the greatest injuries and injustice, and know there are many who entertain, without cause, the utmost enmity towards me. For the most part I feel only contempt for my enemies, for some others who have wronged me most, I feel a sort of sorrow, and am mortified that they could act as they have done.

[The most important event of the year, and not mentioned by Hammond in his diary, was the ending of the Mexican War in the Spring of 1848.]

[Silver Bluff] 22 Sept. 1848

I had 1000 copies of "Anti-Debt" printed in pamphlet form [published in Charleston in 1848] and have sent them all over the State. . . . For the last five or six weeks, however, the excitement about the [upcoming] Presidential Election has absorbed every thing. Gen. [Lewis] Cass was nominated by the Democrats in May and was terribly denounced by the people of Charleston at a meeting and by all our SoCa papers. Gen. [Zachary] Taylor was nominated by the Whigs in June. He professed to be a moderate Whig and an Independent candidate who would accept support from all parties, but bind himself to none. As [Taylor is] a Southern man and slaveholder, I thought the South should support him without regard to party, especially as Cass was openly anti-slavery. And circumstances made this question the great matter at issue. Mr. Van Buren's friends, disappointed at his not receiving the Dem[ocratic] nomination, raised a new party, which they called the Free Soil (abolition) Party and nominated him for the Pres. Shortly after, the Compromise Bill, which would have probably driven the agitation from Congress to the Courts, was rejected in the House by Southern Whig votes, and, after that, the Proviso of 1787 was carried in the Oregon Bill, mainly by Southern Dem. votes. The Slaveholders, thus assailed and betrayed, should by all means have united on the Slaveholding candidate, whose political opinions were moderate and who had virtually no party ties. I was sure they would and in SoCa, Florida, and Alabama, and, in fact, in all the States there was a strong disposition to do it. But the Democratic leaders saw in this union the destruction of their hopes for office, through Dem. nominations. Mr. Calhoun, who should have here shown his patriotism and courage, shrunk from Gen. Taylor after his nomination by the Whigs (tho' unpledged). He dared not touch a Whig, though he had before the nomination expressed himself in favour of Gen. T. and continues still to abuse Cass. He took the sulks. Came home [from the Senate] and advised the state to vote but refused to say who for. Butler [in the Senate] and [Armistead] Burt [in the House] the same. Two of our Congressmen came out for Cass and one for Taylor, I have not heard from the others. Before 1844 it was rare to find a man in SoCa who would take the name of Democrat. The foolish Polk agitation of that year removed the disgust entertained for it. Some of our dirty sheets and low men came out for Cass soon after his nomination. They gradually gained courage and strength as no one at Washington has rebuked them or come out for Taylor. Mr. Calhoun at least did not. And when he came home and declared himself neutral there was a rush to the Democratic nominee. The men and the papers in Charleston who had been most active in abusing Cass took him up. There however the majority of the respectability were and still are for Taylor, and through out the State nearly all the *gentlemen* are or have been for him, and so were three fourths of the voters at first. But the mad-dog cry of "Democracy" has prevailed, and there will be a large majority for Cass in the Legislature. I am however fully committed for Taylor. But he has himself recently since my committal changed his ground. The Northern Whigs were offended at his accepting a Southern Dem. nomination, especially one in Charleston, with Butler (of Ken.) for Vice [President] instead of [Millard] Fillmore. And Taylor seeing that no great number of Southern Dem. were going for him has been forced to declare himself a "decided Whig" and to compliment Fillmore highly. Thus by the cowardice and selfishness—I may say absolute treachery of leading Southern Democrats and especially Mr. Calhoun, the chance of breaking up the miserable Whig and Democratic Factions and electing a Southern Slaveholder at this crisis has been thrown away. The issue is again Whig and Dem[ocrat]. For myself I cannot support Taylor as a Whig, because I do not approve of any of the leading measures that have been proposed by the Whigs. But Cass being antislavery and a man who will do any thing for popularity, Taylor a slaveholder, pure, firm and patriotic and of sound judgement, I still prefer him and would vote for him. For this I should be read out of the Democratic Party, to which however I never have acknowledged any allegiance.

My friends have always professed an intention to run me again for the Senate. I have never given in to it. I have fully determined never to take any part in setting myself up for any office or canvassing for one. Not being anxious to go to the Senate, I was resolved to refuse positively when the time came to let my name be used, unless I could be elected without an effort. My being a Taylor man will relieve me from any difficulty. I shall not be now thought of. So be it. I will not capriciously throw any obstacles in the way of having office thrown upon me. It is the duty of every citizen to serve his country if the country *desires* his services. I acknowledge this in theory and am ready to abide by it in practice. But I have no sort of *ambition* to perform petty services. If a crisis arose in which I might win immortal renown, I should be extremely ambitious of availing myself of it. But I will not move a finger for any of the little contemporary honors which public life can in these days confer. I feel nothing but contempt for them. If I desire to do any thing, I can always use my pen without asking permission or aid from any quarter and when I choose I can make myself *felt* in that way by friend and foe. Such is my position.

Reviewing the last sentence of what I wrote in January [29] I cannot but contrast my feelings now with what they were then. Since that time I have been a good deal annoyed by the malice and ingratitude of my neighbours here. They are a poor set of ducks—save two or three—who cannot be elevated to the appreciation of any man or any thing. I have tried my best and descended low to improve them as in duty bound and also to make the best of my association with them. But I have at length become utterly disgusted, and I am ashamed to own that I have really given way to much bitterness in my contempt. I ought only to despise them, and indeed I cannot hate them. But I have been unable to restrain a sort of abhorrence of them. I believe it arises from my growing discontent that my lot has been cast among such wretched people and that I cannot without the greatest sacrafices get away from here. Sometimes I entertain serious ideas of removing to California. I would not remain here another year if I could sell my land. But I cannot. It was valued at $40,000, twenty years ago. I have invested more than $30,000 in improvements on it. And I could not, I believe, realize $30,000 for it. Thus my life is wearing out in improving poor lands among unimprovable savages, to whose society a wilderness would be preferable. But I am wearing out fast myself and shall not long have to contend with my difficulties. I look forward with anguish, however, at the prospect of my children living in such a place and among such people.

[Silver Bluff] 16 March 1849

I have been so busy—had so much company and latterly have suffered so much from illness that I have not found time or been in the humour to write anything here and must now write briefly. . . . My friend Simms has taken the Southern Review under his charge and I have promised to help him. I have four articles planned and have begun one. The College Societies have also again requested me to deliver an Oration for them in December and I have consented. I delivered this Oration in 1828, declined it in 1841 or thereabouts and again I believe in 1845. I have thus intellectual labour enough on hand. Yet I never felt less competent to it than now. I am irritable, legarthic [sic] and almost paralytic, while I have nothing more than I have long had to cheer me. I lost my poor son [15-year-old] Christopher in October. It was a heavy blow and threw a dead weight on the already overburdened springs of life.

[Silver Bluff] 15 Dec. 1849

I have not had time and felt like writing for a long while that I did not have much more to do in that way than I could, and now I have letters enow on hand unanswered.

I wrote one article for the Review in the July no. which was much approved and I think added somewhat to my reputation. I wrote and delivered an address for the So Carolina Institute on the 20 Nov. in Charleston. It was highly applauded on all sides. I received a public dinner from the Board of the Institute and another from the Chamber of Commerce. The latter was spontaneous and the first dinner the Chamber ever gave to any one. In fact I was lionized to my heart's content and a little beyond.

On the 4th inst. I delivered my Oration before the two [college debating] societies [Clariosophic and Euphradian] in the College Chapel [at Columbia]. It was, I think, much the best production of the two, and the best thing I ever did. The encomiums passed on it by those capable of judging were perfectly satisfactory and the multitude were not backward in echoing them. But there was no lionizing then. Besides that the Legislature was in Session and innumberable diverse interests in active play, my enemies were there in force. W. C. Preston threw off the mask and he and his wife openly exerted themselves [against me], but, as in Charleston, I had an audience that filled every cranny of the room and more than a full proportion of ladies. But the social cordon was drawn close in Columbia. Tho' my room was constantly crowded with visitors, only four or five of the town people called on me, and these in fear and trembling. I called on no one. I had every evidence however of the highest consideration from friend and *foe*. I left Harry [his eldest son] there in College. His position is very painful to me and will be difficult to him. But it is one of those trials which, if he meets it fairly, will prove of immense advantage to him. It will be a gentle storm in which he may learn to stem the hurricanes of life. I trust he will not sink under it. If he does, there will be nothing brilliant in his career. I feel pained that he should be exposed to it and in consequence of my past errors. But my judgement tells me it is a good school for him.

Since my return home, I have been appointed by a Legislative Caucus one of the State Delegates to the Southern Convention to be held at Nashville next June. It was suggested to me when in Columbia, and I requested my friends to remain silent so far as I was concerned. I have not heard particulars of the ballot, but the papers name Elmore first, myself second, Barnwell next, and then Judge Cheves—he was not chosen on the first ballot and was probably a compromise on the second.

This Convention may turn out nothing or may be the greatest event since 1790.

My private affairs do not prosper and they make me melancholy. I think I am one of the doomed in that respect. I cannot reproach myself for want of industry, or judgment, or economy, but providence clearly interferes, to blast all my plans and sweep off the fruits of my energy. If I live a few years longer, and thrive no better I must make a great change. . . .

My friends are of the opinion that I now, after all the past, occupy a better position in the State than I ever did, and at length fully appreciate my resolute enduring and self sacraficing silence in the Hampton business. I am not myself assured that I have fully passed the long crisis now in its 7th year, but if I had vigorous health, I believe I could accomplish all that would be desirable by any South Carolinian.

[Silver Bluff] 16 Dec. [1849]

So far as I can judge the world sets me down for a practical man—a shrewd calculator, gifted with rather an uncommon share of hard common sense. To me this is somehow a most odious character and I am heartily sick and disgusted with having it ascribed to me. It makes me unhappy at times to think that if I were to die now and my eulogy were to be pronounced these phrases would form the staples of it. Whether it would be added that I possessed extraordinary energy and perseverance is doubtful, tho' those who know most of me accord me these. That I should be praised for enlarged views is still more doubtful, but that I have a speculative mind, keen sensibility, ardent sympathy and a brooding imagination few if any dream, I fear. If I were unmarried and had no children to take care of, I would actually run into all sorts of extravagancies and ruin or nearly ruin myself, just out of spite against the world that has dubbed me a sort of utilitarian.

The fact is that from my childhood I have been led by my impulsive speculative turns to taking all sorts of false steps. Both sense and sensibility apprized me of these traits in very early life. I cannot remember when I first felt that I was no match for the keen worldly wise boys and my sufferings and losses led me early in life, first to conceal them from others and next to endeavour to prevent them. In concealment I have succeeded far better than in prevention, and hence the world judging by appearances, by my bearing and conversation, have been wholly deceived in my character.

Not to recount the errors and mishaps of boyhood, I made first the great mistake of settling as a lawyer in Columbia, which I did purely because I loved the place and the society. Next I took charge of a newspaper mainly to oblige a friend, which would have destroyed my practice. I was saved by marrying and leaving Columbia. It was an impulse that led me to run for Congress and another carried me from Washington—where I took no care of my health—to Europe, where I took no better care of it. There I followed every fancy.

Returning home, another fatal impulse led me to re-settle in Columbia, where I spent immense sums in follies, and allowed my feelings to betray not only my judgment but almost my honor. The consequences of this weakness are known to all and has [sic] been at least a drawback on my reputation for shrewdness and calculation.

In my business affairs, it was little more than a whim which made me continue to plant these poor pine lands at Silver Bluff, when I could have done better any where else and at any other business. I loved SoCarolina and I loved this place—that was all. Here I have gone into marling, putting on my land some 400,000 bushels at an expense of at least 5¢ a bushel or $20,000, and losing almost as much more in planting short to rest the lands and give the marl a chance. As yet this operation is, I fear, in arrears. Next I commenced reclaiming, with a rush, near 600 acres almost at once. This has already cost me in labour at least $20,000, and in loss of crops besides, nearly or quite as much.

If in these works I have exhibited persevering energy, as all must allow, the common sense displayed has not been so obvious as the bold *speculation* and unbounded *faith*. And in the meantime I have made many hazardous loans and have been led purely from sympathy to do this and to endorse for friends by whom I have lost $20,000. I have also been swindled a thousand times in trades, have allowed agents to injure me materially rather than mortify them, and made, to gratify another, a ridiculous purchase of Texas Scrip, which cost me some $8,000.

In short I have, I think, shewn myself on almost [all] occasions to be deficient in shrewdness and mere practical sense.

[Silver Bluff] 17 Dec.[1849]

I have rec^d from Col. L. M. Ayer a member of the Legislature the following statement of the ballotting for Delegates to the Nashville Convention. [The Nashville Convention was a convention of slave state representatives who met in Nashville in June 1850 to consider what their position would be on a series of resolutions that were then being debated in the United States Senate—resolutions that dealt primarily with the slavery question. Southern secession was one possible outcome of their deliberations.]

1 Ballot – 113 votes		2nd Ballot – 99 votes	
Cheves	91 chosen	Barnwell	82 chosen
Elmore	57 [chosen]	Hammond	55 [chosen]
Barnwell	49	Pointsett [sic]	17
Hammond	47	Richardson	12
Pointsett [sic]	34	Rhett	9
Judge Huger	25	Scattering	17
R.B. Rhett	24		
F.W. Pickens	20		
Richardson	19		
T.N. Dawkins	15		
B.F. Perry	14		
Robt. Cunningham	15		
Scattering	34		

I feel greatly mortified by this state of things and regret most sincerely that I was not withdrawn after the 1st ballot. Whoever nominated me ought to have done it. I told my friends distinctly not to press my name and that I would not go unless spontaneously called on. As it is I have rec^d less than one third of the votes of those entitled to vote in a Legislative Caucus, and those only after a scramble. The whole thing puts me in a false position, as one battling for honors. I feel very little like going. If I knew who to decline to, I would decline. But no provision appears to have been made for such a thing, and therefore it would give offence and be used against me if I were to do it. It is no sort of consolation to me that I beat others who were anxious for this post. What perhaps gives me most pain is to see how stern the opposition to me still continues. Altho' I want nothing, I was in hopes I stood better and my friends in Columbia flattered me that I did. I have no doubt this blow comes from the Bank party chiefly and that Elmore pulled every wire to defeat me. But the anti-bank men did not stand up to me. There are 60 in the House and 20 or more in the Senate. I feel on this and on many other grounds no disposition to work for them. I think I shall not touch the Bank again.

[Silver Bluff] Dec. 30 [1849]

They write me from Columbia that no effort was made by my friends in the caucus and that, in consideration of what I had said in Columbia, none of my immediate friends would put me in nomination. It was done by others from different quarters. There must have been lukewarmness as two of the Barnwell Delegation were absent and several more that I thought would have been there. Gen. Quattlebaum writes me that ten Senators were absent who would vote for me for Senator.

I have started the Geo. Constitutionalist and the Republic to agitating for a Convention to send Delegates to Nashville.

I have written to ask Prof. Brumby to lecture on Tobacco and shew the young men by analysis how much more injurious Spanish tobacco is than American.

These things and most things I do from momentary impulse. I never felt more incapable of all sorts of exertion in my life than I do now. It grows on me month after month.

VI

I have heard it from an hundred sources that the almost unanimous opinion of the state is that I am the first man in So. Ca., that is as a Statesman and man of intellect.

---

17 MARCH 1850 — 31 DECEMBER 1850

[Silver Bluff] 17 March 1850

The Session of Congress has been stormy and thus far nothing has been done but to debate Slavery and the Union. The South has threatened dissolution through many Representatives, in doing which Toombs of Geo. and Clingman of N.C., both Whigs, have taken the lead. SoCa rather silent. In the Senate Clemens of Ala., Downs of La., Foote and Davis of Miss. have been most violent. Many calculations have been paraded showing the advantage of disunion to the South. On the other hand threats of coercion have been freely made by minor men. There have been some terrible scenes in the House. On one occasion, on a motion to force up on California by the previous question, the House was worn out with calling Yeas and Nays until after midnight, and adjourned only because of the resolution day had expired. The North has given up the Wilmot proviso for the present, on the *avowed* ground that Slavery is naturally excluded from the newly acquired Territories. The main question is on the admission of California as a State—the adventurers there having without any of the usual forms, made a Constitution, excluding Slavery, and asked for admission into the Union. Clay has brought in a long string of what he calls compromise resolutions, which surrender every thing in issue to the North. He has denounced the South bitterly and prophecied, if not threatened, Civil war and coercion. The South contends that the admission of California [as a free state] destroys her equality in the Senate—already merely nominal there, for Delaware belongs to the North. That deprived of equality there [in the number of slave vs. free states] and already in a vast minority in the House and Electoral College, she will be undone. Mr. Calhoun has made an admirable speech, showing that the equilibrium between the North and South is utterly annihilated, and must be restored or we must seperate. As such a restoration is well known to be an impossibility—his proposition is plainly—Disunion. At this, [Senator Henry] Foote—a poor devil—hacked at once. [Foote was a Unionist from Mississippi.] Webster followed with a most eloquent speech, denouncing the free-soil and anti-fugitive movements, but denouncing slavery and yielding nothing. But the North calls him "dough face" and the South alarmed apparently at her own recent boldness, and the raw head and bloody bones of Civil war paraded by Clay and Webster and Cass, and perhaps not less by the inevitable alternative, presented by Mr. Calhoun so clearly, of seperation—appears to be giving way. There is an evident shrinking from their own threats, and Webster again denounced the right of secession as also Clay did—and no one took them up. Calhoun has not strength. He is worn out. In bed most of the Session and even had to get his speech read.

I have had great hopes that an impassable breach would be made before all was over. At this moment however my impression is that they will enter into another fatal truce and stave off the difficulty for the present. If so the Nashville Convention will probably not meet. I have had drawn up for a month passed [sic] resolutions which I intended to propose there, if I could get a backing. They are short and to the effect that Conventions should be immediately called in the Slave States to send Delegates to a General Congress, empowered to dissolve the Union, form a new Constitution, and organize a new Government, and in the meantime appoint a Provisional Government until the Constitution could go into operation. It is not my intention to make a fool of myself, or acquire the reputation of a madman, etc. I shall not therefore in any public capacity do anything hasty, or prematurely if I know it. Privately I both right [sic] and speak freely, precisely what I think and believe.

[Silver Bluff] 7 April [1850]

Mr. Calhoun is dead. He expired at Washington on the 30 ult. [Calhoun died on March 31 having been in public office for over forty years.] For a year or more it has been supposed that he could not live long, and he certainly sacraficed his last chance by going to Washington. I feel his death even more sensibly than I expected. Our intercourse for the last twenty [years] all recurs to me. Our agreements—our disagreements. I grieve for the loss of the man more perhaps than I do for the Statesman. Pre-emi-

nent as he was, intellectually above all the men of this age as I believe—
he was so wanting in judgement in the managing of men, was so unyielding and so unpersuasive, that he never could consolidate sufficient power
to accomplish anything great, of himself and due season. He was a wall of
granite in resisting, and the good he has done in preventing evil is incal-
culable. But after all, evil has become intolerable and the jealousy of him,
his towering genius and uncompromising temper, has had much effect in
preventing the South from *uniting* to resist it. There will be more union
now, many petty politicians who lived on the jealousy of Mr. Calhoun
existing in their sections will sink into contempt. But who shall lead our
united forces? That is a question which time only can answer. I know of
no one. The platform must soon be swept of Mr. C's leading contemporaries, Webster, Cass, Benton, Berrien are all as old [as] Mr. C. and Clay
much older. In five years most or all of them will go. A new regime and
a far inferior [one] will take their places. The results will be as great as the
changes. I think these men as diverse as they were and are, are the last
links of the chain of the Union.

I have heard that Governor [Whitemarsh Seabrook] will not appoint
me, or Elmore, or Rhett as Mr. C's successor [in the U. S. Senate], looking upon us as the prominent candidates before the Legislature and not
wishing to give either [sic] of us an advantage. This is fair and safe if he
can as well fill the place, if not too small a reason for a Statesman. I think
he should appoint Rhett, as Elmore and myself have been chosen for the
[Nashville] Convention. I am very willing that he should, and equally
willing that the Legislature should elect Rhett. I should feel the compliment of being chosen and be bound to go. But besides that, the difficulties
and responsibilities of the Station are serious and solemn, and my health
not sufficient to cope with them at Washington. I know too well how
much happier I should be here and how essential my presence is to my
affairs. I will not lift a finger to promote my election.

It was thought in Charleston that the Governor was inclined to appoint
Gen. [James] Hamilton to the Senate. But for 6 or 8 years Hamilton has
resided in Geo[rgia], Alabama, and Tennessee. He has scarcely kept house
in SoCa for 10 years. In addition he is a swindler and is notoriously one
now. He has recently swindled me out of $2100 after having heretofore
swindled me out of $18,000. Moreover he is now moving heaven and
earth to get the U. S. Govt. to assume the debts of Texas, and his very
scheme is that of Bell, Clay & Co, to make it part of the Compromise at
Washington. In other words to sell [out] the South to get his Texas claims.
Seabrook is a rather uncommon fool, whose itch for notoriety makes him
supremely ridiculous and in his present position somewhat dangerous. I

am inclined to think he wishes to be Senator himself and will appoint some one who cannot stand in his way. If he appoints Hamilton he will bring an awful storm upon himself. I can't suppose he could get a vote for Senator out of his own family connection.

[Silver Bluff] 18 May [1850]

Since my last entry the most unexpected and among the most, if not the most, painful events of my life have occurred—all of a domestic character. But first of politics. The Gov. did appoint Hamilton, but the people of Charleston rose and he had to withdraw it. He then appointed Judge Cheves who declined—next Elmore who accepted

[Several pages removed, evidently by the same hand as the one responsible for the removal of a portion of the diary entry of December 9, 1846. In this instance, the passage excised contains Hammond's sharp criticisms, as the text makes clear, of his son Edward Spann. The diary was in his possession until his death in 1921.]

. . . .ultimately into very bad habits. In all other respects I have been excessively indulgent to him. He has genius of rather an uncommon order, but is very perverse and always prefers to do any thing rather than what was expected or required of him. Latterly he has been much petted by the females of the neighbourhood, who formed a sort of temperance society and made him their orator. I did not think all this was of much service to him and would not encourage it, tho' I let him go on. Latterly he had written some rather humourous letters for their Fair on the 1st April and also some doggerel verses. For all these things, these silly people complimented him highly. I was not pleased with his writing under a mask at all, and pointed out the impropriety of it. He has no poetical genius and I told him to read poetry rather than write. The fact was I felt it wrong to countenance any of these things, but did not wish to repress any thing like mental effort too far. But the result was that because I did not flatter him as others did, he took up the idea that I did not like him. Thus his prurient vanity, which I was very culpable in not checking at once, has been at the bottom of the whole matter, and the scene with my brother [Marcellus, who defended Spann] doubtless fixed a determination, which I now learn was in his mind before. I have laid down my course. Apart from all feeling of indignation at his undutiful course and language about me and repudiation of my name, I am convinced by my judgment that it will never do for him to return here. I have not flogged [Spann] since he was very small. He is now sixteen. It is too late for that. I can exercise no control over him. Yet if I furnish him with the same means to live away from me, I may expect that my other sons from any whim will pursue the same course. I have therefore through a friend sent him word that I would henceforth allow him $300 a year until he was of age, when I would pay him his Grandmother's Legacy of about $3,000 and that henceforth he must act for himself.

These are the facts of all these most painful cases. I could fill a volume in the expression of the thoughts and feelings they have given rise to in my heart. But why should I when they may be concurred by every one who will place themselves in my situation.

What strikes me is, What can be the meaning of all this infliction, and desertions at this juncture, when my future and position appear to be on a pivot and likely to settle very soon one way or another forever. Are they warnings to me to prepare for the worst? But can there be anything much worse than they themselves? Man can do no worse, but God can. May He have mercy on me and mine—Amen.

[Silver Bluff] 26 May [1850]

I expect to set off on the 28th to attend the Southern Convention in Nashville. I am loath to go, believing nothing will be done to repay the trouble. But as something important *may* be done, it is my duty to go. At Washington they have a Compromise, reported by Mr. Clay, under discussion. ["The Compromise of 1850" has been the name applied to laws enacted by Congress between September 9–20, 1850, which were intended to solve the basic divisions between the slave and free states. It included the following measures: the admission of California as a free state, the organization of New Mexico as a territory without restrictions on slavery, the adjustment of the Texas-New Mexico boundary, the provision for the payment of $10 million to Texas in return for the abandonment by Texas of all claims to New Mexico, the "popular sovereignty" provision on slavery in regard to New Mexico's admission to the Union, the establishment of the Utah territorial government with an identical provision concerning popular sovereignty, the strengthening of the Fugitive Slave Act, and the abolishment of the slave trade in the District of Columbia.] It is denounced by the Abolitionists as surrendering every thing to the South, and by some of the Southern men as conceding every thing to the North. Yet others, N[orth] and S[outh], support it and it may pass. Certainly it has lowered

Southern tone so much that the Convention cannot venture on any very decisive measures. I feel pretty sure that the utmost they can be brought to do will be to propose amendments to the Constitution limiting the power of laying duties, and excluding slavery from discussion in Congress. But I have little hope they can be brought to this, and it is probable that nothing more will be done than pass resolutions and vote addresses, which will be mere folly in my judgement. To me it seems to be the one thing needful [is] to *unite the South* on some measure of resistance looking to action. And for this important end, I will concur in any such measure however mild, and however distant the action may be apparently postponed. If the *initiative* is once taken, I do not fear that events will not be rapid enough— far more so than most persons can imagine. As [it is,] if nothing is done at the Convention, the North will be sufficiently encouraged to push its aggressive spirit promptly and vigourously to a point that cannot be borne. So I am content that the Convention should fail, only I do not wish to go so far to see it do so.

The folly of Mr. Clay's compromise may be demonstrated in a very few words. The Northern Abolitionists have brought about the present state of affairs. They do not accept the compromise. They will press agitation. It will go to extremes unless there be something in this compromise giving us the power to arrest it. But there is nothing. It presupposes a desire on both sides to be at peace, when such is not the fact and, if it were, no compromise would be necessary. The whole effect of it will be a temporary suspension of abolition agitation with a few who have never yet done much in that way, while it takes from the South a vast amount of real strength and power from the first.

[Silver Bluff] Aug. 10 [1850]

I went to Nashville and returned 21 June. It has been too hot and dry and I have had too much to do to write since. The Convention laid down the line of 36°30 on which it would agree to the division of the New Territories, and the South having expressed a very general concurrence the Compromise Bill has been defeated. Nine states met. SoCa, Vir. Geo. Flo. Ala. Miss. Ark. Tenn. and Texas. No Delegation was full but ours. I was on all the Committees and worked hard to lay down a foundation for future Conventions, as well as to save the credit of this. R. W. Barnwell and myself were on the committee who reported the Address and Resolutions. Rhett wrote the Address. I carried it through the Committee and made the closing speech on it in reply to Judge Sharkey, the Pres. of the

Convention, in which it was universally agreed I demolished him. It was wholly unpremeditated. Tho' I knew he was to speak, I did not go into the Convention until he had been speaking some time and did not intend to answer him, until a few minutes before he closed. Our Delegation pushed me out. It was our policy to remain quiet. Pickens and Rhett were for speaking and being active. Judge Cheves, Barnwell, and myself were opposed and most of the delegation went with us. Pickens however made two grandiloquent speeches which were much admired by the mob. It was generally expected that SoCa would go there violent for a dissolution of the Union, and all were prepared to resist or nearly all. Our policy was to shew that we were reasonable and ready to go as far back to unite with any party of resistance as honor and safety would permit. In this we succeeded perfectly and won golden opinions and, what was better, laid the foundation for wielding hereafter great influence among the Southern States. But Rhett has overthrown it all. As soon as he came back, in a meeting in Charleston called to respond to the Nashville proceedings, he openly hoisted the Banner of Disunion. He, a Delegate and known to be the author of the Address. He has been, of course, denounced throughout the Union, and SoCa along with him. In the U. S. Senate Clay and Foote denounced him as a traitor, and Foote also went out of his way to attack me for my Nashville speech, a meagre and unmeaning skeleton of which appeared in the papers. He also attacked Judge Tucker, who came home with me and wrote out here a speech he made in the Convention skinning Clay and Foote. Rhett's speech has given every one a handle to abuse SoCa and to endeavour to hold her up as the leader of the Southern Movement and its aim as disunion. For this the South is not yet fully prepared, and many may be alarmed and kept out of it by this course. Nothing could have been more injudicious than Rhett's speech, especially connected as it was with the Nashville proceedings and opposed as it was to the policy our delegation adopted and pursued there. It was criminal. He was led to it partly to vent himself after his restraint at Nashville, partly from love of notoriety and ambition to go further than any one, but mainly to draw down on himself denunciations for expressing what are believed to be the sentiments of the State, in the expectation that the sympathy, indignation, and defiant spirit of the State would in return send him to the Senate. He must have had more sense than to suppose such a speech could do any *public good*. I made as strong a speech at Barnwell C. H. on the 4th July, but expressly requested that no account of it should be given to the papers.

I must not omit to state that poor [Senator Franklin] Elmore died at Washington on the 30th May [Elmore died only several weeks after taking Calhoun's senate seat on May 29] and that [Robert] Barnwell was appointed to succeed him. I am quite apprehensive that after all Rhett's movements I shall be sent to the Senate. In every way it would be disagreeable to me. I had rather go to the field of battle, considering merely the hardships and dangers as compared with the chances of glory. But in addition my comforts and interests will be most materially sacraficed, and probably my little reputation will be destroyed. It might mortify me to be passed over, but sincerely I do not want to go.

[Silver Bluff] 29 November [1850]

I cannot pretend to keep a journal. My time is so occupied with other writings and my cares so burdensome and my health so feeble. I have had a vast deal of sickness to contend with this summer, not on myself alone but others, for my family black and white never suffered so much. I have been both physician and nurse, tho' I could hardly get about.

I delivered in Charleston on the 21st an Oration on Calhoun, written under these circumstances. I was ill all the time I was in Charleston and have been more so since my return. It was said on all hands that it was the best thing I have ever done and from what I can learn has added materially to my reputation.

I did not go to the Nashville Convention which met a second time on the 11 ult. For this I had many reasons. 1. I was not bound to go from the first, owing to the manner of the election as heretofore stated. I went however for fear the absence of one vote might in some way injure SoCa or the cause. As the Convention agreed to vote by Delegations my presence was not necessary, and I never intended to return unless I thought it important. 2. I did not think it of any consequence that the Convention should assemble again as it had been treated with contempt before. I really feared the Union men would crowd in and pervert the Convention to their own purposes, as far as it could effect anything. They however staid away and left it to the Resistance men to do as they please. Thus it has lost all chance of doing much good as it will be said that only a few Ultras came together. 3. I did not go because I wished to shew that I was not seeking political offices. 4. It was a long and very fatiguing journey which I was not well enough to undertake and 5. If there had been no other reason, my daughter Bet [their youngest child, born in 1849] was too ill for me to leave her, and I had 12 cases of severe fever on the plantation, several of which are not yet well.

My enemies have made a handle of my not going to the Convention and some pretended friends have used it as a pretext for falling off and some real friends have regretted it. They threatened me that I should not even be run for Senator if I did not go, for which I thanked them and said that after that I would make no excuse but pay the penalty. My declining to go was well known before hand. I informed the Governor in time for him to have supplied the vacancy, but he said he had no power and I did not think he had myself.

Judge [Langdon] Cheves made a noble and powerful speech in the Convention in favour of Secession, which has been its best fruit. They passed resolutions affirming the right of Secession, and also requesting the Southern States to call a Southern Congress, not naming time or place [this Congress would never meet] and adjourned in haste and to avoid being mobbed by the galleries. Rhett was there and arrived in Charleston the very afternoon that a dinner was given to me by the City Council. He was brought in, and, knowing the anxiety of all to hear from Nashville, when I was called on for a Speech I declined making one and brought him out by toasting him, for which I gained as much credit as if I had made a fine speech myself.

I don't know to this moment whether I am to run for the Senate or not tho' the Legislature met on the 25 ult. My friends seem lukewarm and I have rather discouraged them by expressing my indifference and determination not to go over there to help myself. The public is still burning with curiosity to know all about the Hampton affair and is disposed to taunt us both in order to get at it. I shall not gratify them, Hampton may. This and my not going to Nashville and my opposition to the Bank will lose me so many votes that I don't see how I can be elected [to the Senate] and most sincerely do I hope that I may not be.

[Silver Bluff] 30 Nov. [1850]

I did not state quite fully last night *all* my reasons for not going to the Nashville Convention [November 1850]. Although my isolated social position in the State, arising partly from my residing in a solitary corner and partly from the rupture of family ties under circumstances heretofore referred to, and my want of health, render it wholly uncertain whether I can, if I live, take the stand I might hereafter wish, or maintain it if taken, still I see clearly that the true crisis is not yet, and that he who husbands his strength now can expend it to much more effect a few years hence. The fruit is not ripe. Perhaps it is necessary to its more rapid maturity that the tree should be shaken often and vigourously, and if there were none to shake, it might be my duty as I have in times past thought it to be. But situated as I am now, I am willing to let the eager spirits get in advance of me and gather all the fruit, immature and imperfect as I know it will be, that may fall from their blows, reserving myself for a more propitious season. Last Summer after the Convention [Nashville, June 1850], Rhett declared for disunion openly in a speech in Charleston. Cheves has long been for it. There is a strong party in our State for immediate secession. I should be if I thought it judicious, as I have, for near or quite twenty years, been in favour of disunion and believed it inevitable. But no state save our own is ready to go to such lengths. No state would no[w] follow us. This I saw clearly at the Convention and before and since. But in all the cotton states this sentiment is spreading rapidly, and I think that, aided by the aggressiveness of the abolitionists, in a few years it will predominate so far that we will be sustained in open secession from the Union. I have therefore declared myself against our State's seceding now as impolitic. If I had gone to the Convention [November 1850] with Rhett and Cheves, entertaining sincerely the same opinions they do and differing only as to time, I should have embarrassed my position and thrown myself almost inevitably into the same category with them. This I feared. It turned out that I might have avoided it. In fact I am not sure that even Cheves is for instant action. But he is so regarded, and so are all our people who went to the Convention. But as it is, if I had gone and should have to go to the Senate, I should be there in a different and less eligible position after attending this Convention as Rhett's colleague since his Speech in Charleston last Summer. I have not yet appeared in print as an avowed Secessionist. And it is not my policy to do so yet. I think I can do more good at present by appearing to be cautious, and in fact being so. I prefer to choose my own time and one better suited than the present, in my judgement, for taking my position. And hence I did not desire to be mixed up with the proceedings at Nashville at the late meeting. If as I said before there was any difficulty about it and men could not be found to lead the van-guard— the pioneers—the forlorn hope as I may call it, my opinions and principles would have forbade me from shrinking from it. But while such are to be found who are fully competent and extremely eager for it, I may, I think with propriety, follow the dictates of my own judgement as well as inclinations and hold back a little for the present. Personally I may suffer for it. They may win the battle and reap all the glory before I think the time has come to begin, and I may be cast off forever. These are the risks I have knowingly encountered, and I am willing to abide the result. Let them reap the whole harvest if they can. I will cheerfully yield to them and will rejoice if our independence can be achieved without any aid from me.

[Silver Bluff] 14 Dec. 1850

This is the last day of the third week of the Session and I have not yet heard who has been elected Governor and Senator, if the elections have taken place. They had not on Tuesday last. It is unprecedented, I believe, for a Gov. to hold on to the third week. Whether Seabrook, conscious that he will immediately sink into contempt, prolongs his term from a morbid love of office or whether he is playing the game for some of the intriguants whose schemes are not matured, I cannot, at this distance, tell. Doubtless the [gubernatorial] election has taken place and the probability is that Gen. J[ohn] H[ugh] Means has been elected over Pickens and Gadsden. He is the least qualified of the three for the times. Means is a very respectable country gentleman of very moderate parts and cultivation. His statesmanship is derived from newspapers and two years service in the Legislature. His general knowledge from light readings. He would in war make a fair Colonel. In peace a good citizen. He will be ruled by the Preston clique entirely. The Gens. Jones and Jamison brought him out. I appointed him one of their colleagues when I organized the Military Academies of the State in 1842–3.

[Robert Barnwell] Rhett is probably elected Senator unless he gave way for his cousin [Robert Woodward] Barnwell as the rumour last week was that he would. It is doubtful whether I was even run or not. I know nothing. I had a letter from Ayer dated 1st. Sept. which spoke doubtfully and another from Felder of the 9th which said in these words he "hoped I would be elected." This is all my information save a letter from Walker in Charleston of the 9 or 10th (not dated) saying it was reported there that Rhett would have no opposition. This election should have been made the first week of the Session as a vacancy was to be filled and Congress just assembling. But a puerile proposition was made by J. J. Middleton not to fill the vacancy at all, and then proposed that our whole Delegation sh^d be requested to remain at home. I have not heard the fate of the proposition, but in the meantime [Senator] Butler and our Representatives have quietly taken their seats at Washington.

In placing Means and Rhett in the two principal political positions of the State, the Legislature have given *their approbation to abortive violence.* For they are both of the violent bugle blast section and neither of them capable of effecting any thing. They want all the requisites of Leaders and Statesmen. As far as these men can go, rash and windy measures will be proposed, and though they may not have power and probably will not have to carry them, they will at least throw prudent and efficient measures into the background. What the results will be, without providential interposition, may be easily foretold—distraction, weakness, and failure. If real truth lies at the bottom of our [secessionist] cause, and God favours its successful development at this time, these men and their whole set must be swept away. But as this cannot be done in less than two years, it may be considered that every thing is put back for that length of time. If God is against us, then these are the suitable instruments to work out our defeat. I do not despair because I am not in a hurry and have never expected to see this revolution accomplished in a day. But two years, that should be devoted to correct and judicious preparation, thrown away, is a great loss. And it will be worse than thrown away for their ridiculous vapouring will lower the position of SoCa. And they will doubtless waste a large sum of money to give it some shew of reality. I very much fear our foolish State will be led to establish Factories of arms and powder, which will entail a heavy and useless expenditure on us. I have given my views against them to several members of the Legislature. . . .

As for myself various causes have combined to put me down completely, I suspect. The first and greatest is, I fear, that I am not the destined instrument. God for my sins rejects me. Of course man must do the same from whatever motives. Of secondary causes, I am almost wholly in the dark. I have heard vaguely that the Hampton set was making every effort against me, but what they have said or done in particular I know not. I have no reason to suppose they have pushed matters farther than in 1846 or that any new development has been made. My not going [back] to Nashville has told strongly. The fact of my sickness and that of my family, which would have stopped me had I been ever so anxious to go, has been overlooked. In fact I have said nothing of it, but took the grounds that I was not bound to go on a vote of 55—by no means bound to return as my personal vote was not required, and finally I denounced the whole affair as an *abortion*, which had neither awed the North nor harmonized the South and which should be allowed to sink into oblivion as soon as possible. In reply to a letter of Col. W[illiam] H. Gist of the [state] Senate, I wrote him to this effect on the 2nd Dec (copy kept) and also denounced any breaking openly with the Fed. Gov^t now or calling a Convention or doing anything out of regard to the action of the Nashville Convention. I also stated to him my views generally of the proper course for our State to take, and for myself declared that I claimed nothing, asked nothing, and would have nothing unless it was tendered to me in such a manner as to indicate clearly that I possessed the full confidence of the State. I took high grounds—the higher for the opposition shown to me, that it might be fully understood I was not one to pick up crumbs and be thankful for small favours. It was said in Columbia that I was for the Compromise—

for submission etc. That there was no sort of reliance to be placed on me. My rupture with the Hamptons—with my Brother [Marcellus]—with my son Spann—all were used in a thousand ways and the impression made very extensively that I was a *Monster*. My talents could not be denied, but that was my sole qualification for any position in life, and these deprived of all moral support were rather to be feared and suppressed than to be cherished. The result has been—as I take for certain—that I am utterly broken down and prostrated forever. The Hamptons and all my enemies triumph over me. This should be a deep humiliation to me, and I cannot understand myself when I find it is not. I do of course feel much bitterness of spirit, but it is neither a violent nor a melancholy bitterness. The all prevailing feeling is one of *relief*—of exulting freedom from a thousand petty ties that bound me in every direction.

There are periods in all men's lives when they can of themselves do no more—go no further, and the only wisdom for them is to throw themselves entirely upon God and surrender their fate wholly to his direction without a selfish struggle for themselves. This was exactly my case. Since 1843 I have felt that I had but two courses in which I could expend my energy—the improvement of my Estate and the cultivation of my mind, embracing only such opportunities for displaying my mental resources as were clearly thrown in my path. I have avoided every thing like self-seeking, and given myself up to God and his usual worldly agents, my friends. I have not said this to my friends because it would have been an ungenerous method of stimulating them to make efforts and incur responsibilities. And I do not believe that any of them have taken such views as lead them to the conviction that I had no other resource but themselves and could do nothing for myself. I am glad they have not and have not in consequence got into trouble on my account. Thus resigned to Providence, I have long left my destiny, as far as my weak and sinful nature allowed me, to be shaped by Him who made me; and if my failure in this world is—as it now seems to be—complete and final, it is His will. I have no right to complain. It would be worse than folly—criminal and sinful, to allow it to wreck my happiness, if I must turn to other sources for it. The excitements of public affairs, the enjoyments of what is called society, are no more for me. I shall endeavour not to waste another thought on them—never to allow another tendril of my heart to stretch in these directions. In the improvements of my Estate I have met with such immense difficulties that I have for the most part thought Providence was against me there also. But I have striven on and still indulge fond hopes. But these hopes are now dashed by fresh and untoward domestic difficulties, which render my pursuits in this line scarcely a higher source of happiness than what mere active and agreeable occupation gives. Results have become of less consequence. In fact I may ere long abandon the vocation altogether and become a wanderer over the world seeking solitude in crowds where I may be alike unknowing and unknown. If my life is spared long, even this may be in reserve for me. I will not now explain all this. But I have from my early life tutored myself to surrender any and every thing without surprise and without disappointment. Existence has ever appeared like a dream to me and no turn of it has been so sudden, no combination so incongruous, that some vague glimmering of it cast before has not somewhat prepared me for it, and broken its effect. My suspense for the last few weeks has been more intense and more painful than any I ever encountered. It has been as far as I can judge—the very greatest crisis of my life: my turning point in the world. Up to this period I have ever held myself subject to the call of the public to perform my part on the political stage. I have not since I left Congress felt any keen desire to be called on, for I knew my health has been incompetent to any long continued political career. But after being beaten for Governor in 1840—signally elected in 1842 by only 7 majority when there was no candidate opposed to me— beaten for Senator in 1846—chosen for Nashville by a small minority in 1849, I thought that if my services were now rejected when tendered for the Station to which I have been designated by public opinion in and out of the State—I should of right be *Free-forever!* and never more bound even to answer the most pressing call, should any be made for me. On the other hand if elected now to the Senate, an entirely new career would be opened to me and the whole current of my life be changed. This has been undoubtedly the most critical era of my life, and even yet I feel uneasy tho'— morally sure that I have been beaten—*unbound* and *turned loose.*

One thing I ought to add here. I have heard it from an hundred sources that the almost unanimous opinion of the State is that I am now the first man in SoCa, that is as a Statesman and man of intellect. I have also heard that this opinion prevails very generally in several other states. I may say that even before Calhoun's death a few at least did not except him, tho' generally I was placed second to him. I will further state my own firm belief, that with the help of God, and tolerable health, I could guide the State and the South through all their present difficulties. And if there is another man who can do it, I do not know him—he is unknown now.

After this, if So Carolina refuses my services—drives me from public affairs—is it she or me that will suffer most in opinion, in fact, in the long run? Shall I submit to play a subordinate part, degrade myself to an inferior rank, and have the responsibility of that ruin which I see to be inevitable, if those now in the ascendant are to be the Leaders?

[Silver Bluff] 15 Dec. [1850]

The report has reached here from Hamburg yesterday that Rhett has been elected Governor and that Barnwell will be Senator. This being the first time I have ever heard Rhett's name mentioned in connection with the Governorship, I was taken by surprise, but am inclined to think the report true in all respects. Rhett I did not think until very lately could be elected Senator, and he has wisely taken the Chiltern Hundreds as the most honorable post at this time, as it is commonly said to be, though I think very differently. Barnwell has hitherto expressed himself decidedly opposed to going to the Senate. I wrote to him last summer that he must be Senator, Pres. of the College, or Governor and to take his choice. He averred that he would not take any of them. But I have thought he would not be adverse to the Senate if his Cousin Rhett were out of the way. I have no doubt the matter has been thus arranged and two years hence he is to give way to him. I think it probable also that my friends in the Legislature to whom I have spoken highly of Barnwell, and perhaps mentioned my proposition to him, may have had some hand in making this arrangement, and regard it as letting me down easily. This they would not have done if they had thought I could be elected so that I have been *virtually* beaten and may still claim the privileges of defeat. I should have preferred to have run and [been] beaten openly, for I fear that my friends have taken such a course as to weaken the availability of my plea of repeated defeat and may themselves, after all I have said of my indifference (which is real) towards the Senate, denounce me as capricious and maintain that I take it ill that this post has not been *forced on me*. This will certainly be said of me, if I take the ground I propose, if my friends have in any way lent themselves to this arrangement of affairs. Nevertheless I will take it, though perhaps not so early and openly as I might have done. *Yet in time.* I have been longer and more generally designated for this post than Barnwell, and under all the circumstances it is a decided slight, however it may be glossed over, to pass me by.

The question is how will all this work? Barnwell will be a dignified, able, manly, and unexceptionable Senator, unless a storm arises in the Senate in which a very religious man, scrupulous in his bigotry, can take no part. Then Barnwell will fail utterly, as he did in some passages last Summer. And it is probable that such storms will occur next session, if not during the present. Such a failure will prostrate him. In any event however, he is too *over-refining* in his notions of propriety for the rough and tumble of politics. This delicacy would not be so detrimental in one a little removed from the actual conflict or where another might be substituted to do what he scrupled about. As a Judge, Counsellor, Governor, or President he would answer well, but he is not the man for hand to hand fighting. Besides, tender as he is, he loses his temper and coolness in a crisis and can neither do nor advise then. On the whole however he is a good choice and will be highly acceptable for the present, at least, to all parties. As to Rhett, he will no doubt aim to signalize his administration and will do all sorts of violent things. His violence however will be restricted by the powerlessness of his office, to vapouring, and spending the money subjected to his control. These he will do to the utmost extent and may get the State into difficulties. Whether he will usurp any power I cannot tell. In *some* things he is scrupulous. . . .

Strange things turn up. Eleven years ago I took the field against Richardson, to break up the "Rhett Clique," who evidently aimed to get possession of the State. I broke them down by 1842. Little has been felt of their political power since. Albert Rhett, the ablest of the Rhetts, died soon and Elmore the soul of the clique is gone too. Yet here, just 10 years after the close of the first combat in which they won a Phyrrus [*sic*] victory, behold them at the head of Affairs, dividing among themselves the political power of the State! This is the fruit of my defeat in 1846 to which Rhett's enemies contributed largely. No one but me could keep them in their proper places. And men have gone with them now against me, who do not dream of what they are doing and will repent at leisure—such is this world.

I feel disposed to have as little to do with it as possible. I feel like burying myself in the deepest recesses of Cowden [Plantation] or flying off to the utter-most parts of the Earth. The fact is difficulties of the most serious character have again arisen in my family. Difficulties betwixt my wife and me. I am wholly to blame, not so much, as I view matters, for what I have done as for what I left undone, for want of caution which led to discoveries. Yet I have been as cautious as I could, both in word and deed. Ever since the Hampton rupture I have [been] watched with lynx eyes [by my wife] and harrassed [*sic*] with suspicions until I ceased to be polite to females or to speak a kind word to a servant. But *Fate* so willed it that I was caught at last—as I always am. The result is yet in the future. My wife has been gone to Charleston for a week or more, when to return is uncertain. Concessions are demanded to which I am averse, because they involve injustice and cruelty to others concerned and because I have already borne with more surveillance than I am willing to undergo again. And because also it is useless and painful to re-commence a life of deceit and hypocrisy again. I was born—as I presume most are—to love and be beloved again. The great craving of my nature is for the beautiful—both the ideal and the real. With me I fear it stands before the good—though I will say not far before it, for I think they are almost inseparable. Yet in all my life I have enjoyed no beauty but the ideal. My love has been either lustful or purely platonic. There has been no mingling in its stream of the vital essences of being, of the body and the soul. And I have passed the stage of life to expect it. Not that I am myself less capable of it than I ever was, but that I doubt if I could ever excite in a proper object that reciprocity which is essential to it. My wife loves me. I believe I approach her ideal in person, at least, and she has unbounded admiration of my intellect, though unable to appreciate it or comprehend its range. A purer, more high minded and devoted woman never lived. I esteem, I revere her, and I have—though silently—made sacrafices for her that I could never explain—that she and the world could never understand. I have surrendered my heart if not to her—*for her*, again and again. I have extinguished its emotions and cauterized their sources. As the mother of my children and mistress of my household I would not exchange her for any in the world, and I have never failed in kindness and respect for her. If God has given me tastes and appetites which she was not fitted to satisfy, I have sacraficed the tastes, at least—I have sought to love no other. I do not love any other. But I have not been immaculate. I could not be. I tried it— oh, I tried it fully, fully and failed wholly. I should fail were I to try it again. Shall I pretend to do it, knowing I cannot succeed? If not, what then? Here is the question before which I feel like flying the world and probably shall do it.

Thus situated—thus feeling—my political annihilation, which before would hardly have cost me a pang, gives me now a sort of bitter joy. One more tie that bound me to courses out of my control is snapped. My children and my God remain. I pray for light and strength to perform my completest duty to them.

[Silver Bluff] 16 Dec. [1850]

The mail today brings accounts of the Governor's election which took place on Thursday and Friday, one ballot each day. Means was elected on Friday having 88 votes against Pickens 67. Buchanan, Barnwell, and Treville rec^d votes on the first ballot and perhaps the second.

Thus the report yesterday is blown up and all my views founded on it have failed. They write me from Columbia on Thursday that my friends were growing sanguine of my election, and I am really becoming apprehensive myself. The excitement is abating, and the views I have expressed are now becoming acceptable. Rhett's violence must lose him influence in proportion. My friends are also beginning to congratulate me on my staying at home and refraining from all sorts of electioneering. From this I infer that the intriguers are beginning to excite disgust. On these two grounds rest my apprehensions that I may be elected. The [Senatorial] election may have taken place to-day—may not take place until Thursday. On Friday they adjourn.

[Silver Bluff] 20 Dec. [1850]

There was a ballot on Tuesday the 17 inst. for Senator and another ordered for the day following the result of which must have reached Augusta last night and may be here before night. On Tuesday the vote stood as follows:

Rhett	56	This is a very curious exhibit and entirely in-
Hammond	50	comprehensible to me. The first apparent fact is
Barnwell	27	that two thirds of the Legislature are opposed to
Chesnut	15	Rhett and myself seperately and probable to Rhett
Woodward	9	or me as Senator, for we were the only avowed
J. Preston	2	candidates and the others have been picked up
Richardson	2	to shew the dissatisfaction existing towards us.
Blank	2	

Under these circumstances I don't think either of us should accept the office if elected to it. The decided inclination of my mind is to refuse it should the choice fall on me. I shall certainly do so unless a fuller knowledge of the circumstances of the case and maturer reflection should change my views.

Woodward, Preston, and Richardson have been *talked* of before for Senator, and it was supposed Barnwell had only to say the word to [be] elected. But Chesnut has been sprung on the occasion and how two could vote blank in such a field to choose from is a riddle. Perhaps Chesnut and Preston themselves voted blank. James Chesnut Jr. [husband of the famous civil war diarist, Mary Boykin Chesnut] is a man of 33 to 35 who has often been in the Legislature and has always been regarded as an amiable, modest gentleman of decent parts. He was in the Nashville Convention [June 1850] where I first became acquainted with him, though I have known him ever since he was a boy. I found him a very quiet and apparently unpretending man, but I thought nevertheless quick and keen, with a strong turn for *management*. Being wealthy, of good family, and sound sense with a tolerably cultivated mind, I have thought ever since I discovered his shrewdness at Nashville that he would yet play an important part in public affairs. When I proposed to our Delegation, before the Organization of the Convention, that we should press for a vote by States, Barnwell and Rhett urging some over-refined notion of justice, opposed it. Chesnut suggested to me the *equivoque* of voting by *Delegations*. I rejected it, but he proposed it openly to the Delegation. It *took* with them. It *took* with the organizing Committee when suggested by Pickens, not by me. It *took* in the Convention and I think it was owning mainly to this *ruse* that we carried my proposition. Such is Chesnut.

From the 1st Ballot I can really form no conjecture what the result may be. If I had been there I should have had my name withdrawn. But as I had always supposed that Rhett or myself would be elected on the first ballot, I never thought to instruct my friends specially on this point—tho' I repeatedly requested them in general terms, not to press me against the wishes of the Legislature.

[Silver Bluff] 21 Dec. [1850]

Rhett is elected. At the Second Ballot [.   he United States Senate] the votes were Rhett 65, Hammond 48, Barn ell 28, Chesnut 15, some scattering. The third ballot I have not seen as I get this from a Telegraphic Dispatch in an Augusta paper. On the fourth ballot the vote was Rhett 97, Hammond 46, Scattering 10. Thus the long agony is over. My career as a public man is over, I am crushed—*annihilated forever*. God's will be done.

Ever since my rupture with Hampton, and the consequent damage to my reputation, I have entertained the hope that the State would some day raise me from the dust and cleanse me from every stain. To do this effectually it must have been the *Act of the State*, performed without any prompting from me. I have endeavoured on every proper occasion to prove myself worthy of being thus redeemed. But I have felt that any self-seeking, much less truckling on my part would destroy the healing virtue of this act and I have there[fore] scrupulously avoided it, and not to[o] scrupulously in my opinion. At length it is clear that this hope has utterly failed and there is nothing more for me to do but bow in humble submission to God and my destiny. With a heart so proud and sinful as mine it was doubtless wild and weak in me to indulge the slightest expectation that God would interpose to save me from the ruin I have brought upon myself. I have indeed had, particularly of late, too many evidences of his displeasure with me to place much confidence in any such hope. But still it did seem to me that he had not endowed me with the high talents and the many noble qualities which I am conscious of possessing, to wreck me forever, on what I deemed mere foibles, and having been most severely punished for them in many ways already, I did allow myself to encourage a belief that He would yet restore me to my true position and use me as a fit instrument to work out some of His designs in this world. But the dream is over. My fate is fixed. I shall make no further effort.

The question now is, whether I shall for the good of my children withdraw myself from the country and retire to some remote corner of the world to spend the few miserable days I have to live in solitary obscurity: or remain here in almost equal solitude and work to accumulate wealth for their use. This question I cannot solve now. I will watch developments for a time before I determine. I will endeavour from these to gather the Will of God. At this moment I feel prostrated and overwhelmed—too exhausted in body and spirit to resolve on any thing.

[Silver Bluff] 24 Dec. [1850]

I have received from Columbia a full statement of the Ballots for Senator and they are as follows:

	1	2	3	4
Rhett	56	65	77	97
Hammond	50	48	54	46
Barnwell	27	28	20	5
Chesnut	15	15	10	2
Richardson	2	0	0	0
Preston	2	0	0	0
Woodward	9	1	0	2
Blank	2	0	0	1
	163	157	161	153

The Third Ballot in which I did my best has not been printed in any of the papers but the Courier. The 1st was on the 17th the 2 & 3rd on the 18 and the 4th was on the 19th inst. My friends were for concluding the ballots on the 17th and they write me there was no excitement. But in this they were taken in. They did not, as I had requested, make any exertions, but my enemies were doubtless active enough and arranged matters fully on the night of the 18th. The Legislature has also called a Southern Convention to meet at Montgomery, Alabama, in Jan. 1852 and the State has elected Cheves, Barnwell, Richardson, and *Hampton* on Second ballot. [This convention was to be the meeting recommended by the Nashville Convention. The legislature selected four delegates-at-large and scheduled the election of two additional delegates from each congressional district for October 13 and 14, 1851. This convention never met, but the elections were held.] I have not seen the ballots and don't know whether I was run or not. It is the Nashville Delegation with one substitute for Elmore, who is dead, and one—Hampton—for me who am politically crucified. This is another blow at me and evidently *intended* by the election of Hampton, who was never thought of before. It is very clear that my enemies do not mean to do things by halves, but to put me out of the way forever. The people are also to elect Delegates next October. I have no doubt I could be elected, but I will not offer or permit myself to be brought out. The tide has now set fully against me and I give up altogether. I believe I could now change the current by an appeal to the people, but I want the heart, and above all the physical strength to do it. With my shattered health such a contest would be madness. I want *quiet* above all things.

The State [legislature] has also called a State Convention to meet after the adjournment of the S°. Convention, or before if called by the Governor. The Delegates are to be elected next February. I have no doubt I could go there too, but I will not. [This State Convention had the power to commit South Carolina to immediate secession from the Union. The delegates were elected on February 10 and 11, 1851, and it eventually met in April 1852.]

The Legislature has also raised taxes 50 per ct. and in various ways appropriated half a million for the defence of the State.

I am opposed entirely to every one of these measures and believe they will be very disastrous. They will either end in degrading the State into utter contempt, or forcing her into a rash secession which may end almost as fatally. I can only conjecture the views of those who favoured them— that is of the Legislature, for every thing was passed almost unanimously. There seems to have been a rivalry among the Members as to who should propose the most violent measures, and if there were any men of prudence and sagacity there, they were overawed and compelled to come in. All feared the fate of the union men of 1832–3. The opinion undoubtedly was that these high measures would strike terror into our adversaries. That the taxation and appropriations would shew we are in earnest and that the Conventions held over them *in terrorem* would force them to come to our terms. The indefinite time of meeting for the State Convention and the remote one for the Southern Con. were intended to exhibit our prudence—to give our opponents time to reflect—our Southern sisters time to come in—ourselves opportunity to prepare for advancing or retreating according to circumstances. It is expected that the South will come to the rescue either out of admiration of our gallantry or sympathy or a common interest. The truth is however that Rhett and his set want confidence in the people. They believe that they are now excited enough for any thing, and they [are] determined to commit them *irretrievably* [to secession] at once. Rhett himself told me in Charleston that the people would cool down unless we pushed onwards and kept them excited. Hence the calling of Conventions *now* which are not to meet until *after another session of our Legislature,* and which just as well [could] be called next session, under the additional experience of another year.

My own opinion is that the North will laugh at these conventions as mere powder guns. They no longer fear SoCa and the more she lashes herself into a fury, the more they will ridicule her and press their schemes. Some will be anxious to try whether a State cannot be forced to keep in the Union and would prefer SoCa to all other states for the experiment. The South I think will refuse to follow SoCa. I doubt if a single state will send members to the Montgomery Convention. Mississippi may. Alabama may out of mere courtesy. No other state will. This will make the whole affair ridiculous. Our State Convention will then meet in a state of high exasperation and probably secede. For this step she will not be at all prepared. The half million appropriated will be squandered for useless guns etc.—a very large part of it going into the pockets of Agents. A million and a half is indispensable for a fair prepa[ra]tion for secession *alone,* and that should be expended almost wholly in Naval Munitions including steamers to prevent blockades. A secession under the circumstances that cannot but exist in a year or 10 months will be an act of madness, the results of which no one can foretell further than that a ruinous failure must inevitably occur. . . .

There are many who deem themselves qualified to take Mr. Calhoun's place and very few who do not desire to have at least their share of the power heretofore concentrated in his hands. They united with the Bank and my personal enemies to crush me, because public opinion had pronounced me the most worthy to succeed him. They would have no new master. Hence my fall on the pretext of my not going [back] to Nashville, for it is now said I would have been elected [to the Senate on] the first ballot if I had gone. But I anticipated long before Mr. Calhoun's death these squabbles for the purple and resolved to have nothing to do with them. I am done for—unless I should survive for the Dictatorship, being entitled to it as the *first victim.* Rhett will probably be the next. Somebody will turn him out two years hence. If indeed he and all his fine measures do not explode before then. In what a position I should have been had I gone to the Senate and been compelled to defend them there? I feel curious to see Rhett do it. It is late, I must break off here. But if I feel like it I will continue this subject, state what I would have done had I been sent to the Senate, and pourtray [sic] the Revolution which I see impending over the internal affairs of SoCa.

[Silver Bluff] 25 Dec. [1850]

Merry Christmas to all, especially to you my dear, dear children for whom alone I live or desire to live and many, many, happy New Years, happier than any I have ever enjoyed.

Every hour's reflection leads me more and more to the opinion which is now almost a conviction, that the present state of things in SoCa is not only temporary but likely to lead to great results which are now but little anticipated. The late rash measures of our Legislature will put back, if they do not occasion an indefinite postponement of, the disruption of this confederacy by the action of the South. At present and for a long time past such a jealousy has existed in the South towards SoCa that it was enough to discredit and put down any measure or movement in every other S° State, by attributing its origin to ours. It was laboured to stigmatise the Nashville Convention as a SoCa measure and not without success, and the measures of its last meeting have stamped it with our seal. By carrying Cheves with me, I kept our state in the background before, against Rhett and Barnwell and the other prominent members of our Delegation, Pickens concurring with me in *opinion*, but taking the most prominent part himself that he could. SoCa from her long training and the unanimity of her people under Calhoun was alone capable of seceding with effect, and had she remained *firm*, quiet, and prudent, in a year or two more she would have been called on from all quarters by large minorities, if not majorities, to take the lead and break the ice. Already thousands of *individuals* were calling her. Rhett & Co. have mistaken these voices for those of the *people*, while as yet the[y] have arisen chiefly from those entangled by their own course among their people and crying out for *help* to disembarrass themselves—men excited and embarrassed themselves, and injudiciously demanding more than we could prudently yield to them. But the cause was growing rapidly and in a very few years we should have led the South, with the consent, and by the appointment of the South. I fear our action now is so premature that the other states will recoil and avail themselves of the plea of our usurpation of the lead, our rashness, our arrogance, to drop down into a quiet acquiescence of the measures of Congress. If they do, they will not be stirred again until the Abolitionists perpetrate some new and great outrage. They have only to be prudent and move by slow degrees to prevent any action of the South for many years—probably until it is *too late*.

If such results follow our measures in the South, what will be the effects among ourselves. Violent excitements will arise as the truth developes itself. An effort will be made by Rhett & Co to precipitate the State into secession, which will probably prove so abortive a movement as to be regarded as an insurrection only, and bring some necks into a halter, establishing the full triumph of Federal Consolidation. If the State does not go so far, it will be in consequence of a Re-action, which will annihilate those now at the head of affairs—but will not stop there. It will change the Government and, I fear, the whole character of the State. It will amount to a complete Revolution here. A thing I have been actually labouring for eleven years to prevent by effecting the needful reforms.

The Government of SoCa is that of an aristocracy. When a Colony, many families arose in the Low Country who became very rich and were highly educated. They were real noblemen and ruled the Colony and the State—the latter entirely until about thirty years ago and to a very great extent to the present moment. Our Legislature has all power. The Executive has none. The people have none beyond electing members of the Legislature—a power very negligently exercised from time immemorial. The Legislature governs and the old families ruled the Legislature. The abolition of primogeniture in 1790 was a severe blow to them. Extravagant, bad managers, and degenerating fast, they have been tottering with the death of every one who was in active life or at least had his character formed in the last century or the first fifteen years of this. When the Bank was established, the more needy of them took possession of that. That has kept them up. But for that, most of those engaged in public affairs or exercising any political influence would have been swept away long ago. On the other hand, they dignified and elevated the Bank rule and kept it from degenerating into a low timocracy and exploding, as would have happened long before now. But in spite of all, even the old family aristocracy is sinking to nothing, and the Bank, though it has apparently acquired strength in the late elections, must go. It has fallen, in a measure, into the hands of inferior men—men inferior in intellect and character and is likely ere long to follow the career of all such Banks and blow up. But just now, during the session, the Bank and aristocracy availing themselves of the strength of the *hot bloods* of the Legislature have managed every thing in the present Legislature, and carried all the leading measures. If they fail, the fate of the Bank and aristocracy will not be left to time. They will be annihilated by sweeping changes in the Constitution. These changes have been long proposed. I and hundreds in my position have opposed them and arrested them thus far—preferring Reform to Revolution. But we could not do so, if we desired, should the people become thoroughly disgusted with the Legislature and its managers. The[y] will demand the election of Governor, of Presidential Elections, and perhaps of Judges to be given to them. They will probably break down the Parish Representation and thus crush the Low Country with its Rotten Boroughs and aristocratic Incubi at a single blow. They will increase the power of the Governor and make him and the Public Officers responsible for the Public Treasure instead of entrusting it to a *Secret Conclave* of twelve men in a Bank Parlor. These changes or almost any one of them will be a Revolution. And I think such a Revolution, inevitable in time without great Reforms, will be much hastened by the late measures of our Legislature.

If I were now to set down and write a pamphlet exhibiting these measures in their proper light, and elaborating the sketch I have given of the history of our State Govt. and making perfectly apparent the present condition of our people, I believe it would require only that every man who could read should have a copy to establish this Revolution, if not perfect it, in two years. I am much inclined to think that something will be proposed in the State Convention [April 1852] should it ever meet, that will lay a groundwork.

I have been for preserving the Parish System, the Election of Gov[ernors], Electors, and Judges, all as they are. I have wished the Gov. to be made immediately re-eligible and his powers increased, the double set of State Offices to be consolidated, and the Bank—the source of the real corruption—to be broken down. My views have not succeeded. Other and more sweeping measures will I think be soon adopted.

If I gather the correct view from the few glimpses the papers can permit of such matters, John Preston [Wade Hampton II's brother-in-law] entertains very much my opinions of the late action of the Legislature and opposed it as far as he *dared*. I have no doubt he did not vote for Rhett at all and that he and his set are terribly galled by the whole course of things save my destruction and Hampton's election. The fact is that to secure my ruin they have themselves brought all this about, tho' opposed to it. I am very curious to see what they will be at next. They can never be any thing *under Rhett*, that is clear. But would serve the Devil to ruin me. So the world and *Statesmanship* goes.

[Silver Bluff] 27 Dec. [1850]

The character of a Senator in the U. S. Senate is always that of a Minister from his State. At this particular juncture, a Senator from SoCa chosen by a large majority such as Rhett ultimately got and chosen in reference to the crisis becomes an Ambassador, and is virtually placed at the head of our Affairs, since the seat of operations is still at Washington. But I believe that a large majority of our people and of our simple politicians sincerely think—as they avow—that the post of Senator is now one of little consequence—meaning thereby only to express *their* indifference to the Federal Government, while they really exhibit their entire ignorance of the true condition of our country. If I had been elected I should have soon changed their views. My plan would have been this. I should have immediately invited all our delegation to dine with me—the only way to assemble and keep them patiently together. Inquiring then of them as to the State of Affairs, I should soon have ascertained the opinion of each as to what was best to be done and what left undone to further a dissolution of the union as to which all, I believe, are agreed. Digesting these views and modifying them to accord with my own as nearly as possible, I should have [been] able at a subsequent meeting to present to them a practical plan of operation in which all could concur, and in carrying out which all could heartily co-operate, having for its object the dissolution of the Union, sooner or later according to circumstances. To this plan I would have got all to agree sacredly to adhere in all they did at Washington and to urge their Constituents respectively to unite in aiding to carry it out. Any well digested scheme of action in which our whole Delegation could concur, and cordially and zealously recommend to SoCa, would as a matter of course almost be adopted by the State. Thus we should have got SoCarolina to move harmoniously onward in a well concerted and consistent course of action. And we could have done more. From time to time we could have brought *reliable men* from other Southern States into our Consultations and induced them to act with us at Washington and *at home*. In this way the foundations of a Stable party might have been laid even in this short Session and before the end of the next long Session we might have perfected our organization and embraced in it every truly Southern man at Washington. Time would have been the main ground of compromise. Altho' I think that the sooner we dissolve the Union the better, ten or twenty years are nothing in so grand an operation provided we can then *secure* our object, and this idea would have pervaded my whole scheme. The great point is to *unite* the South, and the next to prepare it fully for the catastrophe. Time is wholly secondary so we *suc-*

ceed. I should not have been anxious to bring in any States after our own but Georgia, Florida, Alabama, and Mississippi. But our plan would be to conciliate all the South and bring in as many states as possible. The more of them the stronger we should be both morally and physically and the more likely to affect our purpose not only without conflict in arms, but without any violent change of any sort.

In this manner I should have acted. But *I* do not believe there is one of our Delegation who would lay out $50 on a dinner or in any way to take the initiative in such a scheme. It will never enter Rhett's head. He has been elected on the top wave of a high excitement. On the least calm he must sink. He will therefore have but one object in view—to keep the waters troubled as long and to the utmost extent that he can. The rest will each one keep his sails trimmed to keep his own course as well as he may be able. The result will inevitably be division at Washington on minor parts and division at home, which will soon grow into ruptures and anarchy will follow.

Mr. Calhoun by the mere incubus of his vast superiority of mind and of influence at home, kept them down and crushed dissension. Yet there was always a lack of cordial co-operation with him at Washington. There was always some one or more of the Delegation in a state of mutiny against him, and most of them were in a state of apathy towards him. He not only overshadowed them, but drove them to measures they did not approve and in fact did not comprehend. The reason of this was that he did not consult with them *beforehand*. He did not tell them what he intended to do—ask their advice—and conciliate their support of his propositions by argument or modify them to meet their views. He took his own course of his own will and expected them to follow and often compelled them against their will. Hence his frequent failures when he attempted to lead. I should have guarded against them in the manner I have suggested.

And what will Rhett do? Never stood any politician in greater peril. He was elected to represent the noisy, vapouring, gasconading spirit now in the ascendant in SoCa—mainly through his own efforts. If he does not represent it, but pursues a sensible, quiet, prudent course, he will be denounced by the Hotspurs and immolated, for he cannot calm the tempest he has raised to blow him into the Senate. If he does attempt to bully, he not [only] degrades himself and SoCa, in the eyes of all out of our State, but Clay, Foote, Benton, Clemens, and others will instantly mount and demolish him. Even if he tries to be prudent there, he will be twitted by Foote, Hale, and others and driven from such a course. It seems to me he has got himself into a circle of fire, and one he has kindled chiefly himself. I am curious to see the result.

The ultimate result I think will be such a State of things in SoCa as will require a Dictatorship to extricate us.

[Silver Bluff] 31st Dec. [1850]

The last day of the year and to me every thing concurring as tho' it was the last day of the world. Cold, cloudy—raw and rain in the early morning. The old Fitzsimons clock stopped at 1 A.M. and I have always observed that some one of the Fitzsimons family dies when that clock stops. Above all, my boys left to-day. Mrs. H and the two children [Katherine and Elizabeth] are in Charleston having left me near three weeks ago. Harry came over from College (at Columbia) by way of Charleston and arrived here on the 28th. He left to-day to return there. Spann and Willie left to go to College at Athens [Georgia] for I am sick of SoCarolina, and little Paul, dear fellow, went to Augusta to go to school there—all gone, and I am alone. This is a real breaking up. Never will my family met [sic] again as they have met before. The Boys will return as men—men of the world with their views and feelings no longer confined to this spot and those here. The girls will never be much more at Silver Bluff.

These are events in the course of nature which one ought to be prepared to meet, but which no one ever meets without sad and painful emotions. Upon most they steal gradually one by one and are the less noticed. But here they come on me at once with their catastrophe, as it were, falling on the last day of the most eventful and afflicting year of my life, at the moment that my worldly downfall is consummated and when my hearth was most desolated from other causes. My God, my God. What trials are mine. Oh give me strength in proportion. But no I am weak and feeble—torn down bodily and mentally with fatigue, anguish, and unremitted disease. The least able, it seems to me, of all earthly creatures to stand up under the accumulation of griefs. I have erred and sinned. I still err and sin. Is this the retribution? To me it seems unequal. But doubtless an all-seeing and all merciful God has not punished me to my deserts.

I wish I could hope that the New Year would open with better omens. But this side the grave I have No Hope.

VII

*Whatever ability I may have exhibited in my career
was developed and fostered by and for my native
state. . . . when she frowned, my genius deserted
me and my intellect dried up.*

2 JANUARY 1851 – 10 JANUARY 1854

[Silver Bluff] 2 January 1851

In whatever point of view the late Senatorial election is looked upon, it furnishes materials for serious and interesting reflection. My enemies regard my course, I know, as a sort of shrinking from the pursuit of honors, which they think I covet, from a fear of coming in contact with them or a consciousness of my unworthiness. Some think the first the cause, some the last, and some both. My friends—those not in close communication with me—perhaps even those, [think] that I have pursued a course of dogged and haughty straightforwardness to which I expected everything to bow, and that could not fail to end in my defeat. None of them however have watched my course narrowly or thought so deeply of my affairs and my position as I have. The sincerest of them take only somewhat obvious views, and so does the world generally. It rarely takes the trouble to penetrate deeply into another's feelings, thoughts, or situation unless for some selfish views. But, not to inquire now into my particular motives or actions, let me consider the bearing of the grounds alleged for my defeat.

1st That I did not go [back] to Nashville. What of that? Could any sensible man suppose from that, that I had turned traitor? With a whole life of proofs that I was devoted to the South—to So.Carolina—to the Cause of South[ern] resistance it seems to me impossible. Besides there was *recently*, my speech of course at Nashville, my speech at Barnwell on 4th July, several letters I wrote in the summer, my Calhoun speech in Charleston, my letters to Columbia, and my conversation with every one I have met this year and for years past and but a few days ago in Charleston. The proofs were abundant and conclusive and at hand that I am a disunionist. No one could have doubted that. Rhett would have vouched it himself. Then there were the causes I assigned—sickness that made it impossible if I had wished to go—the opinion I entertained (and still entertain) of the impolicy of a full delegation and act[ive] part from SoCa— the fact that my attendance was not absolutely necessary—and that from the vote I got in Caucus, the right I had to absent myself when my presence was not indispensable to secure to the State her full weight. Were all these to pass for nothing? If these good excuses and my known devotion to the State could not avail anything against my great offence in not attending that Convention [Nashville, November 1850], in what did that terrible offence consist? If there was *really* any, it was this, that I had ventured to think and act for myself. That I had not implicitly without hesitation surrendered every other consideration and acted promptly and strictly up to the mark of excited feeling of SoCa. And what is that feeling—so excited—so exacting—so wanting in reason and reflection as to regard the present impulse in every matter however trivial as the only rule of action, and which discards and crushes all who are not infected with it not only in kind but in full degree? It is the *Mob* feeling! The Sans Culottes—Red Republican feeling—which overrides and tramples down every thing in its revolutionary frenzy. And has SoCa already got so far? Is this already the spirit which animates those who control her destiny? If I was beaten for the Senate because I did not go to Nashville, it must be so. And I fear that to some extent it is so.

2. My quarrel with Hampton. If the denunciations simply of one family are [sufficient] to put down a man, and denunciations professedly on private grounds, what is the State of things. SoCa is prepared to receive a Despot. In fact she already has a Master—a Reigning Family. But if the rumours current as to the grounds of these denunciations are to be believed—as I have little doubt that in the main they are—and I was beaten because I had committed the faults alleged, what then? Why SoCa has turned prude. She surrenders herself to be ruled by gossip and gossippers and discards her best servant, because he does not pass immaculate through the hands of the Tea Table Goddesses. Where was a Statesman ever put down before for his amours and conjugal infidelity. When I was in London in 1836 L^d [William Lamb] Melbourne, Prime Minister, was docketed for crim. con. and was caricatured—Mrs. [Caroline] Norton and her *Lamb*-kin in every print shop in the City. Public sentiment has in this country and in most country [sic] permitted the party injured in such cases to take exemplary personal revenge—but never before did a miserable craven call upon a Government to redress him, except through the Courts,

and never was there a Government that would have stooped to do it. Undoubtedly however SoCa has done *something* of the sort, for this alleged ground for repudiating me, has had its weight.

3rd. That I did not go to Columbia during this [Legislative] Session. My presence there was demanded for two reasons. 1st to meet Hampton's expected charges. That is to challenge him to bring forward his private griefs, *expose them to the world*, and make or provoke a war with me. What a miserable *prurient curiosity* to penetrate a scandal must govern the minds of those Legislators who could be influenced by a view like this. 2. I should have gone there to canvass the Members and electioneer for Senator. How degraded must SoCa be if my not doing this could influence her in the disposal of her highest office—an office utterly despicable when filled by a Demagogue or procured by Demagogic arts, but not so despicable as those who appoint to it, when such a course is necessary to obtain it. Has SoCa sunk so low as this? To some extent, I fear she has. There are now few Districts in which any but Demagogues can be elected to the Legislature. One must play the Demagogue himself to secure the votes of men elected in this manner. To disdain to electioneer is in effect to condemn them. Such is the downward tendency of our Democratic Institutions. It was very different in SoCa until quite lately. To canvass for Senator, Governor, or Judge would have insured a man's defeat 30 years ago and would have been severely criticised even 10 years ago. Some do it still but even the most fastidious now give up that it is "the only way to succeed" and *success* is every thing. If the old aristocratic association and clique [who] rule with their wits were broken down by this influx of demagogism, it would be some slight compensation. But it is the old families and the cliques who have brought it about in a great measure by their gross fawning on the vulgar, and have made it *fashionable* and *genteel*.

4th. If the Bank influence defeated me—and no doubt it had its full share in the achievement, it is proof that no one in the State can hold himself independent of and opposed to that Institution without being put down, and that we have a corrupt government money power in SoCa which controls the political. I fear there is too much truth in this. I once thought we had the Bank down. In 1847–8 I made an appeal to the people against it so strong as to bring into the Legislature of 1848 a majority against it in both houses. I turned it over to Memminger as Leader there, and he has so frittered it [a]way in these two years, that the Bank has now a majority in the House and will soon have one in the Senate and run over every thing and every body. I saw, when I was over there last year, that my work had to be done over again, by somebody else however. I told them then that I was done. Memminger and others were *jealous* of me and would do nothing in accordance with my views, and this leads me to the 5th cause to which my defeat is to be ascribed.

5. That the jealousy of rivals for the succession to Mr. Calhoun as the first man of the State caused me to be put down. I have assumed all along that I was considered as the most capable candidate for the Senate. This my friends all write me was conceded by my enemies, and I have heard it from so many quarters at home and abroad that, whether it is true or not—much more whether it is deservedly so or not—I have reason to believe that there is a very extensive impression that I am better qualified to take the lead in this crisis than any one who has been brought before the public. This being so, and the People through their Representatives having without hesitation or compunction sacraficed me, at the bidding of the rival aspirants for the leadership—alleging any or all of the 4 *pretexts* previously discussed—what must be the moral condition of SoCa and what [are] her future prospects. Governed by Rival Chieftains who will only unite to immolate the most prominent, and invariably doing that with promptness, what can she look forward to but misrule, anarchy, and utter loss of all moral influence in the South and the Confederacy. The ultimate result is obvious and inevitable. It is *Revolution*, to be reached through the usual miserable process of division, contention, loss of influence, and natural degradation. The People in the last resort will rise—sweep off the Terrorists and change every thing, perhaps through the last process of a Dictatorship. Certainly through one if the times, as they forebode now, are troublous.

These views are all mournful to me. I ascribe my defeat to each and all of these causes operating in full proportion, and their combination shews clearly, that unassuming merit—the highest *conceded* ability—can no longer expect appreciation in SoCa. To be any thing—to do any thing—to serve and even save the State, a man must throw off all reserve—all delicacy—all dignity—every refined and conscientious scruple and thrust himself forward amid the crowd of vulgar combatants, toiling, sweating, striking here and fawning there, a common soldier, using brawn and brute courage as his surest weapons, and hypocrisy as his constant shield.

Who that has a mind and a soul can do these things. Few, very few, indeed. SoCa then must henceforth be ruled in the main by men who have not minds and souls. I know this has ever been the case in other States and countries in all ages, with now and then a brilliant exception. It has been my dream that SoCa was one of these exceptions. I lived—admired, worshipped, and was proud, proud of her, because I thought so of her and believed the world thought so too. But the dream is over.

Thus it is that the death of Mr. Calhoun has been the greatest calamity to SoCa. He kept her in check. He held up her high pretensions. He put his foot upon her evil passions and restrained her degenerate tendencies. He has gone and already the flood of passion, pretension, folly, and corruption has broke lo[o]se from its barriers and pours in on all sides sweeping every thing before it. I am the first victim. Like the feather in the gale my fate has been to shew which way the current flows. It will soon engulf others, and others, and in no long time engulf all our Institutions.

[Silver Bluff] 25 Jan. 1851

On the 14th inst. a nomination of me for the Convention [State, April 1852] appeared in the Charleston Mercury. As soon as I saw it I wrote to the Editor requesting him to state that he was authorized to say that I declined the nomination. He made the announcement saying that he did so with regret. Simms also declined the same nomination, and in Charleston Col. Gadsden declined. There seems to be a general apathy among the people and I doubt if half of them have heard of the election which takes place on the 15 prox. Hordes of Rag, Tag, and Bobtail Candidates are put forth every where however. It will be a motley Assembly. I will have nothing to do with it as present advised. Let those who put the State in her present critical and dangerous situation get her out of it. Already however my friends are beginning to advise me to take a part in Affairs. The same old song, that the State needs me and the people are with me and will call for me as Leader etc. etc.—all stuff. Our people belong to the Demagogues—the Bank and certain family and political cliques, all of whom are deadly hostile to me. I have written to several that when the State wants my services she must come *cap in hand* and *beg them* and that I *may* then *consider* the matter. If I were beaten for offices by men of more merit, it would of course be very unpatriotic and unbecoming in me to refuse to serve my country or to complain. But they beat me with the almost universal acknowledgement that I am far superior in qualification to my opponents. This alone would absolve me from every obligation. But ever since 1846 a majority of the Legislature have openly and avowedly taken sides in my quarrel with Hampton and linked themselves with him against me. When a State descends to interfere with one's private quarrels and leagues with one's personal enemies, She not only releases him from every bond of duty, but fairly entitles herself to his disgust, contempt, and hatred. He may justly esteem and love even his enemies more because they have some grounds for hostility. A State can have none *justly* in such a case. This view my friends and enemies equally forget to take.

[Silver Bluff] 9 March [1851]

The election for Members to Convention [State, April 1852] took place the second Monday in Feb. The Mercury says 127 members out of 169 are pledged to seperate State Action by the Convention. I think it likely that this is a true estimate. The policy of Rhett & Co has been to commit the State and commit the Members as *irrevocably as possible while the* excitement was up. I believe however they are now in low spirits. The votes for Convention did not probably amount to half the legal votes in any district. In Charleston not over a fourth and in Barnwell two fifths. The numbers were not stated in the papers except for Charleston and Richland. This manifested so great an apathy that in Charleston it is regarded as settled, that the Convention will not carry Secession. I am inclined still to think it will, but there will be great hanging back. So much that ultimate failure and disgrace to the State and destruction to those who have precipitated it into its present condition are all inevitable.

Rhett has made a speech in the Senate. He denounced the Compromise [of 1850] and neither Clay nor Foote made any serious reply. The former in a few words sneered at him. They probably think—as is generally thought—that their denunciation of him last Summer for his Charleston Disunion Speech made him Senator and that further notice would only elevate him more. It may be his speech was not thought worth answering as it was very commonplace, where it was not silly. His main point was that the Fugitive Slave Bill was Unconstitutional, Congress having no power over the Subject—but the States. This as a Constitutional argument is as [sic] absurd simply. But as a matter of policy in a Disunionist, it was a fatal error. Georgia, by Convention, and the people of the other Southern States in various forms have pledged themselves to Disunion if that Law is Repealed. Yet Rhett a disunionist endeavours to convince them that the Law is unconstitutional, and that they ought rather to demand its repeal. He does not *say* this last, but the inference is irresistible. It would be a bright idea to seperate from the Union for the repeal of an Unconstitutional Law.

[Silver Bluff] 25 May [1851]

For some months past, dating from perhaps as early as the 1st Nov. last, but more especially for the last two months, I have been undoubtedly in a state of partial derangement. The utter annihilation of my political prospects has had but little to do with it. But the *causes* of my prostration, and like causes which have destroyed my domestic peace, not to say happiness forever, have upset me. I have written little here of late because I could not write or even talk [about] what has been uppermost in my thoughts, and has torn my heart to pieces. The end is not yet. I see no end this side the grave. The result thus far is that I have lost all I had and gained nothing. Miserable beyond expression myself, I have made all miserable, almost as miserable, whose happiness depends in any way on me. I am not perfect tho' I have striven as hard as any one to be so. I have no art to conceal my faults. And no one *not one*, exercises the slightest indulgence towards me. Nothing is overlooked, nothing forgiven. I am never spared. So I have become reckless. I feel outlawed and abandoned. Probably I have provoked all this, not so much by my errors, which seem to me venial and in others are generally so considered, as by my self-will and unyielding temper. I can yield only to kindness and that is never shown— or if so *too late* and *too reluctantly*. Somehow I have lost the love and confidence of all—*yes all*—every one, even those for whom I have made the greatest sacrafices.

About two months ago, I drew up and gave to A. P. Aldrich (afterwards) a Plan of State Action in the form of an Ordinance of the Convention [State, April 1852], he being a Member. It was published in the Mercury of the 2nd inst. A Southern Rights Convention [May 5, 1851] met about that time in Charleston and a wild fever prevailed [in favor of immediate disunion] so that my plan did not produce any sensation. But it is there and the public mind will come to it when the period has arrived "to think precisely on the event." The plan is simply to cut every tie between SoCa and the Fed. Gov. which can be cut without affording a pretext for Collision and to remain thus with one foot out of the Union until a sufficient number of States take the same ground.

On 1st inst. I moved with my family to the Sand Hills near Augusta, giving out that I had left the State forever. [The Sand Hills served as a summer residence for the citizens of Augusta and became the town of Summerville, Georgia, in 1861. Mrs. Hammond had left home in November, 1850, because of his affair with his slaves, Louisa and Sally, and refused to return home for several years, settling for this period in the Sand Hills, where Hammond made frequent short visits. He did not admit publicly the reasons for the separation, and even in his diary he does not admit the truth, but eventually in letters to his brother, Marcellus, it is revealed.]

[Silver Bluff] 28 May [1851]

Rob. Anderson Esq. and Capt. G.C. Cunningham came down yesterday as a deputation from the citizens of Hamburg, and its vicinity, opposed to seperate Secession, and requested me to address a meeting to be held there on the 31st. I stated my views pretty fully and gave them each a copy of my "Plan of State Action," but refused positively to address or attend the meeting, on the ground that the State had excluded me from political life and that I very cheerfully and finally abandoned it.

[Silver Bluff] 30 May [1851]

We are all superstitious and delight in questioning the future. I do it often times but rarely remember the answers a moment after. The next wave of thought usually sweeps away the whole impression. Sometimes it is otherwise, and I always regret when it is so, as no good ever comes of placing confidence in any revelations thus obtained or dreamed, and often much evil. We cannot act on such vague conceits but they frequently paralyse us.

Every one has heard of the "Sortes Virgiliano" though in modern [times] the "Sortes Bibliano" are more frequently consulted by the anxious and unhappy. I now remember that on the first day of January last I opened the Bible with this view, and my [eyes] first lit on that passage—I cannot quote it now—where Abraham buried his wife Sarah. A few days ago for the first time in my life I tried the "Sortes Virgiliano." I sought first to know the results of a very recent act, that of sending to my wife a long discarded servant, knowing that they must have a most important and perhaps decisive bearing on my domestic peace. I took the first line on the right hand page of J. H. Jaeck's edition of Virgil. It was as follows "Infensi; facta pariter nunc pace feruntur," [Now make peace and ride on side by side.] 587 line 5th Book, *Eneid* [sic]. I then inquired in the same manner what was reserved to me in the future so far as my public connection with the world was concerned, and this was the answer: "Tyrrhenas, I, sterne acies; tege pace Latinos" [Tyrrhenas go, scatter the army (of his enemies), protect the Latins (his friends) with peace!] 426 l. 7th B.

If there is any truth in these respective indications, I shall bury my wife this year, but in the mean while our re-union, in peace all around, shall be completed, and I shall also once more be called on and take my post in the line of battle against my enemies and the enemies of my peculiar country and shall be able to secure peace and prosperity to my own people.

I must say that no one of these things seems to be probable or scarcely possible. There is no symptom of decaying vitality in my wife and I feel every confidence that she will long survive me. [Mrs. Hammond lived until 1896.] As to my domestic quiet and happiness, it is gone irretrievably and forever in my opinion, and for the world, my warfare with it and in it is closed never to be opened again.

I do not record these ratiocinations here in the secret expectation that they will be verified in the least particular. I cannot have any faith in them. But [they] are strikingly appropos [sic] to my inquiries and more direct and clear than most oracular responses, and therefore somewhat curious. I put them down on an impulse. Possibly I or some one else may recur to them hereafter.

While on this subject I might as well record a dream I had sometime since. In brief, my late friend Gen. Montgomery of Augusta appeared to me, and, being conscious of his being dead, I asked him when I should die and where. He said I would die in Alabama and perhaps in two years, but if not, in fifteen. I can't remember when I had this dream. It did not recur seriously to my mind until last June when I stood on the bank of the Tennessee river at Chattanooga, debating whether I should take a boat and go down the river through Alabama or take the Stage over Cumberland Mountain to Nashville. I think I must have dreamed this 6 months at least before that time. It might have been a year before. The impression made on my mind at the time was very strong, but I made no men. of the date and the whole matter soon passed out of my thoughts and but for that trip [to the Nashville Convention] might never have returned again. [Hammond died fifteen years after having this dream.]

[Silver Bluff] 7 Sept. [1851]

My life for the last ten months, more especially for the last six, has been the most peculiar. It has passed like a dream. Judgement and judicious connected energy have slumbered. The Will has been powerful but spasmodic, shewing itself only by fits and on [only] a very few subjects. Memory too has slept, a long sleep. Only prominent events here and there are left on record. Much the larger number of them have vanished entirely, and scarcely any one is retained with all its particulars. I can rarely ever tell the current day of the month or even of the week and sometimes yesterday appears as remote as a year ago. And a most painful and exciting dream has it been.

The utter wreck of all my political prospects which occurred last December could not have produced alone this strange and unsound state of mind. I had never wedded myself to them, and other things remaining as it were, I could have surrendered them, I think, cheerfully. Though uncertain and faint as they were, the[y] occupied a corner of my mind and gave a stimulus and an interest to all my studies. I have felt their loss more in this than in every thing else, for now I see no practical use to which I shall ever apply any knowledge I may acquire out of the common mixture of life. In fact I have left off reading any thing but novels and newspapers, until lately I have been dipping a little into religious philosophy and its adjuncts.

A little more than ten months ago—only a few days more—a breach occurred in my domestic relations [when his wife left him because of his illicit relationships with the slaves Sally and Louisa]—jealousy—not wholly without cause, but violently and absurdly pushed to a length that awakened a disposition to give still more cause, which has been met with increased violence, until peace and happiness at home are gone, I fear forever. This backed by my political prostration, of which it was in no small degree the cause, might have made me desperate without other causes, which have not been wanting. My boys in college have proved prodigals and expended sums which, inconvenient in themselves, lead me to believe that they will squander all I can accumulate for them, and of course my interest in accumulating is gone, and my whole range of industrial plans paralysed. Add to this that my crop this year has from the first been beset by a series of disasters so peculiar and severe as to make on me the impression that they are Providential and, in the present state of my mind, lead me to believe that all the harrowing events of the last ten months or more are of the same character and designed by Heaven not merely to try, but to crush me. And crushed, annihilated do I feel. I am not the same man I was a year ago. I can hardly feel my identity. I thought then my burden was a grievous one. But I bore it and struggled forward with hopes which, though not bright, gave me a future and I could look forward. Now I have no hope. I close my eyes to the future I cannot bear. I do not desire to look into it. If I fall into one of my old days I soon awaken with a start. One or more of the many demons who now rule my life, has cast his black shadow across the imaginary landscape and shut out all light.

While I am thus, the world is going on, and I am constantly reminded that I am still of it by appeals to take a part in it. The State is now divided regularly into two parties, one of which is called the "Secession" and the other, the "Co-operation." Various shades of opinion are embraced in each. Some would secede without any delay whatever. The most of that Party are for seceding certainly within the year after the State Convention [April 1852] meets and this is I believe the test. The rank and file of it know no more however than that they are for doing something, and their Leaders proclaim that there is no alternative but Secession or submission. Rhett is the great leader of this [immediate secession] Party, tho' strange to say no one is willing to own him. Still he leads. Colcock, Wallace and Mc Queen (Congressmen) back him, and after them comes the Governor (Means), Maxcy Gregg (the Adjt. Gen. of the Party), Gen. Adams, Gen. Jones, Bellinger, and others of less note. Of the Co-operationists some are for entire submission, others, and, a large number, will not secede without a previous agreement with other States—one—two or more. Others are for taking measures very decisive now and waiting the turn of events without any limit of time say two to ten or more years for Co-operation and then seceding alone as a last and desperate alternative. Among these last I rank, and, in fact, I founded this section by drawing up a schedule of measures in March and giving it to Maj. Aldrich of this District for his use as a member of the Convention [State, April 1852], but he published it anonymously in the Mercury about 1 May [see entry of 25 May 1851]. The Co-operationists have no leader. In the front are Cheves, Barnwell, Butler, Woodward, Orr, and Burt (Congressmen). All the Judges save Chancellor Dargan are with them, and Judge [Thomas Jefferson] Withers has taken a prominent part. I think I may add that generally the ablest and most judicious men throughout the State are with them. In this District Aldrich and Owens, Manning, Preston and all that set are with them. I have received from Manning and another Hampton toady Torre a pressing request through Aldrich to come forward and aid them. I have also been invited to attend various public meetings. To none of these have I even returned answers. Charleston is two thirds Co-operation and their Corresponding Committee there wrote the other day for my views for publication. I answered declining on the grounds that I had been driven from the political arena by repeated blows from two thirds of the State—had no influence therefore, and self-respect forbade my thrusting myself upon the Community. I have received similar appeals from various other quarters— from Butler through my relative Spann. And I have also received them from Gregg, Jones, and others on the Secession side. But I have sturdily kept aloof. My personal friends are much divided—perhaps about equally so that friendship cannot claim me on either side in especial. The State has repudiated me and she cannot. If I had fallen with a party or on a political question there would have been some obligation, at least some propriety, in my fighting up my side. But I have been ostracised on merely personal grounds, and no political triumph could re-instate me so I have no personal interest. The very party in this case whose victory I might achieve would be free to turn a cold shoulder to me, as a leper—which the Bank Party actually did in 1849, when it thought itself triumphant without assigning a reason. If I should bring success to the Co-operationists, Preston, Manning, and that set, while reaping the fruits, would still continue to denounce me. Shall I serve them, and [Judge] Butler who gave me the first decisive blow. Magnanimity might suggest it, but I have not only found no magnanimity of late in the State, but believe that she is incapable of conceiving, much less, of appreciating it, and still less of exercising it. Bitter personal experience has convinced me of this. Patriotism might require me to serve the State. But she, in full view of this crisis and when patriotism required her to put forward those who could best promote the public welfare, has kicked me off on personal and frivolous grounds and chosen before me those confessed to be my inferiors, as [Senators] Butler and Rhett now are and Hampton who took my place in the So Congress [Montgomery] always was. I cannot under such circumstances act from magnanimity and patriotism, being sure it would be said by a vast majority that I was only trying to sneak back into the arena out of which I have been ignominiously driven, and meanly aiming to take advantage of the excitement to regain a position from which the State in its cooler and more judicious moments had expelled me.

But apart from all such considerations, what business have I to carry my desperate fortunes, my Heaven blasted hopes, my shattered constitution, my debilitated mind, my broken heart, into a great political struggle at a vital crisis? I cannot do it. I have no desire to do it, I feel no sort of impulse to do it. I feel held back by every consideration of public policy, and much more strongly by every feeling and sentiment of my heart. There must be a great, great change in circumstances, and, in me, before I can take any part. But I cannot [sic] can conceive now of [only one] any [sic] possible change of importance to me, and that is the great one from this world to the next.

The two parties here are now nearly equally divided, with a large preponderance of talent on the Co-operation side, which is gaining ground and with a good Leader would carry every thing. The Secessionists claim however a large majority.

I have had several invitations to make speeches in Georgia and openings enow would be promptly made for me if I would shew an inclination for a political career there. But I have no heart for it.

[Silver Bluff] 1 October [1851]

I have just finished reading the first vol. of Mr. Calhoun's works containing his "Disquisition on Government" and his "Discourse on the Constitution of the U. S." It has been published only a few weeks and I received it but a few days ago. I never saw it before in print or Mss. and Mr. Calhoun never informed me of any thing it contained, except that in 1843 he told me he had commenced the Disquisition and written some 70 pages. He also stated that he set out by investigating the nature of man. I record these things here and mention also that since the Spring of 1836 I have met Mr. C. only four times: in 1838, in 1839, in 1843, and in 1846, and that our correspondence has been only occasional, and in relation usually to current events. My motive for these statements is to shew that I had not this book before me and never had had when I wrote my Oration [On the Life, Character, and Services of John Caldwell Calhoun] at this time last year. If the Oration should be read 20 years hence it will be supposed it was written after the book, on account of the many co-incidences between them and particularly on account of my reference to his writings at the close, in which I very accurately anticipated the character of this book. From Mr. Calhoun's conversations many years ago, and from his speeches, I gathered his theory of Government, and where he had not fully expressed his ideas, I ventured to anticipate them and with success. Since finishing his book I read over my Oration to see if there was anything to alter and did not make a single correction.

[Silver Bluff] 14 Oct. [1851]

There was a public meeting here on Thursday last near our two churches. It was for free discussion. [Edmund] Bellinger and Aldrich spoke on either side [of the secession question] and it is generally conceded that Aldrich made the best speech by far. I have been stuffing him for the last nine months, and he has for the last three been practising with great advantage. He has very decided talent. Bellinger as usual consumed his time in stale anecdotes and dry jokes which constitute the staple of his "dead lively" style. He has memory and has amassed a great many facts. Where he understands his subject at all, he groups these around it and in this suggestive way gets along pretty well with Judges and Juries who are compelled to reason on them, and with the masses who are overwhelmed by such displays. But he is utterly incapable of digesting, arguing, and drawing a legitimate conclusion in regard to any matter whatever in private or public affairs. As to political matters, he is utterly ignorant of the bearing of either facts or arguments. He takes his side from one motive or another and collects all the facts and jokes he can and jumbles them into a mess that amuses the vulgar. He alone—long professing to be my warm friend—has attacked me in this controversy. He has quoted my message of 1844, which proposes no measure but refers clearly to nullification, as proof that I was a secessionist then and should be now. He denounced my "Plan of Action" with the base insinuation that its object was to destroy the Senatorship because I was beaten, as if Secession did not also destroy the Senatorship, with the difference only that it gave the Senator he worships *now* (Rhett) a fatter office in SoCa and will provide for all his followers, Bellinger, among them, at the expense of SoCa. In 1844, about the time of my message, Bellinger denounced Rhett and the then [Bluffton secessionist] movement and declared for the Calhoun view—he being then at the head of affairs—and also said publicly that he was caught in a minority in 1832 and never would be so caught again. This is the key to his present position. I felt very anxious to take hold of him and skin him when this meeting was first proposed. I thought I would. But on reflection I saw it would not [do] to suffer myself to be twitted into taking a part in this controversy, when I had so often and so publicly declared in answer to the entreaties of my friends, that I would not. To have answered Bellinger, I would have to launch at once into the contest and at a very inauspicious time, for yesterday and to-day was a *test* election for members to the Southern Congress. I did not therefore even attend this meeting. Bellinger made no attack on me, further than to read and eulogise an extract from my speech in Congress and to say that whenever he felt despondent and wished his spirit stirred he flew to my writings for inspiration and excitement. Nor have I voted at this election. I was not competent to vote without declaring that my residence in Georgia is temporary, and that, I am not prepared to do. Moreover I wished to abstain wholly from this affair. The Co-operationists have erred in holding this election up as a *test* one to the public, because they might have [been] beaten in it without losing any ground, as they have been recently organized and have not had time to canvass the State fully. They have grown rapidly, are growing more, and should not have risked any thing material in a trial of strength until they had reached maturity. I apprehend they will be defeated in a majority of the Districts—

perhaps in all but one, and if so, after tendering this issue, they will be much thrown back.

[Silver Bluff] 8 Nov. [1851]

The half occupied and half dreamy life I lead has delayed me in noticing the important events which have occurred since my last. Contrary to my expectation and that of nearly all on both sides, the Secessionists were *annihilated* by the election last month. The Co-operationists carried 20 out of the 28 Districts and all the Congressional Districts save our own, where Rhett and Duncan were chosen. They beat even in Barnwell and would have beaten Rhett but for the want of hope. In the State their majority was over 7,000. The turnout was not a large one. Had it been, their majority would have been larger. Thus ends this wild scheme, put down at the first opportunity simply by the good sense of the people.

Since the Election, the Secessionists have properly and inevitably resigned *the lead* to the other Party. Rhett—no doubt anticipating the result—fled to Europe a few days before the election. The Co-operationists are non-plussed by their own victory and do not know what to do. There was a meeting of the Leaders lately in Charleston, but the result has not reached me. The "Standard", their newspaper, has thrown overboard my "Plan of Action" and opened—at the suggestion I suppose of Aldrich from me—on Calhoun's Presidential amendment. [In his "Discourse on the Constitution," posthumously published, Calhoun proposed a dual executive (from North and South) each armed with a veto.] If they press it from SoCa it is inevitably lost and it was not my suggestion to open here, but get it brought forward in other States.

The Secession Leaders have also met and agreed to fall back—as I always thought they would have to do—on my "Plan of Action" [to cut every tie with the Federal Government which could be cut without going so far as to secede and to remain in the Union until the other Southern states approximated South Carolina's secessionist views], and Gen. Jones was informally deputed to communicate with me about it. We met in Augusta on the 6th. Their object was to get it before the Convention [State, April 1852] *from a Co-operationist* and then carry it by the Secession Majority. I have agreed to aid them in this and have no doubt I can get Aldrich or some one to offer it. I have written to A. But I have no heart for politics or anything, having *no hope* for myself, and it is hard to be patriotic even with some personal views, immediate or remote. But I will do this much—if I can.

[Silver Bluff] 21 Nov. [1851]

The Secessionists hold a caucus in Columbia to-night, and the Co-oper-ationists will hold one on the 25 inst. at the same place. The purpose of each party is to decide on future operations. I have had letters from Gen. Jones, Col. John Cunningham, and Col. Maxcy Gregg and have seen Col. Arthur Simkins, Editor of the Edgefield Paper. The body of the Secessionists are ready and anxious for my "Plan" as the best they can now do, which is what I have foreseen from the first—that is ever since I saw Secession could not carry and therefore drew it up. The three first have warmly solicited me to come out openly and take the lead. I have declined this, though I have given them my views in full to use at discretion so they do not publish them as mine. I have seen Aldrich. He will endeavour to bring the Co-operationists to this "Plan." If he cannot, he will never-theless bring it forward if he has sufficient assurances of a strong support from the Secessionists. In all this I have been very busy and active *sub rosa*, but am beginning to tire of it and to hope that my part of the perfor-mance is over. It would be something to me to have laid down, when the State was in the greatest confusion and alarm and I in the deepest disgrace, far in advance of all others, the "Plan of action" which the State was ultimately brought to adopt, and thus save her, and, as it were, rule her from my deep retirement in these woods. Few however would ever see it in this light and my gratification would be confined to myself and limited only to a consciousness of having done good and my duty under the most adverse circumstances—something to be sure. But it seems very little to my conceit, which is that I am a head and shoulders above them all, and they are pigmies to me. But the Lilliputians had Gulliver fast down and so these people have me. I own myself conquered—but I will not openly serve *them*.

The Union submission wing, the most active and influential tho' least numerous portion of the Co-operationists, are making great efforts to avail themselves of the late Co-operation victory to organize a permanent party: yclept the Co-operation but really the Submission. As the defeated St Rights Parties in Geo., Ala., and Miss. have all retired again into the Great Dem-ocratic Party, many well meaning but too timid men, such as Barnwell, and, it may be, Cheves, will probably fall in with this movement of the Union men here, though they are disunionists. The Spoilsmen of that Party such as Hayne, Butler, Burt, Orr, Magrath and others will probably hold back to see how things work, and thus it is not impossibe that the Union men may control the Party. In the meantime, Rhett, it is said, declared that the Convention [State, April 1852] ought not to meet if

Secession was abandoned, and some secessionists may follow his lead still, and thus play into the hands of the Union men. If they succeed now in preventing any action and thus disgrace the State, I have little doubt that in two years a re-action will take place that will sweep them out of existence. The party that should be formed now and adopt my plan is a coalition of the reasonable and practical Secessionists and all the Co-operationists that ever contemplated resistance. If such a party does not arise now and at once carry a majority of three fourths in the State, it must arise on the first aggression of the North and in two or three years at furthest.

[Silver Bluff] 30 Nov. [1851]

The Legislature met last Monday and I have had accounts to Wednesday. The Secession and Co-operation leaders had held caucuses and adjourned to hold others. Nothing done and every thing in confusion. The Secessionists instead of openly and manfully acknowledging that the late vote of the State was a veto on their measure and taking ground promptly on the next strongest position, which is my "Plan", consult me in secret, demand of the Co-operationists to propose their measure, and keep up the Secession Organization. Nothing could be more weak in policy or unpatriotic in principle. It is true that if the Co-operation Party makes any *new* move it must split at once. Every body sees this and the Secessionists are not at all ahead of the world in discovering it. But why attempt to *force* it? If the Co-operation Party ceases to exist *as a Party*, will Secession gain any thing? Can any be so blind as to believe it? The people are decidedly against it, and the moment it is brought forward again the opposition to it will rally again and put it down by a larger vote than before, for it is not the *true* measure and the more it is discussed the weaker it will be. It is therefore mere wanton juggling with the people to attempt to compel the Co-operation party to disband. If there is any real aim in it, it is to produce dissension among the Co-operation Leaders and thus secure to the Secessionists all the Offices of the State. What a paltry game for the Magnanimous Party which has risen up to bid defiance to all the other states of the Union and to take SoCarolina from among them by force of arms if need be. But the absurdity of the policy of the Secessionists is more striking than its folly or its meanness. The only bond that hold[s] the Co-operation Party together for a moment is Opposition to Secession. Until all apprehension of the revival of that question is dispelled it cannot disband. And that apprehension cannot cease while the Secession party is lying secretly in wait, maintaining its organization and refusing to declare its further views. The Co-operationists will naturally expect that they intend to renew the Contest; and unless they are satisfied on this point, will consolidate their Organization. The Union submission men among them are actively playing on the fears, and the Staunchest resistance men cannot say they are without foundation. Thus the Secessionists are building a Co-operation Party instead of destroying it, and the Co-operationists have only to stand still to checkmate them completely. As the Secessionists do not see what they are at, so the Co-operationists do not understand their own position. Both are blinded by the miserable desire to control the State Offices. What will be the result of so much folly, and cupidity, the Lord only knows. Neither Party has a man capable of extricating them from their difficulties or even pointing them out.

I have given my views fully and very plainly to Aldrich on one side and Gregg and Jones on the other. It certainly is no business of mine, occupying the position that I do. But in spite of myself I feel constantly that public affairs are part of my vocation, and when personal friends call on me for aid, I cannot restrain myself. What I write and say, however, is not, it is distinctly understood, to be printed. I believe I have now however done all I shall do in the premises. I doubt if anything I have said will have any effect, and look, as I did this time last year, to see the very worst possible course taken.

[Silver Bluff] 4 Dec. [1851]

I received no letters to-day from Columbia, but see by the papers that the Co-operation caucus there have resolved that the late election has decided 1st that the State is not to secede 2nd That it is to co-operate and that therefore that party will wait on the other States. The sole question in the election was Secession. That was decided against, and every thing beside left open. It is a bold and fatal assumption that it is also decided to do nothing. Yet every thing is in such confusion, the leaders of both parties so weak, and influenced by such paltry motives of personal promotion, that I cannot predict the result. I am glad I am out of it. I am sorry my "Plan" was ever attributed to me, which I never intended it should be.

I received from Columbia however a new Newspaper with a caricature likeness of Gov. Means and another of Hampton with short biographical sketches. Reading Hampton's, he appears a sort of model of a citizen. Now this man I knew. He has committed higher offences and many more against female virtue and the marriage tie than I have. Yet here he is a "model man" while I am *outlawed*. An exile from public life, from the social, from the domestic circle. How is this. I believe there is a God who rules. *He* has stricken me. The Eternal fiat has gone forth and I am crushed in every way. Driven from the pursuits for which all the training of my life had prepared me and in which it seems to me I might have shown—from Society which no one enjoyed more—from my family to which I was devoted, the Earth has been parched or flooded these eleven years so that I have reaped no rewards for my labors in Agriculture. Every thing fails me. I myself am a total failure. Such is clearly the Will of God. I am not conscious of doing any thing *or desiring to do anything* to merit such dire punishment. I record this as my *deliberate Consciousness*. It is vain to attempt to fathom the mystery. All that is left me is to do what my hands find to do, and my only happiness is in that toil which makes me forget every thing beside. Such is my life now and will be to its ignoble close. God be more merciful to my children!

[Silver Bluff] 6 Dec. [1851]

Rhett was generally expected to resign [as United States Senator]. I knew he would not. He has returned from Europe and has been in Columbia. He declines to resign. He says his mission is not fulfilled until he has "rasped Clay" and with this puerility our poor pitiful Legislature is perfectly satisfied. I knew Rhett would not resign nor favour my "Plan." To do either would have been suicide, and he has no idea of retiring or being pushed off the scene. His idea now is doubtless that having fired he will fall back—carrying his squad with him *into the rear*. This will prevent any further *action* and my "Plan" falls of course. In due time I shall not be surprised to see Rhett re-appear, leading his cohort in the Democratic Line and perhaps into the very next Baltimore [1852 Democratic National] Convention and ultimately becoming himself an *Union Leader*, on the plea that it being useless to kick against the pricks, and equal folly not to kick at all, so he will go for the only practical [course] and sustain the Union, one and eternal.

Had the Bank been broken down, and the rotten family and political cliques which it supports had fallen with it, as they *would have done*, so that the People could have exercised a *real and steady* influence in Affairs, I might perhaps have again been called into Public life in an acceptable manner. Of this there is no prospect now, for I presume the Bank will be re-chartered this Session, and its war on me will never cease. I do not at all repent drawing down upon me the hostility of the Bank and its myrmidons. My attack on it was *right* and it was not impolitic. It would necessarily have been hostile to me for my course would have been open, independent, honest, and patriot. The Bank will always oppose those who attempt to exercise State Power, unless they form a meretricious connection with itself, and rule through and by its aid. This of course I could not do. Indeed I have long regarded it as the settled design of Providence in reference to me that I was not to [be] its instrument for any great or useful purpose. When I married and became independent of professional labor, I naturally desired to enter public life. In three years after, I was elected to Congress at 27 years of age (not quite). I had not been there three months before I was stricken down with disease—suddenly and almost fatally, and compelled to abandon my career. Four years after that I was started for Governor and beaten by that senile Richardson, but elected his Successor under rather mortifying circumstances. This is an Office in which I believe no one before or since me has *acquired* reputation or influence, and most have lost much of both if they [had] them before. Still I did gain reputation in it and would have laid the foundation of strong and durable Power, but that the unaccountable caprice of a girl who for years had loved me devotedly and to whom I never gave any just cause of serious offence, prostrated me completely before my first Message was delivered, and only the moment before. This was another clear visitation of Providence. My defeat for the Senate [in 1846] by Butler followed this and was avowedly occasioned by it. I have by no means gotten over it yet and never shall. I attacked the Bank after this more vigourously than ever and actually by my writings got up a Legislature with a majority in both Branches opposed to it. By the most ridiculous mismanagement of Memminger, the Legislative Leader, this majority was frittered away and the Bank stands.

When the late troubles came up, men's eyes were turned on me once more, and I was *squeezed* into the Nashville Convention through the Legislature. But just as I was about to be forced forward again by dint of circumstances, came this absurd domestic *contretemps*, which paralyzed me at the critical moment [by his wife's leaving him and taking the children] and I was thrown back once more and forever. Here was clearly, as in the Bank case also I think, a Providential interposition. I did all that man could do with my means in both cases and in fact in all cases, but sudden, surprising, and resistless blows from unexpected and powerful quarters, instigated by frivolous causes, the occurrence of which were among the most common events, but the perversion and exaggeration of which was most extraordinary, will strike down the strongest and ablest and most prudent of created beings, unless they are warded off or he is supported by God. On me they fall with full—with even preternatural force, and I should be a fool to expect to recover from them. God only relenting towards me, and bringing about a desperate state of things to put me forward as His instrument, can restore me. I have not the slightest hope that such will be the case.

It is natural that every one should be curious to ascertain his Mission upon earth. Of course I have thought much about it. As yet I have no inkling of mine, unless it is to drain morasses and convert them—without profit to myself—into the most fertile land. But I think I see what I was *not made to do* and why perhaps Providence has interposed to change my apparent destiny. I believe that with the help of Heaven, if my career had not been so often cut short, I could and would have dissolved this Union. In my day, it has only required *The Man* to do it. And I have seen so clearly how to do it, that I believe I could have done it, if it had been God's Will. But it was not his Will to destroy it *now*, at all events, and he has chained me down.

On this subject I will say what I have long talked and recently written to [Maxcy] Gregg and others. Order is a prime necessity in every community, especially an Agricultural one and most especially a slave-holding one. To the great body of the Southern People, the Union is the only tangible and appreciable Representative of Order, and it is solely on this account that they love and sustain it. Its oppressions must be grievously *felt* before they will violate Order to resist them. Two things then *must* be done. They must be enlightened so as to appreciate these oppressions and all its dangers in future with the *mind's* eye and not wait for physical demonstrations. And *pari passu* steps must be taken to carry on resistance and insure the rupture of the Union, *which do not in the first instance involve any violation of Order.* Thus and thus only can the Great Revolution be gradually carried forward and ultimately accomplished. Calhoun I think must have taken this view of the matter. But either he did not see the way clearly and fully, or he was afraid to avow his object and initiate his measures. My "Plan" is the first proper measure yet propounded. It goes further for the first, than I should have proposed, but that the measures of our last Legislature had opened the veil too far to attempt to close it entirely again, and tho' they are defeated now, the state of things they have brought about in the South—the apathy and panic and submission, demand some rather startling measure to prevent the utter extinction of the Disunion Course for the present at least.

Why do I write these things? What eye will ever rest on these pages? Of what use can such thoughts as I place on them be to any? I can answer none of these questions. Yet I write, write. It is not to vent myself, for when I need that most I cannot write, but only talk. And [when] I do write

I never can say the hundre[d]th part of what I wish to say. I could fill volumes right on and I am so disgusted with the meagreness of these jottings down, that I have never yet [read] a page of one of them after I have written them. To this day I have never read a line of my European Journal.

[Silver Bluff] 6 Jan. 1852

I went to Charleston about the 12th of last month and remained there some 8 days purchasing negroes. The Legislature broke [in Columbia] and the Members came down [to Charleston] while I was there. I was informed by [Richard De] Treville and others that the understanding was I would not under any circumstances serve the State, and this I have heard from other sources. I neither admitted nor denied it, but said the State had most emphatically discarded me, and that under existing circumstances it was impossible for me to serve her efficiently—that I had no desire for public life, etc., etc. I was asked and have often been asked whether I would take the leadership of a Resistance Party to be formed on middle grounds, if offered. I have said it was too improbable an hypothesis that such a position would be offered me for me to entertain the idea, etc., etc. It is evident that many in the State feel the want of me—that many think I could do a great deal and desire to see me do it. But it is also clear that for me to have a party, I must *make it*, and it is also equally clear that my ability to do this is less now than it ever has been. The majority I think consider me dead, and *all*, without exception, overlooking the fact that I have been *killed*, agree in reproaching me for dying. It may be true that I have not fully performed my part towards myself and have not pressed my pretensions with the vigor I might have done. But I have not thought self-seeking either a virtue or a duty, but the reverse. And moreover I have not for years had the heart to push myself before the public. The miserable stigma, which my enemies have been able, through the assistance of the State, to fix upon me, of loose morals as regards the sex has placed me more or less at the mercy of many. I may be coldly received and even cut with impunity—for one cannot arrest such things by resenting them. I might prevent direct insults—and in fact none have been offered me—but to *compel* cordiality and kindness—to *force* friendship, sympathy, and support are out of the question. I have therefore made no attempt and have shrunk from the public all I could. Since I returned from Charleston, I have received letters from R. K. Crallé and D. H. London of Virginia asking me to write A Memorial setting forth the injuries done the South by the Action of the Fed. Govt. from the beginning, to be presented by the States Rights Association of Virginia to the State Legislature and by it to Congress. [Richard K. Crallé had been Calhoun's private secretary and chief clerk at the State Department, and was an early editor of Calhoun's papers.] It was a great compliment to select me for this task, and it offered me much the best opportunity I ever had for distinguishing myself. [If] I had undertaken it and succeeded I would have become the Leader of the South. But I declined it. Repudiated by my own State, how could I attempt to foist myself on the South? And broken up as I am in my own household, and have been for so long, how could I bring my mind to bear on a State Paper of such importance, requiring a close review of all the political studies of my life—an accurate and verified history of the whole action of the Fed. Govt, thoroughly digested, logically and lucidly condensed, and clothed in pointed, vigourous, and burning language. I could not forget myself long enough even to begin it fairly. No, it is no use. I am done for. My mind, I believe, is going. Every day I become more morbid, more contracted.

I have heard nothing from Jones or Gregg. They have not even replied to the letters they drew from me. I infer they wished to get from me the views of the Co-operationists and to influence them through me. Finding they could not effect anything in these matters, they have drawn off again. Evidently both parties in the Legislature degraded themselves into mere personal and sports clubs, and neither would listen to any "Plan" which did not promise the ascendancy to their own side and the division of the State offices among themselves. The State—the South were both forgotten in the wrangling and scrambling by both parties. And so things stand. The game now is to get control of the State. One party aims at it through virtual Revolution—the other through virtual Submission. The true course, the real welfare of the State and of the South, are all very inferior considerations. Ehew!

[Silver Bluff] 8 Jany. [1852]

The circumstance may possibly become historical and therefore is worthy of notice now, that, in the recent debate in Congress on the Compromise Resolution of Foote, Mr. Rhett declared himself to be a Disunionist and in favour of immediate Secession by SoCa. It is the first time any one has declared deliberately in favour of Actual disunion in either House. It looks like a very bold declaration. But it was about as bold as to shoot at a man and then run away. Whenever a position is taken by a Statesman, leading or even prominently identified with a great cause, true courage, sound policy—common fidelity and decency—require that he should maintain it and the dignity of it at every cost. But Mr. Rhett permitted Foote and also Clemens of Ala. to denounce and ridicule both him and his cause in a manner so violent and personal and [sic] it must have rendered both comtemptible in the eyes of the whole country, while he replied to them in words—*mere words*, and those well considered and inoffensive. Rhett's object simply is notoriety. He was willing to be spurned, to be called a traitor and a windy demagogue to his face, and by his tame truckling to bring Disunionism into disgrace, that he might have the distinction of first avowing himself a Disunionist in the Senate. If reduced to that necessity, he is one of those morbid lovers of public attention, who would commit murder, and suffer on the gibbet to produce a sensation.

[Silver Bluff] 31 January [1852]

The Convention [State, April 1852] is to meet in April and the *Thinkers*, one would think, should be programing its proceedings. But save a pretty constant croaking by the Standard (Co-operation) with little meaning and less apparent purpose, dead Silence seems to reign. So far as I know, or hear, which indeed is not far, no one has made up his mind as to what will be done or what should be done. Abroad the silence is equally unbroken. The Convention appears in short to be forgotten both in and out of the State. The unusual cold weather, Kossuth and Intervention, Louis Napoleon and his Coup d'Etat, are the absorbing topics. Yet this topic—the Convention—must very soon come up again and shake the State to its centre, if not the Union. And the excitement will be all the greater if this calm continues, and it comes as it were by surprise. Heavy responsibilities have been incurred by those who called this Convention and for, and I may say by, the State, out of which there can be no sneaking, unless ignominious. In fact it will soon be found that Affairs are dreadfully entangled in SoCarolina. To set the[m] right again—and they cannot be set aright wholly, for damage has been incurred that cannot be entirely remedied so far as the credit of the State is concerned in this matter, but to accomplish such disentanglement as may [be] effected—requires first A Man such as the State has not got on the Convention or elsewhere in public life, if, indeed, anywhere. And trust this Man must have, not only the full confidence of the State, but more actual political power than the Constitution has entrusted to any man. More than the Legislature, comprised as it is, of small, narrow minded, ignorant and envious men, would agree, unless compelled by necessity—which, by the by, the[y] could not foresee a single moment in advance—to permit to any man. Perhaps the People would not yield it to any one. Under these circumstances I anticipate nothing but a break down. If Secession is attempted, as some think, and not without reason, it may, utter confusion must ensue, which will lead soon to violence within the State. If ill digested half-way measures are adopted—such as my Plan, patched, dovetailed, and deprived of Unity, and true Vitality—failure must follow that will be both ridiculous and disgraceful. If nothing is done, the State loses caste and sinks into contempt for a generation without some very fortunate turn of events. Such are difficulties of the present position of SoCa, over which every one seems to be sleeping profoundly.

At and after the first meeting of the Nashville Convention, there was every prospect of the formation of a Progressive Resistance and Disunion Party that would extend its ramifications throughout the South, and which if prudently and patiently managed, would in great time, control the whole South. But Rhett snatched the helm, backed by the over ardent patriotism not to say recklessness and excited ignorance of this State, and in less than twelve months he scattered the party to four winds—prostrated it in every Southern State, even in this, and reduced it to a mere faction, about to dwindle into a conspiracy. His Charleston speech in June 1850, on returning from the Convention [Nashville], was his first move, and that gave him the Command of SoCa by putting him at the head of the extremists here, then a majority or supposed to be. His Macon speech, soon after in Georgia, gave the Resistance party a severe blow and helped the Union party to carry the Georgia Convention. That state recoiled from his violence. He was the prime mover in the second Nashville Convention and brought out Cheves speech, all of which was in advance of public opinion out of SoCa. Then he called the State Convention [April, 1852] about to meet here, and started the project of arming—at least his party did. This alarmed the South terribly, which was not yet prepared for open war, and when in the May Convention [Southern Rights Association, 1851] his Party resolved on Secession and he went forth preaching it all over the State, the Resistance Party was immediately crushed throughout the South. He thus made the question of Union or Disunion the actual question in every Southern State in which the Resistance men attempted anything, when no State except this was within five, perhaps ten years of active and judicious preparation for it. I saw and said, as soon as the Legislature of SoCa passed its violent measures in 1850, that Disunion was postponed *indefinitely*. Events make this clear now to all. Rhett has done it. He is morbidly ambitious of notoriety. He may be a good patriot, but with such propensities no man can be a good Statesman or Party Leader. Rhett has other glaring disqualifications besides his impatience and reckless ambitions. He is narrow minded, ignorant, and excessively rude and assuming in his manners. Personally he is extremely unpopular, and the Party in this state, which has implicitly followed his dictation and enabled him to ruin the cause, have all the time openly and indignantly disavowed him as a Leader. But he cunningly placed himself just before them on every step that they seemed inclined to take and managed to decide them to that movement. He has sense enough—just enough for this, and manages very adroitly to promote himself. He is now crushed however, I think, and it will be clear soon. Still he is so cunning and managing that I should not be surprised if he is re-elected to the Senate, though every body hoots at that idea now.

In reference to this Convention [State, April 1852] this may be said. All Public Bodies meeting without a specific object well understood before hand, and measures which have not been pretty thoroughly digested by some leading character or characters, are sure to do mischief. And they are dangerous in proportion to their power. When they have all power as this Convention has in SoCa, they should [be] regarded, under such circumstances, with the most profound apprehension.

[Silver Bluff] 27 Feb. [1852]

On the 13 of this month, a few minutes before midnight, my dear son William Cashel expired after a lingering illness, with typhoid fever, of 31 days. No apprehensions were entertained until a few days before his death. He was a member of the Sophomore class at Athens College and was taken ill at the Sand Hills only the day before he was to have returned to College after the long vacation. He was sixteen years old last October. I can make no comments on this calamity. I feel overwhelmed by it and attendent [sic] circumstances. My thoughts and feelings are unutterable.

It has struck me as worth noting the singular series of accidents of the last three days. On the 25th a fire broke out in the rear of my smokehouse from coals in ashes placed on a hopper there. It was discovered and extinguished before it [got] good ahead. There were two kegs of gunpowder in the smoke[house] within perhaps 3 feet of the fire with on[ly] a plank wall betwixt. Yesterday riding to Cowden [Plantation], I first tore my coat sleeve against a nail in a tree in a swamp, next dismounted on a snag which rent my pantaloons badly and very nearly crotched me, subsequently leading my mare along the road ditch she pushed me in it and ran off so that I had to walk two and a half miles home partly through mud and water. To day having hitched my buggy at my plantation, the little boy I carry along to open gates, got into it in my absence and alarmed the horse—a very gentle one—in some way, so that he dashed off and broke the buggy to pieces. The boy, miraculousness, escaped with many bruises. What next?

[Silver Bluff] 24 March [1852]

About the first of this month, or a few days before, Rhett replied very formally to a speech made by Clemens of Alabama, during his absence from the Senate in December, in which he said in pretty plain terms that he was a "Traitor and a Knave." Rhett showed Clemens up well and undoubtedly got much the better of him in that. But Clemens in reply added very emphatically to his former epithets, those of "Coward and Liar." Rhett then declared that he could not fight him as might be expected for two reasons 1st Because he was identified with a great cause and stood alone and 2nd Because he had been for twenty years a member of the Church. This was very disgusting—egotistical in the last degree in the first reason and hypocritical in the second, for he has talked more of shedding blood and fomented quarrels, both political and personal, more than almost any man living for all these twenty years. It is however a striking example of the Eunuch Spirit which now rules in SoCa and of which he has proved himself a faithful representative *in undertaking what he could not perform* and *ignominiously backing out.* I am quite avenged on him.

[Silver Bluff] 24 April [1852]

I rec^d a letter some two weeks ago from Col. M. Gregg asking me what was to be done and saying that Rhett had written to him to beg me to prepare the leading documents of the Convention [State, April 1852] which meets on the 26 inst. Thus even Rhett at last, in his extreme, comes to me, the other Leaders of both sides have done so before. They forget the persecution I have been subjected to for eight years past, and the injuries that they have done me personally, and think I have also forgotten all. I might forget both the persecutions and the injuries, but what I cannot forget is that I am *powerless, blasted* and that not only is there no possibility that I should rise again, but that whatever aid I could render them must be done secretly, by stealth as it were, lest what is right and expedient, *coming from me* might be rejected. Nor can I forget that unable to propose, carry through the Convention, and put in execution any plan of action I might conceive, all I could do would be to submit it to them and subject it to their stupid alterations which would ensure its ultimate failure, when they would of course make me the Scape-Goat. If what I proposed succeeded the credit would be entirely theirs. It is asking too much of me to ask me to do this for them, nor has the State at large treated me in such a manner as to make it my duty to incur such risks. If the State would destroy me, the least that she can expect is to have to do the best she can without me. I wrote to Gregg positively declining to write any thing for the Convention or to advise any thing, or even to express any opinion upon the present State of Affairs. I even had no opinion *now* as to my "Plan of Action."

The mail of the 22nd inst. however brought me a letter from Aldrich. He was here lately, and I suggested to him to consider whether the best thing he could do would not be to move an adjournment of the Convention *sine die* the moment it was organized and before any thing else was proposed or any speech made. It would be a sort of *Coup d'etat.* His letter indicated that he was inclined to do this and if he failed, then to introduce a resolution which he sent me and ask[ed] my opinion about. I did not approve the resolution, and it was due to his friendship to me not only to say so, but to emend it, sitting down to do that immediately, I found I could not. So I drew up a Preamble and two Resolutions which I sent him as a substitute. And thus at last I am in the business fully. I dubbed this Project "A Schedule for Submission." That is what under all the circumstances the State has to do, and what I wrote was a formula for doing it in the most graceful manner I could think of. I told him however that I neither recommended him to offer it, nor the Convention to adopt it, and that he must not throw any responsibility on me in any shape. Alas I can bear none—nothing. Another feather would now crush me into the earth to which at best I am sinking very rapidly. I am no longer fit for any thing. It wearies and oppresses me even to read novels or talk twaddle.

[Silver Bluff] 12 May [1852]

The Convention [State, April 1852] met [in Columbia] on the 26th. Judge Cheves moved a Committee of 21 to prepare business and in this was smothered perhaps twenty one projects. The Judge called the Convention an "Infernal Machine" and used his influence successfully to break it up without coming to any explosion. Debate would have been dangerous and every amendment to the Report of the Committee was laid on the table on the Judge's motion. That Report was only a few sentences to the effect that the State had ample cause to secede but did not deem it expedient, and solemnly declared her opinion by Ordinance that a State has a right to secede when she pleases. The report and ordinance were finally carried, without debate, with only some 19 dissenting votes and the Convention adjourned sine die. Efforts were made by some secessionists to adjourn without even adopting the report—according to my suggestion to Aldrich, but *too late*. Barnwell wished the Committee—so Aldrich says—to adopt the last preamble I sent A. and would have been glad to have adopted the resolutions also with one or two more of his own.

The incident of the Convention was the resignation of Rhett. He was there and wished to address the Secession caucus when it met, but they would not hear him, and he resigned [his Senate seat]. Thus he was literally kicked out in disgrace and infamy. And so ends the whole series of measures instituted against my warnings at the time, and so terminates the career of the man then used to destroy me. The man used against me in 1846 [Judge Butler] fared little better. He carried an Address and Project, of 100 pages, which no body would listen to, and he could not venture even to bring it forward.

The Governor [Means] has appointed Wm. F. DeSaussure (little Billy) to succeed him [Rhett, in the Senate]. He is a dapper fellow that I dare say no one even dreamed of for Senator before. He will hardly be a candidate for election in Dec. Yet why not? He would fairly represent the hollow, pretentious and shuffling spirit which now characterizes SoCa.

I have heard from no private source about the Convention save from Aldrich, and he writes under some restraint. Doubtless as an avowed friend of mine, he met some galls in Columbia. I am inclined to think he has struck his flag and that I shall see and hear but little more of him. He has hung on well. Simms, of all my friends, only remains now. I was under promise to Aldrich to write a memoir of him for some catch-penny concern in N. York. I wrote it last Saturday night and sent it off by a private hand next day. It was a duty I owed him for his past friendship to me, but it was a hard task, for though a fine fellow and likely to do something, he has done absolutely nothing as yet. There was no single act or event for biography and no salient points of character or mind to describe and analyse. I did the best I could, but dare say it will not please. I could not *lie*.

[James D.B.] DeBow has written to me to ask for my memoir and portrait for his Review, which I declined. The Town Council of Moultrieville have invited me again to deliver their Anniversary Oration—declined also. I have done with the Public forever, in every form and shape so far as it is in my power to keep clear of it, unless indeed by some marvellous turn of event I could be placed in the position which I feel myself entitled to occupy—and placed in it *in all respects* and without condition.

[Silver Bluff] 21 May [1852]

The Gov. has appointed Wm. F. DeSaussure to Rhett's vacancy. He is a respectable worthy man who will make a decent Senator, but no one probably thought of him. I presume the Gov. was embarrassed by applications and selected him to avoid giving offence. I am not aware that any applications were made on my behalf and presume there were none. I would not have accepted it. Rejected so often by the State, I could not take the place from a single man, and I would [not] feel at all complimented now unless elected almost unanimously by the Legislature and without a movement on my part. I could then only value it as a reversal of past condemnation. But I shall never get any thing. My wife, who paralysed me by her arrogance and violence at the critical moment in 1850 and who has ever since kept me in torment, has, at last, managed to make our domestic difficulties apparent to the world, which of course throws all the blame on me. This I have fully anticipated ever since Oct. 1850 and it is no surprise. What a fatal thing it was when I connected myself with that low-Irish [Fitzsimons] family. They have been stupid and purse-proud enough to think they had *purchased* me. With the usual low-Irish insolence they have cherished the idea that I was an inferior who they had raised. Hence their rage whenever I have done any thing to displease them. And finally they have been mean and base enough to expose what families of real pride and proper tone would have concealed [by publicizing his domestic troubles with his wife], and, in blind, vulgar fury, and a conceited idea of their own elevation, they have for petty revenge utterly sacraficed themselves to ruin me. Their sacrafice and my ruin are equally complete, and equally unnecessary. But what better is to be expected of low-Irish, exalted by recent wealth, even though that wealth was acquired by the meanest and most accursed perhaps of all vocations—distilling and selling whiskey.

My health has been bad and getting worse ever since my trip to Charleston in December. I am now laid up. Confined to the house and ill indeed, though not confined to bed. I apprehend hourly apoplexy or paralysis, and it seems to me that this attack must end in one or the other. I am alone—alone. Not a relative near me to call upon. No physician worth any thing in reach. No friend any where. I feel that it is time for me to take my leave of the world and that my departure is near at hand. I cannot retard—I will not hasten it. I resign myself to God. He placed me here for a purpose. When it is accomplished, whatever it may be, he will call me away. I should like to live a few years to complete my swamp drainings and leave my children, as that would do, entirely independent of the world.

[Silver Bluff] June 7 [1852]

I am dreadful ill. I never lie down at night but with the most serious apprehensions that I shall die or be stricken with paralysis before morning. My right side from my toes to the crown of my head is numb almost habitually—even at this moment. My brain is confused by it and I feel more desolate than tongue can tell. I am left alone. My mother never comes to see me. My wife never even sends a message, unless it is something to annoy. Friends I have none. Neighbours none. My employees do nothing to save me trouble or thought. Having an hour or two almost daily during which I feel better, I crawl about, and no one knows what I suffer or my critical condition, and will not heed my complaints. My son Harry has been with me some days, which has been a great comfort, but he does not comprehend my condition and leaves to-morrow. The servants shun me for I am, I suppose, querulous. Great God! how awful it is to be thus isolated, thus abandoned and to die thus—steeped too in infamy and a bye word in the world. I, who never wilfully harmed or desired to harm a human being, who never wronged one that I know of. I have been guilty in indiscretions—venial ones in the judgement of all history and in the practice of every social system until my case. But with me they have been magnified into crimes because I have been betrayed, exposed, and denounced by my own family and abandoned by my own kin. Of course the envious and jealous rivals and enemies have built on this testimony, though wholly ignorant of facts, and piled up calumny mountain high. My God! what have I done or omitted to do to deserve this fate? I trace it all to the horrible connection which Satan seduced me into forming with the vulgar Fitzsimons family, whose low-Irish deceit and hypocrisy can only be compared with their low-Irish pride, selfishness, and utter want of refinement and tone. I feel deeply for my poor dear children, so deeply tainted with this blood. I trust mine, aided by my precepts, may master it in them. Though it has mastered and destroyed me by appealing to the popular prejudices and the interests of my rivals.

[Silver Bluff] July 29 [1852]

I left here on the 10 inst and returned yesterday, having been nearly all the interval on Sullivan's Island. I consulted Geddings about my health, who said there was no organic derangement and, ignorant of my mental horrors, attributed my symptoms to tobacco mainly. I took this book with me expecting to write much in it while there, but I wrote nothing, not even a letter. There is a perfect stagnation in politics there, as elsewhere in the State. Men seemed palsied by the apprehension that they might commit themselves, in this moment of no question, to something that might injure them and spoke little in general.

What I did see, however, very clearly was that I am no longer looked to by *any body* as a public man. My friends have given me up and lay all the blame on me—of course. They do indeed need explanations to understand more fully, yet these I cannot give because they would require domestic exposures and exposures of females, which I must endure any fate rather than make. One would suppose my friends at least would comprehend this from the reports in circulation, and realize in some sort my embarrassments, but they do not. It is a coarse and vulgar era in which exposures of all kinds are the rage, and no delicacy tolerated or understood. So much for democracy and so much also for bringing men's private or rather *secret* lives into public affairs. It is no consolation that those who have denounced and exposed me, suffer in every way as much as I do, which is the case. Suffice it—that I shall never again be called on to take a part in politics, that I can consent to take.

I have also entirely lost social caste. All the women, and the nice men shun me. My touch would be pollution. I should be subjected to all sorts of unpleasantness if I attempted to enter the circle of Society in which I formerly moved. Of course I shall never do it.

Can a Steam Engine work without fuel or water? Can a man do anything more on earth, who is driven from the field of politics and blackballed by Society? I have lost my interest in every thing. My private business has no charms for me—it has lost all its relish, and I cannot get on with it. My family is broken up. The Skies are all closed in upon me in pitchy darkness.

[Silver Bluff] 28 Aug. [1852]

The same dead apathy in regard to politics pervades the State as has done since the Convention [State, April 1852] sat. The General Election now near at hand appears to excite no interest any where. The Papers are dull to stupidity. I was lately a week at Aiken, in the Hotel, and scarcely ever heard politics alluded to. While there, no one called to see me, though Bauskett, Carroll, Magrath, and Finley are residing there just now and were all at home. Having business with Finley, I called on him. He seemed a little surprised and quite shy. All my former friends shrink from me. It is now generally understood that I feel deeply resentful of the conduct of the State towards me and have denounced her openly and often. Of course no one supposes the *State* will make any acknowledgment or concession and as far as I know no one seems to think she ought to do it. This view necessarily leads to the conviction that my career is over, and I am abandoned as utterly prostrate, and not only that but blamed universally as having wrought my own ruin by my perversity. Such is the tenderness and discrimination of the public—the most intelligent of it—in a Democracy. And such is the inevitable result under any Government when a political inquisition is made into a man's domestic affairs. He cannot explain. They are matters of too much delicacy for any but a brute to be willing, even to sustain himself at the cost of laying them bare to the public. He may say this and decline. But however respectfully, the public will not be satisfied. Curiosity is piqued. The mystery must be solved to gratify the vulgar appetite of scandal, which all high and low possess more or less. He is goaded for explanations. In his torture he complains. This is treason. His best friends fly from him to avoid being themselves attainted. He falls and is crushed forever. It is a horrible fate. *Yet it is mine.* I cannot help it. If all were to go over again, I could not act otherwise than I have done so far as the public is concerned. I could make no revelations. I could not avoid giving some expression to the bitterness of my feelings for the triumph which the State has wantonly given to my enemies and persecutors. I do not feel that I have done wrong and do not regret the course I have pursued. It was my destiny. It must have so happened. God made me for this end. But why he should have made me or any one for such a purpose is what I cannot understand. Of course if it is His Will, it is for the good of the whole, possibly for my own good. That it is His work I can see clearly. The whole series of events from the very origin of the whole matter down to its latest phase, grew up and has been developed, if not in an unnatural, certainly in a most unusual way. All concerned, men and women, politicians and private citizens have acted as no one could suppose *a priori*, or from experience or history, they would have acted. And this not in one or two instances, but in all. It was in human nature to act this way undoubtedly, but there have been throughout extremes of conduct without parallel. If it were all worked up into a romance it would be pronounced overstrained and improbable. Alas for me, my life is blighted. I feel as though I never wish to see any acquaintance and least of all old friends. It is part of the sad fate which an offended Deity has imposed on me that my family ties too should be all rent, and all my affairs visited with fatal disaster. I cannot make a crop. For 13 years I have not, with all my determined efforts, made an average crop, and often I do not make the third of one. Within this month past, while every other part of the State has had too much rain and the river has drowned some of my corn, I have been cut off by drought from every surplus bale of cotton, tho' now in debt and needing a large crop. I think at least 250 bales have been thus destroyed, altho' the cold spring had already insured that I could not under ordinary circumstances make over three fourths of an average crop. My powers of endurance are, I fear, gone. I feel as though it is impossible for me to stand it much longer.

Dec. 11 [1852]

An election for Senator for 6 years from 4 March next took place on the 29 Nov. and 1st inst. The following is the ballot as reported:

				1st inst.
J. J. Evans	41	42	50	86
F. W. Pickens	31	36	27	
James Chesnut Jr	24	33	41	59
A. G. Magrath	18	14	3	
John S. Preston	15	15	18	
W. F. Colcock	12	13	7	
R. B. Rhett	7	0	0	
J. H. Woodward	3	0	0	
C. G. Memminger	2	4	2	
R. F. W. Allston	2	0	0	
R. W. Barnwell	1	0	0	
	156	157	148	145 – 169 members

My name was not among those voted for. I am it appears finally dropped. I might comment much on all this, but I am sick of it and forbear. My Career is of course closed forever.

My friends, it seems, had ascertained that I should get my usual vote— about one third and *no more*, and they would not allow my name to be brought forward. [Josiah James Evans served from March 4, 1853 until his death in Washington on May 6, 1858.]

[Silver Bluff] 22 Feb. 1853

I close these remarks. For long they have been painful to me. I cannot endure to continue them. Every hope of life has now utterly failed. Full of toils and cares of the commonest and vulgarest sort—of mere business. I have no leisure to write. Every ideal crushed and forever destroyed, I have no inspiration. Living in a populous region and surrounded by near three hundred persons dependent on me, I am more solitary than any hermit. In the wide world there is no being who comprehends—no mind that mingles with mine—no heart that responds to my own. No one cheers—no one sympathises with me. Labour and sorrow are all I have on earth. The blows dealt me by my wife's kindred first—then by my wife herself—have proved mortal, annihilating. My faults and weaknesses thus betrayed, have been magnified by my enemies, and the unthinking multitude have ratified every rumour, until I have sunk to the lowest position any man, not convicted of crime, can possibly occupy. Thus lonely—thus degraded, I hate to think, much more to write, and in search of obliviousness, I toil, and when that fails I eke it out with the fragrant weed, and the exhilarating yet soothing draught.

Think kindly of me if possible, Whoever may read these pages. I was created for a man—and in all respects a man. The extreme difficulties of early life lead [sic] me to grasp, without sufficient discrimination, at means of extrication, not dishonorable, that my instincts would have resisted—but involving still greater ultimate difficulties which I could not foresee. Utter want of help, even of sympathy, from those nearest to me and finally household treachery have precipitated my ruin and brought my career to a final close at the age of forty five in—*infamy*.

Whatever ability I may have exhibited in my career was developed and fostered by and for my native state and devoted almost exclusively to the promotion of her interests. When she frowned, my genius deserted me and my intellect dried up. Not at once. For seven years [1843–1850]—magic cycle—I bore up and hoped. But when at the close of that long period—during which perhaps my excitement had drawn from me the best efforts of my life—her brows contracted more fiercely than ever and the conviction penetrated my heart that she would smile on me no more—all was over—my annihilation was complete. I sunk into a common—an inferior man.

It is a very great misfortune to be too keen and clear sighted. All Happiness in this world is a delusion. The greatest source of it is self-delusion. Miserable indeed is he who can drink of few or none of the thousand fountains of error—no not exactly of *error* in its accepted sense—but of beguiling, thirst allaying, soul soothing Delusions which a Beneficent Creator has opened around him.

After all Religionists, Philosophers and Misanthropes may say, the sweetest pleasure of this mortal life is the applause of Men—its bitterest grief Their censure. A consciousness that the praise bestowed is not our due may detract from our enjoyment or that the condemnation is unjust may mitigate our sufferings. But right or wrong we rejoice in the approbation and wither under the rebuke of our fellows.

Of the many Religions—a thousand or more—which have flourished or flourish now upon Earth, all—so far as my research extends—without exception have claimed or claim to [be] founded on Revelation. Although the Jews crowded Athens, and Rome, and all parts of the then most civilized portion of the world, and it is impossible that Plato and Cicero could have been wholly ignorant of their peculiar religious opinions, it does not appear that before the time of Christ, and indeed until several centuries after, the Revelation to the Jews was placed in a different category than that vouchsafed to other Peoples. To men of information and reflection in all ages and countries, the traditions of the many Gods who ruled in heaven—their councils, their intermarriages, their contentions, their amours and their children, legitimate and illegitimate, mortal and immortal—must always have appeared absurd, and the idea of One God, the Creator and Ruler of all Things, Spiritual and Invisible, must have appeared most reasonable. This Idea the Jews alone seem to have possessed and why the Thinking Men of Antiquity did not fasten on it and embrace their Theogony is a mystery that can be solved only by conjectures and which I will not stop to discuss. They did not do it until Constantine made Christianity Imperial, and from that time not only this Idea, but all the facts, traditions, theories and records connected with its origin, its history and its precepts have so taken hold of the minds and so controlled the governing Powers of the most enlightened nations, that men can question nothing and propose nothing relating to religion without being denounced and excommunicated, whether in Catholic or Protestant countries. I don't see the justice much less the logic of this, and as *Belief* is *Involuntary* my opinion is that nearly all men and many women—women, by the by, being mostly fools and savages and not to be called either civilized or thinking or reasonable Beings—who acquiesce in this State of things are either indifferent to Religion or Hypocrites. I claim the privilege denied to most men in Ancient and Modern times to have a religion of my own. I cannot risk my Eternal condition upon the Authority of any or of all the mortal men who have lived before or with me. I believe that Jesus Christ was the greatest, grandest, and Truest Expounder of Religion who has ever lived, that is Christ as we have Him—the author of the Sermon on the Mount. I believe that all men are Inspired more or less according to their intellectual Endowments. But that any One who ever trod the Earth had any *direct communication* with God any more than I have had and all have had, I do not believe and never can be made to believe. It is therefore my privilege as much as that of Moses and the Prophets, of Christ and the Apostles, to seek God and search after his Designs and Will through Nature and the workings of the Human Mind and Sentiments and Passions—my own and others.

Thus thinking and in accordance, observing, searching, analysing and building up, my conclusions are that all Human and possibly all Sentient Beings are endowed with a something, Soul, Life, Reason, whatever it may be called that has existed always and will exist forever. I believe in One Supreme Being who made this Earth, perhaps this Universe, who also Rules despotically all the Inferior Beings within his Sphere. I believe that all the Human, possibly all the Sentient, Beings, who inhabit or ever did inhabit this Earth, have been placed here *for Punishment* in consequence of their having violated some of his Laws or Commands. Hence the Evil which predominates a thousand fold on Earth, the Good being only a delusion and a snare to make the evil more pungent and more torturing. Hence some die early, having expiated, by loss of Heavenly Bliss if no actual suffering has been endured. Hence some live on in grief and pain. Hence some appear to achieve much and to enjoy much whose offending has been of a milder type and whose careers are necessary to conceal the Truth. Hence is implanted in us that predominating love of life which keeps us here, it and the concealment of the Past and Future from us, for if we knew the Past we should anticipate the future and leave our Prison House at once since we could at any time "with a bare bodkin our quietus make."

It follows that I believe that our Future depends more or less upon our Conduct here. If we atone and "do works meet for repentance" we may regain our lost status with our Master. If we do not we may aggravate our offences and be plunged hereafter into a "still lower depth."

[Silver Bluff] 27 *Sept. 1853*

Formerly I could in some measure relieve myself by committing my thoughts to paper. But then I felt restrained from saying *all* I thought and felt, lest I might appear extravagant, and this from mere habit of appearing like other people more or less, because I rarely wrote for another eye. Now I could say anything that I thought true, whether apparently so or not, but I cannot. It is torture to use a pen, and *my mind is a boiling cauldron of unutterable ideas.*————Aye! Aye!!

[Silver Bluff] 13th Dec 1853

Until within the [last] few weeks I have never read anything about the "Spiritrappings," except occasional newspaper accounts which held them up as so absurd that I made no inquiry into them and had no notion that any religious system was in any way connected with them. I have just read Judge Edmonds' "Spiritualism." I cannot say that *I believe* he has had any communications of the other world. But that now seems to me less impossible than I lately held it to be. [Hammond shared with his friend William Gilmore Simms, the novelist, an interest in Spiritualism, a highly popular movement in the 1850's.] I must *see* and *hear* myself to believe. I think however the testimony in favour of his and thousands of others having recently established "Spiritual Intercourse" to be far stronger than any which the Bible offers *us* to prove that its teachings are revelations from God. The witnesses are more numerous, infinitely more enlightened and here among us in our day, while the facts, if they be facts, are of a more important and substantial and tangible character, while the teachings are incomparably more consistent with reason, with nature and with truth, so far as we know it. If these things be delusions—I mean the spiritual communications now daily and hourly made—if honest and enlightened [people], much such [as] I now find, put in them faith founded on their own personal experience, and yet it is all the work of their imaginations, then I am more than ever convinced that the Divine pretensions of the Bible are also delusions, if not frauds.

At all events, to the Religious System propounded through Judge Edmonds, if I comprehend it, I am prepared to yield my entire conviction, as the most rational, the purest, and in my opinion the truest ever yet propounded to the Human Race. It is in all *essentials* the very same that I have hammered out for myself, without the aid of Spirits, and does not differ from what I have said in the last few pages except as to the origin of man and his destination, about which we can only conjecture the particulars. I have called this world Hell. It may [be] only the worst state of probation. And instead of our being fallen angels we may be merely undeveloped ones. I wish to see more of all this.

I came into this world without my knowledge or consent. If chance or mere development occasioned my existence, there is no alternative and I must "stand my chance" and fulfil the law of Development. I have no one to blame or to praise about it. My duty and my law is to be *as content* as I can. If God—that is a Superior and Designing Being—created me and placed me here; if this is *all* or the best, *I do not thank him*. I wish I had been let alone. I should not object—hating the pain and lurking fear of death, to be remanded at once to my original nothingness, for this is a world of ineffable misery and from my experience I abominate it and most that it contains. If there is a Hereafter, then the God who placed me here owes me large compensation for the sufferings I have *involuntarily* undergone on Earth.

Were I *sure* of an existence beyond the grave, I should feel almost equally sure of this vast compensation, and I should feel grateful to God who created me and adore Him—not for placing me *here*, but for entitling me to a higher Sphere hereafter.

[Silver Bluff] 3 Jan. 1854

God is Love—Ah—If you are wise never *love* anything or any body in this world.

[Silver Bluff] 10 Jan [1854]

Can any man, Theologian, Philosopher, Skeptic, or Fool tell me why God should place a Man in and confine him to a situation in this world for which he is wholly unfit, causing thereby misery to him and to all concerned and perhaps entailing eternal Curses on *all?* The only answer that can be made is that it is done to *try him*, it is his *ordeal* (and that of *Others* too?) and that if he *wakes* he will come through. This is false. I have *wrought faithfully*. I have fallen short *once only*. Thus to go on I must have met a *bloody* and infamous grave, or what is more probably— as I am a brave and cool man—I must have bathed my hands in the blood of those I respected, even loved. Could either of these alternatives be the desire of a Good God? I thought not and acted accordingly.————and GOD *deserted me!!!*

VIII

*I record now the strangest and most unexpected chapter of
my history, or of almost any history.*

---

3 OCTOBER 1854 – 20 SEPTEMBER 1862

. . . .[Silver Bluff] Oct. 3rd 1854

Wherever I look around me I see a wall of Fire. Wherever I place my foot
the earth crumbles. God hates *me*. No wonder the Bible pourtrays [*sic*]
him as a God full of Wrath, exacting the pound of flesh *and the blood*,
since he has the *power*. No wonder Christian Preachers proclaim him as
an infuriated Demon seeking whom he may destroy. Such and such only
is my experience of him. Can it be the horrible experience of *all* men?
And he expect[s] us to love him, when he shows to us nothing but malignity, *wanton* hatred, and vengeance? When all our efforts to do good
and to be good turn to ashes—do harm: and our slightest peccadilloes
bring us torture extreme and never-ending? Love begets Love. If Love be
the rule of God, he must shew love to us. He should at least set the
example. Does he? The result of my experience of Life and Him is that I
pant for *Annihilation*. Would it might come and *easily this night*.

I have erred in my career of life, often from defect of judgement, often
from ignorance, often from passion, often from weakness. Oftenest from
ill-health which has clouded judgement, compelled ignorance, excited
passions, and begot weakness. That ill-health is chiefly constitutional, the
work of him who made me. But I do not remember that I ever inten-
tional[ly] did wrong, and I do not think that I ever deliberately, or otherwise, wronged any human being. If any accuse me of it, I am ready to
meet the accusation openly, before any Tribunal. Human or Divine. Where
all the facts can be elicited and the Judgement is perfect.

264

[Silver Bluff] 15 Nov. 1854

This is my birthday. I am forty seven years old. I have most earnestly entreated the Great and Good God, whom alone I worship, to be merciful to me, to grant me knowledge, especially of Right and Wrong, to help me to love the truth, and to constrain my animal propensities to subordination to it, to help me to do better in all respects, not only for myself but for all others, and to fulfil, not merely but heartily, all my *duties* in this world.

I cannot tell whether my prayers are heard. I *believe* they are not. If I may augur from the *incidents* of the day, there is no hope for me here or hereafter. It closes in the *deepest gloom*.

[Silver Bluff] April 19th 1855

My two eldest Sons, Harry and Spann, have within the last two weeks returned home from Philadelphia, where they have graduated at the Medical University of Penn. The former had previously graduated at the SoCa College and the latter at the University of Georgia. They have completed their education, in the view of the world, though in mine they are now only prepared to commence. They possess now acquirements much beyond the average of young men and their minds are well disciplined. They have fine talents both. I think very superior. As far as I can judge their sentiments are as pure and elevated as I could wish, and their dispositions excellent. I am very proud of them. I do not think them inferior, take them all in all, to any other young men in the world. I do not know—I never knew any two superior to them at their age. [Such complimentary remarks by Hammond about his sons' accomplishments are especially rare.] I thank God that I am able to give them property that with proper management will enable them to live in a manner so independent that they can pursue truth and cultivate their affections and sentiments without fear and without reproach. May the Good God constantly impel them to do these things and guide and guard them through this world, develope them for the highest attainable sphere in the next, and send his Angels to meet them at its threshold. Dear, precious boys may you be far, far happier in this world than ever I have been, and may you in the next be able to advance me, as I have laboured and desired to advance you here.

For me I feel more and more every day that my earthly career *ought to close*. I have felt and I may say known for nearly 12 years that I was utterly and forever debarred from pursuing that path for which I had during my previous life assiduously trained myself and on which my highest earthly hopes were concentrated. The rarest combination of unexpected events had affected this, and though not without fault myself (Who ever is?) I did not think and I do not think I deserved to be so blasted. If I ever indulged in any hope that things would and I should be restored to my proper sphere, that hope has faded and waned day by day until at last I can truthfully say that I have now no more expectation of such a thing than that I shall be raised and brought to earthly life again after death.

What is very strange, is this. Having almost from the first entirely surrendered what constituted, I may say, my identity—having given up all that I was or was prepared for by my first 36 years of life and all that I hoped to be—I turned to other pursuits to employ myself usefully for my family—I may say for the world and for my own happiness in a minor way—yet the same fate has still attended me. I have failed throughout. With all my intellect and energy, which none depreciate and which I feel to be equal to any man's, I have not been able to compass and consummate any thing, even the smallest expectation. I can't do anything. I am bound hand and foot by an inexorable destiny. Every error, every fault breeds fruit an hundred fold for my wretchedness and ruin. But what is good in me (and surely there must be something: in my judgement there is much) breeds none.

And thus what a wreck have I become! Oh fallen! fallen! I am calm. I am stating soberly facts that are really awful to contemplate and think on. Yet whatever I have done for many long years—what I am doing now, whatsoever I may yet do ere I shift off this mortal—all—all, let be remembered, has been and will be done from the impulse or in defiance of *Despair*.

[Silver Bluff] 12 May [1855]

I purchased not long ago Dr. Milledge Galphin's residence in Beach Island and named it Redcliffe from the red bluff in front of it. I came down there day before yesterday with some furniture and yesterday Mrs. H. came there with more and to-morrow I propose to join her there and take up my residence there. [The separation of the Hammonds ended sometime before the purchase of Redcliffe.] It is a beautiful situation, susceptible of magnificent improvements and has the finest view in the middle country. I wish I had purchased it before I went to Columbia and put up my Columbia house there. How would my career differed from what it has been!!

If I live and prosper I will improve this place, lay my bones there, and leave it for a family mansion. But I am now too old, too infirm, too heart broken to do any thing with spirit or look forward to any earthly enjoyments.

1856

[Redcliffe] 22 Feb.

I have never enjoyed such health as since I have been residing at Redcliffe, nor undergone so much labour and suffered so much anxiety in the same time. I rather think however that I am now about to die though I have accomplished much business to-day and shall have ridden 25 miles when I get back to Redcliffe. But I have symptoms, which may pass off, but which the turn of a hair will convert in to a sharp and fatal disease, and I have no power in the matter.

[Redcliffe] 21 May [1856]

Every thing in the world is *Relative*. In judging of men and Human Affairs, errors chiefly arise from our ignorance or obliviousness or error in estimating these Relations. We are apt to think that men are happy, or at least should be happy, and are wicked if they are not happy if they possess those things we ardently desire to possess ourselves. We do not take into our account, the possibility, nay the probability, that if *we* possessed all these things and could attain suddenly all we *now* desire, we might not realize happiness. Much less do we consider that what *we* think desirable others may not think so. Least of all do we remember that the accomplishment, even of our own highest ambition, must be complete in all its relations and without condition to make us happy. And who ever did achieve this? What does it boot a man to be an Absolute Emperor, if he has no Heir or having one knows him to [be] a fool or uncontrollable? What boot it to a man to grow rich if his wants or his enterprise grow at even pace with his wealth, so that he has no more farthings to *throw away* than the poorest around one. Why should a man stake his happiness on being more virtuous, more wise, or braver than his fellows, when he is sure to find at the end that his Courage, Virtue, or Wisdom are infinitely below his ideal, and compared with perfection, amount to nothing? [Later in a letter of Hammond to his son Harry, dated July 16, 1859, he wrote, "I am like Charles V, wishing and resolving *to abdicate*," but being unable to retire because Harry was a college professor at Athens, Georgia, and his two younger sons, Spann and Paul, were "dead weights" who "growl, grumble, sulk and do nothing. . . . They shoot birds, buy fish, and gerrymander the County. All the negroes see they are mere dilettanti—theatrical planters." HBC, SCL.]

[Redcliffe] Aug. 26 [1856]

Every body knows the story of Sysipphus [sic], who was sentenced to roll a stone to the top of a hill, which before he could secure it there broke loose and rolled again to the bottom forever and forever.

My life has been in all its phases a mere illustration of that fable, with this additional. The Stone rolling back has always broken some limb of mine and utterly crushed some body connected with me.

[Redcliffe] 6th May 1857

A capricious turn of affairs as regards myself has occurred which may be worth a brief record or sign. In Feb. [January 27] Preston Brooks, the representative of this Congressional District, into which I came two years ago on purchasing this place [Redcliffe], died. Some dozen candidates were very soon announced—among them myself—to fill the vacancy. I had my name withdrawn quietly from the papers. Soon letters came pouring in upon me from all quarters, and all the prominent candidates offered to withdraw if I would run. I declined explicitly and decidedly. Nevertheless, an organization was made to elect me without my consent, and some 10 days before the election, it was announced in the papers that I was to be run *anyhow*. I was then forced to say I would not serve if elected. I wrote this to a prominent man in each District and to Col. Simkins, Ed. of the Edgefield Advertiser, authorising him to say so for me in his paper, if he thought it absolutely necessary. In the next paper he did so in a very graceful manner. The election came off yesterday and the day before. I actually forgot it and did not go to vote.

[Redcliffe] 6th June [1857]

I have just had a conversation with my Wife which induces me to record this. [Senator Andrew Pickens] Butler has died and I am again [put] up and run for Senator, and the question is, will the Hamptons move against me again.

My Wife, who might have played a very important part in this matter and, as I think, have in a measure reconciled every thing, has always been negative, a passive nobody, [has] done nothing, and [yet] *apparently* sided with me and been too indignant to act.

I have always suspected—I now *know* the reason. She says, I *declared that* if ever I came [again] in contact with the Hampton girls, I would carry my point—and *use them*. It is *utterly* false. I never said, never thought such a thing. Nothing could possibly have induced me ever to have taken a liberty with one of them, of all people on earth. I did all I could to avoid them, when we were on the best terms. I availed myself of Cathy's rebuff (the first and only) to discontinue them entirely.

But my Wife's jealous mind suggested this result, and She has done all she could *passively* and *negatively* to keep the breach open, for fear I should do what she dreamed, but [which] I never said and never *thought*. This idea, haunting her, she has throughout acted the part of a *jealous Wife*, forgetful utterly of me and my prospects and those of my children, as well as those of her sister's children and all concerned. What devils women are! How their jealousy blinds them to all other things hell, heaven, and all. [The breach between the Hamptons and the Hammonds continued for decades. However in 1894 there is a very sweet letter from Kate (Cathy) Hampton (her rebuff of Hammond is mentioned by him above) to Hammond's granddaughter, Julia. HBC, SCL.]

[Redcliffe] 29th Sept. 1857

I have written—dated to-morrow—a communication to the Charleston Mercury peremptorily refusing to be a candidate for the Senate or to serve if elected. I wish I had done so months ago. I have been waiting for an occasion. None occurs or is likely to occur so I do it any how—*tour de force*. It is too late in life for me to go again into politics. I have not the *Vim*.

It is, I know, political suicide to send this card. I commit it, I want repose, an utter end.

I feel conscious that I have the capacity equal to, if not superior to, any public man in this country. I feel also that it is my duty to exert all my faculties for the good of my fellow creatures. But I believe that God has endowed me with political capacity out of mere profuseness and does not wish me to use it. I believe so because he has deprived me of the necessary health, because he has permitted hitherto unheard of obstacles to thwart me, such as dalliance with women, and because he has—what is equally unheard of—made my family and my wife's family my worst enemies. It is impossible in this or any country for a man to be a public man with all his domestic support crumbling under his feet or deadly hostile. Hence it is not my *duty* to exert my talents in any public way.

The letter was ultimately dated 2 Oct. and appeared in the Charleston Mercury of the 5 Oct.

[Redcliffe] 9 Oct. 1857

It is wonderful that God should have made and placed in this world such a Soul as mine, to be quenched, aborted, and ended it in *Nothingness*. I have long apprehended, but until now never fully *believed* it. Petty, pitiful trains of instances have brought about the catastrophe. I am too disgusted with them to be able to trace them. I despise, I loath, I vomit on them. Yet they are Fate. I succumb and bare my neck to the "Coup de grace."

With fair health and due support I could regulate the affairs of this Country and thereby of the World better than any man living. *I feel sure of this*. Others believe so too. But I have no health, the support with that, I could soon recruit. Could I count upon *myself*—had I confidence in that Stomach and, by consequence, nerve and muscle were at any time under my control, I would throw every obstacle right and left as a lion shakes the dew drops from his mane, and rule this world. But a spoonful sometimes of this, sometimes of that, and sometimes of the other—God only knows beforehand which—prostrates me for days. Who made me thus? God. Why did he do it, and yet endow me with a mind to rule under Him the Universe? Eternity only can answer.

[Redcliffe] 9 Dec. 1857

I record now the strangest and most unexpected chapter of my history, or of almost any history.

The Legislature met on the 23 Nov. The Senatorial election was ordered for the 27th and the actual vote was J. H. Hammond 65, F. W. Pickens 39, James Chesnut 24, John S. Preston 18, R. B. Rhett 6, and some Scattering. The Legislature after ordering a ballot for next day adjourned. The 2nd ballot was Hammond 71, Pickens 50, Chesnut 36, and some Scattering. Sunday intervening there was no other ballot until Monday the 30th and the result was Hammond 85, Pickens 59, and Scattering 14. I was elected by 12 over all and 26 over the foremost opponent.

I had gone to bed the night of the 28th, before any news of this reached me. I would have telegraphed to withdraw my name the next day but for the entreaties of my family and because I did not suppose they would do it.

All this is most extraordinary and to me astounding. I have been too unwell to digest it, for I have been fading away rapidly for two months, and I fear this comes too late.

This is a signal triumph over all my enemies and, speaking as a mere mortal, a full compensation and more for all I have endured. It wipes off every calumny and puts my name among the foremost of SoCa without a stain. Indeed since John Rutledge was appointed Dictator in the Revolution no man of SoCa has ever been *forced* against his *expressed refusal* into so high an office.

Is this a caprice of the People, or the *Will* of God. If it is a "caprice" I nevertheless thank my God for this bounty to my beloved family and my devoted friends. If it is His Will and I have a Mission yet, Oh then He will surely sustain me. He will give me the health, the strength and the Inspiration. Oh Lord, I have struggled earnestly and honestly amid all my trials and temptations, my suffering and agony to do right and not to do wrong. Thou hast fully repaid me already according to my estimate of deserts and overpaid me. Oh that having confidence in me Thou mayest see fit to enable me, with Thy Support, to do *all* that one, placed as I am, might do, if in addition to my willingness, he had the required health, strength and inspiration.

[By the time Hammond was elected to the Senate in 1857, the North and South were polarized over the issue of the expansion of slavery into the territories. The Compromise of 1850 had temporarily settled the slavery question, but the Act had been undermined by the passage of Stephen Douglas's Kansas and Nebraska Act of 1854, which raised again the general question of the expansion of slavery and, in particular, the status of slavery in Kansas. The outcome was a civil war in Kansas. President James Buchanan and Senator Stephen Douglas became embroiled on opposite sides of this controversy. Their confrontation over Kansas was splitting the Democratic Party. At this point, Hammond entered the Senate.

Much as after his gubernatorial victory in 1842, his diary abruptly stops with Hammond's election to the United States Senate in 1857. After following "the utter wreck" of his political career from 1845–1857, the reader must await Hammond's belated account of his Senatorial "triumph" until after the firing on Fort Sumter in April 1861.]

[Redcliffe] 16 April 1861

Until within the last hour I have not opened this book since the last entry [in 1857] and never expected to open it again, though the events that have occurred in the mean time have been the most important of my life and the most momentous to my country. I shall try to make a faint record of them, but my hand, my health, and my eyes fail me utterly and I am little more than an imbecile. I have written heretofore to indulge in the expression of my thoughts and feelings and perhaps have made little more than a record of my own selfishness, morbidity, and conceit. It is now so painful to me to write (and even to read) that I shall hardly indulge myself so much in these regards. Yet here [in this diary] I have painted myself as I am and must continue the picture as originally designed, so far as I can.

Feeble in health and overwhelmed with a sense of my responsibilities, I took my seat in the Senate on (I think) the 6 Jany 1858. I was well received by all, and the manner of my election gave me at once a high position in the Senate. But I soon found that I was surrounded—with a few noble exceptions—by a vulgar set of mere sharp shooters, County Court lawyers, and newspaper politicians, who made the smallest, meanest, and falsest points imaginable and pressed them feircely [sic], to be reported for their benefit among their lowest and most ignorant constituents, who would never see their refutations, even if one would stoop to refute them. Their weapons were pins, but they thrust them mercilessly. I soon found too, while I received every personal consideration, no one believed that I could sustain the reputation that my friends had given me. One Senator I know said—and he was friendly to me of old—that an angel from heaven could not do it. It happens so often that Provincial reputations fade away in Metropolitan arenas that I thought this very natural and took no offence whatever.

I made no speech until the 4th of March [1858]. It was in answer to the speech of Sen. [William] Seward of N.Y., made the day before.

[Although the occasion was the debate on Kansas statehood, Hammond used his speech to compare the resources of the North and the South, making two major points. In his inventory of Southern assets, he touched upon the importance of the South's production of cotton in world commerce, concluding "No, you dare not make war on cotton. No power on earth dares to make war on it. Cotton *is* King." In making his second point, he said in the defense of slavery that, "in all social systems there must be a class to do the menial duties, to perform the drudgery of life. That is, a class requiring but a low order of intellect and but little skill. Its requisites are vigor, docility, fidelity. Such a class you must have, or you would not have the other class which leads progress, civilization, and refinement. It constitutes the very mud-sill of society and of political government; and you might as well attempt to build a house in the air, as to build either the one or the other, except on this mud-sill. Fortunately for the South, she found a race adapted to that purpose to her hand. . . .We use them for our purpose, and call them slaves." While in the North, he claimed, "Your whole hireling class of manual laborers. . .are essentially slaves." But he argued, "not cared for, and scantily compensated." Hammond achieved national prominence with this speech. In his diary entry on 16 April 1861, his recollections continued:]

I had carefully prepared myself, made full notes, and written out much. Of what I had written, I spoke only a few passages verbatim. I could not memorize and deliberately omitted all reference to more than half. But I had mastered my notes and did not show them. Fortunately Seward's line of argument exactly suited mine and I had no great changes to make. The speech was extremely successful in the Senate and in the country. It justified my friends and my State in sending me there. It fixed me at once as the Peer of any one upon the Senate floor. That was glorious to me. But it finished me. I have long known that any great and severe mental labor prostrates me for months and months with my feeble health. Could I have left the scene at once and come home I might have recuperated. As the best evidence of the effect of my speech in the Senate, not a speech in that great debate made after it on the other side did not purport to answer it. I think there were 15 or 20 very long ones—a folio at least—launched at me. I did not reply though I fully intended and even promised it. Passing one day by a knot of Senators and others, among whom was the British Minister [to the United States], Lord [Francis] Napier, while some one was pitching into me, some one said they are giving it to you again. Oh yes, said I, but I will return the compliment. "Oh no" said Lord Napier, "Never reply." I was much struck with the remark and said, "My Lord that is a very sensible suggestion." Reflecting on it, I adopted it. The mover of a measure should reply. A mere debatant never or rarely. Speaking of Napier

—Interrupted here, before I resumed, or rather expected to resume my pen, my health became unusually feeble and my eyes very weak. I think I am slowly recruiting now and, if I can, will try to finish this.

Speaking of Lord Napier, he was a thoroughbred, genial, and very sensible Gentleman. He had a sweet quiet wife just like my own and they naturally took to each other and our intercourse was very pleasant.

If I have not said it before, I say it now that when the Session ended I despaired of the Dissolution of the Union, and it was because that, except [for Clement] Clay of Alabama, and one or two other men, I knew no Southern man prepared for it, except we of SoCarolina. They talked large but shrunk from action, [James] Mason of Va. and [Muscoe] Garnett and [William] Goode and perhaps [R. M. T.] Hunter [all of Va.] would *accept* it cheerfully but could not move for it. Napier was very anxious on this point of Seperation and sought my opinion. I said frankly, "there will be two Presidential Elections in seven years. We may not seperate on the first if the South is beaten, if we do not if beaten on the Second, the Union is perpetual." But said he "Seward thinks it an impossibility to sever the Union" to which I replied, "he may think so." After that Seward said to me in the presence of Mason, that "the Union was stronger at the South than Slavery and at the North than Abolition." I said "You may speak for the North, but as to the South you [are] wholly mistaken if that Issue [of slavery] comes up."

On my return home [in late June 1858] my neighbors in Beech Island gave me a public dinner [on July 22]. I made of course a speech in which I said, "the Union will not be dissolved by the *first* election of a Black Republican President." I said this for reasons that I could not make public but had often given to those concerned at Washington. They were: first, the giving way I had experienced in our men, but secondly, and chiefly, there were 15 or 20 Southern men who had been named for the [United States] Presidency, who were anxiously working for it, and who would not be convinced by one defeat. These men were, Houston, Slidell, Davis, Brown, Johnson, Bell, Cobb, Toombs, Stephens, Crittenden, Breckinridge, Mason, Hunter, Orr, Floyd, Wise, and even Jake Thompson. Without these men there could be no Disunion, and from my knowledge of them I fully believed and believe now if they had not been *co-erced by the People*, this Revolution would not have been inaugurated.

This Speech here in Beech Island produced a sensation, but was so miserably reported that I repudiated it and gave notice that, at a dinner which was tendered me at Barnwell C. H., I would prepare myself—for in the B[eech] I[sland] speech I had not committed a line to paper—and report myself.

The Barnwell occasion, after much delay came off [October 29, 1858], and I had my speech written off that there might be no mistake of reporters. But I left out of it and therefore repudiated the opinion I had expressed [earlier] that the first election of a B[lack] R[epublican] President would not dissolve the Union. I did so because to specify my reasons for the opinion [that certain Southern Leaders wanted to be President of the United States], which I still retained, would have been very unpleasant and injurious. But despairing of a Union of the South *for Disunion*, and accepting the phase of affairs, I tried to show that the South, *if united*, Could *in Union* maintain all its rights. To strengthen this position I dilated on the errors of the South, in the hope, hopeless of a Dissolution, to unite them to control the Government on our principles. I had no doubt that we could do it. [The Southern states, Hammond concluded, could have a "magnificient future" within the Union]. I believe now (22nd Oct. 1861) that we could have done it *if the South had been faithful to herself*. Not that I preferred *that*. For myself I preferred *the other* [secession] and even the desperate warfare now raging. I had lost my confidence in others and, I propose to shew, not without cause as later events exemplified. I may as well say now as I may not live to conclude this that, *God*, not *Man*, *inaugurated this Revolution* putting to shame all Human expectations, mine among the rest.

This speech of mine [at Barnwell Court House] produced an immense sensation throughout the Country. It was published in every leading paper North and South. It was read publicly in the streets of the great Northern Cities to immense crowds. I rec^d showers of compliments from all sides. Even President Buchanan, who, without heart, sentiment, or principle as I soon found out, has brains, complimented me and said that no speech in his time had been so universally read and admired. I was nominated at once for the Presidency by an hundred newspapers of all sides. I had *overts* in abundance, but my health did not permit my assuming such a toil, and I gave a cold shoulder to it and political intrigue, which still follows me and fears me, stepped in to aid me in arresting that. All this was in 1858–9.

In 1860—May, I think, [April 23] the Democratic Convention met in Charleston to nominate a candidate for the Presidency and fix a Platform of Principles for him. The Alabama Convention to nominate Representatives to the [Charleston] Convention passed Resolutions to the effect that if that [Charleston] Convention did not put in its Platform so and so [a federal slave code to protect slavery in the territories], they should at once secede. The Convention met in Charleston. It refused to put "so and so" in its Platform but put something very different—utterly and essentially different [non-intervention by Congress on the question of slavery in the territories]. Wm. L. Yancey had lead [sic] the Alabama Convention and was a Delegate to the Charleston Convention and Leader of those who demanded "so and so." I confess I thought it nonsense, but when I saw the imbroglio, I telegraphed to the SoCa Delegation to go out then if any State seconded Ala. Some State did and our State went off 3rd. [Eight southern states withdrew to meet in a separate convention]. The Seceders met, with their fingers in their mouths. Yancey and Ala. had no plan. The talk was of Disunion and before the next meeting half the Seceders had gone home. A beautiful fix and a hopeful inauguration of Disunion. Just what I feared. It would require a graphic pen to delineate the long faces and lugubrious notes of the Southern Fire Eaters at Washington on the news of this Rupture. And oh they recovered when the news came that the Seceders had dispersed. I was there and utterly disgusted with the whole. I saw—I had seen two years before—that it was all a *political game* of the aspirants.

Well the South had a meeting of her Reps. and Senators. My views, notwithstanding my B[eech] I[sland] and Barnwell Speech, were so well known that I was not invited, having declined to attend many such before.

Another time if I can come to it.

We have by the latest telegraph (afternoon of 23 Oct [1861]) the most exciting news. The Enemy are moving on us every where in most tremendous force and desperation. They are playing their last card. A great victory at the odds of one to four was won day before yesterday by a S.C. General (Evans) near Leesburg, but on the same day the Enemy attacked us 200 miles lower on the Potomac at New Port News and we have not heard the result, which is ominous. The main body at Fairfax has perhaps engaged us to-day, and along the whole line of the Potomac, of Kentucky and Missouri, and our Sea Coast doubtless immediate advances and attacks have been ordered so that in this week and the next the full strength of the North and the South will be fairly tested and the war virtually ended, if we are victorious, but not if we are not. For us there is no avoiding the dire issue of "Victory or death" in its most literal and practical sense. I fear our people do not know that, and that even Jeff Davis and his Cabinet do not. Politicians, Intriguers, Time Servers, and timid Ignorance never face that, I fear, or apprehend it until *too late*.

After the Southern Address of 1860 was ventilated with its names to it, I confess that I lost all hope of a manly and united resistance to the aggression of the North on us. I began to believe with Seward that the Union was stronger at the South than Slavery and I came home utterly desponding. My grieving broke down the little health I had. I wished to die. When I met W. L. Yancey, a So. Carolinian and Leader of the Charleston rupture, at Washington on his way to Baltimore, [the Democrats reassembled at Baltimore in June 1860] after the suppression of the Richmond Convention of the South and asked him "Why do you go there: how can you enter that Convention unless they change their platform?" and he said we go there to help them change it, I grew sick at the stomach and turned my back on him. He and his set, acting according to the advice of the Southern Address, were treated by the Baltimore Convention of the Northern Democrats with the contempt and contumely that I expected. They [the southern delegates bolted again] then met elsewhere in Balt. and nominated [John C.] Breckinridge [of Kentucky] for Pres. and—I forget who for Vice—Al Lane, [Joseph Lane of Oregon] a noble fellow more ignorant than most of my Overseers, but as pure, as high and as true a man to the extent of his knowledge as any man who ever lived.

The nomination took place late one Saturday night and I did not know of it until about 11 o'clock next day. W[illiam] H. Trescot of SoCa came to see me and informed me of it. I then occupied the House [in Washington] known as the Maynard House (on the pavement of which Sickles murdered Key) and opposite Jackson Square. [Daniel Edgar Sickles, a congressman from New York and later a famous Civil War general, on February 27, 1859 shot and killed Philip Barton Key, the son of Francis Scott Key, because of Key's attentions to the wife of Sickles. Sickles was acquitted using the then novel defense of temporary insanity.] Soon after Trescot arrived, I saw Breckinridge, with his hat over his eyes, starting out for a meditative walk around Jackson Square. At the same moment Mrs. [Benjamin] Fitzpatrick [of Alabama] drove up and hailed him. Her husband had been nominated as Vice P on Douglas' ticket. [He declined.] They had half an hour's talk, which I did not interrupt but as soon as Breck. left her and drew down his hat again, I hailed him and asked him to come over and take a Julep. We had many, and others came in and we persuaded him as he had been nominated for it to lead the "forlorn hope"— rather against his will I think. But he did it. Now for the results——(Another time)

I did think that Breckinridge [on the Constitutional Democratic Party ticket in 1860] would be elected. I supposed that the South was aroused enough, firm enough and pure enough to unite and beat the Northern Black Republicans. We had the cards in our hands and it required no skill, but simply common sense and common integrity. The South would not unite. It was corrupt and foolish enough to go off on Bell and on Douglas, and we were beaten by a *Minority*.

I confess I prefer the results—with a most terrible Armada now at Port Royal, which if it gets a foothold, can ravage my plantations—I prefer that to the plan I then had in view as the only one practical. That was to keep the South United, to control the Govt. as it stood for the most part, abiding the occasional loss of that control, in the belief that the North had no statesmen—went solely for the loaves and fishes—and never could control it, as it never has for more than one to two years, at long intervals. I wished to be *Indepen[den]t* of it. In [not] so much that I feared the Abolitionists, who never could have effected any very serious annoyance, but I feared its corrupt and ignorant Politicians, and its Capitalists, who have built up and would continue to sustain its Commerce, its Manufactures, its whole Mercantile and Financial System, *at our Cost*, and in the Union *in despite* of *us*. I wished of all things to be free of this grinding bondage in all its parts. But from what I can see at this date (7 Nov. [18]61) I apprehend that the attempt is to be made to bargain for our mere political freedom by binding us to this other horrible despotism, by those we have put in power and our financial City men. [In the Confederacy's general election on November 6, 1861, Jefferson Davis, the provisional president since February, was elected President for a six-year-term.]

[Redcliffe] 20 Sept. 1862

About May 1861, my health failed me completely that I gave up writing and even thinking [if] that was possible, and therefore ceased to continue my sketch of the immediate events that caused the Great Revolution now just culminating, from an inside view. In fact events became so grand and so exciting that the past, even of a month, was a bore, and speculation for the future equally so. I shall not probably go further in my story, although in some respects my health has improved, but it [is] dreadful in the main and feeble at the very best. They are again putting me in nomination for Gov. and it is said I can run without opposition. This is quite a temptation to one who has for 30 to 35 years been zealously advocating our "Cause," but now in its crisis, when a man can put his name on the historic in 5 minutes of good fortune, Fate has so contrived it that mine will appear no where. But, as an honest man, I cannot undertake to do what I know I cannot do as it should be done. My health will not improve materially I know, and I see no alternative but to surrender to Fortune with as good a grace as I can. I am the more reconciled to it, because I believe in God and Immortality, and that [th]is miserable world is but a poor Affair compared with even the next.

IX

*The hard world looks on calmly, unconscious
apparently that its destiny is wrapped up with
that of the South, & that we are overwhelmed.*

---

20 OCTOBER 1861 — 13 NOVEMBER 1864

Plantation Journal

Redcliffe 20 Oct. 1861

A year ago owning to ill health and failing eyes I transferred my Plantation Journal to my Son Paul. My health has improved but little & my eyes are weaker, but I cannot get on with any satisfaction with[out] making some note of the weather & of my operations in the Garden, Vineyard, Orchard, Lawn, Shrubbery, etc., etc. So I recommence a Diary which I shall hardly add to daily. . . .

November 2. Too unwell to attend the [Beech Island Agricultural] Club—the first time I ever missed when in reach, either this or the Bluff Club. Had a haemorrahge [*sic*] as badly as yesterday. [On November 1 he recorded, "I have lost today over a pound of my blood."]

Not much rain, but raw & windy, some appearance of clearing to night & a killing frost to-morrow. Cut up Peppers & Imphee [a sugarplant].

Mess E & T. Watley, T. Davies, & R. Pryor.

November 8. . . . .Bad news in town about the enemy at Port Royal. [On November 7, 1861, the Union Navy seized the Confederate fort on Hilton Head and by November 10, Union forces occupied Beaufort and Port Royal, gaining a base for the naval blockading squadrons.]

November 12. Fog, clear and quite warm. Mrs H to town. I went to Cowden today. Bush Howard [Hammond's overseer] to carry Harry's horses and buggy to him at Pocotaligo. The wildest enactment. Every man from 18 to 45 ordered to rendevouz at White Ponds tomorrow night to meet the P. Royal Invaders. Woodard among them. Nonsense.

November 15. My Birth Day. Fifty Four years old. President Davis had appointed this day, for Fast, Prayer, & Humiliation. I went to the Presbyterian Church & heard very interesting discourses from Dr. Davies & Rev. E. Whatley. Really fine, clear, bright, summer weather but growing cooler to-night. T. J. Davies & Dr. Cook to dinner.

Last Mess of grapes from Vineyard—Sowed early York in Cold Frame.

[On this same day, James Henry's fifty-fourth birthday, his eldest son Harry, away in the Confederate army near the Union forces at Beaufort, South Carolina, wrote a letter to his father describing the flight of the Sea Island planters into the interior, abandoning plantations and slaves to the Union invaders.]

Gardens Corner 15th November 1861

Dear Father:

I have been so busy that I have not had time to write to you before. The Regiment is on the road leading from Pocotaligo to Port Royal Ferry, and stationed just where the road to Combahee Ferry forks off to the right. All over the Cossaw river has been abandoned to the enemy so that we are near them, but not I think on the track they will pursue.

You know probably as much about the state of affairs here as I do, but you do not know perhaps what a miserable set these low countrymen are. I think this war will sweep them out and I say they will be no loss. They have fled like sheep leaving all their property in the hands of the enemy, many without even a change of clothes. No man had the courage to burn his cotton or his house before he left—and with one or two exceptions scarcely a negro has been saved. They make no hesitation in saying that they will get pay for all this from the Confederate government. Those who have saved anything are selling it at the most extortionate prices to the troops. Here was Gov. Seabrook's son this morning—a man who was worth $100,000 a week ago—standing in a wagon and trying to sell a miserable marsh turkey, a rifle, and some turkey, to our common soldiers and all at the very highest market prices. And every day our contempt for such smallness overcomes the pity we feel for this panic striken [sic] people. I am in the greatest want of horses. My business is suffering for it, and I may any day lose their full value for the lack of them. Besides if we have to make a rapid move I have nothing to depend on, but my feet, which I would not complain of if it was not that I am required to look after many things which demand some more speedy manner of locomotion. If you have not already sent my horses to me I wish you would do so as soon as possible. If they are sent to Pocotaligo to report to Maj Hankel the Quartermaster I will get them. But whoever brings them should have such a paper as would prevent them from being impressed by some foolish Militia officer.

It is impossible to say how long we shall remain here. Everything is uncertain but my own expectations are that we will stay here some time.

I wish you would write to me to Pocotaligo Station putting my title and the 14th Reg S.C.V. on the letter. I had intended to have written to you more fully, but it is after the tattoo and I feel overcome with sleepiness these nights. Tell Mother that everybody enjoys good health here at this season and that we apprehend nothing from the enemy.

Give my love to all, Very affectionately,

Harry Hammond. . . .

[James Henry Hammond Papers, SCL.]

[The mail traveled rapidly, for only two days later, James Henry replied.]

Redcliffe, November 17, 1861

Dear Harry:

I started Bush Howard from Silverton House on Tuesday about 3 o'clock and told him to make Pocotaligo and you or the Q. M. by Thursday night. If no accident happened he must have done so. I gave him no permission to go any where else unless to carry the horses to you. As he had on the uniform of the Edgefield Rangers etc., no one would be likely to press his horses. Your letter was dated Friday night. It must have been written Thursday night for surely on Friday you got the horses.

I am very sorry to hear your account of the conduct of the low country people. You must make great allowances for people who have just fallen in a day from affluence to poverty. It is a terrible collapse and slackens every nerve, moral and physical. Genius and imbecility, Chivalry and poltroonery and meanness were always strangely mixed up among the Salt water people—not in each one,—but in classes. There were old families undecayed, decaying, and decayed and new families founded by successful overseers and factors and then an unusual amount of loafing fishermen, hunters etc. The Chivalry has mostly gone to the wars and the sense probably also. What was to be expected of the rest? Save Paul, whom I have held back, there is scarcely a man of any spirit left from Hamburg to the River. Fifty armed men could sack every plantation. This miserable scheme of carrying on a war by Volunteers is utterly suicidal. The Chivalry go at the tap of the first drum and get badly cut up and physicked out the first campaign. Little remains for a second. Draft and *force* off your Boyds and John Lottys, or hire them off, if the lot of a common soldier is drawn by you or Paul and any gentlemen. They will make just as good common soldiers as you would. Volunteers are only good for a 30 days' campaign— that is, cannot be properly called on for a longer period on any large scale. I doubt not we shall have to review our past decision against a Standing Army to see if we cannot invent checks and balances that will enable us to keep on hand a tolerably respectable one even in times of peace—if we are ever to have such times again.

Pickens had good sense enough to disband the Regt. so summarily called together at White Pond the other day and all have returned save Woodward. Paul expects him. It is however agreed to form a volunteer company and 33 have joined from Pen Corner Company—Tom Beggs among them. I think it will fall through because every man wants to be Captain.

Howard thinks he will finish corn this week at Cowden. I suppose he has some 25,000 bushels housed. I am saving the shucks which loses time. Last week he had to kill a hog to save his life for he was so fat he could not get up. The little fellow weighed 280 lbs.

No sickness worth mentioning. Dr. Davies was down and preached on Friday the best sermon I ever heard from him and I have been hearing him for over 40 years. Loula [Hammond, his son Paul's wife,] left yesterday for Macon.

Yours affectionately,
J. H. Hammond
[Hammond-Bryan-Cumming Papers, SCL.]

1862

January 30. Overcast & some drizzling—still spring weather. Went to both places. The firing at Savannah on 28th distinctly heard there & by the negroes here, & it is said as high up as Union Point. Results not known here yet, & I greatly fear that Savannah has been or will be taken.

Our Generals & Engineers, who have said all was safe, are I apprehend fools & drunkards. . . .

February 11. Clear & cold. Went to town. . . .

Town very gloomy—things look blue for certain localities on navigable waters—this for one. Fools & Sots leading our armies which are the same & all paralysed by Serenade-Orator for President who having predicted a five years war has done all he could to verify his prediction.

March 4. . . . .People woefully despondent in Augusta. I do not feel so, though our silly Serenade & Shrew President have been outgeneralled *everywhere.*. . .

April 6. Sunday. No serious sickness. Weather so cool as to make fires comfortable, breezy & occasionally cloudy—a little colder will bring frost to-morrow or next day & as the moon fills on the 14th if the wind or clouds do not protect we are likely to have a killing frost about that time.

I omitted details as regards melons planted on 1 April and not long before & not mentioned at all—199 hills of watermelons from good seed—50 of seed from Quattlebaum & 58 of a large melon purchased in Augusta, 20 of Cantelopes [*sic*], 15 of Cucumbers & 10 of Syrian Squash. I also replanted Beets, Carrots & Parsnips (omitted mention) about 20 days ago. Set out to day a few Marblehead cabbages brought me by Redmond yesterday, in vine acre no. 3. Yesterday I finished planting in Sorgho my 2 acres.

I feel very, very sad more so than I have felt in many years. It has been growing on me for some weeks, & I have had much to cause it. My cold of 12 days ago shook me severely, & yesterday though I went to the Club I was quite ill from the fatigue & exposure the night before with my poor mare & grief for her death [on April 4 from lockjaw, according to Hammond] was an actual bereavement. But my spirits drooped when all my sons became volunteers for the war leaving me to manage—imbecile as I am this large estate, then came our reverses, then our lamentable Victory of the Virginia or Merrimac. If that thing answers expectation it will be the greatest curse that has befallen man since the fall of Adam. Nations unable to resist assualts [*sic*], must make reprisal & ravage each others Coasts. Sea Coasts & Ports, must be abandoned to mere piracy, Commerce destroyed & all nations compelled to close in like Japan with banditti forever on the water frontier. The Yankees can build 3 of these machines to our 1, & take our Coast & Ports from Norfolk to Matamoros & our only & poor recompense will be to shell their Cities & Coast. Humble Warfare!! Next mother's servants hall was burnt & all disorganized there & the dear old Lady remains here, unwilling to do [so] permanently & yet dreading to go home. Then my good friend Simms is burnt out of house & home, one of the direst earthly afflictions & peculiarly so to him. Every day brought tidings, of the weakness & demoralization of our Armies under this weak, impracticable & termagant Jeff Davis. And finally the loss of my means of locomotion. I could go with my mares. They went with the strength of a locomotive & as fast as I wished. It was a joy to sit behind them. It is over. I cannot supply the place of the lost one & am tied down. I did not go often, but I felt I could go & it was a comfort. Now I feel I cannot.

In addition to all this, I cannot sell cotton. I am just now—the check is drawn—to turn over to the Confederate Produce Loan, the nett sales of 10,000 bushels of Corn ($12500) subscribed by me which leaves me only $4,000 in hand & $8,000 in expectancy, unless cotton can be sold which I don't expect unless the Govt. takes it all *as it should*. In the meantime I have $19,000 borrowed money, drawing interest in the Bank. $1,500 of Tax to pay. Mother, Cousin Augusta, all my children, & family to support, & some 7 or 8,000 due Harry & Paul as their shares in the last crop, & every thing I need at four prices. There is also a reasonable prospect that the Enemy taking Savannah will come up the river [to Augusta] & sweep me out. All depends on the events of this month. There will be the hardest fighting on the Potomac & on the Mississippi, in No. Ca. perhaps, & probably in Charleston & Savannah. Oh sad—sad for an invalid who tires in 10 minutes walk, in 30 minutes horseback, 1 hour in a Carriage, and not a soul to comfort—sad—sad—sad.

April 26. Overcast early and coolish from 10 to 12 o'clock, a very heavy and washing rain. None since but every appearance of a deluge and cold enough for a fire all day and now. Set out 84 Cauliflower and 50 Brocoli [*sic*] also tomatoes. Harry [on leave] and Emily [his wife, here]. New Orleans said to have been taken. I won't believe it.

May 12. . . . .These are terrible times. All our young in the Armies, not [any] men left to suppress an negro insurrection, of which however there are no symptoms yet. Salt is $40 a sack, Bacon 40¢ per lb. Common Sugar 25¢. Rio Coffee 75¢, Beef in Market 30¢ & Mutton the same. All kinds of Dry Goods & Hard at proportionate prices. With this I have 1200 animals to feed—300 & odd negroes to feed & clothe & some 70 white families deriving all or nearly all their support from my earnings besides 4 families that I [supply] bread around Cowden & Silver Bluff & more ready to require it. In addition I have sent to the Con[federate] Govt $12,500 the proceeds of 10,000 bushels Corn subscribed to the Produce Loan, & must send 200 bales of Cotton (the proceeds) when I can sell it. As yet I have not sold a lock of Cotton. These are indeed *hard times* & especially so on me. Last of Corn sold to Govt. taken. . . .

June 1. Very hot but breezy. Thunder & a short big drop shower about 3 o'clock. *Sunday*. No serious sickness. I went to Church and there heard that the great Battle for Richmond began yesterday our men having attacked 3 Divisions of the enemy & driven them on the rather after a terrible [fight] in which we took their Camp & 3 Batteries. Such is the Telegram. God grant that so far may be true. It is only the beginning of this *murderous* battle or series of battles. Doubtless blood has been flowing in torrents all this day & probably for many & at Corinth. My 3 precious boys [Harry, Spann, and Paul] are in these awful fields. Merciful God preserve them.

September 11 . . . .We are intensely excited here about the War. Rumors innumerable & mostly false. The Cin[cin]nati rumour not confirmed, but certainly all our armies are advancing, & it is highly probable that Jackson with a large force has crossed the Potomac a week ago. But all is mystery, which is doubtless right for the present but very painful. The War is gradually becoming on both sides one of fire & sword & extermination. Dreadful, dreadful. The hard world looks on calmly, unconscious apparently that its destiny is wrapped up with that of the South, & that we are overwhelmed. France, England, Belgium, Spain & Italy must go at once into *liquidation*. We ask nothing but Peace & to be let alone. The North seeks to subdue, plunder, confiscate & enslave us. Unless with our present effort we can conquer our Independence, there must be enacted in the next 12 months a history, which the genius of all the Historians from Moses to the present time could not, if combined in one man, adequately depict.

September 18. Thanksgiving Day for our late victories. Went over to Baptist Church. The sad news confirmed, that Tom Beggs, Joe Bates, & Tom Rowel, my immed[iate] neighbors at Silverton who have grown from children just by me, were killed at Manassas, in the great battle of the 30th ult. They were in the Holcombe Legion (unhappy name) in Capt. Crawley's Company. He was wounded. Bates was his 1st Lieut. Beggs his 2nd Lieut & his 3rd Lt. Holland was also killed. Sad, sad.

September 24. Still coolish, but warmer & cloudy, but no rain, which is already needed. Terrible fighting going on. Five Battles in Maryland last week all heavy & one of them [Antietam] the fiercest of the War it is said. We cannot get particulars all we know is that we held the battle fight [*sic*] a day after the last engagement buried the dead & the second day recrossed the Potomac without any molestation whatever. Both armies appear to have been whipped & both retreated—nothing decisive.

October 16. Pleasant day & to-night augurs frost soon. . . .
    I fear Paul was in the great battle of Perryville. Accounts are meagre & conflicting—none from our side yet. The War is awful. I dare not express my apprehensions nor take the measures I would for my own safety. It would depress others too much. I do seriously apprehend that Charleston will be taken by Christmas, unless the War is ended by successes elsewhere. A Cavalry foray to Augusta will follow speedily which will come or return thru my possessions & lay every thing low. The Enemy are bent on Charleston & will concentrate upon it all their forces. May the Good God preserve us.

November 8. Most delightful day. Harry & family, Paul & family & friends dined with us today. Very pleasant indeed. Banked up earth on potatoes. Sent hands back. . . .

November 13. Warm & cloudy. Went to Town & closed cotton sales & got a receipt or check on Govt for $32,778.25.
    Dear Paul, with his friend & brother in Law Maj. [Lawson] Clay, went up & took the cars for Knoxville. They went off in high spirits. Poor fellows, what hardships sufferings & perils they will encounter before we see them again if we ever do. My heart bleeds. Oh the infamous war of the Vandals.

November 15. Cool wind, and rain threatened all day and tonight. Fifty Five years old today and a dreadful attack of hemmoerahge [*sic*] this morning, that I thought would carry me off.

Harry and Emmie, Mrs. Fitzsimons and Mrs. [Virginia] Clay to dinner. Mr. Wm White, brother of Mrs. Gill Fitzsimons, John Clarke, and Mr. Bell before dinner.

Gill F. and Mr. and Mrs. Hughes, his brother and sister in law came.

December 15. Warmer. Cloudy but no rain. A load of Corn from Cowden 105 bushels. Terrible fighting on the Rappahannock. Harry in it; his Genl. Gregg killed—still going on. Awful hemorrages [*sic*], dead man. Hauling dead logs for fuel.

December 16. Cooler & breezy but bright—no better—no more important details. Harry's Chief—a sort of pet of mine from his infancy— named by my Mother, Gen. Maxcy Gregg died of his wounds on Sunday [at Fredricksburg].

T. J. Davies & my nephew Charley—Charley going to the Wars. Tom to the West. Terrible times these.

December 21. Sunday. One child died to-day & several ill. Colds which [are] epidemic & severe. No abatement of my Hem. Dr. Gibbard of Augusta came & put me under medicine—not less than 4 lbs blood in 7 days—feeble of course.

Christmas. A pleasant but no bright day. The Girls & Boys went to Bluff to see Barbecue. Delighted. Two children died there this week. Epidemic colds badly treated. What can I do. In the last 10 days 22nd to 25th [*sic*] I have passed as Dr. Cook estimates from my discharge of to-day 10 lbs blood & really scarcely have the use of my limbs. Have not sat at table in a week yet have a good appetite. Weak, weak: must eat to supply the 10 lbs, but don't smoke (for 4 days now) & drink little. Really feel better to-day. Can't tell why.

P.G. Fitzsimons & Mr. White, his wife's brother, came late last night. All the family dined here today. . . .

1863

March 19. Raw easterly weather and towards night quite cold & threatening snow. Peach trees are about in full bloom & corn coming up.

Went to both quarters Mrs. H. with me. Both overseers off getting corn. I [am] killed & racked for [son] Paul's late injudicious sales. The corn would bring *now* $2 to 10,000 more & the other sales several thousand additional. He is so sudden in his acts, not consulting me before, nor after, & abrupt, reticent & wanting in fullness of explanations on inquiry made, that I am all the time in uncertainty & anxiety about my Affairs in his hands—& he has taken *all* in hand, for he sold over half my Cowden Corn & all my forage that I had to sell. I am greatly troubled. He is poor help. The Lord only knows now when I shall get rid of this corn.

April 29. Delightful morning, & pretty heavy rain this afternoon. Season enough. Went with Dr C. F. to Silver Bluff where I found four *demented negroes absolutely crazy* of different ages & sexes—Minos, Tenate, Daphne & Jim. Kate died of the same way on 27th. Seized with tremendous headache & in a few hours they become maniacal. I fear all will die and perhaps many more. The Drs call it typhoid fever, but [I don't] know. I think it general congestion of the system, which I have more or less myself most of the time. They have very little fever. Old Bob found dead at Brick House this morning.

May 3. Sunday. Six deaths last week from this terrible epidemic, but it is evidently subsiding since I covered the compost heap with plaster, charcoal & straw. T. Davies & R. Starke [here]—Moved people to Lower Quarter.

May 20. Weather unchanged. Mr. Scruggs returned from Va. Mrs H & I went through Augusta to visit Mother & returned in the afternoon on the side of the river. Very pleasant. Mother getting dropsical I fear. My neighbor D. Walker had a daughter married last night & a parcel of the *gentlemen's* sons of the neighbourhood to wit, John Wright, Jack Everett Sr., Geo. Walker, Geo. Pace & Wm. Hankinson, got up a serenade in [which] they made themselves perfect blackguards ending in insulting females & taking possession of Paul's house & ordering breakfast & liquor & maltreating servants.

June 28. Sunday. No serious illness. Heavy rain about 4 o'clock at Cathwood & Silverton, little at Bluff & not much here. Went to both places. Grass & hard work but that does not account sufficiently for the heavy gloom which seems settled on all the negro faces. I have seen this gradually thickening ever since the Richmond battles of last year & more especially since the late repulse at Charleston. They seem utterly subdued as if by blasted hopes. Yet there is a peculiar furtive glance with which they regard me & a hanging off from me that I do not like. I have no doubt they have all along been well apprised with the Abolition version, of what is going on, & may thus shut up their faces & cease their cheerful greetings in view of the future, not the past. They would wish to be passive & take what comes. But the roar of a single cannon of the Federal's would make them frantic—savage cutthroats & incendiaries.

July 10. [Hammond made no mention of the Confederate defeats at Gettysburg and Vicksburg.]
　No rain to-day but thunder, clouds & very sultry. Learning that Charleston was attacked this morning—in fact hearing the guns here— went up with Dr Kit to Town—no news. Heard guns at the Ferry as we came down. Lamar's Boat loaded with corn to-day from Cowden but only about 400 bushels. Mother & family came down
　If Charleston falls Augusta will be taken. *& for us*——

July 19. Sunday. No rain—no sickness
　News from Charleston confused & uncertain. Bombardment said to be on Fort Wagner & unsuccessful? Awful management there. . . .

July 20. Hot & sultry but more sun then usual. Clouds enough. Went to Town. Great Victory at Morriss Island & great Riots in the North, resisting drafting. . . .

August 17. Coolish & pleasant morning. Sultry noon. About 5 o'clock a terrible blow & rain. The wind has lulled but at intervals the rain still pours. Such an explosion of guns never before heard here, which ceased about 4 o'clock, from the storm there (Charleston) I take it or the discomfiture of the enemy. The sounds were awful even here.
　Gill Fitzsimons left carrying to work on the Charleston batteries five of my negroes viz. Henry Fuller & Johnny from Cowden, Adam Hornsby, Adam Robert & Sancho from Silver Bluff.
　Paul Fitzsimons came down. Mrs. H to Bluff.
　Bush [Howard] to town with brass castings for Engine.
　Sowed some more Cabbage & also Turnip seed, ploughed new vineyard and worked in the garden.

August 18. Cool & pleasant, overcast. Heavy showers between 1 & 4 o'clock. Went with Kit to Walker's [barbe]cue & had a pleasant day. Sent Bush to Town with Wheat.

The result of the grand bombardment yesterday was the retreat of the enemy's fleet at *half-mast*—perhaps Admiral Dalghren [*sic*] killed— most likely a mere *ruse* & the attacking vessels "hurt." No doubt *we* are badly hurt ourselves.

August 20. Coolish, hot, cloudy, clear all sorts. Jobbing here. Fort Sumter nearly breached—certain to be. Europe gives up our "Rebellion."

August 30. Sunday. Wesley quite sick at Bluff—no one at Cowden. Cloudy, cool & drizzly. Fires to-night. Went to both places. Negroes demoralized greatly, stealing right & left. Corn & salt now. Found a closed hole apparently of old standing in Bluff Barn through which any quantity of corn has doubtless passed & Frank my plough driver implicated in salt stealing & confined in the Barn escaped to-day & run away. Trouble enough.

September 27. Sunday. Child died at Cowden & sickness at both places. Went to both. Clear & cold, fire again to-night. Low spirited about affairs—see no end *Charleston will fall,* in ruins though. Rosecrans in Chattanooga & I fear cannot be driven out, but will advance again. Signs of peace no where. Foreign Intervention only (I fear) can prevent our being overrun & ruined—*not subjugated.*

November 15. Sunday. No serious illness. Most pleasant day. My birthday. 56 years old. No company without the inclosure save Mr. Chisholm.

November 17. Rather colder. Mrs. H. returned. Mother ill. Bloody discharges begun on me.

November 18. Weather very fine. Blood yet for me. All hands at potateri yet. Mr. Chisholm left—a very agreeable visit. The Maj. Gen. [his brother, Marcellus] to-night.

November 19. Weather delightful. Quietly at home with the Major. Paul to town & got me 20 galls whiskey for 300 lbs. of Bacon. Money price of Whiskey $45 per gall. of Bacon $3 per lb.

November 26. Clear, bright & cold. At potatoes again, & sowed 2 acres of wheat in this inclosure after potatoes.

Bragg has been defeated at Chattanooga with great loss—abandoned Look Out Mountain and fell back we don't know where. The worst news of the war for us here. It looks as if we are to be exterminated. I now anticipate nothing better. The cause—as far as human—utter incapacity in officials civil & military, who have sacraficed the noblest people of the world & in my view the noblest cause. . . .

December 25. Christmas such as it is. It used to be Christmas this day. The weather has been finer, clear, crisping cold. Some flakes of clouds indicating rain or snow. But no smiling faces & merry hearts. Instead of a Barbecue below, I gave an extra week's allowance on each place & left the people to enjoy themselves as they liked. Only those in the inclosure including Harry & Emily to dinner to day. Very dull.

December 27. . . . .Harry & Emily left this afternoon. He returns to the Army. Congress is about to pass a most dishonest bill that will send Paul there—a common soldier. Oh sad, sad. In this bloody war the chances seem to be against every one. I shall hardly [see] both the dear & noble fellows again. While I am left to manage a business which at this distance from it, I did not feel able to do in my primest days. Sixteen years ago this very place & all the land attached was offered me for a song. I would not take it (& Cowden w[as] not then touched) because [it was] too far off & I was not able to manage Silver Bluff from [here]. Now, in the most difficult of times, with superannuated overseers & no sub agents attainable, both places are suddenly to be thrown on my hands (& really no Overseer at S. B.) while I can't walk a mile or ride there on horseback, & I lie on my back at least 20 of the 24 hours.

God protect my poor dear boys: restore them to us & give peace & independence to this miserable, bleeding Country.

December 30. Weather as yesterday in forenoon. Cloudy after & drizzling to-night. Killed at Silver Bluff 30 hogs, weighing 5768 lbs nett titheable 4200 lbs. . . . The worst of News. The Generals & officers of the Army of Tennessee have sent to Congress a memorial which has been published & amounts to a *"Pronunciamento."* The Senate Finance Committee have reported a Bill equally desperate & Foote of the Con[federate] H[ouse] proposes Lee instead of Davis for Dictator. *It seems that all is over.* . . . .

1864

March 2. Not much rain but enough. Went to Town. All in confusion. . . .

March 26. A good deal of rain last night, but none to-day, yet mostly overcast & breezy. Strange weather. Went to Bluff Place & the River. A small freshet stopping fishing. Saw a Steam Boat come down—the first I have seen in 10 years. It carried me back 30 years when it was a daily sight with 18 boats on One River & looking around for my wharf & wood of those days—all gone, large willows where the Wharf was & all the stream filled where it was 30 ft. deep then. Houses & trees gone, & all my feelings & views of worldly affairs so changed since I was accustomed to see Steam-Boats round my Island, & to receive a bow from the Captain, if he did not stop, that I fell into a melancholy that I cannot shake off. This SteamBoat—called the Leesburg—was painted black, the first vessel I ever saw so painted. Is it ominous. I saw but one man. He sat on a chair on the upper deck. He reminded me of the "Ancient Mariner" & passed steadily looking at me without a Salutation. I was dressed [in] glaring homespun or perhaps he might. Put out over 400 little peach trees to bud.

April 14. Bright morning & warm—cooler overcast at noon & cold drizzly afternoon & to-night. Went to Augusta to sell something having no money. Found that there was no *current* money there & every thing down & dull & utter want of confidence in Govt. finances. We are literally without money in the whole Confederacy. The old issues depreciated one third, & not wanted by any, & of the new none of consequence, & not esteemed more highly. It is a serious state of things & no prospect of much relief. . . .

April 22. A pleasant Spring day, but for a keen breeze which brings up clouds to-night.
Went to Bluff. Hands here engaged in replanting potatoes, which under the Season have rotted in the ground & I have only slips to replant a third. The Elements are Yankee—as cruel & destructive. God appears to be utterly against us, but it must come all right tho' we may all perish. In arms we are ever now successful but it is in a small & indecisive way, but as far as it goes thorough.

June 2. I was not with Mother at her death [Catherine Fox Spann Hammond, 1785–1864, died on June 1]. I was with her on the 30th ult & thought it not unlikely she might hold on for months. All her other relatives immediately around, were there, save Betty [his youngest child] & me. I did not attend her funeral & interment in Augusta to-day. I have too little vitality to undergo the fatigues of crowds & ceremonies. If the services had been as I proposed at her own house, with a few near friends & her relatives, & the interment quietly performed, I would have gone up. I remember that when her predecessor in her House—Mrs. Starke, Mother of my brother's wife—died there some 8 to 9 years ago, when I was that much younger & doubly vigorous, it required me to make a most painful effort to attend the service in the house & the burial near by. But to go into a Church, in a demoralized town of refugees, soldiers, & idle citizens, & go thence in a procession, to the grave, I could not undergo. Had I gone I would have been the prominent actor & Spectacle in the show. If there is any just, pure & sacred secret it is grief, & of all, the grief of a son for a Mother, whose life has, to his remembrance, been linked to hers for over half a century. To attempt to personify that grief & *act* it with a view to the applause of an assembled mob seemed to me to be sacralegious [*sic*]. Ostentatious grief is, if not a pitiful weakness, an hypocritical mockery. A hard & stern, or gross & frivolous attempt at concealment still leaves it doubtful if there is any reality. All who die should be appropriately buried, if possible: but a son should not enact before the public, the part of burying his Mother. While I feel on one side that I have lost the dear Mother who bore me, who has been my best & kindest & purest, & oldest friend; who protected my infancy & whose old age I have done every thing to make comfortable, & that there is now a final end, for my life, to all those fond sympathies, those old reminiscences of years past known only to us two & so often referred to, I feel unconsolable. But on the other side my Mother has been spared to us, & in good health until lately, for a longer period than is allotted to our race. During this long period she has exemplified every human virtue, for she has had severest trials, of which, for the most part, none living knew but me. But no trial ever blanched her cheek, as no prosperity ever developed exultation. In all her long life she never made an enemy, or had a detractor. No one who ever enjoyed her society, even for an hour, will see the announcement of her death without emotion. Thus loved, respected, revered, it is simply selfish in me to grieve that she has left us, when it was so clear to all of us that age had become a disease with her & the pains of longer life infinitely surpassed the enjoyments. In one point of view I can hardly refrain from rejoicing that "life's fitful fever over. She sleeps well." The White Savages of the North & N.W. who are waging on us an exterminating war, which does not respect sex or age, but inflicts the most cruel & degrading deaths—upon all who fall into their hands— save those required for exchange of prisoners—are in full force 120 miles south of us, & at 200 miles West & are advancing on us with overwhelming numbers & increasing ferocity. It has been a great burden to me though, how to shield her from this storm of horrors. The Good God has relieved her some, by taking her away to the abodes of Peace. I humbly thank Him. She was buried in the Augusta Cemetary this afternoon very near her own Mother buried there in 1827 & her daughter buried in 1828. Her half brother Capt. Turner & her ancient friend & companion Mrs. Jones lie the[re] also. Her Father, my Grandfather died in Augusta 1794 or 5 & was buried in St. Pauls Churchyard, but his brother-in-law Fox, seizing all his property omitted to mark the grave & it cannot be distinguished now. I made diligent search there in 1827. Rev Dr Wilson performed the funeral services in the Presbyterian Church & at the grave. . . .

June 13. Rain, rain to the ruin of crops & starvation soon. Wind N.E. & to-day very brisk. Fires, comfortable yesterday, requisite to-day. Work no where. Good God! in this crisis is there to be no fruits from fields, vineyard, orchards, or gardens to support life & our Cause. Why not slay us & all of us at once & *forever*, which is for *myself*, my constant prayer being weary of this farce.

June 24. Weather as yesterday. . . . All overwhelmed with the anxiety about this awful & decisive crisis now impending. Can't think or act.

June 28. Went to town. The people seem cheerful, not so much from confidence as from don't care—business hardly practicable. The idea is that Sherman & Grant are both whipped. I think so myself, but I wish no body else did & if too many do we shall soon [be] whipped back fatally & finally.

July 5. Weather cooler & more breezy than yesterday. No rain any where. Every thing is burning about here. D.J. Walker. Mr. King (to buy corn) corn $18 today in Augusta.
The war is so exciting & confused that one is stunned. [Gen. Jo-

seph E.] Johnston is falling back again, the enemy attacking Islands near Charleston with great vigour & all rail communication cut of[f] on the two Southern roads in Virginia. The crisis is now—may be decided this week, if not yesterday.

July 20. . . . .Yesterday seven corn raids, two of them by letter, Col Miller of N.C. & Dr Cook. At night, Messers & Capt Riley, Hay, Wilson & Hamilton after Corn. Army Agents. I had sold out to Gregg, Major May, & H. Moore, who could not be impressed. Yet Hamilton left on my desk last night a notice of impressment which this morning I tore up & threw out of the window in his presence, saying I paid no respect to the order of Hanckel, his principal, & simply defied him— not meant to offend and not offending I hope. They want to take my Corn at much less than half the price I can sell it & have sold it to Consumers. I will sooner Consume it with fire if my poor neighbors wont make way with it. . . .

July 28. The weather yesterday & to-day & for near 40 days has been not only a coquette but a whore & is not worth any further notice. To War & Pestilence, Famine is soon to be added. Yesterday Dr. Large [here] for corn & is refused. Then Dr Berckman, who went with me to Cowden where I closed up corn sales, having no more to sell. To day Cap. Hanckel & Lt. Hewlit & another man, armed, invaded me here & I understand they left 40 soldiers at my plantations & have taken military possession. I defied them. They left & the Dr. also. . . .

July 31. War news very bad from every quarter. A portion of the for- tifications at Petersburg blown up & Sherman's raiders dashing through the heart of Georgia. The Oconee bridge on Central R. R.—a mile long—burnt. Communication from Atlanta to Augusta & to Macon cut off entirely. They meet no opposition. It is also reported that At- lanta is virtually surrounded. Heavy fighting there on 29th of which we hear no particulars. All this is owing to the want of capacity in the President to which he added the lowest jealousy, the most malignant temper, the most perverse & mulish obstinacy, spleen, spite & illim- itable conceit & vanity. If I had not known from the first that he had all these disqualifications for his position & that besides he is, when pushed, an abject coward, I should think he is a Traitor. The veriest bought-up traitor could not have played affairs to suit the Yankees [better] than he has done. I denounced him before he was made even

Provisional President; during the first 4 or 5 months, I questioned my judgement of him, but never after the battle of Manassas, July 1861.

August 2. I can scarcely say I was surprised that Messers Hamilton & Wilson—Hanckel's strikers were announced about 10 o'clock to-day. They brought May's & Moore's certificates by which they relinquished all the corn they contracted for (in writing) but had not paid for. They took care to get that. This it was supposed threw some 5,000 bus. into the hands of the Impressors. Then there was Lamar's & Gregg's some 5,000 bu. more which gentlemen could protect but did not seem to care to do it. They had a Steam boat prepared to carry the corn & a sufficient force to seize it. They made the issue to have the corn conceded *or they would take it,* thus branding upon my forehead "Slave." They [got] it at just half the price it was sold for. They finally proposed to leave the price to arbitrators to which, as the best alternative, I agreed to. The arbitrament to-morrow at Cowden. Rain ceased. Very hot.

August 3. After getting ready & my carriage [at] the door my wife persuaded me not to go to Cowden to day. Reflecting, the first time, that all being arranged for Mr. Howard he could carry on the matter very well, that it would be unpleasant to see this pollution of lands & prying into my barns, & allowancing me for 90 days, & that my patience was exhausted, & I should probably get into some difficulty with these fellows, I concluded not to go. The thing went on. John Foreman was my arbitrator, Charles Tutt their's: differing in price, Wm Turner was called on & it was immediately fixed at $10,000. They then examined all my Cribs & estimated my Corn & after releasing Gregg's, Moore's, & Lamar's & making up my allowances, there was only May's & Kinchley's Corn—then Sacked & in the barn, 2408 bushels to take. So they substituted themselves as purchasers instead of these, & *at the same price.* So they have got [not]hing & I have lost nothing but perhaps my temper. Very hot.

August 8. Very warm and also very windy. Clouds abundant, but no rain. Dr. Cook and my Brother to dinner, an important settlement with him as to the Estate of my Mother. Both left after.

The names of the Impressors who have so annoyed me are Hay and Riley on the first part and John A. Hamilton and Leroy Wilson, M. Hanckel and Leut. Hewlett on the second. Yet all agents of same Maj. Guerin and zealous both to have the credit of fleecing me. After the arbitrator had fixed the price of my corn etc., my overseer allowed Hamilton and Co., who prevailed, to take my corn without receipt etc. Learning this I directed Mr. Howard to get receipt. He sends me one from Hamilton acknowledging the amount of corn, but not the price adjudged by the Umpire. That he says, after making no objection to the decision, is to be tried by law. Thus the whole thing is to be done over. I have defeated them twice and will again, but it seems they will push it to bloodshed.

August 9. A moderate shower about noon & coolish after.

Alonzo—a very valuable fellow of mine, died after many weeks illness of this mysterious disease which paralyses brain & body, called by the Doctors some sort of *Meningitis.* Quite unwell myself—have not for some time slept well of nights. The War, the impressment, & Sickness here, & altogether too much to do, have altogether used me up. Mobile attacked & in eminent [*sic*] danger of capture.

August 28. Sunday. Negro barbe[cue] yesterday & dance last night— no sick of course, very hot out of the pleasant, but unwholesome breeze. Bush came up to say he expected to be seized to-morrow or next day for the war. His father will soon come. I must turn my negroes loose & will there then be soon a raiding by them of me & mine—ruin to me & what is worse ruin to our Cause & Country.

September 3. Cool & cloudy. About 2 o'clock heavy shower. Mr. Beale returned home on past terms. Club day & all enjoyed save me. I was very [ill] all day as I have [been] more [or] less for 10 days. Hear most disastrous new[s] from Atlanta. Gregg and daughter left.

September 4. Sunday. Hear of no illness. Weather pleasant.

Nothing further from Atlanta. Hood there is cut off & Hardee badly flogged at Jonesboro.

Dr B & Charley left here. Still quite unwell. D.J. Walker this afternoon. Atlanta evacuated [by Confederates on September 1]—terrible disaster.

September 26. Clear bright & very pleasant weather, the air cool & crispy rather soon. Bad Army news from all quarters, & nothing but the direct intervention of the Good God *very soon* can save the South from subjugation. All may be attributed to incompetence, & monstrous temper of Jeff Davis, who a few day[s] ago in a Stump Speech, evidently well prepared, denounce[d] Gen. Johnston openly as a liar & a scoundrel, & otherwise used language about him as would have disgraced a Corporal of Zouaves. He behaved like a plug ugnly [*sic*] minus his club which he would be loth to use. . . .

October 3. A very heavy [rain] about day break & after & much rain all day. River rising, dull of course. Have had serious hemorrage [*sic*] beginning on the 29th ult. Throat better but very weak. Who can recuperate under our present perilous state of affairs. God alone can save us.

October 12. Most delightful weather. Very unwell but I ride out. . . .

October 14. Weather still fine. Spann came.

October 22. Weather very fine, bright sunshine & cold, but frost does not appear to injure. Drs Pettigrew & Berckmans yesterday. Mr. Walker, Davies & others to-day. Too much company. Sent Mrs. Whatly 100 bushels of corn for a year's use of the ferry with all the privileges of the same use as before the war.

[The last entry on October 22, 1864, was in an unsteady hand. Hammond died at Redcliffe on November 13, 1864, two days before his fifty-seventh birthday. As his death approached, he played out the final act. An eyewitness account written by Spann to his brother Harry provides what is normally missing in a diary, the final chapter.]

Last Moments of J. H. Hammond

Father's strength failed daily from the time of my arrival home, about the middle of October. Remaining later and later each morning in bed, he declined entirely the fatigue of dressing about a fortnight before his death, changing his bed in his chamber every few days for one he had placed in the library. About ten days before his death he experienced an attack, very alarming at the time, variously attributed to the effect of disease, or an overdose of narcotic accidentally administered, after which his mind wandered greatly and, in general, was clear only after sleep and quiet, becoming confused after a few minutes conversation, or the presence of several persons. The day before his death I received a message in Augusta of a serious change, and to assist the bearer in finding and bringing Dr. Steiner to see him at once. The Doctor and I reached Redcliffe about noon. Father's reception of us was very warm, but he expressed surprise at our arrival and seemed concerned at Mother's anxiety. He conversed on various topics for an hour, most of the time with clear mind, when the Doctor left with ominous looks, but encouraging words. After the Doctor's departure Father called me to his bed-side and asked "what it all meant—the Doctor's sudden coming and mine, and Mother's anxiety?" He bade me raise and prop him in his bed, and hand him a small looking glass. He told me he did not feel as badly, that Mother's and the Doctor's anxiety was unnecessary and, looking at himself, remarked how well he looked, that he looked better than the day before, better perhaps than in twenty years past—his complexion clearer; but, on inspecting his tongue which was dry, engorged and darkened, "ah," said he, handing back the glass, with a depressed countenance, "that's a very bad tongue, very bad: lower me." He then told me to sit by him and proceeded calmly: "I have something to tell you; now listen. I may live three days; it may be only three hours. Over in the woods," pointing in the direction, "are two large hickory trees, one just in the field, the other some 60 or 70 yards back. They are notable trees, larger than any others around, a little way from the head of a gorge and near the top of a hill almost as high as this. I wish to be buried near those trees, within 50 or 60 yards of them, on the highest ground around. By cutting pines, perhaps a dozen, in the gorge, there will be a fine view of Augusta and the Sand Hills. Clear up a space, say 60 or 70 yards square, and enclose it, and I wish you to place my Father and your Brothers there. As to a monument, I have nothing to say of that; you boys do as you think best. But, mind," and he uttered it with a thrilling earnestness, looking at me and pointing his finger, "if we are subjugated, run a plow over my grave." He went into some further particulars, and had repeated again most impressively the last injunction when the entrance of others interrupted the conversation. He sent for me soon after and desired me to play on the fiddle for him, which I was dissuaded from as the Doctor had enjoined quiet. He repeatedly in the afternoon sent messages to me to play, which was disapproved by his attendants, until at night, when he became more urgent. I played for an hour in an adjoining room. When I had ceased playing, he summoned all the negro children from the yard and made them sing around his bed, but not being able to recall a favorite hymn, nor they to hit upon it, he became fretted and Dr. Cook, who had arrived, dismissed them. He then summoned me again and rebuked me for not having gratified his wishes for music. He added,

"I can relish neither food nor drink; only music. Give me music. It is all I want." I sat up in the adjoining room until near day-light, in company with Miss Mary Wimberly [a companion to the family], Dr. Cook and Maj. Thos. J. Davies, one or another of whom was nearly always with him. He conversed incessantly, at times wandering and disconnected, running with sudden fancies on religion and politics, and at other times discussing various subjects with power and clearness. He entered with Dr. Cook upon a discussion of the value of the bitumen bed on Hollow Creek; the uses it might serve the public and the country, the probable extent of the bed, its quality, the expenses minutely calculated of excavation and transportation and for two hours continued the subject lucidly and full of sound suggestions. Near day break I fell into a doze and was aroused by a groaning noise in the adjoining room. It was full day and the Doctor and Maj. Davies had left. I peeped into Father's chamber (the library) and saw him lying squarely on his back, his eyes closed, knees drawn up and apparently dozing with deep, but very deliberate, groaning respiration. I was struck with the pinched appearance of his features. Mother was seated by him and motioned to me to preserve quietness. He continued in this situation for several hours, occasionally opening his eyes and addressing a few words to those around him. After breakfast, as Mother resumed her seat near him, he turned and playfully poking his finger at her exclaimed, "Booh! is that you Catherine?" Some ten minutes after Mrs. Fitzsimons [Catherine's sister-in-law] stepped softly in when he called out "Who's that?" but, giving a look of recognition, dozed on as before. Mrs. F. immediately whispered to Mother his changed appearance and the settling at the finger nails. A few minutes after, I heard his spring and immediately came in. He seemed endeavoring to rise, with a disturbed, glaring countenance, soon followed by violent spasmodic jerking of his arms and lower limbs, accompanied with short, sharp and rapid groans. He seemed appalled at something mysterious and terrible and his movements were as if to avert or dispel it. Thinking he wished something, or was in a spasm, we called for persons from the adjoining room and set severally at various things for his relief. But he waived [sic] them all off and exclaimed, "help, help, raise me." He had been supporting himself on his right elbow. We raised him, and he surveyed his books and busts, then gazed intently from the rear side window, which was open, and bade us lower him. In lowering him, this time to the left elbow, his struggles were renewed with equal or greater violence, the whole movement, manner and tone as if something over-powering had pounced upon and was grappling furiously with him. But turning upon his right side he instantly became calm. Seeing Mother as he turned he exclaimed "My dear Wife!" and folding his arms on his breast passed away without a gasp or groan. So life-like was his appearance—the features calm and placid, lips closed naturally, eyes wide opened, brilliantly but not unnaturally luminous, and a look of profound thought and brightest intelligence, as if something most curious and interesting was just unraveled—that none of us conceived it was death until Miss Mary remarked to Mother, who was preparing to administer a dose of medicine, that she thought all was over. The struggle lasted perhaps two or two and a half minutes: a half minute after Miss Mary had spoken I felt the pulse. It shot for an instant to the wrist, and I observed a slight twitch on the left upper lip. I instantly ordered rubbing and called for mustard and restoratives, but before they could be applied it was evident all was over. He passed away about 10 minutes before 10 A.M. (13 Nov. 1864). Mother simply exclaimed "What! Dead? Dead?" but seemed incapable of realizing it. Seeing her stand bewildered, scarcely a tear on any eye, so sudden and une[x]pected was the scene while all were busy in getting remedies, or in attendance, I led Mother to the other room, but she soon returned. Just after our return Mrs. Fitzsimons threw herself by Father's side and exclaiming with a flood of tears,"my best friend, you have left us," closed his eyes. . . .

[Edward Spann Hammond to Harry Hammond, The Last Moments of James Henry Hammond, November 13, 1864, James Henry Hammond Papers, SCL.]

Epilogue

The readers of *Secret and Sacred* have shared almost twenty-five years of Hammond's life and are well aware of his aspirations to found a long-lasting aristocratic family. However, for one so concerned with posterity, Hammond imprudently committed too much of his wealth to the Confederate war effort, at the end of which, all that was left was the land. His son Harry struggled through the Reconstruction period and afterward to hold the legacy together, but in impoverished South Carolina his efforts were far too feeble. By the time John Shaw Billings, Hammond's great-grandson, purchased the property in 1935, all that remained of James Henry Hammond's holdings of 14,000 acres was the house, Redcliffe, on 373 acres.

Billings, a gifted journalist and the first editor of *Life*, restored the plantation house to its former grandeur. Before he died without surviving children in 1975, he bequeathed it to the state of South Carolina. All that stands today as a haunting reminder of James Henry Hammond's vast dominion is his last home, Redcliffe, now preserved as a state park.

James Henry Hammond died in 1864; almost one hundred and twenty-five years later the core of his "secret and sacred" diaries are now published. Although no one study of a single document or of a single person can capture the world view of the Southern planter class, let alone of the whole South, Hammond's private views on the destiny of Southern society, expressed during the two decades prior to the Civil War, offer some of the best insights we are likely to have from a single source. Several aspects of his thinking are clear from what he writes or can be inferred from what he does not write.

His view of slavery can be deduced from the fact that in his private diaries he never questioned the institution or expressed any guilt over being a slaveholder. He was presumably a complete racist, totally accepting the proposition that blacks were inferior and that slavery was the only condition appropriate for them. His view of white society can be derived from his frequent paeans to South Carolina, where, in his view, families of culture, wealth, and breeding were the leaders of the state (due in no small part to many state offices being open only to holders of sufficient property), and his aspiration was to place his family first among them. His view of the future was one which preserved in perpetuity all that he found good in the present, an aristocratic white society based on a foundation or "mudsill" of black slavery.

This set of beliefs, respectively immoral, outrageous, and incredible, if widely held, as they undoubtedly were, seem sufficient to have spelled disaster for the South. Hammond, living through and benefiting from the early stages of the industrial revolution—the English manufacture of cotton cloth, the factory system, the steam engine, the steam ship, the railroad, the telegraph, and the Atlantic Cable—failed to appreciate these changes and their portents for the future. His reading lists included the latest in modern science—archaeology, astronomy, geology, physics, "Dr. Faraday's latest works on electricity"—but his vision of the world seemed to look back to a romantic re-creation of the Middle Ages, to a world created and dominated by an aristocracy. Through most of his career he sought to achieve this by secession, freeing the South from Northern control and freezing it in time, presumably never to change. Incredibly shortsighted as we now know this to be, it is perhaps understandable for Hammond, who looked back to cultures and civilizations lasting hundreds if not thousands of years. Egyptian society and culture, for instance, were stable for nearly three thousand years, a fact that is virtually incomprehensible to the modern world, but which was perhaps more important to Hammond than the burgeoning auguries of change around him. One year before Hammond died, Henry Ford was born. Idealizing the past, fixated on preserving the present, he never gave a thought to the whirlwind of change which was even then sweeping up him and the South. Hammond seems to have succumbed to the myth of the Old South even before the South was old and there was a myth.

Secession he always argued for, but preferably a peaceful and bloodless one, and certainly only a successful one. When finally the South was ready to secede, it was too late, and Hammond for one drew back or at least stood aside as his world at last followed the course he had so long advocated, but now it was a disastrous course which totally destroyed all that he had sought to preserve. Hammond was clearly one of the intellectual leaders of the South. Widely read, articulate, learned, he remained completely oblivious to the need for change presented by the two greatest challenges facing the South—the moral question of slavery and the coming of the modern industrial world. Looking backward, trying to preserve unchanged his world, he and his peers led the South to Armageddon, losing all that they cherished.

Biographical Directory

JAMES HOPKINS ADAMS (1812–61), Richland District cotton planter at "Live Oak" plantation, owner of many slaves, governor, banker, and state legislator, was graduated from Yale University in 1831. Adams, possibly was a member of the Nullification Convention of 1832–33, served in the South Carolina House of Representatives 1834–38, 1840–41, 1848–49, and in the South Carolina Senate, 1851–53. A brigadier general of the state militia (ca. 1840s), Adams, between 1854 and 1856, served as governor, and during his administration he urged that the slave trade be reopened. Adams was a trustee of South Carolina College, 1841–61, and during his governorship forced the resignation of South Carolina College Professor Francis Lieber. Adams was a director of the Exchange Bank of Columbia, 1854–61, and of the Bank of Chester, 1858–61. As a delegate to the Secession Convention, Adams favored immediate secession, and the convention appointed him one of three commissioners to treat with President James Buchanan for the return of property held by the Federal government in South Carolina.

WILLIAM H. AIKEN (1806–87), planter, governor, United States congressman, banker, state legislator, and railroad magnate, was graduated from South Carolina College in 1825, a classmate of James Henry Hammond. Aiken, who inherited his father's large fortune in 1831, developed a highly successful cotton and rice plantation on Jehossee Island near Charleston; he owned also 878 slaves. Aiken served in the South Carolina House, 1838–41, the South Carolina Senate, 1842–45, and resigned from the Senate to become governor in December 1844, the successor to James Henry Hammond. Elected to the United States House of Representatives in 1851, Aiken served until 1857. Although Aiken opposed nullification and secession, he supported the Confederacy financially. Aiken held the directorship of the Planters and Mechanics Bank, 1833–36, 1849–57, promoted railroad development in the state, and was elected in the fall of 1865 to the 39th Congress of the United States but was denied his seat.

ALFRED PROCTOR ALDRICH (1814–97), judge, lawyer, and state legislator, attended the College of Charleston and in 1835 was admitted to the bar. Aldrich settled in Barnwell and practiced law. Aldrich was a protégé of Hammond, his confidant during the scandal with Hampton, and a cooperationist who put forth Hammond's "plan of state action" during South Carolina's secession crisis, 1850–51. Aldrich served for five terms in the South Carolina House, 1858–65, and as speaker, 1862–65. He resigned from the House in December 1865 upon his election as a judge to the court of pleas and general sessions, but was removed from the bench in 1866 by Brevet Brigadier General E. R. S. Canby. He was reappointed to the court in 1878 by Governor Wade Hampton.

ROBERT FRANCIS WITHERS ALLSTON (1801–64), planter, governor, state legislator, and author, was graduated from West Point in 1821. He owned numerous plantations in Georgetown District, including "Chicora Wood" and "Brookgreen," and purchased in 1857 an elaborate mansion at 51 Meeting Street in Charleston, once owned by Nathaniel Russell. At his death an inventory listed 590 slaves as part of his estate. Allston, as a nullifier, served in the South Carolina House, 1828–31. He was a member of the South Carolina Senate, 1832–56, being president of that body from 1850 to 1856. Allston lost the 1842 gubernatorial race to Hammond but served as governor, 1856–58. Allston, a supporter of states' rights and nullification, urged the annexation of Texas, opposed the Wilmot Proviso, which would have prevented the expansion of slavery into the territories gained from Mexico, and was a delegate at the Nashville Convention in 1850 which openly discussed secession. Author of two works on South Carolina rice cultivation, Allston also served as a South Carolina College trustee from 1840 until his death at "Chicora Wood" near Georgetown. Allston was the father of Elizabeth Waties Allston Pringle (1845–1921), the author of *Woman Rice Planter* and *Chronicles of "Chicora Wood."*

JOHN ALGERNON SIDNEY ASHE (1796–1868), planter, banker, and state legislator, was graduated in 1814 from Union College in Schenectady, New York, studied law under Langdon Cheves in Charleston but never practiced as an attorney. Ashe inherited the plantations "Roxbury," "Hywassee" or "Rotterdam," other plantations, and a house at 26 South Battery in Charleston. He served in the South Carolina House, 1826–29, and in the South Carolina Senate, 1830–35, 1845–49. Ashe was a director of the Bank of the State of South Carolina, 1842–45, and, in 1850 he served as a guard of honor in Charleston at the funeral of John C. Calhoun. It was Ashe in the South Carolina legislature who shared with Hammond's supporters the incriminating documents on Hammond that were held by Hampton. A duelist, Ashe frequently acted as a second and it was alleged that he had been the referee "in fifty-one difficulties between gentlemen."

ROBERT WOODWARD BARNWELL (1801–82), United States congressman, planter, lawyer, state legislator, and educator, was graduated with first honors from Harvard College in 1821, studied law, and began a practice in Beaufort in 1824. He was a member of the South Carolina House, 1826–28, a member of the United States House of Representatives, 1829–33, and president of South Carolina College, 1835–41, succeeding Thomas Cooper. Much more moderate in politics than either Cooper or his fire-eating first cousin, Robert Barnwell Rhett, he was chosen to fill the United States Senate seat originally vacated by the death of John C. Calhoun. Barnwell held this seat during the last six months of 1850. A delegate to the Nashville Convention of 1850, he was also a member of the state Secession Convention meeting in December 1860, and was appointed along with James Hopkins Adams to treat with President Buchanan in 1860 for the return of property held by the Federal government in South Carolina. Throughout the Civil War, Barnwell was a member of the Confederate States Senate.

JOHN BAUSKETT (1794–1867), lawyer, planter, state legislator, banker, and businessman, was admitted to the bar in 1817. Initially he resided and practiced law in Newberry District, but moved to Edgefield in the 1820s and to Columbia in the mid 1850s. He served in the South Carolina House, 1822–23, 1830–31, 1844–45, and the South Carolina Senate, 1834–38. A member of the Nullification Convention, 1832–33, Bauskett was director of the Hamburg Bank, 1836–44, and part-owner of a cotton factory at Vaucluse.

EDMUND BELLINGER, JR. (1808–59), legislator, lawyer, and educator was graduated from South Carolina College in 1826, admitted to the bar in 1829, and began the practice of law at Barnwell Court House. He was a member of the South Carolina House, 1838–41. Bellinger campaigned for secession in 1851, and at a barbecue on July 4 in Barnwell District he spoke for the secessionists. At that same affair, Alfred P. Aldrich, a cooperationist, debated Bellinger and presented Hammond's "plan of state action" as an alternative to separate state secession. Bellinger in 1854 moved from Barnwell to Columbia, where he continued his practice of law and inaugurated a law school.

MILLEDGE LUKE BONHAM (1813–90), United States congressman, governor, lawyer, state legislator, businessman, and Confederate soldier, was graduated from South Carolina College in 1834 and was admitted to the bar in 1837. Bonham served in the South Carolina House, 1840–43, and was solicitor of the southern district of South Carolina, 1848–57. From Edgefield District, Bonham was originally elected to the United States House of Representatives in 1857 to fill the unexpired term of Preston S. Brooks. Reelected, he resigned his seat in December 1860 upon the secession of South Carolina. Bonham commanded troops during the Seminole, Mexican, and Civil wars. From 1862 to 1864, Bonham served as the war governor of South Carolina, and was appointed a brigadier general of cavalry in February 1865. After the war, Bonham resumed the practice of law, planted, and represented Edgefield District in the state legislature, 1865–67. In

1878 Governor Wade Hampton appointed Bonham a state railroad commissioner, a position he held until his death.

KER BOYCE (1787–1854), banker, state legislator, businessman, and railroad magnate, began as a poor boy working as a clerk in a Newberry store, was a deputy sheriff and a tax collector in Newberry, and moved to Charleston in 1817. In 1825 Boyce became a factor on East Bay in Charleston and a director of the Bank of the United States, Charleston branch, 1826–35, Bank of Charleston, director, 1836, 1849–54, president, 1840–42, and director, South Carolina Canal and Railroad Company, 1839, 1841–42, 1850–54. Boyce represented Charleston in the South Carolina House, 1832–39, and the South Carolina Senate, 1840–48. A member and president of the Charleston Chamber of commerce, Boyce was also director of the South Carolina Insurance Company, a director of the Louisville, Cincinnati and Charleston Railroad, and one of the founders of the Graniteville Manufacturing Company in Edgefield District. His factorage company and his subsequent investments in numerous banks, railroads, manufacturing companies, and other businesses yielded extremely high returns, and after Boyce's death inventories listed his assets as totalling $998,337 in stocks, bonds, and notes and over $160,000 worth of real property.

PRESTON SMITH BROOKS (1819–57), United States congressman, lawyer, state legislator, and a cousin of Senator Andrew Pickens Butler, attended South Carolina College but left in 1839, was admitted to the bar in 1842, and served as an aide-de-camp to Governor James Henry Hammond, 1842–44. Brooks served in the South Carolina House, 1844–45, and in the United States House of Representatives, 1853–57. In 1840, during the South Carolina gubernatorial campaign, Brooks fought a duel with Louis Trezevant Wigfall. Both men were from Edgefield District—Brooks's family supported the candidacy of Hammond while Wigfall supported his opponent, John P. Richardson. Wigfall had already dueled with two members of the Brooks's family, killing Thomas Bird. In the duel between Brooks and Wigfall both men received leg wounds. Congressman Brooks physically attacked Senator Charles Sumner of Massachusetts in the U.S. Senate chamber on May 22, 1856, and beat him with a cane because of Sumner's "Crime Against Kansas" speech delivered in the Senate on May 20. In this speech Sumner had insulted Brooks's cousin Andrew Pickens Butler, senator from South Carolina. The House of Representatives censured Brooks for the caning, he resigned his seat on July 15, only to be reelected to fill the vacancy caused by his own resignation. He died suddenly in Washington on January 27, 1857. Hammond noted to a friend on Brooks's death, "he dies just at his culminating point. The decadence to you and I was clear but not to the world. . . ."

ANDREW PICKENS BUTLER (1796–1857), United States senator, judge, lawyer, state legislator, and a cousin of Preston Brooks, was graduated from South Carolina College in 1817, was admitted to the bar in 1818, and practiced law. He served in the South Carolina House, 1824–31, and in the South Carolina Senate, 1832–33. Butler resigned his seat in the South Carolina Senate upon his election as a judge of the court of general sessions and common pleas, where he served from 1833 until 1846. On the court, Butler was considered a wit, but could be very caustic. Elected to the United States Senate in 1846, having defeated James Henry Hammond, Butler served until his death in 1857; Hammond was elected to fill Butler's vacant seat.

PIERCE MASON BUTLER (1798–1847), governor, soldier, banker, planter, Indian agent, and brother of Andrew Pickens Butler, was in the United States Army from 1819 to 1829 before becoming the executive director in 1833 of the Bank of the State of South Carolina, Columbia branch. During the Second Seminole War (1835–43), Butler served briefly as a lieutenant-colonel before returning to South Carolina in 1836. Governor of South Carolina, 1836–38, Butler was appointed in 1841 agent to the Cherokees and remained until 1846 at Fort Gibson, Arkansas. Hammond's brother Marcellus served at Fort Gibson from 1839 to 1842. At the beginning of the Mexican War, Butler was elected colonel of the Palmetto Regiment and was killed at the Battle of Churubusco in August 1847.

JOHN CALDWELL CALHOUN (1782–1850), statesman, planter, and political philosopher, was graduated from Yale in 1804, Litchfield (Connecticut) Law School in 1806, and was admitted to the South Carolina bar in 1807. After a term in the South Carolina House, 1808–09, he served in the United States House of Representatives, 1811–17, where he became a leader of the "War Hawks" and also supported nationalistic legislation after the War of 1812, including the protective tariff of 1816. In 1811, Calhoun married his cousin, Floride Bonneau Colhoun (1792–1866), a member of the low-country planter aristocracy. He served as secretary of war under President Monroe, 1817–25, was a presidential candidate in 1824, and was elected twice to the vice presidency, serving first under John Quincy Adams (1825–29) and then under Andrew Jackson (1829–32). In his "South Carolina Exposition and Protest," secretly written in 1828 when he was vice president of the United States, Calhoun postulated the principles of states' rights and nullification, and in 1831 at his plantation "Fort Hill" (now the campus of Clemson University in upstate South Carolina) he penned the "Fort Hill Address" in which he publicly declared himself for nullification and proposed the process by which it could take place. Breaking with President Jackson in part over states' rights and nullification, Calhoun resigned the vice presidency in 1832 and was elected to the United States Senate from South Carolina, replacing Robert Y. Hayne. As an United States senator, 1832–42, he remained the principal political figure in South Carolina. In 1842 he resigned from the Senate to seek the 1844 Democratic presidential nomination and again he was unsuccessful; however, Calhoun became secretary of state following the accidental death of Abel P. Upshur in April 1844. While secretary of state under President Tyler (1844–45), Calhoun secured the annexation of Texas. Calhoun, again senator from South Carolina from 1845 until his death on March 31, 1850 (in the midst of the congressional debates on the Compromise of 1850), had remained an unyielding defender of Southern rights. He opposed the compromise measures, yet pleaded for the preservation of the Union. In his "Disquisition on Government," posthumously published, Calhoun proposed a dual Executive (from North and South), each one armed with a veto. Hammond along with many other South Carolina political figures, including Robert Barnwell Rhett and Francis W. Pickens sought in the 1850s to inherit from Calhoun the mantle of leadership.

THOMAS JAMES DAVIES (1830–1902), a planter from Edgefield and brother of Harriet Pamela Davies, wife of Marcellus Hammond, became after the marriage of Harriet and Marcellus in 1842 a life-long friend of the Hammond family. He was present at "Redcliffe" when James Henry Hammond died.

JOHN MCPHERSON DESAUSSURE (1807–83), planter, state legislator, and lawyer, was graduated from South Carolina College in 1825, a classmate of James Henry Hammond. DeSaussure was admitted to the bar in 1828, and over the years in Camden was elected justice of the peace, justice of the quorum, warden, and intendant. A wealthy planter, DeSaussure owned "Laussane" plantation. He served in the South Carolina House from 1858 to 1864. His brother was William Ford DeSaussure and his father, Henry W. DeSaussure (1763–1839), was director of the United States Bureau of the Mint in 1795 and also was very instrumental in the establishment of South Carolina College in 1801. The third building constructed at the College, a Robert Mills designed three-story Federal, was named in 1809 for Henry William DeSaussure.

MARY DAVIE DESAUSSURE (1821–58), niece of John McPherson DeSaussure and daughter of William Ford DeSaussure, was James Henry Hammond's "Miss Mary." Mary DeSaussure married William Izard Bull (1813–94) of "Ashley Hall" in Charleston in 1842. They were the parents of seven children. Mary DeSaussure Bull died of yellow fever in Charleston in September 1858; her husband lived on for thirty-six years.

WILLIAM FORD DESAUSSURE (1792–1870), United States senator, judge, lawyer, state legislator, older brother of John McPherson DeSaussure, and father of Mary Davie DeSaussure, was graduated from Harvard in 1810, admitted to the bar in 1813, and practiced law in Charleston and Columbia. DeSaussure served in the South Carolina House, 1836–39, 1842–47, and was appointed judge of chancery court in 1847. A delegate to the Nashville Convention in 1850, he was a delegate to the Democratic National Conventions of 1852 and 1860, and also represented Richland District in the South Carolina Secession Convention in December 1860. DeSaussure in 1852 was appointed to fill the United States Senate seat vacated by the resignation of Robert Barnwell Rhett and served until March 3, 1853, when he returned to his law practice.

RICHARD DE TREVILLE (1801–74), lieutenant governor, lawyer, and state legislator, was graduated from West Point in 1823, admitted to the bar in 1825, and practiced law first at Beaufort and later in Charleston. He served in the South Carolina House, 1830–31, and in the South Carolina Senate continuously from 1835 to 1853. He was elevated to the post of lieutenant governor, 1854–56, serving with Governor James Hopkins Adams. During the early 1850s, De Treville opposed separate state action on secession because he feared it would result in both failure and armed Federal intervention and would also impede future cooperation among the Southern states. In 1860 he signed the secession ordinance, and during the war he served as a Confederate colonel of the 17th Regiment of S.C. Volunteers.

JAMES DE VEAUX (1812–44), a painter, born in Charleston, was a close friend of Wade Hampton III. De Veaux studied art in Philadelphia with Henry Inman under the sponsorship of William Hassell Gibbes and Washington Allston. De Veaux, sponsored by Gibbes, Allston, and Wade Hampton II, set sail for Europe in 1836, the same year as did the Hammonds, and James met up with the artist in Paris and in London. After De Veaux returned to South Carolina in 1839, he spent the next three years painting the portraits of the members of prominent South Carolina families, including the Mannings, the Hamptons, and the Gibbes. In September 1841, De Veaux returned to Europe to study and to paint and was sponsored on this trip by the Hamptons, Mannings, and the John S. Prestons. In Italy the artist contracted pneumonia and died in Rome. During his brief lifetime, De Veaux painted 240 portraits.

ELIZABETH FRIES LUMMIS ELLET (1818–77), an author, and the wife of South Carolina College professor William Henry Ellet (1806–59), was educated at the Aurora Female Seminary in upstate New York. As a teenager she started translating works into English from Italian, German, and French literature. Her first published work in 1834 was a translation of Silvio Pellico's tragedy *Euphemio of Messina*. She published a translation of *Teresa Contrarini* in 1835, the year she married Professor Ellet. They moved to Columbia, South Carolina, and lived there until 1849, when they returned to New York. Although Hammond disparaged her work, Elizabeth Ellet wrote several well-known books on American history, the best-known being a three-volume set, *The Women of the American Revolution*, published between 1848 and 1851.

BENJAMIN THOMAS ELMORE (1787–1841), lawyer, legislator, state treasurer, and the brother of Franklin Elmore, was graduated from South Carolina College in 1810, admitted to the bar in 1815, served as the treasurer for the upper division of South Carolina, 1817–21, and was comptroller-general for the state, 1823–26. Elmore served in the South Carolina House from 1836 to 1839, where he was considered powerful in Richland County politics. In 1838, Patrick Noble defeated him for governor. Narrowly defeated for reelection to the House in 1840, Elmore left office in ill-health and died the following year. Hammond wrote in his diary that Benjamin Elmore was "the most bitter and most active enemy I had. His death will do much towards harmonizing of politics in Columbia."

FRANKLIN HARPER ELMORE (1799–1850), United States senator, congressman, lawyer, banker, state legislator, and brother of Benjamin Thomas Elmore, was graduated from South Carolina College in 1819, read law, and was admitted to the bar in 1821. Solicitor for the Southeastern Circuit Court, 1822–36, Elmore was elected to the United States House of Representatives in 1836 to succeed Hammond who had resigned. Elmore served an additional term before resigning in 1839 to become president of the Bank of the State of South Carolina, where he served until 1850. Elmore, described by John C. Calhoun as his "devoted disciple," was appointed early in May 1850 to succeed John C. Calhoun in the United States Senate, but served only several weeks before his own death on May 29. In partnership with Wade Hampton II, Elmore had been a major developer of iron mines in upstate South Carolina near Spartanburg and was a longtime trustee of South Carolina College.

ELIZABETH (BETTY) HAMMOND EVE (1849–1941), the eighth and last child of Catherine and James Henry, married William Raiford Eve in 1871. They had twelve children between September 1872 and January 1891. Hammond lovingly described his youngest child in 1860 as "the brightest creature in the world." He wrote with much pride that in Washington and at "Redcliffe" she was a Captain who "commands a troop of little folks of both sexes, white and black, whom she trains to run over me and the household. Yet she is gentleness itself when by herself, loyal, loving and pure." The Senator's youngest child lived to be ninety-two years old.

CATHERINE PRITCHARD FITZSIMONS (1771–1841), the mother of Catherine Elizabeth Fitzsimons Hammond, was the daughter of Paul Pritchard, a Charleston shipbuilder. She married Christopher Fitzsimons (1762–1825) in 1788 and had ten children. After the death of her husband she spent much of her widowhood at "Millwood," the home of Wade Hampton II and her daughter Ann, and at "Silverton," the home of James Henry Hammond and her daughter Catherine. She died at "Silverton" in her seventieth year.

RICHARD GANTT (1767–1850), judge, lawyer, state legislator, and a South Carolina College trustee, was a native of Maryland who migrated first to Georgia and then in 1794 to South Carolina. Admitted to the bar in 1795, Gantt was Clerk of the South Carolina House from 1804 to 1815, was put on the bench in December 1815, where he served until 1841, retiring at the age of seventy-four. A teetotaller, Gantt was active in the temperance movement.

ROBERT WILSON GIBBES (1809–66), physician, author, educator, art collector, and newspaper editor, was born in Charleston and graduated from South Carolina College in 1827. From 1827 to 1834, Gibbes was a professor of chemistry, geology, and mineralogy at South Carolina College. He resigned to practice medicine in Columbia in 1834, having graduated from the Medical College of the State of South Carolina. A noted author, he wrote many monographs in his field, including in 1842 a treatise on the method of treatment for typhoid pneumonia. His *A Memoir of De Veaux*, written in 1846, is an excellent source on the life of the young artist who had been materially aided by Dr. Gibbes before De Veaux's untimely death. In the settlement of a debt in 1852, Gibbes acquired *The South Carolinian*, a Columbia newspaper. Gibbes took active editorship of the newspaper until 1858, and he continued to own it until the plant was destroyed by fire in 1865. During the war, Gibbes served as surgeon general of South Carolina. In the destruction of Columbia in 1865, it is alleged that Gibbes lost more than two hundred paintings.

HENRY GOURDIN (1804–79), businessman, banker, and state legislator, acquired a factorage business before he was twenty-one years old and remained active in it for over half a century. Alarmed at the failure to recharter the Bank of the United States in the 1830s, Gourdin was instrumental in gaining the charter for the newly formed Bank of Charleston in 1835 and served on its board of directors continuously from 1835 to 1879, resigning only after forty-three years of service because of failing health. He served in the South Carolina House, 1834–35, 1838–39, 1841, and 1852–53. Elected president of the Charleston Chamber of Commerce in 1853, he was reelected for three successive years. In 1852, he became the first president of the Blue Ridge Railroad and was instrumental in its merger with the Greenville Railroad.

MAXCY GREGG (1814–62), lawyer, states' rights activist, and Confederate commander, was graduated from South Carolina College in 1836, admitted to the bar in 1839, and began a law practice in Columbia. A veteran of the Mexican War, Gregg sought in vain to persuade Hammond in 1852 to asssume the leadership of the wing of the state Democratic party advocating immediate secession. A delegate to the South Carolina Secession Convention and a member of the central committee which framed the ordinance of secession adopted on December 20, 1860, Gregg, early in 1861, formed a South Carolina unit which became known as Gregg's Brigade. Hammond's eldest son, Harry, served as a major with Gregg. Gregg fought at Malvern Hill, Second Manassas, Sharpsburg, and was killed at the battle of Fredericksburg.

JAMES HAMILTON, JR., (1786–1857), United States congressman, governor, planter, lawyer, diplomatic agent for the Republic of Texas, state legislator, and land speculator, was admitted to the bar in Charleston in 1808. Hamilton served in the South Carolina House, 1819–23. He resigned upon his election to the United

States House of Representatives in December 1822, where he served from 1823 to 1829. An active nullifier, he was elected governor in 1830, and during his term in office convened the state's Nullification Convention in November 1832. In 1834 he was elected to the South Carolina Senate and served until 1838. By 1836 Hamilton owned fourteen plantations in four states and ultimately acquired property in Texas. Vitally interested in the settlement of Texas, Hamilton lent the new government large sums of money and speculated in land. In 1838, Hamilton became commissioner of loans for Texas, and in 1839 he was made a perpetual citizen of the Republic of Texas and was made diplomatic agent to France, Great Britain, Belgium, and the Netherlands. Hamilton was recalled in 1842 by Texas President Sam Houston. Hamilton had not only lost favor with the government of Texas, but by 1842 he was vastly overextended, heavily mortgaged, and $700,000 in debt. Hamilton returned to Europe as an agent for the James River Company of Virginia. This venture failed too and resulted in more personal debt for Hamilton. In a gesture of friendship, Hammond had agreed to co-sign a loan for his hard-pressed friend. When Hamilton went bankrupt, Hammond lost more than $20,000. Hammond pressed Hamilton relentlessly and recovered a portion of the money owed him, in oil paintings owned by Hamilton's wife. Others lost much more, for example, James Petigru lent Hamilton over $100,000. Despite Hamilton's almost continuous absence from the state after the late 1830s, Governor Whitemarsh Benjamin Seabrook initially named Hamilton to Calhoun's Senate seat in 1850, but was persuaded to withdraw the appointment. From the mid-1840s until the end of his life, Hamilton pressed the Texas government for a settlement of the loans and expenses he had extended and incurred on her behalf. In the fall of 1857, Hamilton decided to make a direct and final appeal for payment from the Texas legislature, but he drowned at sea when his ship collided with another vessel in the Gulf of Mexico.

CATHERINE ELIZABETH FITZSIMONS HAMMOND (1814–96), wife of James Henry, married Hammond in 1831 when she was seventeen years old. Catherine bore eight children, five of whom lived to maturity. After her husband's death in 1864, Mrs. Hammond continued to live at "Redcliffe" until 1873, when she moved into the original house on the property, "Old Yard." She lived there until her death, and her son Harry and his family lived next door at "Redcliffe." Except for a period of about five years when she separated from him, Catherine accepted Hammond's domination of her life with all its stresses and strains, and after his death she devoted her "remaining years to his memory."

CATHERINE FOX SPANN HAMMOND (1785–1864), the mother of James Henry Hammond, married in 1806 Elisha Hammond (1774–1829). Four of their children lived to maturity. Widowed at the age of forty-four, Mrs. Hammond for the remainder of her life lived with or near her son James Henry and saw him achieve wealth and fame. She died on June 1, 1864, just five months before Hammond's own death.

EDWARD SPANN HAMMOND (1834–1921), called Spann, the third son of Catherine and James Henry, was graduated from the University of Georgia in 1853, attended medical school in Charleston, and was graduated from the University of Pennsylvania Medical School in 1855. In the fall of 1855, Spann became engaged to his second cousin Clara Kilpatrick, but James Henry succeeded in breaking off the engagement in 1857, because the bride's dower was encumbered. A half-century later Spann recalled vividly, "the blow that struck me left an anguish in which a life-time is comprised." Elected a member of the state legislature in 1858 for one term, Spann was a major at Manassas in 1861, and he married Marcella Morriss of Lynchburg, Virginia, on June 20, 1861. They had one daughter. Spann left the army in 1862 and sent a substitute in his place. In 1863–64 he edited the *Richmond Whig*. Spann was at "Redcliffe" when his father died in 1864, but after the war lived with his family in Lynchburg and was a planter with his father-in-law. He returned to South Carolina in 1870; his wife, after six weeks' residence returned to Virginia. Marcella died in 1878, and Spann remarried in 1882. He and his wife Laura Hanson Dunbar Brown Hammond were the parents of two sons. In postwar South Carolina, Spann became a planter, practiced law, and was elected a magistrate. Until his death at Blackville, Spann had in his possession the volumes of his father's "secret and sacred" diary.

HARRY HAMMOND (1832–1916), the first child of Catherine and James Henry, was named James Henry Hammond for his father, but was called Harry and is so listed in the family genealogy. Harry received his A.B. degree from South Carolina College in 1852, studied medicine briefly in Charleston, acquired a medical degree from the University of Pennsylvania in 1855, and went on the Grand Tour of Europe for eighteen months. He studied chemistry at Harvard in the fall of 1858 and was appointed a professor of natural sciences at the University of Georgia in January 1859. Harry married Emily Cumming (1834–1911), of Augusta, Georgia, on November 22, 1859. He served during the war as a quartermaster with the rank of major and surrendered with the Army of Northern Virginia at Appomattox Court House on April 9, 1865. After the war, Harry and Emily raised five children and sought to make a success of their plantations. In 1883 Harry authored most of the essays in *South Carolina Resources and Population, Institutions and Industries*, commonly known as "Hammond's Handbook." It was the major scholarly achievement of his life. Harry, as the eldest son, sought to preserve his father's estate, but by the time of Harry's death all that remained of James Henry's vast holdings of 14,000 acres was 500 acres owned by Harry's son, Kit, and the house at "Redcliffe" on 373 acres.

JOHN FOX HAMMOND (1820–86), the youngest brother of James Henry, was graduated from the University of Virginia and studied medicine at the University of Pennsylvania. He entered the United States Army in 1847 as an assistant surgeon. When the war came, John Hammond remained in the Union Army, his brother having advised him to stay, fearing he would return home to "squat on" the rest of the family. In 1862 Major Hammond served as medical director of the 2nd Corps, Army of the Potomac, during the entire Peninsular campaign. On March 13, 1865, he was brevetted a lieutenant colonel and in 1876 he received the grade permanently. He married Caroline E. Lawrence of New York City on April 15, 1863. The marriage produced two daughters, and the family made their home in Poughkeepsie, New York. Hammond retired from the army at the age of sixty-four. He wrote his sister-in-law Catherine F. Hammond in June of 1886 that he was then sixty-five years old and that his health was frail. "I am," he wrote, "much like a sapless old tree that stands the storms for ages and then to fall prostrate in a calm." He died in Poughkeepsie less than four months later.

Marcus Claudius Marcellus Hammond (1814–76), referred to as the "Major" or Marcellus was a younger brother of James Henry and his close and confiding friend. Marcellus, after graduating from West Point in 1836, served in Florida in the 4th Regiment of Infantry, and participated in several campaigns against the Seminole Indians. Later he served in the regiment that removed the Cherokee Indians to the West. In 1840 he was stationed at Fort Gibson, Arkansas. In July 1842, Marcellus married Harriet Pamela Davies (1821–80), of Augusta, Georgia. They had seven children. On December 31, 1842, he resigned his commission on account of ill-health. Between 1842 and 1846 he was a cotton planter in Georgia, but with the coming of the Mexican War he regained his commission; ill-health still plagued him, and he resigned in April 1847. Marcellus returned to planting, this time at Hamburg, South Carolina. Between 1849 and 1853 he wrote a series of articles on California and the battles of the Mexican War for the *Southern Quarterly Review*, edited by William Gilmore Simms. In 1856 he was elected to the South Carolina legislature and served one term. In 1860 he moved again to Georgia, where he was appointed major-general of the Third Division of the Georgia militia. In this capacity he raised thirty companies for the Confederacy, although he himself saw no action. During the 1870s he located again the Cherokee Indian woman by whom he had at least one child while stationed at Fort Gibson. He told her he was once rich but that the war had ruined him. In his last known letter to her written in the summer of 1875, he said, "good-bye— it may be forever. Whatever may happen I have had some good times." He died the following year.

Paul Fitzsimons Hammond (1838–87), nicknamed "Dan," was the sixth and youngest son of Catherine and James Henry. He attended school at Nashville, was in Washington when his father went to the Senate, and met there Loula Comer (1838–1914), of Macon, Georgia, a relative of Mrs. Clement Clay, wife of the Alabama senator. They married in 1858 and went to live at "Glen Loula," a plantation given to them by James Henry. During the war Paul served on the staffs of General Kirby Smith and General John Breckinridge. He continued to plant after the war, and he and Loula were the parents of eight children. He died at the age of forty-nine, a self-confessed morphine addict.

WADE HAMPTON II (1791–1858), planter, greatest turfman in South Carolina, state legislator, banker, and soldier, had great political influence in the Palmetto State, and was also the brother-in-law of James Henry Hammond, John Laurence Manning, Thomson T. Player, and John Smith Preston, among others. Hampton attended South Carolina College, 1807–09, and left without a degree. On the staff of General Jackson at the battle of New Orleans, Hampton afterwards managed "Millwood" plantation near Columbia, and married in 1817 Ann Fitzsimons, (1794–1833), Catherine F. Hammond's older sister. After the death of his father in 1835, Hampton owned over 18,000 acres in South Carolina, Georgia, and Mississippi. According to the 1840 Federal census, he possessed 490 slaves in Richland District. Hampton served in the South Carolina Senate, 1826–29, and as a trustee of South Carolina College from 1826 to 1858. Frequently urged to seek the governorship, Hampton preferred to be the power behind the political scene. He was a director of the Louisville, Cincinnati and Charleston Railroad, 1840–42, director of the South Carolina Railroad Company, 1849–58, and director of the Bank of South Carolina, 1820–24, 1831–36, and 1849–58. When he died in 1858, he, whom Hammond in his diary had accused of being a spendthrift and in debt, left debts amounting to over half a million dollars.

WADE HAMPTON III (1818–1902), United States senator, governor, soldier, and planter, was the eldest child of Wade and Ann Fitzsimons Hampton and the nephew of Catherine and James Henry Hammond. Wade was graduated from South Carolina College in 1836 and studied law but never practiced as an attorney. In 1838 he married Margaret Francis Preston (1818–56), the sister of John and William Preston, and after her death he married in 1858 Mary Singleton McDuffie (1830–74), the only child of Senator George McDuffie. A member of one of the richest families in the antebellum South, Hampton was a planter at "Millwood" near Columbia and in Mississippi where he owned over 10,000 acres. By 1860 he and his family, it was estimated, owned more than 3,000 slaves. However, his lands, including those he inherited from his father, were heavily mortgaged in the 1850s. Hampton served in the South Carolina House, 1852–57, and in the South Carolina Senate, 1858–61. As a legislator in 1859 he opposed South Carolina's reopening the slave trade, and although he believed secession was a constitutional right, he did not think the situation in 1860 justified such a drastic step. He started the war as the commander of the Hampton Legion and ended it as the general in command of Lee's cavalry. He evacuated Columbia on February 17, 1865, as General Sherman entered the capital. Following the withdrawal of Federal troops in April 1877, he became governor and was reelected without opposition in 1878, but resigned on his election to the United States Senate, where he served from 1879 until 1891.

ROBERT HENRY (1792–1856), clergyman, educator, and fourth president of South Carolina College, received his master of arts degree from the University of Edinburgh in 1814, and served as a minister in Charleston and Columbia before joining the faculty of South Carolina College in 1818. Professor Henry taught moral philosophy and logic until Robert Woodward Barnwell was forced to resign the presidency of the college in 1841 because of illness. Professor Henry was appointed acting president and in 1842 was unanimously elected president by the trustees. In 1845 he was replaced by former Senator William Campbell Preston, and Henry accepted a faculty position teaching Greek at the college until his death.

DANIEL ELLIOTT HUGER (1779–1854), United States senator, judge, lawyer, planter, and state legislator, was graduated in 1798 from the College of New Jersey (later Princeton), read law in the office of Henry William DeSaussure, and was admitted to the bar in 1811. A successful attorney, he also owned considerable property throughout the state including "Goodwill" plantation of approximately 5,910 acres in Richland District. Huger married in 1800 Isabella Middleton, daughter of Arthur Middleton (1742–87), a signer of the Declaration of Independence. Huger served in the South Carolina House, 1803–19, and resigned on his election as a circuit judge, serving on the bench until 1830, when he resigned to take a more active part in the nullification issue. Serving in the South Carolina House, 1830–31, he was an influential and outspoken unionist. A member of the South Carolina Nullification Convention, 1832–33, Huger strongly opposed nullification. He retired from politics after the defeat of the unionists on the nullification issue, but in 1838 he was elected to the South Carolina Senate. The respected low-country unionist served in the South Carolina Senate until elected in 1842 to the United States Senate by the same legislature that elected Hammond governor and McDuffie as the other senator in a successful effort to reconcile the nullifiers and unionists within the state. He served in that body until 1845 when he resigned reluctantly to make room for Calhoun, who wished to return to the Senate. Huger was a trustee of South Carolina College, 1813–17, 1818–37, 1841–45.

FRANCIS LIEBER (1800–1872), internationally known political philosopher, educator, and author, was born in Berlin and received his Ph.D. from the University of Jena in 1820. In 1827 he emigrated to the United States and for twenty-one years, from 1835 to 1856, Lieber was professor of history and political science at South Carolina College. During his tenure at South Carolina, Lieber wrote some of his most famous works including: *Manual of Political Ethics*, 2 vols., published in 1838–39, and *On Civil Liberty and Self-Government*, 2 vols., published in 1853. A suspected abolitionist, Professor Lieber was unhappy and unpopular in South Carolina. Subsequently, in 1856, he resigned from the College and moved to New York where he was made professor of history and political science at Columbia College, 1857–65, and professor of constitutional history and public law at Columbia Law School, 1865–72. Two sons fought in the Union army; a third son, Oscar Montgomery Lieber, a geologist and a friend of Hammond's son Harry, died from wounds sustained while fighting in the Confederate army.

DAVID JAMES McCORD (1797–1855), lawyer, banker, editor, state legislator, plantation manager, and husband of Louisa Cheves McCord (1810–79), attended South Carolina College, studied law, and was admitted to the bar in 1818. McCord practiced law and was editor of the Columbia *Telescope*, a states' rights newspaper, in which he wrote articles in favor of nullification. McCord was in the South Carolina House, 1832–37, until he was elected president of the Columbia branch of the state bank, a position he held until 1840. In 1840, McCord, a widower, married Louisa Susanna Cheves, a daughter of Langdon Cheves, and retired to private life and the management of his wife's plantation "Lang Syne" and others which he and his brother owned in Alabama. Louisa McCord is best known for her articles popularizing free trade, defending slavery, and arguing that woman's proper sphere lies within the home. Widowed in 1855, Louisa McCord continued to manage her own plantation. During the war she operated a military hospital in Columbia and turned her plantation to the war effort, raising provisions rather than cotton.

KATHERINE ("Catty" or "Cattie") HAMMOND GREGG McCoy (1840–82), the seventh child and first daughter of Catherine and James Henry, was described by her father in 1860 as "not deficient in beauty," with strong will and spirit, but "purposeless and indifferent to mundane matters." Katherine married James Gregg, son of William Gregg, owner of the Graniteville Mills on October 10, 1861. On April 19, 1876, her husband was murdered for no apparent reason, and, still interesting one hundred years later, this crime was the subject of a television play on the Public Broadcasting System entitled "The Gardener's Son." Katherine's second marriage was to another textile mill owner, William E. McCoy, on April 13, 1878. Katherine, childless and in bad health since adulthood, died a tragic death at forty-two. Her sister-in-law Loula Comer Hammond wrote Alabama relatives that she supposed they knew how Catty died. She had been a "morphine eater for fifteen years and tried under the treatment of Dr. Burchard to give it up and she had died of paralysis of the heart."

GEORGE McDUFFIE (1790–1851), United States senator, congressman, governor, planter, lawyer, and state legislator, was born in Georgia, was graduated from South Carolina College in 1813, was admitted to the bar in 1814, and practiced law. From 1818 to 1819 he served in the South Carolina House, and from 1821 to 1834 he sat in the United States House of Representatives. An ardent nullifier, McDuffie was elected governor in 1834, and in 1842, the year Hammond was chosen governor, McDuffie went to the United States Senate to fill the vacancy left by the resignation of William C. Preston. In 1846, McDuffie resigned from the Senate, and Hammond's candidacy was put before the legislature. Wade Hampton II, however, exerted pressure on that body and brought about the election of A. P. Butler. McDuffie owned a large plantation called "Cherry Hill"; his only child, Mary Singleton (1830–74), became the second wife of Wade Hampton III in 1858.

JOHN LAURENCE MANNING (1816–89), governor, planter, state legislator, soldier, and brother-in-law of Wade Hampton II, attended the College of New Jersey (now Princeton) but returned home at his father's death, and was graduated from South Carolina College in 1837. Manning served as a trustee of the college, 1841–54 and 1865–69. Son of Governor Richard Irvine Manning (1789–1836), Manning married in 1838 Susan Frances Hampton (1816–45), the youngest child of Wade Hampton I. Susan brought to her marriage her large income from the Hampton's "Houmas" sugar plantation, and the couple built between 1838 and 1840 a Greek Revival mansion, "Milford," on Manning's property near Pinewood in Clarendon District. Susan died in childbirth in 1845 and Manning remarried in 1848. Manning served in the South Carolina House, 1842–45, the South Carolina Senate, 1846–52, 1876–78, and was governor of South Carolina, 1852–54. Considered a moderate in politics, Manning upheld the Union until the late 1850s, when his aversion to the Republican party and abolitionism caused him to support secession and sign the secession ordinance. Manning served during the war as a colonel on the staff of General P. G. T. Beauregard and in the Confederate South Carolina Senate, 1861–65. In 1865 he won a seat in the United States Senate but was not seated. Said to be one of the wealthiest men in the South, Manning's wealth in 1860 was reported to be over two million dollars; however, he lost most of it during the war.

JOHN HUGH MEANS (1812–62), governor, state legislator, and soldier, was graduated from South Carolina College in 1832, served in the South Carolina House from 1844 to 1845, and was the predecessor of John Manning as governor, serving from 1850 to 1852, during which time the question of secession was the most important issue in state politics. Means, an active secessionist, was a delegate to the 1860 South Carolina Secession Convention and during the Civil War served as a colonel. He was killed at the second battle of Manassas.

CHRISTOPHER G. MEMMINGER (1803–83), Confederate cabinet member, state legislator, and lawyer, was born in Germany but came to Charleston as a young child. Memminger, early orphaned, was adopted by Thomas Bennett (1781–1865), who from 1820 to 1822 was South Carolina's governor. Memminger was graduated from South Carolina College in 1819, studied law with Thomas Bennett, and was admitted to the bar in 1824. He opposed nullification and in 1836 was elected to the South Carolina House, where he served for twenty years, 1836–51 and 1854–59. Memminger opposed the bank but was an active promoter of railroad development in South Carolina. In the 1850s Memminger came to be an influential member of the cooperationist movement in South Carolina which urged cooperative secession by all the southern states. He was the Confederacy's first secretary of the treasury and served in that post until June 1864. After the war Memminger practiced law in Charleston, served in the South Carolina House 1876–78, and supported the development of the public school system in Charleston.

PATRICK NOBLE (1787–1840), governor, lieutenant governor, state legislator, a cousin and a friend of both John C. Calhoun and Francis W. Pickens, was graduated in 1806 from the College of New Jersey (now Princeton), studied law with Calhoun, and was admitted to the bar in 1809. He practiced law briefly with Calhoun until the latter's election to Congress in 1810. Noble served in the South Carolina House, 1814–23, 1832–35; and as speaker 1818–23 and 1833–35. He was lieutenant governor from 1830 to 1832, served in the South Carolina Senate, 1836–39, and resigned on election to the governorship on December 8, 1838, dying in office. A states' rights Democrat, a promoter of South Carolina's Agricultural Society, serving as the Society's first president, 1839–40, he actively promoted the development of railroads and banking in South Carolina, and he was a trustee of South Carolina College, 1818–24, 1830–32, and 1836–40.

JOHN BELTON O'NEALL (1793–1863), jurist and author, was graduated in 1812 from South Carolina College, taught school, and studied law, being admitted to the bar in 1814. O'Neall received the master of arts degree from the College in 1816, served in the South Carolina House, 1816–17, 1822–28, and was speaker his last two terms. O'Neall became a circuit judge in December 1828 and advanced in 1830 to the South Carolina court of appeals. In 1835 he was assigned to the court of law appeals, became president in 1850, and in 1859 became chief justice of South Carolina. O'Neall was recognized as a scholar who produced many works, including a two-volume study, *The Biographical Sketches of the Bench and Bar of South Carolina*, published in 1859 but still regarded as authoritative. Opposed to both nullification and secession, O'Neall was an active unionist in 1832, but took no steps against the secessionist movement in 1860. Like Judge Gantt, O'Neall was a leader in the temperance movement and made numerous talks for the cause.

JAMES LOUIS PETIGRU (1789–1863), lawyer in Charleston, state legislator, and best known as a unionist leader, was graduated from South Carolina College in 1809, studied law, and was admitted to the bar in 1812, for over half a century he was an acknowledged leader of the law profession in the state. In the South Carolina House, 1831–32, 1836–37, he opposed nullification, and in 1860–61 he opposed secession. It wass said of him in 1860, "everybody in South Carolina has seceded, except Mr. Petigru." At the time of the war Petigru was engaged in the codification and annotation of the laws of South Carolina. Law partner for a time with James Hamilton, it is alleged that Petigru entered into speculative ventures with his partner and also endorsed his notes, leading to losses of nearly $100,000, which Petigru was forced to pay, resulting in the loss of his savings, his Savannah River plantation, and other properties. Petigru, unlike Hammond, never blamed Hamilton.

FRANCIS WILKINSON PICKENS (1805–69), United States congressman, minister to Russia, governor, planter, lawyer, state legislator, and a cousin of Calhoun, was a college acquaintance of Hammond and a political friend from the time of Hammond's editorship of the *Southern Times* in 1830. Pickens attended South Carolina College from 1825 to 1827, but left college before the completion of his senior year. Pickens married Margaret Eliza Simkins, his childhood sweetheart on October 18, 1827, read law with his father-in-law, Colonel Eldred Simkins in Edgefield, and was admitted to the bar in 1828. Owner of several plantations in Edgefield District, Pickens lived at "Edgewood"; he also owned substantial property in Alabama and Mississippi and estimated that at one time he owned 563 slaves. Pickens, an early advocate of nullification, served in the South Carolina House, 1832–33, and the United States House of Representatives, 1834–43. While in Congress, Pickens supported issues favoring slavery and states' rights, advocated an independent treasury, and opposed the Bank of the United States. Pickens also served in the South Carolina Senate, 1844–45, was a member of the Nashville Convention of 1850 and the Southern Rights State Convention in 1852. Pickens lost the election to the United States Senate in 1852, to Congress in 1853, and, in 1857, lost the contest for a Senate seat to Hammond. President Buchanan appointed Pickens minister to Russia in 1858, and he remained in Russia until 1860. Upon his return to South Carolina, he was elected governor, thus, becoming South Carolina's first Civil War governor. Returning to Edgefield, Pickens retired from public life except to serve as a delegate for Edgefield at the 1865 constitutional convention immediately following the end of the war, where he supported President Andrew Johnson's reconstruction plan.

THOMSON TREZEVANT PLAYER (1804–53), lawyer, state legislator, brother-in-law of Wade Hampton II, and cousin of Louis Trezevant Wigfall, was graduated from South Carolina College in 1822, studied law in the Newberry office of John B. O'Neall, and was admitted to the bar in 1827. Player was elected to the South Carolina House, 1828–33, and was elected solicitor of the middle circuit, 1833–41. Player married in 1831 a daughter of Wade Hampton I, Mary Sumter Hampton (1810–32); she died the following year in childbirth. His maternal aunt, Eliza Thomson Player, married Levi D. Wigfall. Their son, Louis T. Wigfall (1816–74), was thus a first cousin of Player. Player in 1840 married wealthy Emma T. Yeatman (1825–1902), a step-daughter of John Bell of Tennessee. Player resigned his position as solicitor in 1841 and moved with his wife first to New Orleans and then to Nashville in 1847. He died of yellow fever six years later.

JOHN SMITH PRESTON (1809–81), lawyer, planter, state legislator, brother of William Campbell Preston, and brother-in-law of Wade Hampton II and Wade Hampton III, was born in Virginia and attended Hampden-Sydney College, 1823–25, and the University of Virginia, 1825–27, studied law briefly at Harvard, and traveled in Europe before becoming an attorney in Virginia. In 1830 Preston married Caroline Martha Hampton (1807–83). His youngest sister, Margaret Frances Preston (1818–56), married Wade Hampton III in 1838. After his father-in-law's death in 1835, he and his wife moved to Columbia to be with her family and he practiced law, 1835–40. After 1840, Preston became a planter at the Hampton family sugar plantation, "Houmas," in Louisiana and built a mansion there. Between 1840 and 1848, the Prestons divided their time among "Houmas," Columbia, and Europe, became collectors and patrons of the arts, and sponsored several artists including the painter James De Veaux and the sculptor Hiram Powers. Returning to Columbia, Preston was elected to the South Carolina House, 1848–51, and to the South Carolina Senate, 1854–57. In 1858, Caroline and John Preston sold Caroline's portion of "Houmas"—12,000 acres and 550 slaves—to a New Orleans merchant for a reported $1.5 million. The Prestons, their children, the widowed Mrs. Hampton II, and several of her Manning grandchildren went to France and Italy, where they stayed for over two years, returning to South Carolina on the eve of the Civil War. Always an ardent secessionist, John Preston was a delegate to the Democratic National Convention in Charleston in 1860, delegate to the South Carolina Secession Convention, and served the Confederacy in both a military and an administrative capacity. Between 1863 and 1865, Preston resided in Richmond as the superintendent of the Bureau of Conscription for the Confederacy. After the war the Prestons resided in Europe for three years, but returned to South Carolina during reconstruction. Preston was a founder of the Carolina Art Association, a promoter of railroads in the state, and a trustee of South Carolina College, 1849–65. At the time of his death an inventory listed only a small bank deposit and $1,000 in bank stock.

WILLIAM CAMPBELL PRESTON (1794–1860), United States senator, lawyer, educator, state legislator, brother of John Smith Preston, brother-in-law of Wade Hampton III, and mentor and friend of James Henry Hammond, was graduated from South Carolina College in 1812. After traveling in Europe and studying law at the University of Edinburgh, Preston returned to the United States in 1819, was admitted to the bar in Virginia in 1820, and moved to Columbia, South Carolina, in 1822. Hammond read law in the office of Preston. At first a staunch nullifier, Preston served in the South Carolina House, 1828–33, and in 1833 was elected to fill the vacancy in the United States Senate caused by the resignation of Stephen D. Miller. Preston was reelected in 1837 and served until 1842, when he was forced to resign his seat because of his support of the Whigs, Henry Clay, and the bank of the United States, all opposed by Calhoun. George McDuffie succeeded him. Returning to the practice of law, William Preston was chosen president of South Carolina College in 1845; he resigned in 1851 because of poor health. Trustee of South Carolina College, 1851–57, he died in Columbia on the eve of the war.

ALBERT MOORE RHETT (1809–43), (family name changed from Smith to Rhett in 1837), lawyer, state legislator, and brother of Robert Barnwell Rhett, was graduated from South Carolina college, ca. 1827. Rhett studied law and was admitted to the bar in 1834. Elected to the South Carolina House, 1834–37, 1840–43, Albert Rhett was a leader in that body and part of the Rhett-Elmore political clique feared and disliked by Hammond, among others. Rhett died of yellow fever in Charleston at the age of thirty-four.

ROBERT BARNWELL RHETT (1800–1876), United States senator, congressman, lawyer, state legislator, was called "the father of secession" as early as 1876. An older brother of Albert Moore Rhett, he attended the College of Beaufort, studied law in Charleston, and was admitted to the bar in 1821. Rhett served in the South Carolina House, 1826–33, was state attorney general, 1832, and was a member of the United States House of Representatives, 1837–49. Hammond believed that the Rhett-Elmore clique had defeated him in his bid for the governorship in 1840. In 1844, Rhett broke with Calhoun to lead the Bluffton movement, which espoused separate state action on the tariff issue and called upon South Carolina to nullify the tariff of 1842 unless its rates were reduced. For Calhoun this seemed the worst moment to wave the banner of disunion in the face of the upcoming presidential contest. In this instance Hammond sided with Rhett and confided in his diary that Calhoun was willing to sacrifice the South in his desire for the presidency. Calhoun temporarily put down the malcontents. Rhett, one of the leading "fire-eaters" in the South, was at the Nashville Convention of 1850 which failed to endorse Rhett's aim of immediate secession of the whole South, but in December 1850, Rhett beat out Hammond in South Carolina for John C. Calhoun's coveted Senate seat with 97 votes to Hammond's 46. In 1852, Rhett resigned his Senate seat when South Carolina turned against his radical party of immediate secessionists. He continued to express his strong secessionist sentiments through the Charleston *Mercury*, a newspaper edited by his son. Rhett was a member in 1860 of the South Carolina Secession Convention, signed the ordinance of secession, and served in the lower house of the Confederate Congress until his defeat in 1863. Rhett throughout the war was almost always in opposition to President Jefferson Davis, whose office he had coveted. Rhett might have been a possible candidate for the presidency had his views been less extreme.

JOHN PETER RICHARDSON (1801–64), United States congressman, governor, planter, state legislator, and arch rival of Hammond in 1840 for the governorship of the Palmetto State, attended South Carolina college but left in 1819 during his senior year. He studied law and was admitted to the bar. A successful planter at "Manchester" plantation in Clarendon District, Richardson owned at least 8,754 acres and in 1860 held 194 slaves. He served in the South Carolina House, 1825–33, the South Carolina Senate, 1834–36, and sat in the United States House of Representatives, 1836–39. A man of moderate unionist sentiments in the 1830s, Richardson beat Hammond out of the governorship in 1840, and his election marked an attempted political reconciliation between unionists and nullifiers within the state. By 1850, however, Richardson supported states' rights and secession. He served as a deputy to the Nashville Convention in 1850, and became president of the state Southern Rights Association in 1851. He attended the secession Convention in 1860 and was a signer of the ordinance.

WILLIAM GILMORE SIMMS (1806–70), nationally known South Carolina novelist, man of letters, state legislator, and very close personal friend of Hammond, never attended college but studied law, and on the day he was twenty-one he was admitted to the bar. He soon abandoned the law for a career in writing. A member of the South Carolina House, 1844–45, Simms was narrowly defeated in 1846 for lieutenant governor. In addition to his own writing, Simms edited the *Southern Quarterly Review* from 1849 to 1855. A prolific and popular author, he married his second wife, Chevillette Roach (1817–63), in 1836 and moved to her father's plantation, "Woodlands," in Barnwell District, making it his home for the remainder of his life. Describing his friendship with Hammond to one of Hammond's sons following the Senator's death, Simms wrote, "your father was my most confidential friend for near twenty-five years. Never were thoughts more intimate than his and mine. We had few or no secrets from each other, we took few steps in life without mutual consultation. We had—I am sure I had—perfect confidence in him. I believe he had in me. I felt there was something kindred in our intellectual nature. Certainly, there was very much in common between us."

BENJAMIN FRANKLIN TAYLOR (1791–1852), planter, and state legislator, attended South Carolina College in 1806 and the college of New Jersey (now Princeton), 1808–09. His father, Thomas Taylor, and his uncle, James Taylor, owned much of the land on which the city of Columbia was built. Taylor served four terms in the South Carolina House, 1820–25, 1850–51. A very successful planter, he owned a plantation near Columbia. He died at "Edgehill," his residence, and reportedly left his widow one of the richest women in the South. His brother, John Taylor, married, in 1793, Sarah Cantey Chesnut, and their tenth child, Sarah Cantey Taylor, married Albert Moore Rhett, making Benjamin Taylor, Rhett's uncle by marriage.

JAMES MURDOCH WALKER (1813–54), lawyer, legislator, and author, was graduated from South Carolina College in 1830, studied law, and was admitted to the bar in 1834. He practiced law in Charleston and served in the South Carolina House, 1840–47. Walker was the author of a number of pamphlets, among them: *Argument in the Case of the State vs. the Bank of South Carolina* (1843), *Theory of the Common Law* (1852), and *On Government* (1853).

LOUIS TREZEVANT WIGFALL (1816–74), United States senator, legislator, lawyer, Southern firebrand, and Confederate officer, was graduated from South Carolina College in 1837, attended the law school at the University of Virginia, and was admitted to the bar in the fall of 1839. In the 1840 gubernatorial campaign, Wigfall, a resident of Edgefield District, was a supporter of John P. Richardson and challenged to duels several supporters of Richardson's principal opponent, James Henry Hammond. He killed Thomas Bird, and in a second duel both Wigfall and his opponent, J. P. Carroll, missed; in a third duel Wigfall exchanged shots with Preston Brooks, both duelists missed with their first shots, but rancor ran too deep for the seconds to prevent a further exchange. In the second round of shots both men were wounded; Brooks in the hip, Wigfall through the thigh. For his services in the political campaign, Wigfall was appointed aide-de-camp with the rank of lieutenant colonel on Governor Richardson's staff. Having generated a reputation as a violent young man and also being deeply in debt, Wigfall, in 1846, for both professional and financial reasons decided to move to Texas. In Texas he practiced law, was a member of the state House of Representatives, 1849–50, a member of the Texas Senate, 1857–59, and was elected to the United States Senate from Texas in 1859. He withdrew from the Senate in 1861 to enter Confederate service on March 23, 1861. During the war, Wigfall was commissioned a brigadier general, but in February 1862 he resigned to enter the Confederate Senate. After the war, he resided in England, but returned in 1873 and settled in Baltimore. He died while on a lecture tour in Galveston, Texas.

THOMAS JEFFERSON WITHERS (1804–65), judge, lawyer, editor, and college friend of James Henry Hammond was graduated in 1825 from South Carolina College, studied law, and edited for several years in Columbia the *Telescope*, a pro-nullification newspaper. He moved to Camden and married in 1831—the same year as Hammond's marriage to Catherine Fitzsimons—Elizabeth Boykin, the sister-in-law of former governor and in 1831 United States Senator Stephen D. Miller, becoming by marriage the uncle of Mary Boykin Chesnut, the famous Civil War diarist. Withers was mentioned quite frequently in the pages of his niece's diary. A successful lawyer of Camden, Withers was elected circuit solicitor in 1832 and reelected several times. In December 1846, Withers was elected one of the common law judges and was a member of the court of appeals, where he served for almost twenty years until his death in 1865.

SELECTED BIBLIOGRAPHY FOR THE BIOGRAPHICAL DIRECTORY

The sources for much of the unpublished research material used to compile this biographical directory have been drawn from the personal and public records at the Library of Congress, the South Carolina Department of Archives and History, the South Carolina Historical Society, the South Caroliniana Library of the University of South Carolina, and special collections at Clemson University. Birth, marriage, and death dates have been extracted from the published volumes of the *South Carolina Historical and Genealogical Magazine*, and from the privately printed family genealogies. Standard reference books and many historical monographs on nineteenth-century South Carolina also have been especially valuable in the compilation of this biographical data, and a list of these works follows:

Bailey, N. Louise; Morgan, Mary L.; and Taylor, Carolyn R., eds. *Biographical Directory of the South Carolina Senate, 1776–1985*. 3 vols. Columbia: University of South Carolina Press, 1986.

Billings, John Shaw, comp. *Descendants of James Henry Hammond of South Carolina*. New York: By The Author, 1934.

Biographical Directory of the American Congress, 1774–1971. Washington: General Printing Office, 1971.

Bleser, Carol. ed. *The Hammonds of Redcliffe*. New York: Oxford University Press, 1981.

Brooks, Ulysses Robert. *South Carolina Bench and Bar*. vol. 1. Columbia: The State Company, 1908.

Carson, James Petigru. *Life, Letters and Speeches of James Louis Petigru*. Washington, D.C.: W.H. Lowdermilk and Company, 1920.

Cauthen, Charles E., ed. *Family Letters of Three Wade Hamptons, 1782–1901*. Columbia: University of South Carolina Press, 1953.

Cyclopedia of Eminent and Representative Men of the Carolinas of the Nineteenth Century. 2 vols. Madison, Wisconsin: Bryant and Fuller, 1892.

Davidson, Chalmers Gaston. *The Last Foray: The South Carolina Planters of 1860: A Sociological Study*. Columbia; University of South Carolina Press, 1971.

Edmunds, John B. Jr., *Francis W. Pickens and the Politics of Destruction*. Chapel Hill: University of North Carolina Press, 1986.

Faunt, Joan Reynolds; Rector, Robert E.; and Bowden, David K., eds. *Biographical Directory of the South Carolina House of Representatives*. 4 vols. Columbia: University of South Carolina Press, 1974.

Faust, Drew Gilpin. *A Sacred Circle: The Dilemma of the Intellectual in the Old South, 1840–1860*. Baltimore: The Johns Hopkins University Press, 1977.

———. *James Henry Hammond and the Old South: A Design for Mastery*. Baton Rouge: Louisiana State University Press, 1982.

Garlington, J. C. *Men of the Times: Sketches of Living Notables: A Biographical Encyclopedia of Contemporaneous South Carolina Leaders*. Spartanburg: Garlington Publishing Company, 1902.

Gibbes, Robert W. *A Memoir of James De Veaux of Charleston, S.C.* Columbia, 1846.

Hammond, Roland. *A History and Genealogy of the Descendants of William Hammond*. Boston: Clapp and Sons, 1894.

Hollis, Daniel W. *University of South Carolina*. vol. 1. Columbia: University of South Carolina Press, 1951.

Johnson, Allen; and Malone, Dumas, eds. *Dictionary of American Biography*. 11 vols. New York: Charles Scribner's Sons, 1958.

LaBorde, Maximilian. *History of the South Carolina College From Its Incorporation, December 19, 1801 to December 19, 1865*. 2nd ed. Charleston: Walker, Evans and Cogswell, 1874.

Meynard, Virginia G. *The Venturers: The Hamptons, Harrison, and Earle Families of Virginia, South Carolina, and Texas*. Easley, South Carolina: Southern Historical Press, 1981.

O'Neall, John Belton. *Biographical Sketches of the Bench and Bar of South Carolina*, 2 vols. Charleston: S.G. Courtenay and Company, 1859.

Oliphant, Mary C.; Odell, Alfred Taylor; and Eaves, T.C., eds. *The Letters of William Gilmore Simms*. 5 vols. Columbia: University of South Carolina Press, 1952–56.

Raimo, J., and Sobel, R. *Biographical Directory of the Governors of the United States, 1789–1978.* Connecticut: Meckler Books, 1978.

Roller, David C.; and Twyman, Robert W., eds. *The Encyclopedia of Southern History.* Baton Rouge: Louisiana State University Press, 1979.

Steadman, Joseph Earle. *A History of the Spann Family with Attached Hammond Connections, Compiled by Edward Spann Hammond from the Notes of James H. Hammond.* n.p., 1967.

Wachope, George Armstrong. *The Writers of South Carolina.* Columbia: The State Company, 1910.

Waklyn, Jon L. *Biographical Dictionary of the Confederacy.* Westport: Greenwood Press, 1977.

Warner, Ezra J.; and Yearns, W. Buck. *Biographical Register of the Confederate Congress.* Baton Rouge: Louisiana State University Press, 1975.

White, Laura A. *Robert Barnwell Rhett: Father of Secession.* New York: The Century Company, 1931.

Wood, W. Kirk, ed. *A Northern Daughter and a Southern Wife: The Civil War Reminiscences and Letters of Katharine H. Cumming 1860–1865.* Augusta: Richmond County Historical Society, 1976.

Woodward, C. Vann, ed. *Mary Chesnut's Civil War.* New Haven: Yale University Press, 1981.

———; and Muhlenfeld, Elisabeth, eds. *The Private Mary Chesnut: The Unpublished Civil War Diaries.* New York: Oxford University Press, 1984.

Index

Platt, John, 59
Player, Emma T. Yeatman, 324
Player, Mary Sumter Hampton, 324
Player, Thomson Trezevant, 319; bio.
   sketch, 324
Poinsett, Joel Roberts, 195
Polk, James K., 122, 124, 127, 144, 145,
   146, 148, 153, 154, 155, 160, 162,
   182, 183, 186, 190
Port Royal, S.C., 280
Poughkeepsie, N.Y., 318
Powers, Hiram, 325
Preston, Caroline Martha Hammond, 185,
   193, 324
Preston, John Smith, 36, 37, 38, 39, 62,
   96, 120, 171, 174, 180, 214, 258, 270,
   313, 319; and Hampton scandal, 169,
   185; political positions of, 221; and Cooperationist Party, 235, 236; Hammond's views on, 54; bio. sketch, 324-
   25
Preston, Margaret Frances. See Hampton,
   Margaret Frances Preston
Preston, William Campbell, 37, 54, 55,
   60, 61, 66, 120, 128, 132, 169, 171,
   177, 179, 180, 193, 207, 216, 319,
   321, 324; views on banking, 28, 52, 53;
   political ambitions, 35, 40, 52; resigns
   from Senate, 116; and Hampton scandal, 185; Hammond's views on, 39, 53;
   bio. sketch, 325
Pringle, Elizabeth Waties Allston, 308
Pritchard, Catherine. See Fitzsimons,
   Catherine Pritchard
Pritchard, Paul, 7, 314
Proslavery argument, xi, 11, 20, 321, 324.
   See also Hammond, James Henry: writings of; "Mud-sills" speech

Quattlebaum, Paul, 30, 74, 196, 284

Railroads, 67, 97, 186-87, 315, 323, 325
Ransey, John, 73; quarrel with Hammond,
   108, 109, 110, 111, 112, 113, 114;
   Hammond's views on, 110
Redcliffe Plantation, 266, 267, 268, 299,
   300, 303, 314, 316, 317; purchased by
   Hammond, 266; Hammond's views on,

266, 267; bought by Billings, 303; as
   state park, 303
Reform, 121, 123
"Regency," 29, 31, 47, 69, 82, 83, 84,
   116, 212, 326. See also Benjamin F.
   Elmore; Franklin H. Elmore; Albert
   Moore Rhett; Robert Barnwell Rhett
Religion: Hammond's views on, x-xi, 64,
   73, 81, 106, 125, 138, 147, 188, 209,
   243, 260-61, 263, 264; the clergy, 98.
   See also Spiritualism
Republican Party, 35
Rhett, Albert Moore, 59, 66, 68, 69, 74,
   83, 132, 326; political views, 29; and
   1842 governor's race, 47, 54, 60, 65,
   115; and 1842 Senate race, 116; death
   of, 120, 212; bio. sketch, 325
Rhett, James (Smith), 83, 84
Rhett, Robert Barnwell, 28, 58, 127, 130-
   31, 141, 155, 161, 163, 195, 199, 203,
   204, 205, 216, 218, 221, 222, 226,
   236, 238, 239, 240, 254, 258, 270,
   309, 312; political ambitions, 60, 116,
   211; support for Hammond in 1842,
   115; 1842 Senate race, 116; Senator,
   1850, 214, 215, 243, 251; resigns from
   Senate, 1852, 253; and Bluffton Movement, 122; political positions, 203, 206,
   207, 223, 230; Nashville Convention,
   202, 206, 219, 249; and secession, 203,
   206, 219-20, 230, 235, 247-48; Hammond's views on, 212, 214, 223, 243,
   249-50; bio. sketch, 326
Rhett, Sarah Cantey Taylor, 327
Rhett, William, 8
Rhett family, 31, 47, 115, 116, 117, 211
Richardson, John Peter, 22, 47, 56, 76,
   82, 83, 84, 94, 132, 134, 136, 137,
   159, 160, 161, 195, 212, 214, 216,
   310, 327; 1840 governor's race, 20, 21,
   29, 244; political views, 28; as Unionist,
   28-29, 116; alliance with Rhetts, 58,
   116; political ambitions, 59, 69, 117;
   Hammond's views on, 20, 57, 59; bio.
   sketch, 326
Richland District, S.C., 28, 76, 230, 319,
   320
Richmond, Battle of, 286, 289
Rives, William Cabell, 35